SKIRMISHES

Before you start to read this book, take this moment to think about making a donation to punctum books, an independent non-profit press,

@ https://punctumbooks.com/support/

If you're reading the e-book, you can click on the image below to go directly to our donations site. Any amount, no matter the size, is appreciated and will help us to keep our ship of fools afloat. Contributions from dedicated readers will also help us to keep our commons open and to cultivate new work that can't find a welcoming port elsewhere. Our adventure is not possible without your support.

Vive la Open Access.

Fig. 1. Hieronymus Bosch, *Ship of Fools* (1490–1500)

SKIRMISHES: WITH FRIENDS, ENEMIES, AND NEUTRALS. Copyright © 2020 by Graham Harman. This work carries a Creative Commons BY-NC-SA 4.0 International license, which means that you are free to copy and redistribute the material in any medium or format, and you may also remix, transform and build upon the material, as long as you clearly attribute the work to the authors (but not in a way that suggests the authors or punctum books endorses you and your work), you do not use this work for commercial gain in any form whatsoever, and that for any remixing and transformation, you distribute your rebuild under the same license. http://creativecommons.org/licenses/by-nc-sa/4.0/

First published in 2020 by punctum books, Earth, Milky Way.
https://punctumbooks.com

ISBN-13: 978-1-953035-20-2 (print)
ISBN-13: 978-1-953035-21-9 (ePDF)

DOI: 10.21983/P3.0293.1.00

LCCN: 2020949501
Library of Congress Cataloging Data is available from the Library of Congress

Copy editing: Lily Brewer
Book design: Vincent W.J. van Gerven Oei

spontaneous acts of scholarly combustion

HIC SVNT MONSTRA

graham harman

SKIR✊ISHES

with friends,
enemies,
and neutrals

(p.)

CONTENTS

Introduction   11

Part One

Tom Sparrow, *The End of Phenomenology*   17
Steven Shaviro, *The Universe of Things*   53
Peter Gratton, *Speculative Realism*   101
Peter Wolfendale, *Object-Oriented Philosophy*   195

Part Two

Alberto Toscano   299
Christopher Norris   307
Dan Zahavi   319
Stephen Mulhall   333

Bibliography   353

INTRODUCTION

The original plan for *Skirmishes* was drawn up some years ago, though for various reasons it fell through the cracks of expanding professional obligations. My first idea for the book was to respond in alphabetical order to nearly everyone who, by that point, had written a critique of Speculative Realism (SR) or Object-Oriented Ontology (OOO). That plan is no longer feasible, given the now sizable literature — both positive and negative — on these closely related philosophical currents. What I will do instead is spend Part One on a quartet of books devoted in whole or in part to OOO, and Part Two on a series of shorter engagements with critics. The ordering of sections in Part Two is neither chronological nor random, but arranged in a way I hope will be useful to the reader.

Let's speak first about Part One. The year 2014 was as a milestone of sorts for my colleagues and me. In that year, the first four monographs on SR and OOO were published. From most to least favorable in tone, they are as follows:

- Tom Sparrow, *The End of Phenomenology: Metaphysics and the New Realism*
- Steven Shaviro, *The Universe of Things: On Speculative Realism*
- Peter Gratton, *Speculative Realism: Problems and Prospects*

- Peter Wolfendale, *Object-Oriented Philosophy: The Noumenon's New Clothes*

As subway officials might say, this map is not to scale. Shaviro is barely more negative than Sparrow, while Wolfendale's ISIS-like assault is far more openly hostile than Gratton's smirking and eye-rolling account. The first three books on the list are slim volumes and quick reads, but the fourth is a tome so massive, and so awkward in typeface and physical form, that I would never dream of taking it to a coffee shop with the others. Yet considered together, they offer a good sampling of the range of attitudes towards SR and OOO found among those contemporary philosophers who have paid some attention to these trends. Ideally, I would have written a quick response to all of these books shortly after publication, so as to maintain the rapid pace of debate once found in the now-dormant blogosphere; against all expectations, it took longer than expected to sit down and finish these pages.

In Part Two, I have added briefer accounts of other critics of OOO. To name them in order of appearance, I will cover Alberto Toscano, Christopher Norris, Dan Zahavi, and Stephen Mulhall. There are others who could also have fit but were excluded for one reason or another. Of these, I especially appreciate the efforts of Ian James in *The Technique of Thought*; maybe I will have the chance to respond to him elsewhere.[1] The critiques of OOO by Elizabeth Povinelli and Adrian J. Ivakhiv have also been on my radar, and I will try to deal with them in the near future if the opportunity arises.[2]

If we provisionally accept the claim of José Ortega y Gasset that a generation lasts exactly fifteen years, then the explosion of critical responses in 2014 came a full generation after the birth

---

1 Ian James, "The Relational Universe," in *The Technique of Thought: Nancy, Laruelle, Malabou, and Stiegler after Naturalism* (Minneapolis: University of Minnesota Press, 2019), 55–120.
2 Elizabeth Povinelli, *Geontologies: A Requiem to Late Liberalism* (Durham: Duke University Press, 2016); Adrian Ivakhiv, *Shadowing the Anthropocene: Eco-Realism for Turbulent Times* (Earth: punctum books, 2018).

of Object-Oriented Philosophy in my Chicago apartment and roughly a half-generation after the Speculative Realists first met in London.[3] We are no longer outsiders who hope for a hearing, but recognized enemies of those who prefer the settled older discourse of 1990s Anglophone continental philosophy, with its ceaseless prayers to Jacques Derrida, Michel Foucault, and a handful of related authors — nearly all of them native speakers of French or German. Further evidence of the ripening public discourse about OOO and SR can be seen in the fact that the four book authors of 2014 all basically know what they are talking about, even in those moments when I find them off the mark. By contrast with our worst-informed critics, even the caustic Wolfendale shows a praiseworthy diligence.

Warm thanks are due to Eileen A. Joy for recruiting me to write this book for punctum and for patiently enduring the unforeseen delays in completing it. And while I'm at it, I am grateful to Lily Brewer for giving the manuscript a remarkably thorough edit, and to Vincent W.J. van Gerven Oei for producing this beautiful object.

---

[3] José Ortega y Gasset, "Preface for Germans," in *Phenomenology and Art*, trans. P.W. Silver (New York: Norton, 1975), 24–70; Ray Brassier, Iain Hamilton Grant, Graham Harman, and Quentin Meillassoux, "Speculative Realism," in *Collapse III*, ed. Robin Mackay (Falstaff: Urbanomic, 2007), 306–449.

PART ONE

1

TOM SPARROW

The End of Phenomenology

The End of Phenomenology is the second of three courageous books already published by Tom Sparrow, the others being *Levinas Unhinged* (2013) and *Plastic Bodies* (2015). By "courageous" I mean that none of these books has been greeted warmly in those circles most capable of benefitting the next decade of Sparrow's career. He speaks what he considers to be the truth and refuses to flatter academic magnificoes of any stripe. *The End of Phenomenology* has already received a stern printed rebuke from Dan Zahavi, the chief gatekeeper of phenomenology in Generation X, who is also a target of riposte in chapter 7 below.[1] *Plastic Bodies* was abused in shoddy fashion by a number of anonymous mainstream phenomenologists before finding a suitable publishing home. Sparrow's head and backbone are strong enough that he has no need of my encouragement; I mention these incidents only for the sake of younger readers who may someday find themselves obstructed in similar fashion.

For disclosure purposes, I should note that *The End of Phenomenology* was published by Edinburgh University Press in the Speculative Realism series that I edit myself. Certainly, we have made a point to include quality volumes in that series by authors

---

1 Dan Zahavi, "The End of What? Phenomenology vs. Speculative Realism," *International Journal of Philosophical Studies* 24, no. 3 (2016): 289–309.

with whom I have significant philosophical disagreement, such as Markus Gabriel and especially Adrian Johnston.[2] Sparrow's book is a different sort of case. Other than my own volume on Quentin Meillassoux, there is perhaps no work in the series with which I agree more wholeheartedly.[3] *The End of Phenomenology* makes the argument that phenomenology is haunted by a disavowed anti-realism, that it is ill-equipped to deliver us "to the things themselves" despite its habitual claim to do so, and that Speculative Realism has raised the banner of *reality* in a manner of which phenomenology is inherently incapable. I agree with all of this, as well as with Sparrow's skepticism toward the supposed showcase moments of "realism" in phenomenology: above all in the writings of Maurice Merleau-Ponty, whose recent influence in the philosophy of mind has made him arguably more influential than Edmund Husserl himself.[4] On the whole, my disagreements with Sparrow range from minor to moderate. One such disagreement is that I am less enthusiastic than Sparrow about Lee Braver's "transgressive realism," a supposed third way that blends the advantages of realism and anti-realism while avoiding the defects of both.[5] Another is that whereas Sparrow doubts whether phenomenology has a clear method at all, I am convinced that it does.

Some who read Sparrow's words about my philosophy in *The End of Phenomenology* might be misled into thinking that he is a fellow practitioner of object-oriented ontology (OOO) in

2 Markus Gabriel, *Fields of Sense: A New Realist Ontology* (Edinburgh: Edinburgh University Press, 2015); Adrian Johnston, *Adventures in Transcendental Materialism: Dialogues with Contemporary Thinkers* (Edinburgh: Edinburgh University Press, 2014).
3 Graham Harman, *Quentin Meillassoux: Philosophy in the Making,* 2nd edn. (Edinburgh: Edinburgh University Press, 2015).
4 Maurice Merleau-Ponty, *Phenomenology of Perception,* trans. Colin Smith (London: Routledge, 2002); Merleau-Ponty, *The Visible and the Invisible,* trans. Alphonso Lingis (Evanston: Northwestern University Press, 1968); Edmund Husserl, *Logical Investigations,* 2 vols., ed. Dermot Moran, trans. J.N. Findlay (London: Routledge, 2001).
5 Lee Braver, "On Not Settling the Issue of Realism," in *Speculations IV,* eds. Michael Austin et al. (Earth: punctum books, 2013), 9–14.

the manner of Ian Bogost, Levi R. Bryant, or Timothy Morton.[6] That is not the case. The intellectual bond that unites Sparrow and me is looser than this, though perhaps it will prove just as durable — namely, we both spent our formative years with phenomenology and treasure its greatest insights while remaining frustrated by its limitations. There is a basic sympathy between us, then, in our agreement that phenomenology is something to cherish, then vigorously critique, then leave behind for something else. This peculiar relation to phenomenology may also explain why Sparrow and I are both drawn so strongly to the work and person of Alphonso Lingis, whose attitude toward the school is similar.[7]

By contrast, consider the case of my one-time colleagues in Speculative Realism. Among them is Ray Brassier, whose visceral loathing for phenomenology — primarily due to its "bracketing" of the natural world — is rarely concealed whenever he mentions Husserl's way of thinking.[8] Iain Hamilton Grant seems mostly indifferent to phenomenology, and his most passionate concerns lie in a totally different sector of the history of philosophy: German Idealism and Gilles Deleuze. As for Quentin Meillassoux, though he sometimes insists on his admiration for the school, his praise for phenomenology is notably vague and faint. As he once put it in an interview, "I am a diligent reader of the great phenomenologists [...] phenomenology remains for me a formidable descriptive enterprise of the complexities of the given."[9] The first problem with this is that phenomenology is not

6 Levi R. Bryant, *The Democracy of Objects* (Ann Arbor: Open Humanities Press, 2011); Ian Bogost, *Alien Phenomenology, or What It's Like to Be a Thing* (Minneapolis: University of Minnesota Press, 2012); Timothy Morton, *Hyperobjects: Philosophy and Ecology after the End of the World* (Minneapolis: University of Minnesota Press, 2013).

7 Tom Sparrow, ed., *The Alphonso Lingis Reader* (Minneapolis: University of Minnesota Press, 2018).

8 Ray Brassier, *Nihil Unbound: Enlightenment and Extinction* (New York: Palgrave, 2007).

9 Quentin Meillassoux, qtd. in Graham Harman, *Quentin Meillassoux: Philosophy in the Making*, 2nd edn. (Edinburgh: Edinburgh University Press, 2015), 219.

solely, or even primarily, about "description." In Sparrow's critical words: "Today, anything is called phenomenology so long as it involves some kind of subjective description of experience."[10] But if this were all it took, Sparrow notes, it would lead to the baffling conclusion that "Melville [is] a phenomenologist of whaling, Thoreau a phenomenologist of walking, or Foucault a phenomenologist of power" (5). The second problem with Meillassoux's praise of phenomenology is that he by no means grants high philosophical status to description, which he treats with relative disdain by contrast with *deduction*. Thus, his compliment for phenomenology's descriptive skills is backhanded at best.[11]

OOO is the only strand of Speculative Realism to make room for Husserlian phenomenology at the core of its approach, and not even the whole of OOO. Among my object-oriented colleagues, Bryant is a Deleuzean who draws nothing from Husserl for his own position, since the phenomenological tension between intentional objects and their adumbrations disappears for him in favor of the single term "local manifestations."[12] Bogost did write a book called *Alien Phenomenology*, but it is certainly not phenomenology in the Husserlian sense of the term.[13] Morton's philosophical background was initially shaped by Derrida, and though he has a deep respect for Husserl, he is not emotionally invested in phenomenology in the same way as Lingis, Sparrow, or I. When Sparrow says in his book that "Harman has no patience for curt dismissals of Husserl" (116), the same can be said of Sparrow himself, even if this proves insufficient for an enforcer like Zahavi. This is the nature of my intellectual alliance with Sparrow, and our admiration for phenomenology

---

10 Tom Sparrow, *The End of Phenomenology: Metaphysics and the New Realism* (Edinburgh: Edinburgh University Press, 2014), 9. Subsequent page references are given between parentheses in the main text.
11 Quentin Meillassoux, *After Finitude: An Essay on the Necessity of Contingency*, trans. Ray Brassier (London: Continuum, 2008), 38.
12 Levi R. Bryant, *Difference and Givenness: Deleuze's Transcendental Empiricism and the Ontology of Immanence* (Evanston: Northwestern University Press, 2008); Bryant, *The Democracy of Objects*.
13 Bogost, *Alien Phenomenology*.

survives our shared critique. It would be a good thing if our phenomenological critics would at least acknowledge this point.

Realism and Anti-Realism in Continental Philosophy

The central argument of Sparrow's book is that phenomenology is guilty of a "disavowed antirealism" (ix), and that by avoiding this peculiar defect, Speculative Realism is the true heir to phenomenology's purported turn to the things themselves. Needless to say, I agree with this assessment. But in order to explain why I agree, we should begin with some general reflections on philosophical realism before returning to Sparrow's book.

"Realism" is a flexible term that has numerous and sometimes opposite meanings in different fields. Political, mathematical, literary, and pictorial realism are not automatic philosophical allies; indeed, they often lead us in opposite directions. For example, mathematical realism is committed to the existence of an ideal realm of perfect numbers and shapes, while political (Thomas Hobbes, Carl Schmitt) and literary realism (Émile Zola, Theodore Dreiser) mock all hope of perfection, asking instead that we face up to brute material existence in all its ugliness. A different case is pictorial realism, which need not exhibit outright ugliness but only a commitment to the illusionism of a plausible three-dimensional scene, as opposed to Byzantine or cubist abstraction or the outlandish figures of surrealist painting. Even within philosophy there is room for confusion about the word. George Berkeley, despite being the most anti-realist major philosopher in Western history, is sometimes called a "direct realist" in the sense that he holds that the images viewed by the mind are all the reality we can hope for and are not just "representations" of something more real outside the mind, as John Locke would have it.[14] But this is a derivative use of the term.

---

14 George Berkeley, *A Treatise Concerning the Principles of Human Knowledge*, ed. Kenneth P. Winkler (Indianapolis: Hackett Publishing Company, 1982); John Locke, *An Essay Concerning Human Understanding*, 2 vols. (New York: Dover, 1959).

What most people understand philosophical realism to mean is the view that reality has an existence independent of the human mind. Though I will claim that this definition is still inadequate, it is a reasonable starting point for discussion; any remaining problems can be dealt with as we go along.

Some years ago, Bogost was visiting the archives of the newly deceased Richard Rorty. He reported an amusing remark from Rorty's unpublished papers, which I quote haphazardly from memory: "Every ten years or so," the philosopher began, "someone writes a book with a title something like *Beyond Realism and Idealism*. And it always turns out that what's beyond realism and idealism is — *idealism*!" Rorty was presumably speaking of intermittent claims within analytic philosophy to have passed beyond the classic realism/anti-realism dispute. But the situation in continental philosophy is much worse, since this entire subfield has long been tacitly committed to the claim that we stand "beyond" both alternatives. In part this can be traced to G.W.F. Hegel, whose claim to have domesticated Kant's hidden noumenon as a special case of what appears is often accepted by continentals without further comment.[15] But even more of the blame must go to the phenomenological tradition of Husserl, Heidegger, and their lesser allies, since here it is customary to treat the realism question as a "pseudo-problem": after all, we are "always already outside ourselves" in intending objects or handling equipment. Although counterexamples are sometimes given of realist trends in earlier continental philosophy (Nicolai Hartmann, or the Munich phenomenologists) these partial exceptions prove the rule, since Hegel, Husserl, and Heidegger have influenced hundreds of thousands of readers, while the others are generally read by a small number of specialists. Neither realism nor anti-realism has ever gained much traction in continental philosophy, since the whole point was to view these two options as naïve and already surpassed. In more recent continental thought, there was an initial realist surge in the early

---

15 G.W.F. Hegel, *Phenomenology of Spirit*, trans. A.V. Miller (Oxford: Oxford University Press, 1977).

1990s thanks to Maurizio Ferraris in Turin.[16] In Anglophone continental circles, realism returned to the forefront in 2002 with Manuel DeLanda's *Intensive Science* and *Virtual Philosophy* as well as my own *Tool-Being*.[17] The controversy provoked by these two books has sometimes led to mockery by analytic philosophers, in whose own subfield the realism/anti-realism dispute has been an openly discussed topic from the start. But we could easily play the ridicule game in reverse, laughing at the shock to analytic philosophy provided by Saul Kripke's theory of reference, given that Husserl's own treatment of "nominal acts" in the *Logical Investigations* more than foreshadowed the insight that led to the vicious priority dispute between Kripke, Ruth Barcan Marcus, and one or more thinkers from Finland.[18] One can always attempt to devalue philosophers by finding predecessors to their insights, yet only in rare cases of outright ignorance or robbery does the second occurrence add nothing to the first. Today's continental realism is a different bird from the realisms of yesteryear, as the present book will show in several distinct ways.

A significant contribution to the theme was made by Braver in 2007, in his outstanding work *A Thing of This World: A History of Continental Anti-Realism,* one of the signal achievements of its decade in continental thought. While Braver's book has numerous merits, two in particular stand out. First, he no longer permits continental philosophy to present itself evasively as somehow standing beyond the realism/anti-realism dispute. For the first time in memory, and perhaps the first time in history, he candidly describes continental philosophy as an *anti-realist* movement (the mysterious absence of Husserl from Braver's

---

16 Maurizio Ferraris, *Manifesto of New Realism,* trans. Sarah De Sanctis (Albany: SUNY Press, 2014).
17 Manuel DeLanda, *Intensive Science and Virtual Philosophy* (London: Continuum, 2002); Graham Harman, *Tool-Being: Heidegger and the Metaphysics of Objects* (Chicago: Open Court, 2002).
18 Husserl, *Logical Investigations,* 2:169; Saul Kripke, *Naming and Necessity* (Cambridge: Harvard University Press, 1980); Ruth Barcan Markus, "Modalities and Intensional Languages," *Synthese* 13, no. 4 (1961): 303–22.

story is the one unfortunate lacuna). More than this, he sees the continentals as having been rather successful along their anti-realist path: "Overall, I think the continental thinkers carry out the implications of anti-realism further and more consistently than do their analytic counterparts."[19] Second, Braver shows exemplary awareness of the ambiguities of the term "realism." Thus, he begins his book with a scrupulous glossary that lists six different meanings of realism (R 1–6), paired with their corresponding anti-realist inversions (A 1–6). In an early review of Braver's book I argued that he was missing a seventh pair, and DeLanda later added an eighth and a ninth.[20] Whatever one makes of our disputes with his list, Braver's initial project remains of crucial importance for the future of continental philosophy, that professionally marginalized but influential subfield. Continental thought needs to face up to the realism question more directly, and should also be more aware of the different inflections of the term "realism" itself. Although Braver does this on behalf of anti-realism, and Speculative Realism on behalf of the opposite term, the two trends share much in common. At the end of this chapter, I will address the apparent shift in Braver's position, since 2007, from overt anti-realism to what looks like a more qualified stance.

While mainstream continental philosophers are generally dismissive of realism — which they usually call "naïve" realism, with no demonstration of why it is naïve — it is just as hard to find a full-blown continental idealist. It is usually Hegelians who come the closest, though even they are quick to insist that Hegel is an "objective" idealist, meaning that he is not trapped in some merely subjective standpoint. In short, nearly everyone in continental circles is confidently "beyond" the realism/anti-realism dispute; in practice, what this means is that thought and

---

19 Lee Braver, *A Thing of This World: A History of Continental Anti-Realism* (Evanston: Northwestern University Press, 2007), 514.
20 Graham Harman, "A Festival of Anti-Realism: Braver's History of Continental Thought," *Philosophy Today* 52, no. 2 (Summer 2008): 197–210. Manuel DeLanda and Graham Harman, *The Rise of Realism* (Malden: Polity Press, 2017).

the world are treated as existing only in correlation with each other rather than independently. Meillassoux once told me that he coined the term "correlationism" in 2002 or 2003 precisely because he was so tired of people telling him that they were not idealists, on the grounds that Kant provides a "refutation of idealism" and Husserl knows that we are always already outside ourselves in intending objects. Though I had earlier used the term "philosophy of access" to mean much the same thing, I was quick to recognize the superior flexibility and relevance of Meillassoux's term, and it strikes me as a permanent contribution to the philosophical lexicon.[21] (However, I should note that Niki Young has recently made a strong case that the two terms ought to be kept distinct.[22]) That said, numerous critics have refused to accept the term "correlationism," for reasons I generally regard as caviling and flimsy.[23] My aim for now is only to set the table for Sparrow's discussion of phenomenology, and thus it is sufficient to repeat what I have written elsewhere about Meillassoux's own attempt, which one can only regard as failed, to escape correlationism.[24] We note first that he distinguishes between "weak" and "strong" varieties of this doctrine. Weak correlationism is exemplified by the Kantian thesis that we can think of a thing-in-itself beyond thought but cannot know it, though at least it is possible to speak meaningfully about the *Ding an sich*. Strong correlationism, by contrast, holds that even this is impossible. If we speak of a thing-in-itself outside thought, this is itself a thought, and hence there is no escape from what Meillassoux calls the correlational circle. To summarize, weak correlationism is a philosophy of finitude, while strong correlationism is strongly anti-finitude, just like Meillassoux himself. OOO proceeds differently. Beginning with Kant's weak correlationism, we radicalize it not by denying finitude but by claiming that it char-

21 Harman, *Tool-Being*; Meillassoux, *After Finitude*.
22 Niki Young, "On Correlationism and the Philosophy of (Human) Access: Meillassoux and Harman," *Open Philosophy* 2 (2020): 42–52.
23 See for instance David Golumbia, "'Correlationism': The Dogma That Never Was," *boundary 2* 43, no. 2 (May 2016): 1–25.
24 Harman, *Quentin Meillassoux*, 14–23.

acterizes all objects, not just humans. This shows additionally that while correlationism is usually treated as an "agnostic" position on reality, it is inherently unstable. The strong correlationist is someone who says, "to think a thing outside thought is to think it, and therefore it is automatically a thing *inside* thought." The thing-in-itself is therefore rendered *meaningless,* and hence the strong correlationist is already an idealist. But Meillassoux attempts to finesse the point by saying roughly that just because we cannot *think* the in-itself does not mean that it necessarily *does not exist.* Yet this argument fails, since Meillassoux is saved from idealism only by the supposed difference between (a) our inability to *think* the in-itself and (b) its inability to *exist.* But by his own assumptions we cannot even conceive of option (b), given that the possibly unthinkable in-itself outside thought was converted in advance — by the correlational circle — into an in-itself *for* thought. For this reason, both strong correlationism and Meillassoux's own proposed speculative materialism are really just forms of idealism, however "materialist" they may claim to be. Meanwhile, the weak correlationist is indeed a sort of realist, since the thing-in-itself is held to exist even though we are unable to access it directly.

If we adopt this realist alternative, as I propose, then it must be distinguished from the realism of *knowledge*: which holds not only that there is a reality outside the mind, but also that we are capable of grasping it. This type of realism nearly always flatters the natural sciences as our exemplary means of grasping the real, as in Paul Boghossian's *Fear of Knowledge,* which is primarily concerned with attacking relativism.[25] By contrast, philosophies that give priority to mathematics (such as those of Meillassoux and Alain Badiou) veer instead towards idealism, usually clothed in the alibi of "materialism."[26] Another typi-

---

25 Paul Boghossian, *Fear of Knowledge: Against Relativism and Constructivism* (Oxford: Oxford University Press, 2006). For a critique of this book, see Graham Harman, "Fear of Reality: Realism and Infra-Realism," *The Monist* 98, no. 2 (April 2015): 126–44.
26 Alain Badiou, *Being and Event,* trans. Oliver Feltham (London: Continuum, 2005).

cal example of a realist confident in his ability to obtain direct knowledge is the analytic philosopher Michael Devitt, who defines "strong scientific realism" as the view that there not only exists a reality outside the mind, but that it "(approximately) obey[s] the laws of science."[27] This differs from what he derisively terms "*Weak, or Fig-Leaf Realism.* Something objectively exists independently of the mental."[28] As to what is wrong with this "Fig-Leaf" brand of realism, Devitt tells us that it "is so weak as to be uninteresting; but it is worth stating, because it is all that many so-called realists are committed to."[29] Presumably the "uninteresting" character of Fig-Leaf Realism for him is that it merely proclaims realism as an alibi against falling into anti-realism, when, as Devitt sees it, a true realist ought to be committed to the natural sciences as our eminent route of access to the "something [that] objectively exists independently of the mental." In other words, the point seems to be that we can either speak of reality in the terms of natural science, or we must pass over it in silence, with the Fig-Leaf Realist confined to the latter option. Continental idealists sometimes make the similar objection that OOO becomes mired in little more than a "negative theology." Elsewhere I have responded to Adrian Johnston's charge along these lines. The gist of my response is that our discussion of the outside world is not "science or bust," nor even "prose discursive propositions or bust."[30] For in fact, much human cognition occurs at a level that has nothing to do with the discursive capture of reality by concepts. Art is one good example of this, and Socratic *philosophia* another.[31] The fact that so many people are happy to turn philosophy into the handmaid of natural sci-

27 Michael Devitt, *Realism and Truth*, 2nd edn. (Princeton: Princeton University Press, 1997), 347.
28 Ibid., 23.
29 Ibid.
30 Adrian Johnston, "Points of Forced Freedom: Eleven (More) Theses on Materialism," in *Speculations IV*, eds. Michael Austin et al. (Earth: punctum books, 2013), 91–98; Graham Harman, *Immaterialism: Objects and Social Theory* (Cambridge: Polity, 2016), 29–32.
31 Graham Harman, "The Third Table," in *The Book of Books*, ed. Carolyn Christov-Bakargiev (Ostfildern: Hatje Cantz Verlag, 2012), 540–42.

ence is evidence of how much they have forgotten the lessons of the *Meno* concerning the difference between philosophy and knowledge, as attested by Socrates' repeated and unironic professions of ignorance.[32]

An alternative model of realism is the sort devoted to something like the inaccessible thing-in-itself, which is probably the unluckiest concept in the history of Western philosophy. The vast majority of philosophers today would agree that Kantian philosophy marked a revolutionary change in our discipline. The thing-in-itself, unattainable to finite human cognition, is surely the centerpiece of his system, insofar as it renders the old "dogmatic" metaphysics impossible. Nonetheless, there is virtually no one today willing to defend the *Ding an sich*, under penalty of being called either a "Fig-Leaf Realist" or a "negative theologian." One distinctive trait of OOO is its insistence on the noumenon, which can never be made directly present through knowledge or by any other means, though it showers us constantly with effects that are detectable indirectly. The fact that a black hole is not directly visible does not prevent us from saying and learning many things about it, and the same holds for the thing-in-itself. We simply need to hold in check those scientistic tendencies that want philosophy to have no other role than commenting, after the fact, on the most up-to-date achievements of science. As a corollary, aesthetic phenomena and metaphorical and rhetorical discourse must have a stronger place in our philosophy than they usually do in our time.

But what is our reason for insisting on the thing-in-itself in the first place? There are several grounds for doing so, some of them involving an explication of Heidegger's philosophy that need not be repeated here. Perhaps the simplest way to explain the need for realism is as follows. Anyone other than a full-blown Berkeleyan idealist will surely agree that knowledge is not the same thing as that which it knows — our knowledge of the sun, however extensive, is not itself the sun. While this

---

32 Plato, *Meno*, trans. G.M.A. Grube, in *Plato: Complete Works*, ed. John M. Cooper (Indianapolis: Hackett Publishing Company, 1997), 870–97.

may sound like a triviality, it becomes more interesting if we ask ourselves *why* any entity and our knowledge of it are different. The practitioner of "Strong Scientific Realism" (or "Strong Mathematical Materialism," as Meillassoux's position might be called) has no other choice than to say that our knowledge of the sun consists of certain formal properties that are "the same" in both the sun and my knowledge of it, but that in the sun's case those forms somehow inhere in something called "dead physical matter." (We will return to this issue in chapter 4 in connection with Wolfendale.) But since no one has ever discovered formless matter — nor will it ever be discovered — this idea of matter is itself little more than a "fig leaf" to prevent the full-blown idealist doctrine that the sun and my knowledge of it are one and the same. In fact, let's call this position "Fig-Leaf Materialism." The alternative, which OOO recommends, is that the form in the sun and the form in my knowledge of the sun are two very different things, and that the sun's form cannot possibly enter my mind without *translation*. In a sense this revives the Jesuit thinker Francisco Suárez's rejection of the Thomist conception of *materia signata*, though the most proximate influence for OOO on this point is Bruno Latour.[33]

Thus, we are not committed to an "uninteresting" existence of noumena, but to the view that there is much to be said about them, even if not in the way of direct propositional discourse. This, I repeat, merely places us back in the honorable lineage of Socrates. It also differentiates OOO from what might be called "realisms of the remainder," which merely accept some sort of residue lying outside human access without letting it play any constructive role in the world itself. Some of these theories of excess or residue involve appeal to the shock, trauma, or resistance of the outside world as proof of a "realism" that they then do little to develop, as in the discussions of "resistance" by Wil-

---

33 Francis Suarez, *On Individuation: Metaphysical Disputation V: Individual Unity and Its Principle,* trans. Jorge J.E. Gracia (Milwaukee: Marquette University Press, 1982); Bruno Latour, "Irreductions," trans. John Law, in *The Pasteurization of France,* trans. Alan Sheridan and John Law (Cambridge: Harvard University Press, 1988), 153–238.

helm Dilthey and Max Scheler that Sparrow mentions himself (43). The Real of Jacques Lacan, though intriguing in purely psychoanalytic terms, is also a fig-leaf realism, since it cannot exist except through being interlaced with the Symbolic and the Imaginary, both of which require a human subject.[34] I would say the same of Jean-Luc Marion's notion of "givenness" and the "saturated phenomenon," Jacques Derrida's trace-structure, and even of "alterity" in one of my favorite philosophers, Emmanuel Levinas.[35] What differentiates OOO from realisms of the remainder is that for us, the real does not exist only to surprise and exceed humans. This is why the usual formulation of philosophical realism — "there is a reality outside the mind" — is inadequate. For the mind is not the only thing with an outside; the relation between the mind and a real thing is just one of many different kinds of relation. In many relations the human mind is not present at all, as with the interaction between comets and moons, or raindrops and tar. What realism truly refers to is the autonomous reality of each and every object in its own right, its untranslatability or inexhaustibility by the effects it happens to have on minds or on anything else. In short, the phenomenal/noumenal distinction is not primarily one between people and non-people, but between any reality in its own right and its relation with anything else. Having clarified how several different approaches to realism and anti-realism bear on Speculative Realism and OOO, we turn to Sparrow's fine discussion of phenomenology itself.

---

34 Jacques Lacan, *The Sinthome: The Seminar of Jacques Lacan, Book XXIII*, ed. Jacques-Alain Miller, trans. A.R. Price (Malden: Polity, 2016).
35 Jean-Luc Marion, *Being Given: Toward a Phenomenology of Givenness*, trans. J.L. Kosky (Stanford: Stanford University Press, 2002); Jacques Derrida, *Voice and Phenomenon: Introduction to the Problem of the Sign in Husserl's Phenomenology*, trans. Leonard Lawlor (Evanston: Northwestern University Press, 2010); Emmanuel Levinas, *Totality and Infinity: An Essay on Exteriority*, trans. Alphonso Lingis (Pittsburgh: Duquesne University Press, 1969).

Phenomenology and Speculative Realism

Sparrow's book loses no time in identifying phenomenology with correlationism. His exclamation point is not in vain when, in the preface, he asks us to "think of how much effort phenomenology has put into fending off the language of realism and antirealism!" (xiii). In more positive terms, "phenomenology [...] is exclusively committed to investigating only those dimensions of human experience that take shape within the correlation between thought and being" (2). Sparrow cites Zahavi's praise of the correlation between subjectivity and world as essential for phenomenology (15) and plausibly depicts Merleau-Ponty as a correlationist ally (35).[36] But which of the two sorts of correlationism do we find in phenomenology, weak or strong? Weak correlationism, with its acceptance of an unknowable thing-in-itself, would surely be a poor fit for Husserl, who regarded the Kantian *an sich* as an absurdity. Yet for the very same reason, Karl Ameriks argues that Husserl is already as realist as one can possibly be. Sparrow summarizes the issue as follows: "Meillassoux specifies that the kind of correlationism defended by phenomenology is *strong* correlationism, by which he means the view that the in itself is neither knowable nor thinkable. If Ameriks is right about Husserl, however, then the latter represents a *weak* form of correlationism." (35). But there are genuine problems with Ameriks's reading, and Sparrow reminds us why: "[according to Ameriks] neither Husserl's rejection of the thing in itself nor his claim that a 'world outside our own' is absurd force him [...] to abandon realism. It is simply necessary for us to see that his transcendental idealism does not end in *subjectivism*" (33; italics added). Here again we have the favorite trick of Hegelians, who often change the topic of conversation from idealism to subjectivism, knowing as they do that the latter is an easier hurdle for Hegel to clear: just consider the subtitle of Frederick Beiser's influential book on German Idealism, *The*

---

36 He cites Dan Zahavi, *Husserl's Phenomenology* (Stanford: Stanford University Press, 2003).

Struggle against Subjectivism.[37] As Sparrow notes, "If it is true that Husserl's position is not metaphysically neutral, it does not, however, lean towards realism. It leans toward idealism, even absolute idealism, in its steadfast commitment to the inescapability of correlationism" (34).

A critical reader might now ask whether Sparrow himself is guilty of shifting the goalposts to his own benefit. He first claimed that phenomenology was a form of correlationism, but now seems to go further and call it a form of outright idealism. Indeed, the same critic might also note that Meillassoux himself is guilty of the same slippage, sometimes defining correlationism in a way that includes Kantian weak correlationism, while at others requiring correlationism to be the strong form which holds that we cannot talk meaningfully about a thing-in-itself at all. But there is no contradiction here, even though Meillassoux later wished aloud that he had been more precise with his terminology in *After Finitude*.[38] For we have seen that the "weak" and "strong" versions are two different and equally legitimate ways that one can speak of correlationism. The weak version defines it as a philosophy which holds that we cannot speak of thought or world independently of each other, but only in their primal correlation or rapport. This obviously includes Kant. But the strong version defines correlationism, as Meillassoux himself seems to prefer, as resulting from the correlational circle — the argument that we cannot think a thing outside thought without turning it into a thought, thereby bringing it back into the circle. This version does not include Kant, but *does* include Husserl and his rejection of the *Ding an sich*. But is Husserl a "strong correlationist" as Sparrow said earlier in the book, or an "idealist" as he says now? As I see it this is no problem for Sparrow, because

---

37 Frederick C. Beiser, *German Idealism: The Struggle against Subjectivism, 1781–1801* (Cambridge: Harvard University Press, 2008).

38 Quentin Meillassoux, "Iteration, Reiteration, Repetition: A Speculative Analysis of the Meaningless Sign," trans. Robin Mackay and M. Gansen, in *Genealogies of Speculation: Materialism and Subjectivity Since Structuralism*, eds. Armen Avanessian and Suhail Malik (London: Bloomsbury, 2016), 117–97.

there is no ontological distinction between strong correlationism and idealism in the first place, despite Meillassoux's urgent need to drive a wedge between them. In fact, strong correlationism is really just idealism with an added fig leaf. To say that we cannot even speak meaningfully about a thing outside thought is tantamount to saying that nothing exists outside thought, no matter what Meillassoux claims on the matter. If Husserl were really just a weak correlationist, as Ameriks holds, then we could insulate Husserl from charges of idealism just as this is done for Kant: that is, by calling attention to his postulation of the thing-in-itself. But not only does Husserl postulate no such thing, he explicitly rejects it. This means he is actually a strong correlationist, and therefore slips into idealism as quickly as the German Idealists — or as Meillassoux, for that matter. It is really rather simple: if you accept the notion that it is "absurd" to speak of a thing outside thought, then you are an idealist. This is why a number of contemporary Continental idealists — Meillassoux, Slavoj Žižek — prefer to change the subject and speak about materialism instead.

Sparrow is correct in saying that "the evidence of phenomenology is complicit with the antirealist streak of post-Kantian philosophy," at least in the continental tradition (80). He rightly notes that when a phenomenologist starts speaking about "extraphenomenal, transphenomenal, or nonphenomenal entities," they are transgressing the rules of phenomenology itself (80). Stated differently, the point is not whether Husserl knows that the world exists when we are not looking at it, but whether *Husserl's philosophy* knows it. This is why token proclamations of faith in "the existence of the outside world" do nothing to alleviate the rampant forms of idealism that are too often proffered by those who proclaim such faith. Thus, we need not look to the later career of Husserl to find idealism, though it certainly becomes more pronounced as time passes. As for Heidegger, Sparrow puts it best: "[although] already in *Being and Time* [he] seems only nominally committed to phenomenology, when he is, it sounds like antirealism" (26; punctuation modified). In the case of Merleau-Ponty, who is often portrayed as a futuristic, quasi-realist innovator, the atmosphere of idealism is overwhelming for anyone who reads him with a clear sense of what realism means. In Sparrow's words, "one of Merleau-Ponty's chief lessons [is that] when it comes to perception, the very ground of all knowledge, it is possible to perceive the in itself, but this in itself is always only the in itself *for us*" (89). As Sparrow comments further, in response to Ted Toadvine's work, "even if Merleau-Ponty's philosophy of nature does not issue from a fundamentally anthropocentric stance, it nevertheless situates the ground of nature, or what he calls 'wild' or 'brute' being, at the center of the human/nature chiasm" (154). These factors prompt Sparrow to offer some radical advice: "phenomenology should give up on realism and package itself instead as a formidable idealism" (12). More specifically, he suggests Hegelian Idealism as a promising new ally for phenomenologists (188–89).

Throughout Sparrow's book, I agree with nearly everything he says about the weaknesses of phenomenology. Yet I am not so sure it is easy to radicalize Husserlian phenomenology into Hegelian idealism. Although both of these philosophies are often portrayed as being "beyond" idealism even while embracing it, I find the realist alibis of Husserlian phenomenology more intriguing than Hegel's. Although Sparrow does a fine job of chasing down Husserl's alibis and exposing them as shams, I still find them charming for reasons to be explained shortly. From the opening of his book, Sparrow is suitably ruthless in insisting that phenomenology "can only underwrite a rhetoric of realism, not a metaphysical realism" (xiv). He pulls no punches with his examples: "just because Merleau-Ponty provides us with a characteristically rich and evocative description of the day's weather, then adds that he sincerely believes in the autonomous, mind-independent reality of meteorological events, this does not entail that phenomenology authorizes him to make realist commitments" (xiv). In metaphysical terms, "phenomenology appears as a dead-end that leaves its practitioners gesturing toward the outside without ever actually stepping out of the house" (1). While much of phenomenology's rhetoric of concreteness is tied up with "embodiment" (13), DeLanda is right when he calls "the body" a realist alibi for otherwise non-realist philosophies, like a token minority member of an otherwise lily-white corporate board.[39] Yes, Merleau-Ponty can always be summoned to testify about the "opacity" of perception (30) and the permanent bondedness of subject and object in the cosmic "flesh" that joins them (49). But Sparrow shows the weaknesses of such claims when he adds that "phenomenal contestation is no proof of the noumenal" (82).

By contrast with these anti-realist failings of phenomenology, Sparrow is sanguine, I am pleased to note, about the credentials of Speculative Realism and especially about OOO. Some of his kind words need to be quoted here simply because they were later denied so vehemently by Zahavi. In his preface, Sparrow claims that "it is ultimately necessary to close the door on phenomenology as an approach to realism. […] Speculative realism signals the end of phenomenology" (xi). Moreover, "only speculative realism can actually get us out of Kant's shadow" (1), and Speculative Realism is "a new, better-equipped vanguard" (12) for the task of returning to the things themselves. The final, short paragraph of Sparrow's book reads as follows: "For too long we have believed that phenomenology is the philosophy best equipped to deliver the things themselves. In the wake of speculative realism this belief seems more and more unbelievable" (190).

To repeat, I find Sparrow's case concerning the "disavowed antirealism" of phenomenology to be conclusive. But as already mentioned, I am not convinced by his view that phenomenology ought to be radicalized into a form of Hegelian Idealism. For there is an important difference between the respective ways that Husserl and Hegel deploy their idealisms. While defenders of Hegel frequently play the "objective idealism" card to soften accusations of idealism against their hero, it is worth noting that no one ever calls Hegel a realist. But while the defenders of phenomenology also do not frequently call Husserl a realist, I mentioned that the realist *alibis* for phenomenology have

---

39 DeLanda and Harman, *The Rise of Realism*, 116.

an undeniable charm and surface plausibility to them. The reason is that even though phenomenology is an idealism, it is an *object-oriented* idealism nonetheless. The same cannot be said for Hegel, despite the efforts of Robert Stern to portray him as a philosopher of objects.[40] In the phenomenological tradition, however idealist its chief thinkers inevitably turn out to be, there is the constant temptation to think we are in the presence of red-blooded forms of realism. Levinas may not secure genuine realism with his discussions of alterity, but his pages are filled with such examples as bread, cigarette lighters, and fine new automobiles. Merleau-Ponty's "opacity" and "flesh" turn out to be mere covers for an ongoing idealist project, and his "house viewed from everywhere" is not the realist house we might have hoped to find in his work.[41] Yet there is a good reason these authors are able to give mesmerizing descriptions of specific everyday objects in a way we would never expect from Hegel. The same is already true of Husserl, even though as a stylist he is not the equal of Levinas or Merleau-Ponty. Specific objects populate the pages of phenomenological writings in a way that would never have interested earlier idealists. And however inadequate Merleau-Ponty's talk of "opacity" may be, it seems to have realist overtones utterly foreign to Hegel, for whom we could never imagine opacity as a central topic.

What is the reason for this phenomenological allegiance to the play of profiles and shadows? We have seen that Husserl has little to recommend him on the question of how the noumenal relates to the phenomenal, since he merely denies the existence of the former in much the same way as Hegel. But *within* the phenomenal realm, Husserl discovers a great deal that was missed by philosophy before him. Recall that the empiricist tradition tried to eliminate objects from the phenomenal by reducing them to "bundles of qualities." Locke is typical of this group:

---

40 Robert Stern, *Hegel, Kant and the Structure of the Object* (New York: Routledge, 1990).
41 Merleau-Ponty, *Phenomenology of Perception,* 149.

> The mind being, as I have declared, furnished with a great number of the simple ideas, conveyed in by the senses, as they are found in exterior things, or by reflection on its own operations, takes notice also, that a certain number of these simple ideas go constantly together [… and thus] we accustom our selves to suppose some *substratum,* wherein they do subsist, and from which they do result, which therefore we call *substance*.[42]

For empiricism, there is no evidence of an "object" over and above the qualities immediately present to the mind, no case for an empty substratum holding the qualities together. Instead, the name of the object is merely a collective nickname for qualities that appear together frequently enough to deserve a proper name: "banana," "gas lamp," "fox terrier." It is Husserl himself who reverses this empiricist notion, by alerting us to the fact that one and the same object supports shifting sets of qualities ("adumbrations") at different times while still remaining the same object. To be sure, Aristotle had already noticed that substances support different qualities at different times, but these substances were located in a real world outside the mind, whereas Husserl's intentional objects are newfound "intentional objects" in the realm of phenomenal experience. In this way he introduces us to a new tension, found solely in experience, between intentional objects capable of enduring for a while and their constantly shifting adumbrations. More than this, along with the shifting accidental adumbrations, Husserl noticed that his intentional objects also have *essential* qualities that they need in order to remain what they are from one moment to the next. These are what we obtain through the famous *eidetic reduction,* in which the phenomenologist strips away the accidental features of an intentional object to arrive, ultimately, at its *eidos*. This is supposed to occur through a direct "intuition of essence," said moreover to be an intellectual intuition and never a sensuous one.

---

42 Locke, *An Essay Concerning Human Understanding*, 1:390–91.

In this way, Husserl's extreme idealism turned out to be salutary for his philosophical development. Unconcerned by the relation between real and phenomenal that has obsessed so many modern philosophers, Husserl was able to find new levels of texture and complexity within the phenomenal sphere itself — with intentional objects torn between eidetic qualities intuitable by the intellect and accidental adumbrations grasped by the senses. This is why I cannot join Sparrow when he goes so far as to claim that "phenomenology really began and ended with Husserl" (xi) and that "the idea of phenomenology lacks a coherent center" (xiii). It may be true that there has been "a failure on the part of phenomenology to adequately clarify its method, scope, and metaphysical commitments" (xiii) and that "no consensus exists" (4) as to the meaning of phenomenological method, even to the point that "'phenomenology' is on the verge of empty signification, if it has not already crossed that threshold" (189). And indeed, Sparrow cites a number of attempts to define phenomenology in ways that are much too inclusive, as when Dermot Moran calls Hannah Arendt a phenomenologist despite little trace of the phenomenological method in her work[43] (4–5). Yet I would counter that most schools of philosophy, art, and literature are subject to numerous rival definitions, most of them insufficiently precise. More than this, it is often the case that the originator of any movement, struggling full-time with the demands of founding it, is less skilled at defining it than are later heirs. In the case at hand, Husserl is actually better than most at explaining the meaning of phenomenology, which he at least attempts to do in countless passages. Even so, it is possible that a better way to understand phenomenology is to read the first hundred or so pages of Heidegger's *History of the Concept of Time*. Although orthodox Husserlians dislike Heidegger's claim that phenomenology is caught up in the notion of being as "presence for consciousness," and that Husserl fails to raise the question of the meaning of being, Heidegger's account of Hus-

---

43 Dermot Moran, *Introduction to Phenomenology* (London: Routledge, 2000), 189.

serl in that lucid lecture course is basically sympathetic. He does a good job analyzing phenomenology into what he considers its three basic concepts: intentionality, categorial intuition, and the original sense of the *a priori* (as an ontological rather than an epistemological concept). Heidegger also gets the phenomenological method right, defining it as "the analytic description of intentionality in its a priori" (79). Yet even Heidegger misses the truly central discovery, a fourth basic concept more important than the three he records: *intentional objects*. Luckily Sparrow himself does not miss it, but realizes it is the key to the OOO interpretation of Husserl (116–23).

Much of the discussion of intentional objects — whether by Husserl, his rivals, allies, or scholars — is focused on whether they exist internal to the mind, external to the mind, or somewhere else altogether. Restated in Speculative Realist terms, it is a never-ending dispute over whether Husserl was an idealist, a realist, or a correlationist. Put differently, it is an argument about whether there is some sort of gap between an intentional object such as a cat and a real cat that exists in some other place than the intentional one. Husserl obviously regards such a gap as nonsensical or absurd, while I side with Kant on the question of the noumenal. But in an important sense, this perennial dispute merely distracts us from two other gaps that are demonstrably found in Husserl: (a) The gap between an intentional object and its countless adumbrations, its various appearances in sense perception, as when the cat is seen from many different angles and distances; (b) the gap between an intentional object and the qualities it essentially needs in order to be what it is — which is not the case with adumbrations, since in that case all are purely accidental or inessential. Whereas the realist/anti-realist argument over Husserl concerns the gap that OOO names *space,* the latter two gaps or tensions are the ones we call *time* and *eidos*.[44]

We can approach this from another direction. It is well known that the notion of intentional objects — meaning objects immanent in the mind — was revived in the nineteenth century by

---

44 Graham Harman, *The Quadruple Object* (Winchester: Zero Books, 2011).

Husserl's teacher Franz Brentano.[45] The intentional acts aimed at these objects come in three basic types — presentations, judgments, and valuations. Brentano treats presentation as the most basic type, since nothing can be judged, loved, or hated unless it is first present to the mind, whether in perception or in memory. While this seems logical enough at first glance, Husserl rejects Brentano's core idea that intentional experience is grounded in presentation. While seldom discussed, this rejection is so central for Husserl's philosophy that in it we find the whole of his advance beyond not only Brentano but the empiricist tradition as well. The problem with finding the essence of intentionality in presentation is as follows. If we are interested in the essential features of an object of experience, as phenomenology certainly is, then presentation always distracts us with too much information. If we intend a cat, for instance, we not only see the cat but see it as sitting on a specific piece of furniture from a definite angle and distance in a specific quality of light. Quite obviously, none of these overly specific details are necessary for us to intend the cat, and Husserl will ask us to strip away these accidental qualities in the course of the eidetic reduction. To intend the cat, we simply need to intend the intentional object that is *this cat* rather than any specific detailed presentation of it. This is why Husserl tells us in the *Logical Investigations* that Brentano is wrong — intentionality is not about "experienced contents" but about "object-giving acts."[46] Stated more simply, we intend objects rather than all the excessive perceptual detail that inevitably comes bundled with them. We have seen that this central teaching of Husserl has a surprisingly Aristotelian flavor to it and is not unlike the classical distinction between essence and accident, though it occurs in an idealist register foreign to Aristotle himself.

---

45 Franz Brentano, *Psychology from an Empirical Standpoint*, ed. Linda L. McAlister, trans. Antos C. Rancurello, D.B. Terrell, and Linda L. McAlister (London: Routledge, 1995).

46 Husserl, *Logical Investigations*, 1:276.

This is why I disagree with Sparrow that the meaning of phenomenology is not sufficiently clear, and also disagree with Heidegger that phenomenology is about "the analytic description of intentionality in its *a priori*." What phenomenology is really about is the way in which intentional objects differ from the numerous qualities or adumbrations with which they appear, as well as how such objects differ from the crucial *eidetic* qualities that can never be encountered by the senses but which make an intentional object what it is. Sparrow is aware of my view, but rather than evaluate it as a candidate for an integral definition of phenomenology, he focuses instead on the widespread inability of phenomenologists to define what they do in any but the vaguest of terms. In ooo we call the intentional object the *sensual* object, which — let the reader beware! — is the collateral adjective for "sensuality" rather than "sensibility." We do not accept Husserl's claim of a crucial distinction between the senses and the intellect. We also hold that Husserl discovered the existence of a tense relationship between intentional objects and their sensual qualities on one side and their real ones on the other. We steadfastly maintain that Husserl is an idealist who refuses to concede the existence of real objects over and above his intentional — i.e. sensual — ones. Yet there is still enough to be learned from Husserl that his idealism is often beside the point.

Braver's Transgressive Realism

Few authors in contemporary continental philosophy have written more important things than Lee Braver. His debut book *A Thing of This World* displays formidable powers of scholarly synthesis and a talent for philosophical speculation beyond the narrow bounds of scholarship. If this were a fair world, Anglophone continental thought would have shifted soon after the publication of his book from the pretension of being "beyond" realism and idealism to a more candid variant of anti-realism. Instead, though his book has been widely read and cited, it seems not to have spawned much added ontological candor in its readers. Despite my admiration for Braver's work, I have found — through his publications and our personal correspondence — that we almost always disagree on philosophical issues. This is true not only of his first book, but also of two important articles published in later years in which he significantly softens his anti-realist position, quite possibly as a result of his encounter with Speculative Realism.

A Thing of This World was a remorseless defense of anti-realism, which Braver presented both as the most legitimate line of development in continental philosophy and as the source of its relative superiority to the analytic tradition. If we glance at the titles of his later articles, "A Brief History of Continental Realism" (2012) and "On Not Settling the Issue of Realism" (2013), we might be inclined to think that after his first, explicitly anti-realist book, Braver shifted positions. The chronology of these articles might suggest that he was first led to consider an omitted realist strand in continental thought before settling in the second article into a more agnostic position. This is not actually the case. Instead, both articles appeal to a new position that Braver calls "transgressive realism," so that neither is any closer to classical realism than the other.

Given Sparrow's generally positive reaction to Braver's transgressive realism, we might ask how different it is from the overt idealism of *A Thing of This World*. The answer? Not as much as one would think. For instance, in the 2013 article Braver speaks as follows: "I'm still too much of an Anti-Realist to embrace Speculative Realism whole-heartedly. It seems right to me that we always bring our thoughts to any consideration of the world as it is independently of us which automatically compromises any absolute independence."[47] Yet immediately thereafter, he makes what sounds like an important concession:

> But the Speculative Realists are right to point out that the Anti-Realists may have exaggerated the comprehensiveness of our pre-forming of experience. If experience were so fully

---

47 Braver, "On Not Settling the Issue of Realism," 12. Subsequent page references are given between parentheses in the main text preceded by NSI.

pre-digested by the ways our minds process information, we could never experience surprise. Specific, ontic surprises, sure, but not radical surprises that violate and transform our very notions of what is. (NSI 12)

He goes on to say that "*lately,* I've become interested in these moments of revolutionary experience, when our whole sense of what the world is like gets turned inside out" (NSI 12; italics added). The word "lately" rings true for this reader, at least. Braver's more recent articles do show heightened attention to surprises that uproot the very structure of how our world seems to be constituted. We should also note that — if memory serves — the term "transgressive realism" does not appear at all in *A Thing of This World,* and hence we must assume it was coined at a later date. Even Søren Kierkegaard, now depicted by Braver as the founding father of transgressive realism, is hardly mentioned in his earlier book, and even then only to explain why he was largely excluded. To summarize, even though the Braver of 2013 says "I'm still [...] an Anti-Realist," his position has certainly shifted somewhat; he does try to make room for a radical outside that would meet what he sees as the partially valid demands of realism.

Sparrow is not entirely uncritical of this step. As he wisely notes, "Just because something surprises us does not necessarily indicate an ontological rupture in immanence" (59). What Sparrow apparently senses here is that a realism of "surprise" is on roughly the same footing as a realism of "resistance," which he already criticized in the cases of Dilthey and Scheler. Any philosophy of resistance is still guilty of domesticating the outside by reducing it to an obstacle for humans, just as when J.G. Fichte confronts the I with an *Anstoß* that checks or limits it or when Lacan — as we have seen — posits a Real that exists as nothing more than an impasse or trauma for the human subject.[48] Yet elsewhere in Sparrow's book, he is more optimistic

---

48 J.G. Fichte, *The Science of Knowledge,* ed. and trans. Peter Heath and John Lachs (Cambridge: Cambridge University Press, 1982).

about Braver's efforts: "I think Braver uncovers something important for the future of continental philosophy: a middle path between antirealism and realism, but one that does not bear the name of phenomenology" (52). And this is my final point of disagreement with Sparrow's book. For while I share his positive assessment of Braver as a scholar, I do not think there is any such thing as a "middle path" between antirealism and realism, and thus cannot see Braver as anything other than a hardline anti-realist, despite the conciliatory spirit of his recent articles.

One oddity about "On Not Settling the Issue of Realism" is that, while Meillassoux is the only Speculative Realist mentioned by name, and I am entirely omitted, this article actually has more in common with my own philosophy. Whereas Meillassoux holds that the primary qualities of the real can be adequately known through mathematization, this is clearly not the sort of realism that Braver has in mind. Instead, Braver talks about surprises, the horror fiction of H.P. Lovecraft, and aesthetics as a privileged mode of access to the real, all of which are important issues for OOO, but — with the exception of Lovecraft — not for Meillassoux. The article also ends with Braver pleading for "openness" about realism, which sounds exactly like one of my own appeals to Socratic *philosophia* over against knowledge: "Couldn't we learn from questions without trying to settle them, resolve ourselves to not resolving them? Couldn't wisdom be found in reconciling ourselves to its perpetual love, and never to its possession?" (NSI 14). The problem is that Braver's transgressive realist position does not really allow for the openness he appears to demand. Like Meillassoux, he agrees with the idealist that whatever is thought is thought *by us,* so that in principle nothing can be placed outside the correlational circle of thought and world. Braver, again like Meillassoux, is also convinced that we cannot talk about the collision of two inanimate objects but only about our *thinking* about that collision. He merely adds the additional claim that we are sometimes surprised in shocking ways that undercut our very sense of reality. But as an ontology this is not especially "open," since Braver asserts that there must always be a human on the scene to be surprised. To summarize, I do not agree with Braver's claim that object-oriented realism is less open than his own mélange of idealism and existentialism. I also hold that in order to be genuine realism, a philosophy needs to be open to something beyond the human–world correlate, since otherwise we end up with nothing more than yet another realism of the remainder. When Braver tells us that "noumena represent the vestigial remains of traditional metaphysics in Kant's system," he conveniently omits that the noumena, through their very inaccessibility, are what allowed Kant to *annihilate* traditional metaphysics (NSI 10). In this way, Braver again shows his true anti-realist colors. His recent tactical shift toward claiming to be beyond the realist/anti-realist dispute altogether actually weakens the chief virtue of his first book — its unremitting frankness in support of idealism.

Let's turn now to his 2012 article, "A Brief History of Continental Realism." We recall that *A Thing of This World* treated the history of continental philosophy as more or less co-extensive with the history of anti-realist thought. He did find numerous subtle examples of lingering realism in major continental thinkers, but these were treated as symptoms of retrograde compromise rather than evidence of a fruitful realist tradition. So, why his sudden interest in continental realism? It seems fairly obvious that this article was motivated by Braver's recent encounter with Speculative Realism. But in an even more puzzling oddity, this school is mentioned nowhere in Braver's article, other than a strange passing reference in footnote 51 to "Speculative Realists and Quentin Meillassoux," in which the disjunction between Meillassoux and the rest of the group is left unexplained. A more generous way of proceeding would have been to name us and take issue with us, rather than pretending that we had nothing to do with Braver turning his attention to a previously unacknowledged strain of continental realism.

In any event, the point of the 2012 piece is to provide a historical basis for transgressive realism. As stated in the abstract, "Kierkegaard created the position by merging Hegel's insistence that we must have some kind of contact with anything we can call real (thus rejecting noumena), with Kant's belief that reality fundamentally exceeds our understanding; human reason should not be the criterion of the real."[49] This is, in fact, an accurate summary of Braver's case. He is fully on board with Hegel against Kant when it comes to the thing-in-itself: "By jettisoning the very idea of noumena, Hegel's Objective Idealism takes the scare quotes off of Kant's phenomenal 'knowledge,' and it does so without resorting to a God's-eye view" (HCR 266). The supposed contribution of Kierkegaard to a germinal form of realism is also convincing enough: "Whereas Kant and Hegel place morality entirely within our reach, Kierkegaard insists that we dare not claim to know all that morality is and can be. In short, ethics and reason acquire an outside. Not only is there an outside, as Hegel denies, but we can encounter it, as Kant denies" (HCR 270). And further, "Kierkegaard's transcendence does not repose in undisturbed isolation but makes contact with us. This experience is not squeezed into our mental structures but violates them, overloading and reshaping our categories" (HCR 271). There is also an unexpected moment when the formerly rabid anti-realist Braver praises Kierkegaard for avoiding Hegel's "arrogant anti-realism" (HCR 272).

Now, what is the supposed virtue of transgressive realism as opposed to the various brands of Speculative Realism? Since Braver never considers this question in his article, we can only guess, though I will try to limit my guesses to direct textual evidence. Here is one such piece of evidence: "Transgressive Realism, I am arguing, offers a *via media,* a way to have our ineffable cake and eff it too. It gives us a reality that transcends our ways of thinking, but not all access to it" (HCR 272). But which sort of realism posits an ineffable that transcends *all* access to it? One might make this argument against Kant, though in his case there is still a sort of indirect access to the noumenal side of humans through the assumption of our ethical freedom, and even an indirect access to artworks and biological creatures through the

---

49 Lee Braver, "A History of Continental Realism," *Continental Philosophy Review* 45, no 2 (2012): 261. Subsequent page references are given between parentheses in the main text preceded by HCR.

faculty of judgment.⁵⁰ But does Braver's critique work against OOO? Not at all, since OOO does not deny all access to the supposedly ineffable real but simply denies that *knowledge* (whether reducing an object downward to its components or upward to its effects) is able to exhaust the real.⁵¹ This is why I agree with Braver that art has a different sort of access to the real that does not reduce it to its givenness, though I also extend the argument to philosophy itself, which must be understood in the sense of the Socratic *philosophia* rather than the *sophia* of those who wish it to be a critical appendage to natural science.

Among his transgressive realist allies, Braver names Heidegger and Levinas, who are favorite authors of mine as well. And indeed, there is a sense in which both philosophers end up with a realism of the remainder in which the real has little role other than to haunt human cognition with its opacity. Even so, I do not think Braver gets everything right about these two figures. For example, he has this to say about Heidegger: "His background in phenomenology, which equates beings with phenomena and being with appearing or manifesting, places him squarely among the enemies of noumena" (HCR 273). While there is a certain degree of truth in this characterization, as seen from Heidegger's frequent dismissive accounts of the realism/anti-realism dispute, Braver follows most Heidegger scholars in ignoring at least one striking counter-instance. I speak of a badly neglected passage from late in *Kant and the Problem of Metaphysics,* where Heidegger boldly declares: "What is the significance of the struggle initiated in German Idealism against the 'thing-in-itself' except a growing forgetfulness of what Kant had won, namely […] the original development and searching

---

50 Immanuel Kant, *Critique of Practical Reason,* trans. Mary Gregor, 2nd edn. (Cambridge: Cambridge University Press, 2015); Immanuel Kant, *Critique of Judgment,* trans. Werner S. Pluhar (Indianapolis: Hackett Publishing Company, 1987).

51 Graham Harman, "Undermining, Overmining, and Duomining: A Critique," in *ADD Metaphysics,* ed. Jenna Sutela (Aalto: Aalto University Design Research Laboratory, 2013), 40–51.

study of the problem of human finitude?"[52] True enough, Heidegger's real emphasis in this passage is on human finitude; he never escaped the basically Kantian correlationism for which Being is of little interest aside from how it reveals itself to *Dasein*. Nonetheless, there is no evidence that Being for Heidegger is exhausted in its manifestation to *Dasein,* despite Derrida's baseless assertion to the contrary, and thus Heidegger's positive mention of noumena deserves our attention.[53] To my mind, Braver also places too much stress on Heidegger's "altering our attitude from absorbed coping to disengaged observation" (HCR 273), since it is unclear that the difference between human practical and theoretical comportment is of much philosophical significance at all.[54] At times, Braver even seems to lose all remembrance of Heidegger's break with Husserl: "Phenomenology's implicit ontology, which Heidegger considers the only legitimate ontology, agrees with Objective Idealism in restricting reality to what we can encounter" (HCR 273).

As for Levinas, there is indeed something of the transgressive realist about him, given his fascination with absolute Otherness. Braver cites the following, highly relevant passage from Levinas: "Husserl's idealism is the affirmation that every object, the pole of a synthesis of identifications, is permeable to the mind; or, conversely, that the mind can encounter nothing without comprehending it. Being can never shock the mind. […] Nothing in the world could be absolutely foreign to the subject."[55] And further, "When the Other enters into the horizon of knowledge, it already renounces alterity. […] It infinitely overflows the

---

52 Martin Heidegger, *Kant and the Problem of Metaphysics,* trans. James S. Churchill (Bloomington: Indiana University Press, 1965), 251–52.
53 Jacques Derrida, *Of Grammatology,* trans. Gayatri Chakravorty Spivak (Baltimore: Johns Hopkins University Press, 2016), 22–23.
54 Harman, *Tool-Being*; Graham Harman, *Heidegger Explained: From Phenomenon to Thing* (Chicago: Open Court, 2007).
55 Emmanuel Levinas, *Discovering Existence with Husserl,* trans. Richard A. Cohen and Michael B. Smith (Evanston: Northwestern University Press, 1998), 68–69.

bounds of knowledge."⁵⁶ But while this argument for "radical alterity" is the most famous aspect of Levinas, I would contest the idea that it is his most important contribution. For precisely due to its "infinity," the Other in Levinas shares one of the biggest problems with Kant's notion of the sublime — namely, if all sublime experiences are taken to be *absolutely* large, it becomes difficult to distinguish one from another. If my brother is one infinite otherness and a menacing stranger in an alley another, then in this infinity they are the same, and any differentiation between them will be a mere surface-effect concealing an *apeiron* of ethical otherness that swallows them both. Lest this sound too extreme, I would note that the problem is more than foreshadowed in the early Levinasian text *Existence and Existents,* in which being itself is treated as a shapeless *il y a* or "there is," with all specific beings resulting from a "hypostasis" performed solely by the human mind.⁵⁷ I am unmoved by Braver's pre-emptive strike against this critique: "Transgressive thinkers are not positing an inchoate chaos howling outside the borders of thought or rumbling beneath the floorboards of experience [...] Rather, that which exceeds our grasp strikes us precisely *by* exceeding it, stretching previous categories until they rip, leaving us with conceptual tatters which get sewn into motley paradoxical categories of the uncategorizable" (HCR 284–85). Insofar as I can make sense of this, his point seems to be that the excess of alterity is to be judged not by its own amorphous surplus but by the way it transforms our own immanent understanding of the world, so that my brother differs from the stranger in the alley only through the different effects they have on me and others. But in that case, we must wonder how they are able to have different effects in the first place, if they are both chunks of the same *apeiron*. This simply means that Braver's Levinas is less a "realist" in any meaningful sense than he is a modern-

---

56 Emmanuel Levinas, *Basic Philosophical Writings,* eds. Adriaan Peperzak, Simon Critchley, and Robert Bernasconi (Bloomington: Indiana University Press, 1996), 12.

57 Emmanuel Levinas, *Existence and Existents,* trans. Alphonso Lingis (Pittsburgh: Duquesne University Press, 2001).

day Anaximander. In other words, to the extent that Levinas is a realist, he is also a monist unable to articulate the various incarnations of infinite alterity in the world. For this reason, I find him much stronger as a thinker of the surface of reality, as in his remarkable discussions of the enjoyment of individual things.

Ultimately, why is Braver so concerned to cut off philosophical discussion of object–object relations and limit himself to the inscrutable traumas faced by human beings? His clearest justification can be found in the previously discussed article, "On Not Settling the Issue of Realism." There he tells us as follows:

> [A]gainst the Speculative Realists, I still think that reality has to make some kind of contact with us for us to be able to talk about it. I don't see how discussion of the ways that inanimate objects "experience" or "encounter" each other in the dark after we've all gone to bed could ever be more than mere speculation. It's just that this contact doesn't always fit neatly into our concepts, [in] the way the Anti-Realists had it. (NSI 12)

This nicely encapsulates the feature of modernism that, in Part Two of this book, I will call Onto-Taxonomy. A brief criticism is already in order. Braver's point seems to be that *because* we humans are inevitably limited to human experience, as Kant famously argued, it is impossible to speculate on what the experience of some other entity might be like. But this conflates two separate issues, and here Braver is far from alone. It is certainly true that I cannot know exactly what it is like to be a bat or dog or slime mold, and to a lesser extent I cannot even know what it is like to be a woman, African-American, or a billionaire in twenty-first-century America. But this expectation sets too high a hurdle, for I do not need *to be* a woman, an African-American, or a billionaire to argue that such people are every bit as finite as I am. Stated differently, I do not gain the sense of my own finitude from more than fifty years experience of living my own life, so that I would somehow have to leave it open as to whether my fellow humans and other creatures are also finite. Instead, finitude is the result of a *philosophical argument* by Kant, to the effect that we did not create the thing-in-itself and therefore (unlike God) cannot know it. This is not the form taken by my own argument for finitude, which simply appeals to the inability of any relation to exhaust its terms, including relations in which no human or other living creature participates. We can deduce the finitude of billionaires, dogs, and slime molds just as easily as we deduce it in our own case. We need not step into their shoes to do it; it is not the kind of lesson that requires any degree of empathy. By closing off this possibility, Braver joins the mainstream of modern philosophy (including Meillassoux) in taking the human–world relation to be the philosophical root of all the others. For this reason, I cannot follow Sparrow in seeing significant promise in transgressive realism.

2

STEVEN SHAVIRO

The Universe of Things

Steven Shaviro has a colorful range of interests running from cinema, to Marxism, to science fiction, to the philosophies of Whitehead and Deleuze. *The Universe of Things* ostensibly owes more to Whitehead than to the other items on the list, though we will encounter a key point where Deleuze seems to be the dominant influence. Shaviro is such a fair and generous critic that I cannot imagine anyone disliking him; at the very least, I would be suspicious of anyone who did. While he is not someone who goes out of his way to agree for the sake of artificial harmony, the blunt New Yorker in him somehow delivers the bluntness in inoffensive fashion. I do not recall having ever been annoyed with him for even a fraction of a second.

Shaviro and I agree on any number of things, and *The Universe of Things* offers numerous examples of intellectual overlap. Otherwise, there are perhaps three points of serious disagreement, and these are likely to be of greater interest to the reader:

1. Although we both stress the importance of aesthetics, Shaviro favors the beautiful over the sublime, since the latter strikes him as a worn-out modernist trope. He follows Whitehead in treating the nature of beauty as "patterned contrasts" and critiques ooo for overinvesting in the sublime. The root of

our disagreement here is that OOO actually does not take the side of the sublime against beauty.

2. What Shaviro admires in both Whitehead and Deleuze is their apparently shared focus on process and becoming. By contrast, he sees OOO as providing a hopelessly static model of the world.

3. When it comes to cognition, Shaviro proceeds in decidedly non-modernist fashion, endorsing a panpsychist theory of Whiteheadian inspiration. He also treats cognition in relational terms and criticizes OOO for its insistence on a non-relational model of beings.

Each of these points deserves a section of its own, though they will not be of equal length. Since the objection concerning the beautiful and the sublime is one I have addressed twice in print already, a brief rejoinder should suffice.[1]

The Beautiful and the Sublime

Let's begin on the final page of Shaviro's book: "The primordial form of all experience, and thereby of all action and relation, is an aesthetic one. This is why Harman is right to proclaim that aesthetics is not 'a local phenomenon of human experience,' but rather 'the root of all relations [...] including causal relations.'"[2] We do agree on this point, which is enough to make us black sheep in a philosophy world still ruled by the Modernist Onto-

---

[1] Graham Harman, "Response to Shaviro," in *The Speculative Turn: Continental Materialism and Realism,* eds. Levi R. Bryant, Nick Srnicek, and Graham Harman (Melbourne: re.press, 2011), 279–90; Graham Harman, *Art and Objects* (Cambridge: Polity, 2020), 45–47.

[2] Steven Shaviro, *The Universe of Things: On Speculative Realism* (Minneapolis: University of Minnesota Press, 2014), 156. Subsequent page references are given between parentheses in the main text. The reference here to my own work is to Graham Harman, "On Vicarious Causation," in *Collapse II,* ed. Robin Mackay (Falstaff: Urbanomic, 2007), 221.

Taxonomy that treats human thought as one sphere and nature as another that only the sciences are permitted to enter, while throwing animals and plants onto whichever side is convenient at the moment. However freely Meillassoux may speculate on the virtual God, he will always be spared ultimate ridicule given his patient observance of the standard modern rift between thought on one side and "dead matter" on the other.[3] Shaviro and I are more likely to be on the receiving end of punch-the-hippie attacks by rationalists, due to our shared concern with "how nonhuman agents, no less than human ones, perform actions and express needs and values" (5). We also agree that Whitehead "is one of those rare philosophers who […] dares to venture beyond the human sphere" (6), although this is not a virtue for those who assume that humans are trapped in a prison of self-reflexivity, unable to think anything outside thought without immediately turning it into a thought. In Shaviro's own words, "No particular entity — not even the human subject — can claim metaphysical preeminence or serve as a favored mediator. All entities, of all sizes and scales, have the same degree of reality. They all interact with each other in the same ways, and they all exhibit the same sorts of properties" (29). This is not something one would hear from the likes of Badiou, Meillassoux, or Slavoj Žižek, who represent the main speculative branch of Modernist Onto-Taxonomy in our time.

Stated differently, Shaviro and I join Whitehead in affirming a "flat ontology" in which all entities are placed on the same footing, unlike the medievals (God) and moderns (thought) who take one kind of entity to be ontologically the most important. We also join Whitehead in treating aesthetic experience as more primary than the intellectual sort, which we both see as an especially complex version of experience that occurs only rarely in the cosmos. Yet we now diverge sharply, though not in exactly the way Shaviro thinks. In his own words:

3   Quentin Meillassoux, "Appendix: Excerpts from *L'Inexistence divine*," in Graham Harman, *Quentin Meillassoux: Philosophy in the Making* (Edinburgh: Edinburgh University Press, 2015), 175–238.

> The difference between Whitehead and Harman is best understood, I think, as a difference between the aesthetics of beauty and the aesthetics of the sublime. Whitehead defines beauty as a matter of differences that are conciliated, adapted to one another, and "interwoven in patterned contrasts," in order to make for "intense experience." Harman, for his part, appeals to notions of the sublime: although he never uses this word, he refers instead to what he calls allure, or the attraction of something that has retreated into its own depths. […] Allure is properly a sublime experience because it stretches the observer to the point where it reaches the limits of its power or where its apprehensions break down.[4] (42)

Shaviro's alternative to allure and its hidden depth is the term "metamorphosis," admittedly a better match for Whiteheadian process philosophy. As he puts it,

> In metamorphosis, it is not the thing itself that attracts me, over and above its qualities; it is rather the very unsteadiness of the thing that draws me onward, as it ripples and shifts in a kind of protean wavering. […] Metamorphosis thus reflects the way that, as Whitehead puts it, "every actual entity is present in every other actual entity." In the movement of allure, the web of meaning is ruptured as the thing emerges violently from its context; but in the movement of metamorphosis, the web of meaning is multiplied and extended, echoed and distorted, and propagated to infinity as the thing loses itself in the network of its ramifying traces.[5] (54)

This beautiful description draws the following distinction: allure is about hiddenness, or the gulf between a real object and its accessibility, while metamorphosis is centered in the rift between

---

4 Alfred North Whitehead, *Adventures of Ideas* (New York: Free Press, 1967), 252, 263; Graham Harman, *Guerrilla Metaphysics: Phenomenology and the Carpentry of Things* (Chicago: Open Court, 2005), 141–44.
5 Alfred North Whitehead, *Process and Reality* (New York: Free Press, 1978), 50.

an entity and its own shifting kaleidoscopic patterns, which do not retreat into any sort of depth at all. Although Shaviro kindly states that his preference for Whitehead's theory over mine comes down to a matter of taste (41), it is more than that, since he happens to think that Whitehead is on the right side of history here. Since my theory of allure so closely resembles the Kantian sublime — or so Shaviro claims — it "fits very well into what is now an extended modernist tradition" (43). By contrast, the Whitehead-inspired theory of metamorphosis is said to be a better match for twenty-first century culture: "We live in a world where all manners of cultural expression are digitally transcoded and electronically disseminated, where genetic material is freely recombined, and where matter is becoming open to direct manipulation on the atomic and subatomic scales. Nothing is hidden; there are no more concealed depths" (43).

Let me now explain why I think Shaviro's contrast between Whiteheadian and OOO aesthetics is not quite on target. First, there is a striking insufficiency in Whitehead's definition of beauty as "patterned contrasts," which I cannot regard as one of his strongest moments as a thinker. It is a flowery approximation too easily subverted with counterexamples, as also happens with many theories of humor such as "sudden incongruity," "benign violation," "defense mechanism," "economy of energy," and the like. For it is not hard to think of examples of patterned contrasts that are not beautiful in the least. Allure, however, offers a precise theory of beauty that does not hide behind vagueness: for OOO, allure results from a rift between a real object and its sensual qualities. While this theory can be opposed just like any other, there are no obvious counterinstances to it.

Second, Shaviro is wrong to identify allure with the Kantian sublime by saying that "allure is properly a sublime experience because it stretches the observer to the point where it reaches the limits of its power or where its apprehensions break down" (42). This equation fails for two reasons. One is that we need not turn to the *sublime* in Kant to find a place where the observer reaches the limits of their power. This is already true for Kant's notion of beauty, which by definition is unparaphrasable and unconceptualizable, approachable only by means of taste. On this point I enjoy the unexpected alliance of Jacques Rancière, who also regrets the excessive focus on the sublime in recent decades.[6] But there is another, more decisive point. For while Shaviro rightly emphasizes the depth and inscrutability of the sublime — while missing that the same is true of beauty — he fails to note that the sublime is also defined in absolute terms. As Kant puts it in Book II of the *Critique of Judgment*, "we call *sublime* what is *absolutely* large [… meaning that which is] *large beyond all comparison*."[7] He goes on to distinguish between absolute magnitude (the mathematical sublime) and absolute power (the dynamical sublime), but both exemplify something that is absolutely beyond the human scale. This is why the Kantian sublime has nothing to do with OOO's allure, which I identify instead with beauty. The best way to see this is to consider Timothy Morton's notion of "hyperobjects," a term coined primarily for ecological purposes, though it can also be deployed as a pointed critique of the Kantian sublime. Morton is not interested in absolutes and infinities, which he takes to be covertly anthropocentric terms. Instead, hyperobjects pertain to extremely large finite quantities. As he puts it, "Infinity is far easier to cope with. Infinity brings to mind our cognitive powers. […] But hyperobjects are not forever. What they offer instead is *very large finitude*. I can think infinity. But I can't count up to one hundred thousand."[8] In short, Morton is interested in the hyperobjective rather than the sublime, and so am I: the "absolutely" large or powerful are simply the night in which all black holes and tsunamis equally eclipse the tiny human form.

What Shaviro calls "metamorphosis" is already accounted for by OOO under the name of *time* (or the SO–SQ tension) and by Kant under the name of *charm*. It has to do with the delightful

---

6 Jacques Rancière, *The Emancipated Spectator*, trans. Gregory Elliott (London: Verso, 2011), 64.
7 Immanuel Kant, *Critique of Judgment*, trans. Werner S. Pluhar (Indianapolis: Hackett Publishing Company, 1987), 103.
8 Timothy Morton, *Hyperobjects: Philosophy and Ecology after the End of the World* (Minneapolis: University of Minnesota Press, 2013), 60.

rippling play between a thing and its various shifting configurations over time, as with the flickering flames in the stove of a snowbound cabin.⁹ Kant views this as a subsidiary form of beauty, incapable of rising to great aesthetic heights. As for OOO, this SO–SQ tension is counted as one of the four basic kinds of aesthetics in the broadest sense.¹⁰ But it cannot account for beauty, which requires the withdrawal of a real object and the beholder's own theatrical replacement of it.¹¹ Since I have already dealt with this topic in other publications, we should move on to other disagreements.¹²

Becoming and Stasis

Shaviro is not the first to have charged OOO with offering an excessively static conception of reality. He places himself instead in the Whiteheadian camp of novelty and becoming:

> Whitehead […] envisions a dynamic world of entities that make decisions — or more precisely, of entities whose very being consists in the decisions they make. Harman's entities, in contrast, do not spontaneously act or decide; they simply *are*. For Harman, the qualities of an entity somehow already preexist; for Whitehead, these qualities are generated on the fly. (40)

For Shaviro, the preference for becoming over stasis links directly with his favoring of a relational ontology over the nonrelational sort embodied by OOO. My philosophy, he holds, "[affirms] the actuality of the volcano only at the price of isolating

---

9 Kant, *Critique of Judgment*, 95.
10 Graham Harman, *The Quadruple Object* (Winchester: Zero Books, 2011).
11 Graham Harman, "A New Sense of Mimesis," in *Aesthetics Equals Politics: New Discourses across Art, Architecture, and Philosophy,* ed. Mark Foster Gage (Cambridge: MIT Press, 2019), 49–64.
12 The most concise argument is probably in Graham Harman, "Materialism Is Not the Solution: On Matter, Form, and Mimesis," *The Nordic Journal of Aesthetics* 47 (2016): 94–110.

it from the world and reducing its dynamism to a sort of sterile display—which is all that it can be, in the absence of its direct effects on other entities" (41). As mentioned, Shaviro is far from alone in this sentiment. For more than a century we have heard the refrain that a theory of constant flux is truer to reality than one of static independent substances that engage in relations after the fact. I too can recall my excitement as an undergraduate when reading Benjamin Lee Whorf's argument that the Hopi language was more suited for up-to-date quantum theory than our sadly static Indo-European noun/verb grammar.[13] More recently, the revival of Bergsonian currents by Deleuze and Gilbert Simondon has led to increased emphasis on the *process* of individuation while instilling suspicion about the OOO concern with "fully-formed individuals."[14] Michael Austin and Miguel Penas López are just two of the younger authors who have approached my work critically from this direction.[15] But perhaps Shaviro's own words are the most damning: "where Whitehead is concerned with both transience and futurity (which he calls 'creative advance'), Harman shows little interest in either of these" (40).

Shaviro himself shows plenty of interest in the inherent instability of things, and in the opening pages of the book he praises Whitehead for doing the same: "The world, [Whitehead] says, is composed of processes, not things" (2). For him the ultimate atoms of experience, known as "actual entities," are

13   Benjamin Lee Whorf, *Language, Thought, and Reality,* ed. John B. Carroll (Cambridge: MIT Press, 1956).
14   Henri Bergson, *Time and Free Will: An Essay on the Immediate Data of Consciousness,* trans. F.L. Pogson (Mineola: Dover, 2001); Gilles Deleuze, *Bergsonism,* trans. Hugh Tomlinson and Barbara Habberjam (New York: Zone Books, 1991); Gilbert Simondon, *L'Individuation à la lumière des notions de forme et d'information* (Grenoble: Jérôme Millon, 2005).
15   Michael Austin, "To Exist Is to Change: A Friendly Disagreement with Graham Harman on Why Things Happen," in *Speculations I,* ed. Paul J. Ennis (Brooklyn: punctum books, 2010), 66–83; Miguel Peñas López, "Speculative Experiments: What If Harman and Simondon Individuate Together?" in *Speculations V,* eds. Ridvan Askin et al. (Brooklyn: punctum books, 2014), 225–47.

"active and articulated processes — experiences, or moments of feeling — rather than simple, self-identical substances" (3). And finally, "the world is never static, never closed, never completed. Each process of becoming gives rise to *novelty*: it produces something new and unique, something that has never existed before. Things do not 'persist in being' (the definition of Spinoza's *conatus*) so much as they continually alter and transform themselves" (4). There is also my own purported failure to do Whitehead justice: "Because he insists on enduring substances, as opposed to relations among 'perpetually perishing' occasions, Harman underestimates Whitehead's account of change" (38).

Shaviro's next step is to assemble a list of allies for his process-oriented view of the world, beginning with a crowd favorite: "the recent revival of interest in Whitehead has also been spurred by an increasing recognition of the affinities between Whitehead's process-oriented thought and that of the French philosopher Gilles Deleuze" (4). While conceding my own resemblance to Whitehead on one point, he distinguishes us on another: "even as Whitehead's actualism links him to Harman, so his insistence on processes and becoming — which is to say, on relations — links him to Deleuze and to [Iain Hamilton] Grant"[16] (35). Shaviro also admires the book on Whitehead by Isabelle Stengers (9), which at least two scholars have called "the book to beat" in recent Whitehead studies, and Stengers too sees an intimate link between Whitehead and Deleuze.[17] But even as Shaviro holds that Whitehead is the master of creative, relational novelty whereas I am trapped in static substancehood, he simultaneously argues that Whitehead is also the thinker who *balances* the opposed claims of relation and individuality. Shaviro can only wish, he tells us, that ontological isolation were as normal as OOO claims. Instead, he reports that "our

---

16 Iain Hamilton Grant, *Philosophies of Nature after Schelling* (London: Continuum, 2008).

17 Isabelle Stengers, *Thinking with Whitehead: A Free and Wild Creation of Concepts,* trans. Michael Chase (Cambridge: Harvard University Press, 2011); Randall E. Auxier and Gary L. Herstein, *The Quantum of Explanation: Whitehead's Radical Empiricism* (London: Routledge, 2017), 18.

fundamental condition is one of ubiquitous and inescapable connections. We are continually beset by relations, smothered and suffocated by them" (33). And further, "To my mind, relation and causal determination are our common conditions and maladies, and self-creation or independence is the rare, fragile, and extraordinary achievement that needs to be cultivated and cherished" (34). I always appreciate those moments when philosophers share the background experiences that shape their arguments, and certainly appreciate Shaviro's words here. If he feels so oppressed by the swarm of relations in contemporary life, one might wonder why his "taste" leads him to Whitehead rather than OOO. The reason, I take it, is that Whitehead's relationism foregrounds the perilous over-connected situation in which Shaviro feels trapped, and that he works his way out of it rather than simply positing its non-existence in the manner of object-oriented thinkers. In any case, he thinks I do not sufficiently honor Whitehead's twofold achievement:

> Whitehead refers to the "'really real' things" that "constitute the universe" both as "actual entities" and "actual occasions." They are alternatively things or happenings. These two modes of being are different, yet they can be identified with one another, in much the same way that "matter has been identified with energy" in modern physics. When Harman rejects Whitehead's claims about relations, he is not being sufficiently attentive to the dual-aspect nature of Whitehead's ontology. This can also be expressed in another way. Harman skips over the dimension of *privacy* in Whitehead's account of objects.[18] (35)

The consequences are said to be serious, for "[Whitehead] also has a sense of the cosmic irony of transition and transience. And this latter sense is something that I do not find in Harman" (36).

---

18 The quoted phrases in this passage are from Alfred North Whitehead, *Modes of Thought* (New York: Free Press, 1938), 137.

Shaviro's root claim in these matters is that philosophies of individual substance inevitably lead to stasis and fixity. This does ally him with Whitehead, who famously dismissed the concept of substance as an example of "vacuous actuality," which in his view "haunts realist philosophy" with the untenable notion of essentially non-relational things.[19] We can leave this particular dispute for the discussion of relations in the next section. But one thing that *cannot* straightforwardly be said about Aristotle's theory of substance is that it is insensitive to transience and change. The point is relevant because OOO, like all theories that highlight individual things capable of enduring for more than an instant, ultimately traces its ancestry to Aristotle. Seen in the context of his era, Aristotle actually looks like a wild advocate of dynamic change. It is not just his proverbial opposition to Plato's eternal perfect forms, his pathbreaking study of corruptible biological things, and his physics so heavily devoted to change and motion. More than this, it would be fair to say that Aristotle was the first philosopher to place *destructible* entities at the center of his philosophy. We recall that the pre-Socratic thinkers competed to deliver the best version of the root element of the world: water, air, the four elements mixed together, atoms, being, or the formless *apeiron*. But note that all of these options exist eternally. Even the two pre-Socratics who believed in an ancient destruction of the *apeiron* found its successor in something that was eternal: number for Pythagoras, and the tiny *homoiomereiai* for Anaxagoras. By contrast, the ranks of Aristotle's substances consist largely of mortal living creatures. This is the first point I want to make about Aristotle, that he is primarily a philosopher of change and movement, not of fixity and stasis. The fact that an Aristotelian primary substance might endure for hours, weeks, or decades before dying hardly puts him in the same camp as Platonic or Christian theories of eternity. Only because Whitehead sets such a high bar for becoming — a "perpetual perishing" in which nothing lasts more than a single instant — can Aristotle look like a static old grump by compari-

---

19 Whitehead, *Process and Reality*, 29.

son. To summarize, we should acknowledge that the Aristotelian tradition generally does a pretty good job of accounting for change, and if someone insists that a philosophy of change requires the abolition of *any temporal endurance whatsoever,* then we ought to ask them why. This holds not only for Shaviro and Whitehead but also for my favorite living philosopher, Bruno Latour, who tells us that "everything happens only once, and at one place," which precludes the endurance of an actor for more than an instant.[20] But there is something else that needs to be said about Aristotle, though it works against Shaviro less directly. Namely, one of the most important dualisms in Aristotle is his distinction between the continuous and the discrete. We know this because two of his greatest works, the *Physics* and the *Metaphysics,* each deal primarily with one of them.[21] Perhaps the central topic of the *Physics* is the continuum. Considering the room in which you are now reading, how many parts does it have? We can divide it arbitrarily into two, seven, nine hundred, or perhaps a billion segments. Some divisions of a given space might make more practical sense than others, but in absolute terms, we can *potentially* divide space into any number of pieces we like, which does not mean it is actually thus divided in its own right. A given space is always a single continuum, not the aggregate product of a definite number of tiny spatial elements. What about the time you need to read this chapter on Shaviro? How many pieces does this stretch of time have? Again, it is a continuum — it has no definite number of parts but can be split up according to our convenience into three spans of time, five spans, one hundred forty-seven, or however many we please. The same holds if we ask how many numbers there are between zero and one thousand, since we can count by integers, halves, tens, or hundreds, with equal justice in each case. Among other

20 Bruno Latour, "Irreductions," trans. John Law, in *The Pasteurization of France,* trans. Alan Sheridan and John Law (Cambridge: Harvard University Press, 1988), 162.
21 Aristotle, *Physics,* trans. Robin Waterfield (Oxford: World's Classics, 1996); Aristotle, *Metaphysics,* trans. Hugh Lawson-Tancred (London: Penguin, 2004).

consequences of this thesis, Aristotle uses it to refute some of Zeno's famous paradoxes, which are shown to rely on a misconception of time and space as made up of discrete units. But what about the *Metaphysics*? Here, the focus shifts away from continua and toward the discrete. How many individual substances are there in the room with you right now? Assuming we agree on our definition of what counts as a substance, then there is some *exact number* of substances in the room, one that in principle can be tabulated. There are either ten, or seventy-five, or nine hundred substances in the room, or some other number. For Aristotle this is not subject to arbitrary whim, unlike when we slice up a continuum. We thus see that the *Physics* and the *Metaphysics* establish a division of labor, with some aspects of reality definable as continua and others as made up of discrete units.

Now, the difference between the continuous and the discrete happens to be one of the central dualisms of human thought in every field; anyone who thinks about anything must reach some decision as to how to integrate these two opposites. But of course, Aristotle's division of labor is not the only way to do it. Thus it should be no surprise that various extremist positions have also arisen over the centuries, seeking either to reduce the continuous to the discrete or vice versa. The clearest extremists of the discrete are surely the occasionalists, who first appeared in medieval Islam and re-appeared — for somewhat different reasons — in early-modern Europe.[22] There are actually two different occasionalist theses, which we might call "spatial" and "temporal," and not all occasionalist thinkers have defended both.[23] "Spatial" occasionalism is the notion that no two enti-

---

22 Majid Fakhry, *Islamic Occasionalism and Its Critique by Averroës and Aquinas* (London: Allen & Unwin, 1958); Dominik Perler and Ulrich Rudolph, *Occasionalismus: Theorien der Kausalität im arabisch-islamischen und im europäischen Denken* (Göttingen: Vandenhoeck & Ruprecht, 2000); Steven Nadler, *Occasionalism: Causation among the Cartesians* (Oxford: Oxford University Press, 2011).

23 Graham Harman, "A New Occasionalism?" in *Reset Modernity!*, eds. Bruno Latour and Christophe Leclercq (Cambridge: MIT Press, 2016), 129–38.

ties can influence each other directly, so that God must be the universal causal agent for everything that happens. "Temporal" occasionalism refers to the view that the world does not exist automatically from one moment to the next but must be continuously recreated by God. But there are also extremists of the continuous, far more popular today. Deleuze and Simondon are two of the leading figures in this tribe, and Grant belongs in this group as well, given his view that what seem to be individual entities are simply "retardations" of a more primal, unified flow of production.

For obvious reasons, it is difficult to unify the opposed extremists of the discrete and the continuous, since each group tries to reduce the central concern of the other to its own obsession.[24] This poses a grave difficulty for Shaviro, as well as Stengers, in their wish to place Whitehead on the same philosophical team as another of their joint favorites, Deleuze.[25] Shaviro is well aware that Whitehead is *at least* a temporal occasionalist for whom the world does not automatically endure from one moment to the next: "For Whitehead, even death and resurrection are commonplace occurrences. Objects endure by refreshing themselves continually. Everything is subject to a rule of 'perpetual perishing,' for 'no thinker thinks twice; and, to put the matter more generally, no subject experiences twice'"[26] (23). I am also inclined to view Whitehead as a spatial occasionalist, for reasons to be mentioned shortly. By contrast, Shaviro thinks Whitehead manages to avoid this second topic completely: "there is […] no gap to bridge between any one […] entity and another" (39). The problem with this claim is that just like the occasionalists of earlier centuries, Whitehead invokes God as a universal causal mediator, with entities prehending each other by way of the "eternal objects" (roughly, universal qualities) con-

---

24 Graham Harman, "Whitehead and Schools X, Y, and Z," in *The Lure of Whitehead*, eds. Nicholas Gaskill and A.J. Nocek (Minneapolis: University of Minnesota Press, 2014), 231–48.
25 Steven Shaviro, *Without Criteria: Kant, Whitehead, Deleuze, and Aesthetics* (Cambridge: MIT Press, 2009).
26 Whitehead, *Process and Reality*, 29.

tained in God. This entails that Whitehead is a spatial occasionalist as well, since he acknowledges that relations occur only by way of a mediator.

Now, it would simply be false to say there is a doctrine of "perpetual perishing" anywhere in the writings of Bergson, Deleuze, or Simondon. These three are extremists at one end of the spectrum, on the opposite side of the occasionalists, who include Whitehead — along with Latour — as one of their more recent leading members. Shaviro concedes this in the case of time, and ought to admit it for space as well. The hasty rallying of present-day authors to the flag of "process philosophy" goes astray when it tries to unite continuum extremists such as Bergson, Deleuze, and Simondon with latter-day occasionalists such as Whitehead and Latour. As for the last-mentioned figure, we need not even hark back to his 1981 remark about everything happening only once and in one place. More recent, and perhaps more compelling, is the explicitly anti-Bergsonian note in Latour's 2012 work on the modes of existence: among the fifteen modes catalogued in that book, we find reproduction.[27] The purpose fulfilled by this mode is none other than the old occasionalist function of continuous creation.

Let's conclude this section with a brief outline of how I see the cosmology of OOO, since it has nothing to do with the stasis or fixity that Shaviro and others see in it. In the first place, it is not a question for me of whether "everything communicates" or "nothing communicates"; some things affect us, and others do not. The singing finches in our Long Beach courtyard make me happy, and writing this book *Skirmishes* makes me feel resolute. The finches and the book are not me, but things outside me with which I am currently in relation, but under other circumstances might not be. It does not follow that everything in the universe is affecting me right now, even if only in a derivative or "negative" sense, as Whitehead imagines with his doctrine of prehen-

---

27 Bruno Latour, *An Inquiry into Modes of Existence: An Anthropology of the Moderns*, trans. Catherine Porter (Cambridge: Harvard University Press, 2013), 91.

sions. The question at hand is this: if the universe is taken to be in total ontological flux, then why is it not changing constantly? Meillassoux addresses this question in his own offbeat Cantorian way, with appeal to the non-totalizability of possible worlds.[28] For my own part, I would say that a thing is what it is, and since there is no reason to reify "time" as an independent destructive force — as Meillassoux and others do — then change is what needs to be explained rather than presupposed. It is intermittent rather than constant, and arises from the vicarious combination of two separate entities into one, which then has retroactive effects on its components.[29] Sometimes these effects cascade through different levels of reality and have profound ramifications: as in a major earthquake, for instance, which destroys numerous structures and changes lives hundreds of miles from the epicenter. But for such major events to be possible, it cannot be the case that every instant experiences a major earthquake. Some teachers, friends, or lovers change us profoundly and others hardly at all. Some books haunt us for a lifetime while others leave us unmoved. Unlike Shaviro, I do not see our lives as oppressed by a constant swarm of relations, but see us and all other objects as in partial retreat from the theater of the world, drawn into it only in a small number of fateful encounters that change us.[30] In Whitehead's ultra-relational philosophy — as in Latourian Actor–Network Theory — I see no way to account for the difference between important and unimportant relations; for Whitehead too, every tiniest event shakes an entity to its core, and every instant is equally catastrophic.

---

28 Quentin Meillassoux, *After Finitude: An Essay on the Necessity of Contingency*, trans. Ray Brassier (London: Continuum, 2008).
29 Graham Harman, "Time, Space, Essence, and Eidos: A New Theory of Causation," *Cosmos and History* 6, no. 1 (2010): 1–17
30 Graham Harman, *Immaterialism: Objects and Social Theory* (Cambridge: Polity, 2016).

Relation and Cognition

We now turn to the key philosophical difference between me and Shaviro: the quarrel between relational and non-relational ontology. Shaviro's relational position unites him not only with Whitehead but also with Latour, the greatest living relational ontologist we have. For Latour entities are essentially actors, and actors are nothing more than whatever they "modify, transform, perturb, or create."[31] By contrast, my non-relational position derives from Heidegger and his one-time Basque student, Xavier Zubíri.[32] I am well aware that many or most devotees of Heidegger and Zubíri do not accept that they are non-relational ontologists in the first place. This comes from my own interpretation of their philosophies, and we should remember that a philosophy is not the same as what the philosopher happens to think is entailed by it. For example, Heidegger would be the first to accept a *relational* interpretation of his tool-analysis, in which all items of equipment are woven together in a total system that ultimately takes its meaning from Dasein's care for its own being, and in which independent or autonomous items are derivative "present-at-hand" instantiations of the system as a whole. What Heidegger and his disciples miss here is that tools also *break* or *malfunction,* and that they cannot do this unless they are already something more than the tool-system makes use of in them. If it is true that human thought or perception of things reduces them to a limited caricature of their innermost being, the same holds for their interaction with other tools or indeed with anything else. In this sense, Heidegger's system *requires* that all entities are a surplus over and above their appearances or interactions. As for Zubíri, while it is true that he is interested in the dynamic activity of things, his central idea is that things should not be taken as "respective" to other things but as having

---

31 Bruno Latour, *Pandora's Hope: Essays on the Reality of Science Studies* (Cambridge: Harvard University Press, 1999), 122.
32 Xavier Zubíri, *On Essence,* trans. A. Robert Caponigri (Washington, DC: The Catholic University of America Press, 1980).

an existence *de suyo,* or "in their own right."³³ It is not that things *cannot* relate, but that their relations are derivative of a being that is never fully expressed in any relation. This is what Shaviro denies, even while claiming that he like Whitehead can account for the "privacy" of things in a different manner.

Nonetheless, Shaviro's basic fairness as a critic leads him to admit that there is something as worthy in my position as in Whitehead's own. As he sees it, we both proceed from valid intuitions: "There is a deep sense in which I remain the same person, no matter what happens to me. But there is an equally deep sense in which I am changed irrevocably by my experiences, by the 'historic route of living occasions' through which I pass"³⁴ (32). He presents this dispute between two "equally deep" truths as a speculative antinomy, difficult or even impossible to resolve. We have seen that he opts for Whitehead's vision largely for personal reasons, given his own view that we are largely oppressed by a swarm of relations, "of relentless implications and involvements" (33). He opts, in short, for Whitehead's notion of the world as "one system of relations"³⁵ (114), and finds additional support in the "paranoia of holism" that Marshall McLuhan diagnoses in both traditional tribal culture and the new tribal culture of electronic media, in which "'terror is the normal state' [... because] 'everything affects everything all the time'"³⁶ (59). Needless to say, it is not our everyday experience that everything effects everything all the time but that *some* things affect some things while *not* affecting others. To move to the Shaviro/Whitehead/McLuhan "paranoid" position requires extra backing in the form of an assumption that everything affects everything else. And even if someone adopts such a view, it would only lead to an "antinomy" if I were making the opposite

---

33 Xavier Zubíri, *Dynamic Structure of Reality,* trans. Nelson R. Orringer (Urbana: University of Illinois Press, 2003).
34 Whitehead, *Process and Reality,* 119.
35 Alfred North Whitehead, *The Concept of Nature* (Amherst: Prometheus Books, 1920), 32.
36 Marshall McLuhan, *The Gutenberg Galaxy: The Making of Typographic Man* (Toronto: University of Toronto Press, 1962), 32.

claim that *nothing* affects anything else. But in fact it is OOO that strikes a proper balance between these false opposites, with its idea that however ubiquitous relations may seem, it is relatively rare for effects to matter to any given thing. Although it is trivially true that even buying a new shirt or drinking a glass of water affects me in some fashion, these actions usually do not affect who I am at any important level. Actor–Network Theory already has a hard time distinguishing between important and unimportant actions, and Shaviro faces the same difficulty. In *Immaterialism,* I tried to show how one specific historical entity — the Dutch East India Company — cannot be read as a swirling set of constant relations, even if it looks that way at first glance. There turn out to be only a half-dozen or so events for any entity that transform it in any significant way across its lifespan. Borrowing a term from the evolutionary biologist Lynn Margulis, I call these "symbioses" as opposed to mere relations, which do occur very frequently.[37]

Needless to say, Shaviro does not follow me here: "Harman, as we have seen, discounts relations as inessential" (40). Drawing on the distinguished support of William James, he asserts that "[r]elations are too various and come in too many 'different degrees of intimacy' to be reducible to Harman's characterization of them as reductive determinations"[38] (40). I have dealt with James's essay elsewhere.[39] Suffice it to say, I do not disagree that relations come in many different kinds and "different degrees of intimacy." But Shaviro is no less guilty of the univocal view of relations that he ascribes to me, insofar as he states baldly that "[i]n the realm of causal efficacy, we have rather to do with a sort of total contact, a promiscuous interchange among objects" (56). If there is total contact, then by definition there are no "de-

37 Harman, *Immaterialism*; Lynn Margulis, *Symbiotic Planet: A New Look at Evolution* (New York: Basic Books, 1998).
38 William James, *Essays in Radical Empiricism* (Lincoln: University of Nebraska Press, 1996), 44.
39 Graham Harman, "Object-Oriented Philosophy vs. Radical Empiricism," in *Bells and Whistles: More Speculative Realism* (Winchester: Zero Books, 2013), 40–59.

grees" of promiscuity, since everything is equally promiscuous from the start. How, then, does Shaviro account for the fact that we do not *seem* to be in contact with everything at all times? Like Whitehead, he treats this as an artifact of the relatively rare and high-grade form of relation found in conscious life: "only in the realm of presentational immediacy, with its inevitable limitations and failures [… are we] faced with Harman's paradoxes of 'sensual objects' that must be distinguished from 'real' ones and of occasionalism or vicarious causation" (56). If we consider causal relation itself, rather than its advanced late form as found in conscious life, we will find that there are no "deep essential properties" in things as I claim (141). Here Shaviro is led, like James, Whitehead, and Latour, to deny what Meillassoux and I both uphold for different reasons — the distinction between primary and secondary qualities. For Locke, this was the difference between the material properties of things (primary) and the properties that arise only when these things are encountered by other, sensing things (secondary).[40] Whereas Locke finds the primary qualities in underlying matter, Meillassoux finds them in what can be mathematized, and I find them in the intrinsic, non-relational properties of things: the properties things have whether anything else encounters them or not. For Shaviro, however, such nuance is irrelevant. As he sees it, the primary/secondary rift "is an epistemological matter, not an ontological one" (116). Strangely enough, he relies in this verdict on an appeal to something very much like the "correlational circle," even though he is usually allied with me — against Meillassoux — in denying that we cannot think a thing outside thought without turning it into a thought. After all, Shaviro thinks "we do not have unmediated access to […] properties, and this is equally the case for those we call 'primary' and 'secondary'" (117).

Shaviro's view entails that on the level of presentational immediacy there is no escaping the correlational circle, but that as soon as we shift to the Whiteheadian cosmic level of unnoticed prehensions, we have escaped the circle in advance thanks to the

40 Locke, *An Essay Concerning Human Understanding*, 178.

direct and promiscuous causal relation of everything with everything else. Since Shaviro knows that I do not limit my theory of interaction to the realm of conscious thought and perception, he can only turn this point against me by claiming that I wrongly reduce inanimate interaction to the conscious sort, whether I know it or not. This is a rather tall order, given that he is not only aware of my constant efforts to show the universal character of relation as caricature, but even cites the most prominent instance himself: the case of fire burning cotton. He starts by agreeing with me that the fire cannot make contact with *all* properties of the cotton any more than a human observer can. This is the sense in which we are both Whiteheadians, after all, a beleaguered minority opposed to the Kantian placement of the human–world relation at the basis of all others. But for Shaviro, this limited encounter of fire with cotton still counts as "epistemological" (106), a term I prefer to reserve for the dominant modern human–world rift. But if the meeting of fire with cotton is merely "epistemological" in an extended sense of the term, then where is the "ontological" level that underpins it? For Shaviro it is found on the level of fire-effects that the fire itself cannot apprehend. As he puts it, "As the cotton is burned, even those properties to which the fire is wholly insensitive are themselves also altered or destroyed — that is, fire *affects* even those aspects of the cotton that it cannot come to 'know'" (106). On this basis Shaviro argues that "knowledge" has an excessively large place in my theory, keeping in mind that he means knowledge in a broader-than-human sense. For example, "Harman gives too much weight to the informational and epistemological limits of contact between entities" (118), and "errs in conceiving finitude — just as Kant does in the first critique — as primarily a matter of the limits of *knowledge*" (136). And furthermore, "whereas [Harman] says that no amount of 'information' about a thing can 'replicate' or 'add up to' that thing, I find it more accurate to say that no amount of information can ever *exhaust* the thing" (117), apparently forgetting that I use the term "exhaust" quite often myself.

The difficulty with Shaviro's argument is as follows. While accepting my expansion of the finitude of interaction well beyond the Kantian human sphere, Shaviro points to the realm of causal effects that occur outside the fire-cotton confrontation itself. For instance, the cotton is destroyed, and this is something completely different from the fire's immediate "contact" with the sensual object, cotton. The first problem with this is that the causal impact of fire and cotton is not infinite, even though it results in destruction. The destruction of a cotton ball need not have any effect on the tides in Long Beach or the political system of Germany; in fact, there is no reason to suppose it has any at all. Whitehead tries to account for this by stipulating that many prehensions are "negative," but it is unclear why he wants to call fire–tides or fire–Germany "prehensions" at all; the need to call them "negative prehensions" is simply a consequence of the self-imposed danger of global prehension becoming an ultraholistic excess.

The second problem for Shaviro is that, although Whitehead does lay great stress on the difference between presentational immediacy and more rudimentary forms of prehension, the point of this is to shake us from our modernist slumber and urge us to include more in our philosophy than the modern human-world correlate. Contra Shaviro's argument, it is not in order to establish a dualism between "epistemological" and "ontological" interactions, each governed by different relational rules: on the contrary, one of Whitehead's greatest philosophical achievements is his deliberate flattening of this distinction. Though I am well aware that Whitehead speaks of separate "mental" and "physical" poles in reality (63), all his prehensions work in the same way: one actual entity prehends another by means of "eternal objects" (which never appear in Shaviro's book) that are contained in God and ensure that no entity ever prehends the entirety of another. The way causality works for OOO, unlike for Shaviro, *is not* through total contact on the causal level that is left undetected by either fire or humans due to their relative obtuseness. Instead, causation occurs because fire and cotton combine into a single new entity that then has retroactive effects on both of its elements. The fact that such effects occur at a level beneath the threshhold of explicit perception does not entail a causal free-for-all at the undetected level. By way of analogy, the city of New York has retroactive effects on its residents, perhaps making them more stressed-out, aggressive, and cynical, but also more sophisticated and cosmopolitan than if they were living in rural Iowa where I grew up. We would not expect the city of New York as a whole to come into contact with these individual effects, but that is because they are not relevant to the city as a system, in a sense familiar to readers of Niklas Luhmann.[41] It is certainly not the case that both New York City and its Iowa-born transplants are finite, limited entities while the whole of causation is *without* such limits. In short, what Shaviro calls "the epistemological" and "ontological" levels really belong to one and the same level, on which everything is limited in what it can and cannot encounter. Here Shaviro's theory sounds less like Whitehead than like Deleuze in *The Fold,* or like some of Bryant's recent work, in which everything is connected on the primal story of being and is split apart only on some derivative upper floor.[42]

Interlude on Levi Bryant

As it happens, a further word about Bryant is in order, since there are important overlaps and differences between his position and Shaviro's. After all, Shaviro openly upholds a level of direct causal interaction — though at the cost of ignoring Whitehead's "eternal objects" — and claims that the inherent limitation of sensual objects is a mere byproduct of presentational immediacy, with human thought and perception being obvious examples. His possible difference from Bryant appears

41 Niklas Luhmann, *Theory of Society,* 2 vols., trans. Rhodes Barrett (Stanford: Stanford University Press, 2012–13).
42 Gilles Deleuze, *The Fold: Leibniz and the Baroque,* trans. Tom Conley (Minneapolis: University of Minnesota Press, 1992); Levi R. Bryant, "The Interior of Things: The Origami of Being," *Przeglad Kulturoznawczy* 29, no. 3 (2016): 290–304.

in the latter's 2015 interview with Kevin MacDonnell. There Bryant states as follows: "Despite our differences, Harman's work has been a tremendous impetus for my thought. While I don't share his distinction between real and sensual qualities and objects nor his theory of vicarious causation, I do nonetheless hold that objects can be severed from their relations."[43] In this respect, Bryant sides with me against Shaviro. For although Shaviro holds that Whitehead allows perfectly well for the "privacy" of entities, this purported privacy is merely the unified sum total of its prehensions from the previous instant, and therefore is not really private at all: except by comparison with the numerous possible relations it might have in the instant to come. It seems to me that Bryant's "virtual proper being" is a good deal more private than this, and thus in some sense Bryant remains an object-oriented ontologist, while this cannot be said of Shaviro despite his broadly sympathetic view of my work.

As seen in the passage just cited from Bryant's interview, he rejects both the real/sensual distinction I draw from Husserl and vicarious causation itself. He does this by way of a position he calls "interactivism," one that is well worth considering.[44] Bryant begins by citing a question I pose in the same journal issue as his interview, concerning my state of perplexity as to whether his concept of "local manifestation" pertains to a single adumbration of an object, or instead to what Husserl would call an enduring intentional object.[45] Bryant's response is intricate and puzzling:

> A local manifestation is not a view of an object, but rather is an event that takes place within an object. For example, the manner in which an elephant encounters an apple in a tree from the west is not a local manifestation of the apple.

---

43 Kevin MacDonnell, "Interview: Some Differences Between Object-Oriented Philosophy and Onticology," interview by Levi R. Bryant, *St. John's University Humanities Review* 12, no. 1 (Spring 2015): 69.
44 Ibid.
45 Graham Harman, "Strange Realism: On Behalf of Objects," *St. John's University Humanities Review* 12, no. 1 (Spring 2015): 17–18.

> Indeed, this is a local manifestation of the elephant [...]. The apple is what it is regardless of whether it's encountered by another entity from east, west, north, south, above, or below. Rather, a local manifestation of the apple would be something like qualitative changes that take place as a result of biochemical processes the apple undergoes in interaction with its environment as it ripens. The softness of a very ripe apple is not a manifestation to anyone else. It would be there regardless of whether or not any other being regarded the apple. Rather, it is a qualitative feature of the object itself resulting from the becoming it has undergone.[46]

Reading this passage was useful to me in understanding Bryant's model. Previously, I had thought of his "virtual proper being" as equivalent to my own "real object," but equipped with powers rather than qualities. And I had also thought that his "local manifestations" were equivalent to my sensual realm, but with an insufficient distinction between the sensual object and its various qualitative adumbrations. I now get the sense that he is doing something completely different, though as a result my puzzlement simply changes form.

For it now seems as if Bryant's virtual proper being and local manifestation both belong to what I call the *real* rather than the sensual. After all, "the softness of a very ripe apple is not a manifestation to anyone else," and I presume Bryant would extend "anyone" to "anything" as well, since he does not limit himself to human manifestation in the manner of philosophical modernists. It is a question of ripeness as a manifestation that is not seen — as the word "manifestation" would normally suggest — but a ripeness inherent in the apple whether encountered by anything else or not. Although Bryant is leery of the world "qualities," this sounds very much like a primary quality to me. What then becomes of the sorts of qualities usually called "secondary," such as Husserl's adumbrations or my sensual qualities: as with the exact appearance of the apple to some-

---

46 MacDonnell, "Interview," 69.

thing from a specific direction? This seems to vanish altogether, along with my sensual objects or Husserl's intentional ones. It certainly looks as if everything secondary or sensual (or their Bryantian equivalent) is on the same footing, which means that for him there is no rift within the sensual realm. Yet what is truly strange is that these secondary qualities of the apple — Bryant does not use the term, but we can do so in his stead — do not belong to the apple at all but are a local manifestation of the elephant who views it. Stated differently, while I had previously interpreted Bryant's "local manifestation" as his version of the sensual realm, he seems to allow for no sensual realm at all. The apple is locked up in its own ripening and softening, and the elephant is locked up in its own perception of the apple. What we have, in short, looks like an even more monadological model than my own. My position is that even though the real object can never be accessed directly, there is still a certain minimal otherness in the sensual realm. The profile of an apple from the west is not "in the elephant," but on the interior of the larger object formed from the elephant and the apple, so that the profile owes its exact features to both. Yet even though Bryant calls his position "interactivism," it is hard to see much interaction going on, given that the various profiles of the apple are said to be just local manifestations — of the elephant! The elephant is trapped in a monad of its own, without even Leibniz's pre-established harmony able to give it access to an apple it is apparently unable to touch even indirectly. Presumably Bryant and I will need further rounds of dialogue to make sure I am getting it right, but as I see it, this is the plain meaning of the blockquote cited above.

To repeat, Bryant's equally monadological conception of virtual proper being and local manifestation, each of them locked up inside the apple, elephant, or human being to which they belong, sounds more occasionalist than anything found in my pages. After all, I do allow for intermittent transgression of the boundaries between real beings through allure. For his part, Bryant offers no explanation of how the elephant and apple could ever come into contact. But given this apparent inclination towards the mutual exteriority of entities, it is all the stranger that he rejects my concept of vicarious causation. As he put it earlier in the same interview,

> Harman argues that real objects never touch nor relate to one another, but rather are "vacuum sealed" and forever behind firewalls. I confess that this is not a thesis I really understand. He seems to argue that real objects never touch one another, yet only encounter one another in the interior of their sensual objects. However, it seems to me that this amounts to saying that they relate without relating, in which case I'm led to think that they do relate.[47]

What would be wrong with such a model? It cannot be a matter of contradiction, since I say that they relate without *directly* relating, which is not contradictory; Bryant knows me well enough to be aware of this. Thus, I think he is left with two possible options. He could say that I am wrong either because (a) objects do not relate at all or because (b) direct relations between objects are so common and easy that they are hardly worth the fuss of a complex theory of vicarious causation. Obviously, most critics of my work will choose (b) at this juncture, especially those of a scientistic bent who assume that physics already tells us everything we need to know on the matter. But as we have seen, Bryant's theory of an apple and an elephant each enclosed in its own local manifestations suggests option (a), in which objects do not relate at all.

Along with the difficulty of seeing how such a theory would work in the absence of a Leibnizian pre-established harmony, there is the further problem that on the very same page Bryant chooses option (b) just like most of my critics. He helpfully diagrams two triangles that touch at a single point, then comments as follows: "Clearly [the triangles] are not relating directly at all points, but why should that lead us to conclude that there's no real relation between them or that they don't touch? This is

---

47 Ibid., 67.

something I don't understand."[48] There now seem to be two different Bryants on the loose, and I have a hard time putting them together. Let's call them Elephant Bryant and Triangle Bryant. Elephant Bryant looks like a radical monadologist who holds that the elephant never perceives the apple but only its own local manifestations, and vice versa. But Triangle Bryant thinks contact between things is as easy as pressing two triangles together at a single point. The contradiction seems so flagrant that it cannot have escaped Bryant's notice, which means that there must be a hidden premise making the two sides compatible in his mind. Before saying what I think that premise is, allow me to explain why the contact of two triangles does not invalidate vicarious causation.

As we have seen, Bryant concedes that "clearly [the triangles] are not relating directly at all points, but why should that lead us to conclude that there's real relation between them or that they don't touch?" This is a variant of the view, often wielded against me in the blogosphere, that contact is "direct but partial" rather than indirect. In order to avoid possible complications specific to mathematics, let's shift our example from a triangle to a handshake. Obviously, in shaking Bryant's hand I do not touch the whole of his being; we would agree on that much. Nonetheless, Bryant seems to regard shaking his hand as touching him directly, whereas I do not; after all, Bryant's hand is not Bryant himself. More than this: it is not even *part* of Bryant himself, even though in the anatomical sense his hand is one of his body parts. We moderns have become so averse to metaphysical problems that we immediately think of contact in the obvious physical sense of one thing bumping into another. Why is it impossible to touch Bryant directly through one part called his "hand," you ask? Because it is not even possible to touch Bryant's *hand* directly — the hand is a real object in its own right, and perhaps at most we only make contact with the epidermis. You will then say that I make direct contact with the epidermis, perhaps somewhat annoyed by now. At this point, you will try to

---

48 Ibid.

get me to admit that eventually we will reach some ultimate minuscule layer of direct contact. Yet there are two problems with this. First, even if you are right that there comes a point of direct physical contact, you will still need to explain the connection between this point and the epidermis, or the epidermis and the hand, or the hand and Bryant. But in doing so you cannot have recourse to the "folk contiguity" of these parts, since contiguity and contact are precisely what is under dispute. This brings us to the second and more important problem. If touching a thing merely means touching the surface of a thing, then this is not merely a physical truism about the impossibility of hands deeply penetrating each other to their anatomical cores.[49] Instead, it points to a more sophisticated problem with contact: to touch a thing is to touch a caricature of it, since you are a finite creature whose hands are simply incapable of directly touching another hand or anything else. You cannot touch someone else's hand, not because of physical limitations pertaining specifically to hands, but because a hand — like any other object — is not directly open to everything else in the cosmos. It is open to sensual reality alone, and this means indirect contact with the real at best.

I said earlier that Bryant cannot simply be offering the flagrant contradiction of a monadology and a theory of easy direct contact simultaneously, so that there must be a hidden premise in his argument that allows for both. That premise, as I see it, is the same one that Shaviro seemed to draw from the Deleuze of *The Fold*: a twofold model in which there is causal directness in the initial relation between entities, followed by closure at a more complex level of presentational immediacy. This is easier to see if we combine the two Bryants (the Elephant and Triangle versions) and imagine that he had drawn not two triangles touching at a single point but an elephant and an apple touching at a single point. From this combined example we can see

---

[49] Manuel DeLanda seems to have misunderstood my argument in this sense in DeLanda and Graham Harman, *The Rise of Realism* (Malden: Polity Press, 2017), 56.

that Bryant is saying the following two things simultaneously: (a) "look, the elephant and the apple are touching. What's so hard about that?" and (b) "although the elephant seems to touch the apple, it is really only touching its own local manifestations, and the same for the apple when it seems to touch the elephant. The two entities are really just touching themselves." Bryant, like Shaviro, happens to be a highly intelligent person. He is not falling into childlike logical contradiction, but offering a twofold theory of relation as opposed to my own onefold theory. In that theory there is a level of causal contact on which relation is not difficult, coupled with an upper story of perception on which relation is so difficult that only sensual manifestations ever occur. It is similar to how Deleuze tries to unify the continuous with the heterogeneous, and how Shaviro limits finitude to presentational immediacy while permitting an orgy of direct causation on the ground floor. Bryant's monadological elephant and apple are "without windows" only in terms of what they *experience,* not in terms of their causal interactions. What Bryant and Shaviro both miss thereby is that indirect relation is not just a result, but also a starting point. We cannot say that the apple and elephant touch at some point and *only then* are locked inside themselves. This is a duplicitous solution to a unified problem, one that equally effects both the initial contact of elephant with apple and their ability to perceive one another.

From Bryant Back to Shaviro

Returning to Shaviro, the situation becomes somewhat more confusing when he tries to turn my own terminology against me. While deeply skeptical of my non-relational real objects, Shaviro contends that "what Harman dismisses as the merely 'sensual' realm of carnality, causality, and aesthetics is in fact the only realm there is" (146). But there are at least three things wrong with this attempt to hoist me by my own petard. The first is that there is nothing "mere" about OOO's sensual realm, which among other things is the only place where causal interactions can be triggered, given the mutual withdrawal of real objects.

For example, what distinguishes my interpretation of Levinas from the usual tiresome focus on ethics and absolutely alterity is my attention to his brilliant account of enjoyment: a sensual immediacy of things that Levinas rightly finds missing in Heidegger.[50] I would also note my strong interest in Jean Baudrillard, despite his being possibly the most anti-realist thinker since Berkeley, given the importance I place on his notion of how the object *seduces* us or draws us into a new sort of reality.[51] Second, the sensual realm in my philosophy is not characterized by the sort of unfettered causal interaction that Shaviro finds so desirable; rather, sensual objects lead a *buffered* existence on the interior of a larger real one, meaning that they too are walled off from automatic interaction with each other. Third and most importantly, the key feature of my sensual objects has no analogue in Shaviro's thinking at all, or in Bryant's for that matter. This is the Husserlian point that even within the realm of direct sensual accessibility, there is a permanent duel between sensual objects and their sensual qualities. A watermelon or mailbox remains the same sensual object for us, no matter how much it changes from one instant to the next—unless and until it changes to such an extent that we no longer recognize it as the same thing, but decide either that it has changed into something else or that we have been deceived by it all along. In fairness to Shaviro, it should be added that he rejects this Husserlian model consciously rather than unknowingly, as we will see when he contests the very notion of intentionality.

For the same reason as with fire and cotton, Shaviro contests my further example of the moon, again finding fault with my "epistemological" account of its limited effects on us. In so doing, he makes the unsurprising claim—for a Whitehe-

---

50 Graham Harman, "Levinas and the Triple Critique of Heidegger," *Philosophy Today* 53, no. 4 (Winter 2009): 407–13.
51 Jean Baudrillard, *Seduction,* trans. Brian Singer (London: Palgrave Macmillan, 1991); Graham Harman, "Object-Oriented Seduction: Baudrillard Reconsidered," in *The War of Appearances: Transparency, Opacity, Radiance,* eds. Joke Brouwer, Lars Spuybroek, and Sjoerd van Tuinen (Rotterdam: V2_, 2016), 128–43.

adian — that the moon is equivalent to all its influences (137). While he is certainly right to say that "there are limits to our independence from the moon" (137), he is wrong to omit the counter-principle that there are also limits to our dependence on it. Even those who listen to a New Age celebrity claiming that the moon affects moods more than we moderns would like to admit, or to an astrologer who derives aspects of their personality from the position of that great satellite at birth, would rightly be alarmed by someone who blames absolutely *everything* on the moon: from lottery numbers, to police shootings, to election results, to their own school examination failures. The fact that the moon has large effects on our planet does not prove the nonexistence of the moon as a withdrawn real object, but only requires that we account for why the moon affects some things without affecting everything. Relations are formed through *work,* even if much of this labor done in advance by other entities. Work may involve engineers and construction teams building bridges and dredging canals on which we rely every day, or it may be the slow labor of gravitational pull from the center of the galaxy. One aspect of my theory is that there can be "dormant" objects that exist without currently being in relation with anything else[52] (83). Shaviro notes the relation of this term to sleep as a way of withdrawing ourselves from relations and closing back into ourselves, and I still think this is a productive way to understand what sleeping is. But Shaviro overdetermines the role of this metaphor in my theory, claiming that since no sleep is perfect and sleeping humans are always involved in dreams and subconscious awareness of what is going on in the room around them, "dormancy" is impossible on the ontological level as well, and only *death* brings about a non-relational state (147). Yet all this really proves is that living creatures might be incapable of pure dormancy: not that everything that exists, such as the moon, must exist in relation to everything else.

Earlier I made brief mention of autopoiesis theory and of some of its leading figures, Luhmann, Humberto Maturana, and

---

52 Harman, "Time, Space, Essence, and Eidos."

Francisco Varela.[53] It is easy to see why Shaviro (like his fellow relational ontologist Latour) is suspicious of this line of thinking, while OOO thinkers tend to appreciate it. Shaviro has a fair amount to say on the matter. According to autopoiesis theory, a system is fundamentally closed off from its environment and tends to process this environment only in terms that make sense for the system itself. For Maturana and Varela, both of them immunologists interested in the behavior of biological cells, the cell aims at "homeostasis," or preserving its interior in the same condition from moment to moment. Thus it follows that the cell for them, like the "system" for Luhmann, has only a limited ability to be changed by what lies beyond its walls. The political consequences of this theory are obviously pessimistic, since for Luhmann the actions of radical protesters are generally just co-opted by whatever system they oppose. This has even led some critics to charge autopoiesis with a form of solipsism.[54] Shaviro's charge is not quite this extreme, though it is still relevant to our discussion. As he puts it, "[The] active persistence [of enduring objects] is more or less what Spinoza calls *conatus,* or what Levi Bryant calls the 'ongoing autopoiesis' of objects. I am not entirely happy with these terms, however. *Conatus* and *autopoiesis* seem to me to put too exclusive an emphasis on the entity's self-reproduction and maintenance of its identity, or on what Bryant calls its 'endo-consistency.'"[55] Shaviro justifiably counters that objects can also change, expand, contract, and otherwise shift their traits or undergo differing fortunes. In a way, this might begin to look like just another speculative antinomy. For example, Luhmann and Latour can probably be faulted for an *insufficient* and an *excessive* focus on relations, respectively.

---

53 Niklas Luhmann, *Social Systems,* trans. John Bednarz, Jr. with Dirk Baecker (Stanford: Stanford University Press, 1996); Humberto Maturana, *Autopoiesis and Cognition: The Realization of the Living* (Dordrecht: Kluwer Academic Publishers, 1980).

54 Jeremy Dunham, Iain Hamilton Grant, and Sean Watson, *Idealism: The History of a Philosophy* (Montreal: McGill-Queen's University Press, 2011), 86.

55 Levi R. Bryant, *The Democracy of Objects* (Ann Arbor: Open Humanities Press, 2011), 143, 141.

Again it seems that a balance must be struck, one allowing for objects to engage in relations but not in too many relations. Earlier I argued that OOO is better equipped than Shaviro to strike a balance between stasis and becoming, given his excessive allegiance to an ontology of constant and unremitting change, one that has a hard time explaining stability, and which is too quick to consign it to the derivative realm of "epistemology" and "presentational immediacy." Shaviro makes the same move here, claiming that pre-presentational causality is practically unlimited in a way that even sub-human cognition is not. Yet he also takes the unexpected step of distancing himself from Bryant on the topic of aesthetics:

> Bryant seeks to explain away what I am calling "aesthetic contact" as a "perturbation or irritation" to the system [...]. But this wrongly assumes that encounters between entities can be fully described in terms of "information" (which is to say, in terms of [George] Spencer-Brown's and Luhmann's "distinctions" or Gregory Bateson's "difference which makes a difference"). To the contrary, transfers and dissipations of energy, provoked by forces external to a system, can never be adequately coded in such informational terms. (145)

Stated differently, Shaviro accuses of Bryant of reducing aesthetics to an "epistemological" level of self-containment, while pointing to an external realm of free causation that aesthetics is somehow able to access. He portrays aesthetics as a form of "contact at a distance" (147), borrowing from Timothy Morton's account in *Realist Magic*. In this way, he tries to join up with Morton and me against our fellow OOO theorist Bryant.

Yet it is not so clear that I belong on Morton's side against Bryant here; my position is better described as somewhere between the two. With Morton and Shaviro, I agree that aesthetics is the way we occasionally escape our correlation with sensual objects, breaking free into an indirect relation with the withdrawn real object. As noted earlier, my term for such events is "allure." Like Shaviro I see aesthetic allure as operative at a far more primitive level than the human, and like Morton I see brute inanimate causation as another form of aesthetics. Also like Shaviro, I hold that the "allusive, external reference is irreducible to myself and resists assimilation to 'myself' as a coherent system [… so that] my own actions or 'operations' *never* 'refer only to themselves'; they always relate directly to things and forces that are outside their power and beyond their reach" (145). Furthermore, I also agree that while Kant's aesthetics does not give us access to the beyond or *au-delà* of the thing-in-itself, it does station us in the hither side of the correlation of subject and object (148). What I cannot see is how this "*en déçu*" could ever bring us into contact with Shaviro's desired realm, which for me does not exist, of a boundless playing field of global interaction between entities. My view, instead, is that the aesthetic contact with an outside occurs through my *becoming* the missing real object, by stepping in as a real object in place of the one that is never accessible. Whereas I merely perceive sensual objects, in aesthetics I perform real ones. But far from allowing me to step out of "epistemological" systems into an unrestricted causal plane, it simply establishes me in a new restricted system. When reading Homer's famous metaphor, I am no longer just the perceiver of the Mediterranean Sea but a thespian *enacting* the wine-dark sea that cannot have a literal, sensual meaning. But I am not thereby in contact with all possible metaphors. I limit myself to this one, and at most to a handful of others simultaneously.

The bigger difference between Shaviro and me can be seen in his view that "aesthetic feelings with regard to an object cannot be *correlated* to that object. An aesthetic encounter takes place without recognition or possession and without phenomenological intentionality or 'aboutness'" (153). This is his critique of phenomenology's intentional model of consciousness. The modern use of "intentionality" appeared, famously, in Brentano's effort to distinguish the psychological from the physical sphere.[56] What

---

56 Franz Brentano, *Pyschology from an Empirical Standpoint*, ed. Linda L. McAlister, trans. Antos C. Rancurello, D.B. Terrell, and Linda L. McAlister (London: Routledge, 1995).

we find in the former realm but not the latter, Brentano holds, is that all mental acts are directed at some object: to perceive is to perceive something, to judge is to judge something, to love or hate is to feel these emotions about something in particular. The formula is often expanded to say that every intentional act aims at an object "beyond" itself, but this expansion is ambiguous and misleading. For it is clear that Brentano is referring to an *immanent* object, an object located within the mental sphere. In a sense it is true that the object is beyond me, insofar as I am not identical with what I intend. But if it is taken to mean that the object in my mind points at an object *outside* the mind, as many readers assume, then this reading not only goes beyond Brentano's own thought but turns it upside-down. In fact, Brentano gives surprisingly little guidance as to what relation there might be between the immanent object and an analogous object in the extra-mental world. This ambiguity led to considerable hand-wringing among Brentano's disciples, and in some ways even gave rise to the ingrained but unacknowledged *idealism* Sparrow finds in phenomenology: given Husserl's attempt to solve the problem by effacing the very distinction between immanent and transcendent objects.[57] This can be seen from his fiery early dispute with the Polish thinker Kazimierz Twardowski, a strong advocate of two distinct levels, one outside the mind (object) and another inside it (content).[58] In any case, we saw that Husserl later modified Brentano's principle to say that intentionality consists not of "experienced contents" but of "objectifiying acts."[59] The difference is that in "experienced contents," we experience an object such as an apple with a highly determinate set of quali-

---

57 Barry Smith, *Austrian Philosophy: The Legacy of Franz Brentano* (Chicago: Open Court, 1994).
58 Kazimierz Twardowski, *On the Content and Object of Presentations: A Psychological Investigation,* trans. R. Grossmann (The Hague: Martinus Nijhoff, 1977); Edmund Husserl, "Intentional Objects," in *Early Writings in the Philosophy of Logic and Mathematics,* trans. Dallas Willard (Dordrecht: Kluwer Academic Publishers, 1994), 345–87.
59 Edmund Husserl, *Logical Investigations,* 2 vols., ed. Dermot Moran, trans. J.N. Findlay (London: Routledge, 2001), 1:276.

ties; this is really no different from the British Empiricist model of a "bundle of qualities." Husserl's innovation was to say that our intentional acts point at a *unified* object that within certain limits endures even as the qualities shift. Whether it is the bright red apple in direct sunlight or the same apple in duller red when clouds cover the sun, in both cases we are dealing with one and the same apple. The heart of the phenomenological method is to scrape away the specific "adumbrations" of the apple and eventually "intuit its essence" by not being sidetracked with its variable and inessential qualities. Husserl identified the difference between essential and merely adumbrative qualities — wrongly, in my view — with the difference between theoretical and sensuous intuition. Heidegger preserves this Husserlian distinction, even while reversing it, when he treats the unconscious practical handling of things as deeper than our theoretical comportment toward them. For my part I hold — no doubt with Shaviro's agreement — that there is no great difference between human handling, sensing, and theorizing, and indeed, all three of these count as relatively complex forms of presentational immediacy in Whitehead's sense.

But Shaviro has a deeper objection to Husserl, one that I do not share, and it involves his outright rejection of intentional objects. For instance, "despite his opposition to phenomenology, Meillassoux still takes for granted, and never questions, the phenomenological assumption that perception and sentience are fundamentally and necessarily *intentional*" (124). Now, I would not agree that Meillassoux is caught up in the discourse of intentional objects, though he certainly overlooks the aesthetic *en deçà* of sense-experience that Shaviro draws from Kant's aesthetics. But it is obvious enough that I myself uphold intentional objects in Shaviro's sense of the term. For when he tells us that "[i]n phenomenology, every act of thinking is directed to an object *beyond* itself" (124; italics mine), he seems to mean "beyond" only in the sense of immanent objectivity, and with that aspect of phenomenology I do concur. The evidence for this is the following statement by Shaviro: "A mental state always *points* to something. This remains the case regardless of whether that 'something' is a thing that really exists in the world or whether it is fiction, or an abstraction, or a mental construction" (124). Yet despite his broad sense of "intentional object," Shaviro rejects it is a necessary constituent of mental life. Why so? He quotes my passage about the moon, which describes our knowledge of it as a more or less accurate model, but one that is not equivalent to the moon itself.[60] Shaviro adds that he agrees with this sentiment, but not entirely. He does not like my use of the word "model," because he sees this again as a mere "epistemological" consideration that is too beholden to the concept of intentional objects. In Shaviro's words,

> I am uneasy with this claim for the same reason that I am uneasy with Thomas Metzinger's argument that consciousness is essentially representational and that conscious perception is really just a sort of virtual-reality simulation. For the notion of a model, or a simulation, tends to oversimplify what is really a more complicated process. […] My prehension (to use Whitehead's term) of the moon is not a model or a representation of the moon but a kind of contact-at-a-distance. [… The notion of an "intentional object"] is [inadequate] to describe the way that the actual moon really and truly *affects* me.[61] (118)

We have now seen two separate ways in which Shaviro tries to counter the role of the intentional object, which becomes the sensual object in OOO. One way is through the hither side of sub-objective experience, a realm presumably made up of not-quite-objective colors, sounds, and the like. But this notion is less developed in Shaviro's work than his truly pivotal commitment to a space of causal interplay to which we always have direct non-mental access without realizing it. The actual moon

---

60 Graham Harman, *Quentin Meillassoux: Philosophy in the Making*, 2nd edn. (Edinburgh: Edinburgh University Press, 2015), 147.
61 Thomas Metzinger, *Being No One: The Self-model Theory of Subjectivity* (Cambridge: MIT Press, 2004), 15ff and passim. See also Graham Harman, "The Problem with Metzinger," *Cosmos and History* 7, no. 1 (2011): 7–36.

"really and truly *affects* me," regardless of how I encounter it as an intentional object. Here we see another crucial difference between Shaviro and OOO. In my philosophy, the sensual object plays a decisive role as a mediator between the real me and the real object, occasionally allowing for experiences of allure in which the sensual object disintegrates by aesthetic means and I am compelled to perform a new real object that replaces the sensual one. For Shaviro, by contrast, the real action always already happens in causal fashion between me and the outside world without my knowing it.

The problem, as I see it, is that under Shaviro's model there is no reason why our sensual experience of objects should occur at all. That is to say, if there is already a direct conduit between me and reality, why should organisms go through the needless labor of constructing a mediated version of the world consisting of cotton-balls-for-fires and cotton-balls-for-humans, whose existence Shaviro by no means denies? Here again Shaviro is closer to Deleuze than to Whitehead. Intentional objects, whose existence Shaviro does not deny, but merely seeks to limit to presentation, would be what Deleuze calls "sterile surface-effects," while the real game of the world takes place on a sort of unobstructed "plane of consistency" where everything meets everything else without difficulty.[62] As a reminder, Whitehead himself does not allow for that sort of causation without representation, as seen from his doctrine of "eternal objects," so strangely absent from Shaviro's account of his thought. Thus it is fitting that Shaviro's main example of a non-intentional object comes from Deleuze instead: "Deleuze's object of encounter is therefore not an 'intentional object' in the phenomenological sense; rather, it is something that is not a correlate of my thought, something that thought cannot possibly correlate to itself" (155). This makes it clear how Deleuze's object of encounter is not OOO's sensual one.

---

62 Gilles Deleuze, *The Logic of Sense,* ed. Constantin V. Boundas, trans. Mark Lester (New York: Columbia University Press, 1993), 124; Gilles Deleuze and Félix Guattari, *A Thousand Plateaus: Capitalism and Schizophrenia,* trans. Brian Massumi (London: Continuum, 2004), 78.

Yet we also know that the object of encounter is not a OOO real object, since it does not have "deep essential properties" withheld from its neighbors. That being the case, it is unclear why thought would need to exist, given the apparent "epistemological" incapacity of thought to do the world justice, even though it is said to do justice to itself through direct causation beforehand. Entities could simply ride the waves of effect and influence, thereby making closer contact with the intensities of the world, without having to be conscious in the first place. Shaviro cites Eugene Thacker as holding that "we can only encounter the world-without-us obliquely, through the paradoxical movement of speculation."[63] Yet Shaviro himself endorses no such limits on contact with the world.

Since we are speaking of intentional objects, a word is in order about George Molnar, the maverick Australian philosopher who died in 1999, and whose interesting book *Powers* was published a few years later thanks to the editorial labors of Stephen Mumford.[64] Shaviro states that "Molnar strikingly anticipates Harman's argument against human exceptionalism," by arguing that intentionality is not just a special human feature but one that belongs to objects in general (80). To this I would say both yes and no, for reasons Shaviro eventually acknowledges himself. For me, intentional objects are found everywhere simply because real objects cannot make direct contact, but encounter each other only as sensual caricatures. That is to say, I strongly uphold the Brentanean premise that intentionality requires *immanent objectivity,* while merely denying Brentano's assumption that this requires a full-blown "mind." Molnar by contrast interprets the term "intentionality" in the lowest-common-denominator sense of "directedness outward." And given his view that *dispositions* are real properties of things, including "physical powers, such as solubility or electrical charge,"[65] it is easy to see

---

63 Here he is glossing Eugene Thacker, *In the Dust of This Planet: The Horror of Philosophy* (Winchester: Zero Books, 2011), 5–6.
64 George Molnar, *Powers: A Study in Metaphysics,* ed. Stephen Mumford (Oxford: Oxford University Press, 2003).
65 Ibid., 80.

why he thinks intentionality is spread far and wide beyond the human realm. Yet for Molnar there is no obvious sense in which physical entities would encounter each other as immanent or sensual objects, and in this respect the gulf between us is unbridgeable. As Shaviro notes, "in the process [of Molnar's redefinition of the term], intentionality also becomes a far weaker and vaguer concept than it was before" (81). He is right, however, that Molnar's position is "at least not incompatible with Harman's claim that objects have a substantial reality outside of, and anterior to, their relations" (142).

Nonetheless, no one would call Molnar a panpsychist, and this gets at the heart of Shaviro's argument in his book — which, unlike the earlier *Without Criteria,* is an open celebration of panpsychist doctrine. As he puts it now, "Once we understand 'thought' in Whitehead's deflationary sense, rather than in Kant's grandiose one, we discover that it is everywhere rather than nowhere" (82). He is untroubled by Colin McGinn's dismissal of panpsychism as "a complete myth, a comforting piece of balderdash" and as "vaguely hippieish, i.e. stoned."[66] Shaviro agrees instead with the view of McGinn's target, Galen Strawson, that thought "is rather the inner, hidden dimension of everything" (101). Like me, Shaviro has had at least one change of heart as to whether or not panpsychism is something to embraced or avoided. He seems to have changed his mind sometime between 2009 and 2014, in part due to David Skrbina's eye-opening book that did much to mainstream the concept by showing its presence throughout Western history. One can see the clear influence of Skrbina's later anthology on the pages of *The Universe of Things.*[67] Shaviro tries to drag me into the clubhouse too, as when says that "vital materialism [as defended by Jane Bennett] and object-oriented ontology both entail some sort of panexpe-

---

66 Colin McGinn, "Hard Questions: Comments on Galen Strawson," in *Consciousness and Its Places in Nature: Does Physicalism Entail Panpsychism?,* ed. Anthony Freeman (Exeter: Imprint Academic, 2006), 93.

67 David Skrbina, *Panpsychism in the West* (Cambridge: MIT Press, 2005); David Skrbina, ed., *Mind That Abides: Panpsychism in the New Millennium* (Amsterdam: John Benjamins, 2009).

rientialism or panpsychism"[68] (63). Shaviro is also right to add that "[t]his is not a step to be taken lightly; it can easily get one branded as a crackpot" (63). The reason for this is the hegemonic Modern Onto-Taxonomy that the present book opposes. But I would rather be called a "crackpot" by such people than join in their unadventurous credo of philosophy as a tarted-up theory of science that draws on science not as a source of surprise, but as a weapon to beat up the naïve and the gullible.

No, there are two other reasons why I hesitate to enlist OOO in the ranks of panpsychism. One is that, despite Skrbina's useful observation about all the many different things that "psyche" might mean, to endorse panpsychism at least suggests that one endorses the ubiquity of the many specific features of *human* psyche. This I am not prepared to do. Among those factors not listed by Skrbina, as far as I can recall, is that when one hears "human experience," *vision* and *thought* too often come to mind above everything else. Thus, when I claim that a rock encounters sensual objects every bit as much as a human does, it is often assumed that I imagine a rock somehow "seeing" a caricature of the dirt on which it sits and then "thinking" about this caricature, even if it were allowed that I claim that this happens in some "privative" form. We still lack the tools to speculate very far about what sub-human or sub-animal experience might be like, despite Shaviro's own pioneering efforts in his book *Discognition*; for this reason, I am inclined to proceed with caution. But there are sufficient grounds to agree — with Shaviro — that Robert Brandom's distinction between "sapient" humans and merely "sentient" animals is just neo-Cartesian wordplay masquerading as insight. On the same grounds it is also fair to suspect that Heidegger's efforts in 1929/30 to distinguish between world-forming humans, world-poor animals, and worldless stones is merely an abortive threefold version of the old modern duality between thought and dead matter, as embraced with

---

68 Jane Bennett, *Vibrant Matter: A Political Ecology of Things* (Durham: Duke University Press, 2010).

disappointing fervor even by Meillassoux[69] (87). The number of basic levels will no doubt be greater than two or three, and the success of twenty-first-century philosophy will be measured in part by how much progress it makes along this front.

Yet there are other points on which I am certainly not allied with panpsychists, and that means not allied with Shaviro. Namely, he seems too sympathetic to Strawson's idea that consciousness alone cannot emerge, and with Chalmers's assumption that "the hard problem" pertains to consciousness and nothing else. But above all, there is Shaviro's idea that the old dispute between "first-person introspection" and "third-person scientific description" should be maintained but reversed, whereas I think it should be discarded altogether. Let's discuss each of these issues, as I did in more detail a decade ago in "Zero-Person and the Psyche."[70]

The younger Strawson has been one of the boldest voices defending panpsychism in the world of analytic philosophy, which (to say the least) is not a naturally welcoming environment for the doctrine. He starts from the reasonable position that eliminativism cannot be true, "because experience is itself the fundamental given natural fact […] there is nothing more certain than the existence of experience"[71] (82). While Meillassoux argues for the *ex nihilo* emergence of thought from life for no reason—though he does think it has to emerge *from life*, rather than directly from inanimate matter—Strawson denies that "brute emergence" of this sort is possible. Therefore, there must be thinking all the way down. Of the original Specula-

---

69 Robert B. Brandom, *Reason in Philosophy: Animating Ideas* (Cambridge: Belknap Press, 2009), 148; Martin Heidegger, *The Fundamental Concepts of Metaphysics: World—Finitude—Solitude,* trans. William McNeill and Nicholas Walker (Bloomington: Indiana University Press, 1995); Meillassoux, "Appendix," 238–40.

70 Graham Harman, "Zero-Person and the Psyche," in *Mind That Abides: Panpsychism in the New Millennium,* ed. David Skrbina (Amsterdam: John Benjamins, 2009), 253–82.

71 Galen Strawson, "Realistic Monism: Why Physicalism Entails Panpsychism," in *Consciousness and Its Place in Nature: Does Physicalism Entail Panpsychism?,* ed. Anthony Freeman (Exeter: Imprint Academic, 2006), 4.

tive Realists, Shaviro plausibly associates me and Grant with this view, and Meillassoux and Brassier with the contrary view that in most of the universe there is nothing like thought at all. Nonetheless, Shaviro also notices something that separates my position from Strawson's in an absolute way. For unlike Whitehead, Karen Barad, Bennett, and DeLanda, Strawson "is radically anti-systems theory and antiemergentist. He rejects the idea that anything nontrivial can emerge on a higher level that was not already present in and linearly caused by microconstituents at a lower level"[72] (99). As Strawson has it, it is easy for science to explain how the chemical known as water causes wetness, and in principle — if not in fact — it is easy to do the same for the emergence of life but *utterly impossible* to do the same for the relation between sentience and non-sentient matter (100). This latter point matches Chalmers's concern with the highly localized "hard problem" of knowing the relation between first-person experience and third-person description. The main difference is that, even though Chalmers courts controversy by going so far as to propose that even a thermostat might be conscious, he never argues like Strawson that consciousness must be everywhere from the start[73] (96). But while Chalmers sees a "hard problem" only in the mental realm, I see it in the physical sphere as well. Many have spoken of a "combination problem" for panpsychism, meaning that it is unclear how smaller minds can combine into a larger one at a higher level. For my part, I see such a problem on the physical level as well. It does not seem so easy to me that many boards would combine into a single table, or at least no easier to grasp than my own idea that the boards and the table as a whole would each confront their own set of intentional objects.

---

72 Karen Barad, *Meeting the Universe Halfway: Quantum Physics and the Entanglement of Matter and Meaning* (Durham: Duke University Press, 2007); Bennett, *Vibrant Matter*; Manuel DeLanda, *Intensive Science and Virtual Philosophy* (London: Continuum, 2002).
73 David J. Chalmers, *The Conscious Mind: In Search of a Fundamental Theory* (Oxford: Oxford University Press, 1996).

Thomas Nagel's seminal essay "What Is It Like to Be a Bat?" proposes a famous test for consciousness.[74] Namely, an entity is conscious if there is an answer in principle to the question of "what it is like" to be that entity. For instance, the common-sense view would be that we can wonder what it is like to be a bat, dog, lion, or snake, and certainly another person. We may find it hard to imagine ever attaining such knowledge, but in some vague way we can think there is an answer to the question if only there were some means of finding out. The same common-sense view is likely to assume that there is nothing "that it is like" to be a rock or a star, though there may be some hesitation about borderline cases such as slime molds, blood cells, or the novel coronavirus. Panpsychists, by this test, would be those who hold that for pretty much *any* entity, we can reasonably ask what it is like to be it.

Enter James Ladyman and Don Ross, who at one point were heroes in continental neo-rationalist circles for their attempted evisceration of individual objects, on the basis of a faulty argument I have addressed in detail elsewhere.[75] For these ruthless eliminativists, there are no things except as correlates of the scientist who studies them: hence the clever title of their book, *Every Thing Must Go*.[76] As Shaviro aptly puts it,

> [For Ladyman and Ross] physical science can only describe relational properties. […] They conclude that since "intrinsic natures" are not known to science, they simply do not exist. As far as Ladyman is concerned, nothing has an irreducible inside; to posit one is to make an illegitimate inference […]. In Ladyman's vision, physical science is exclusively relational;

---

74 Thomas Nagel, "What Is It Like to Be a Bat?" in *Mortal Questions* (Cambridge: Cambridge University Press, 1991), 165–80.
75 Graham Harman, "I Am Also of the Opinion That Materialism Must Be Destroyed," *Environment and Planning D: Society and Space* 28, no. 5 (2010): 772–90.
76 James Ladyman and Don Ross, *Every Thing Must Go: Metaphysics Naturalized* (Oxford: Oxford University Press, 2007).

anything not determined by these relations must be eliminated. (103)

This seems to rule out anything like Nagel's "what it is like" criterion, since Ladyman and Ross leave no room for anything intrinsic in reality at all, much less an intrinsic character of psyche. Shaviro notes my objection to any purely relational theory of this sort. He then pairs my view with those of Sam Coleman and William Seager, who also require consciousness to be something intrinsic, against the usual functionalist duomining maneuver of saying that consciousness means sub-personal neural facts plus observable outward behavior, with no room for anything in between. In particular, "Seager and Harman alike insist, rightly, that entities must have something like intrinsic properties, because relations cannot exist without relata"[77] (104).

This brings us to a final point of disagreement between me and Shaviro, one that makes it impossible for me to embrace panpsychism as fully as he now does. Following his discussion of Seager, he poses the following question: "In just what does a thing's intrinsic nature consist?" His answer follows immediately, "The answer, I believe, can only be that all entities have insides as well as outsides, or first-person experiences as well as observable, third-person properties. A thing's internal qualities are objectively describable, but its interiority is neither a Something nor a Nothing" (104). The claim that the interiority of a thing is not a "Nothing" seems to be a deserved dig at the title of Metzinger's book, *Being No One*. But in what sense is interiority "Something," in view of Shaviro's claim that the interior is "what it is intrinsically like" to be something? He answers by drawing a contrast with my own position:

---

[77] William Seager, "The 'Intrinsic Nature' Argument for Panpsychism," in *Consciousness and Its Place in Nature: Does Physicalism Entail Panpsychism?*, ed. Anthony Freeman (Exeter: Imprint Academic, 2006), 140; Harman, "I Am Also of the Opinion that Materialism Must Be Destroyed," 786.

> Everything in the universe is both public and private. [...] Harman claims that all objects are "withdrawn" from access. As far as I can tell, this withdrawal is nothing more (but nothing less) than the "what-it-is-likeness," or private interior, of a thing that is also outwardly public and available. My problem with Harman is that he seems to underestimate this latter aspect. (104–5)

This does get at the heart of our disagreement, though I think Shaviro gets two points wrong. First, I would agree that every entity has both a public and a private aspect, though unlike Shaviro I identify these with the relational and the non-relational. But when he says that the "private interior, of a thing that is *also* outwardly public and available," I am not sure this makes the point he wishes to make. Granted, my inner experience is not a total mystery to other humans; for someone like my wife who knows me very well, facial expressions are often a perfect indicator of my thoughts. But all legibility of faces aside, Shaviro would surely agree there is a big difference between the experience of thinking a thought and that of interpreting the face of the thinker. For example, to realize that someone's furrowed brow indicates anxiety is obviously not the same thing as to feel anxious. Elsewhere in the book Shaviro seems to make this point himself, so I suspect he is once again claiming that intentional objects are the culprit that prevents us from realizing the free and interrupted causal flow from one point of reality to another. I have argued more than once that this puts him closer to Deleuze than to Whitehead, and will not repeat the exercise here.

The bigger problem is this: I cannot agree with Shaviro that first-person experience is the intrinsic nature of things. It is true that the usual debate in philosophy of mind is between "tough" thinkers (like Dennett) who hold that third-person scientific descriptions are all we ever need and "tender" ones (like Chalmers) who insist that first-person introspection can never be reduced to any account given from outside. Although my sympathies — like Shaviro's — are more with the latter group, I also see a problem with the first-person standpoint. Namely, what first- and third-person descriptions share is that both are *descriptions*. But to describe is to relate, and to relate automatically means to translate or caricature. Throughout his book, Shaviro in *The Universe of Things* shows an awareness that our introspection can go wrong just like our scientific descriptions, and he shows it even more vividly the following year in *Discognition*. This is the reason why I argue, in Skrbina's aforementioned anthology, that both first- and third-person consciousness are derivative of a deeper *zero-person* reality.[78] That is to say, there is a sense in which the difference between first- and third-person is ontologically trivial — not because science gets the last word on everything (so that third-person wins) or because science ultimately has to be done by sensitive human beings (so that first-person wins). Instead, insofar as both are descriptions, both are the polar opposite of what it means for a thing to be intrinsically itself. I am not my thoughts. At best, my thoughts and experiences are sketches from the outside of what I intrinsically am.

78 Harman, "Zero-Person and the Psyche."

3

PETER GRATTON

Speculative Realism

Having considered the views of my friendly acquaintances Tom Sparrow and Steven Shaviro, we now enter terrain occupied by critics who do not always wish me well. Peter Gratton was one of the first outside critics to pay attention to Speculative Realism, and on this basis he earned a not undeserved reputation as an authority on the movement.[1] Productivity, curiosity, and alertness to new trends have long been among his signature strengths, so it was little surprise that he arrived early on the scene. Yet this should not obscure a crucial difference between Gratton and the founding figures of Speculative Realism; although he is somewhat younger than all of us, his intellectual allegiance is to earlier currents of continental philosophy as embodied in the writings of such figures as Jacques Derrida and Jean-Luc Nancy. This is the context for his view, expressed repeatedly in his 2014 book *Speculative Realism: Problems and Prospects,* that the Speculative Realists often merely repeat insights that were already clear to Derrideans. He compares our evident lack of interest in deconstruction to the latter's own dismissal of Jean-Paul Sartre and existentialism, before concluding as follows:

1 Peter Gratton, "Interviews: Graham Harman, Jane Bennett, Tim Morton, Ian Bogost, Levi R. Bryant and Paul Ennis," in *Speculations I*, ed. Paul Ennis (Earth: punctum books, 2010), 84–134.

"Many generations of philosophers suffer from an anxiety of influence, and the speculative realists are no different."[2] We should first note that this is a misuse of Harold Bloom's theory of how different generations of authors interact.[3] The anxiety of influence, strictly speaking, occurs when a later author "deliberately misreads" a predecessor they regard as exceptionally *strong,* in an effort to carve out their own distinct space in the intellectual world. It does not follow that every critique of an older author by a younger one is a case of such anxiety; often enough, the new generation simply experiences the previous one as a stale ruling power whose ideas no longer sparkle. On this note, it is easy to see why the young deconstructionists would have regarded existentialism — if somewhat unfairly — as a tired form of modern humanism. But it would be rather odd to claim that the young Derrida's anxiety of influence stemmed from Sartre, and far more plausible that it came from structuralism on one side and phenomenology on the other. As for the alleged Speculative Realist anxiety in the face of deconstruction, there is no such thing. If one examines our writings collectively, Derrida is simply not one of the central figures with whom we grapple, my frustrations with his critique of Aristotle notwithstanding.[4]

In fact, it is Gratton himself who likely feels some anxiety of influence with respect to deconstruction, the most important school in forming his own outlook. Thus, we are dealing with a case of projection on his part. Rather than calmly identifying the authors who risked overpowering the various Speculative Realists in their youth — as Bloom would do — Gratton invents a theory of secret Derridean influence that suits his own agenda without fitting the case at hand. Elsewhere in the book, he makes the more interesting claim that I am heavily indebted to

---

2 Peter Gratton, *Speculative Realism: Problems and Prospects* (London: Bloomsbury Academic, 2014), 5. Subsequent page references are given between parentheses in the main text.
3 Harold Bloom, *The Anxiety of Influence: A Theory of Poetry,* 2nd edn. (Oxford: Oxford University Press, 1997).
4 Graham Harman, *Guerrilla Metaphysics: Phenomenology and the Carpentry of Things* (Chicago: Open Court, 2005), 110–16.

the philosophy of Levinas in a way that some readers do not realize. This is both true and insightful, though I will show that Gratton misreads the nature of that influence, which has less to do with "alterity" and "the Other" than with Levinas's insights into the sensual hither side of being.

More generally, Gratton's jet drifts too easily into Airspace Snide-and-Cocky. His eleven-page introduction is mottled with so much regrettable shade that the book would have been better served by having no introduction at all. At the bottom of page three, we read the following: "But I've delayed long enough. What is speculative realism anyway?" (3). Under normal authorial circumstances, "What is speculative realism anyway?" would have been the first sentence of the book, or close to it. So, we might ask, what was going on in the three full pages before Gratton finally got to the point? A good portion of those pages is filled with statements reminiscent of "many people are saying…" insinuations. A few examples are in order, starting with this one: "But to make it for real these days, the cynical will claim, you must have a *system,* and it better come with a ready-made politics. Which, *of course,* you'll say, it *does,* since it's the subject of your forthcoming book; anyone can have a book *forthcoming,* and it is best to have several to have a trump card to throw into any conversation at conferences" (1). To whom, pray tell, is Gratton referring here? And what does any of it have to do with a book on Speculative Realism? While there is some ambiguity in the passage as to whether the author agrees with "the cynical," anyone reading a few pages further will conclude that the introduction is designed primarily to generate alibis for such cynicism among readers ill-disposed toward Speculative Realism. Is there really a problem in our discipline, for instance, with people having too many book contracts? Normally, no one has multiple contracts unless they have reliably published actual books, so that publishers come knocking on their doors for more. Gratton would appear to be dog-whistling at someone, and there is little point speculating who. It is his job to lay his cards on the table, not mine.

But perhaps Gratton is aiming his accusations instead at those who actually have published a good deal, despite his own relatively prolific track record. The cat would appear to have escaped the bag near the top of page one: "Philosophy, the fear is, has become even more of a bazaar of self-branding academics pumping out articles and books and pushing new systems of thought with clumsy titles" (1). "The fear is?" Whose fear, exactly? We are never told, though apparently many people fear that "self-branding" academics are "pumping out" too many articles and books. But as a rule, it is a good sign when academics are productive rather than unproductive, and I have mentioned that Gratton himself very much belongs to the productive side of the profession. Nonetheless, he sees fit to consider — or perhaps many people are considering — whether it might be better to behave instead like "[Hans-Georg] Gadamer [...] publish[ing] his first major book at age sixty"[5] (2). Is there really a problem with Speculative Realists publishing too much too early? The evidence suggests not. At the time of the inaugural Goldsmiths workshop, the four participants were relatively obscure, dues-paying veterans ranging in age from thirty-eight to forty-three, which is hardly a premature blossoming. Yet it is difficult to respond to anything in the introduction with much precision; the smoke signals are always mixed, and Gratton never quite tells us where he stands on all this cynicism that many people are said to be feeling.

Unfortunately, the closest he comes to tipping his hand comes when his very first block-quote is original Speculative Realist Ray Brassier infamously referring to SR as an "online orgy of stupidity,"[6] followed shortly thereafter by a false piece of objectivity: "Let us thus make Brassier's analysis our starting point" (3). Why make Brassier's insult — hardly an "analysis" — the "starting point" of the book, when Gratton is fully

---

5 Hans-Georg Gadamer, *Truth and Method*, trans. Joel Weinsheimer and Donald G. Marshall, 2nd edn. (London: Continuum, 2004).
6 Ray Brassier, "I Am A Nihilist Because I Still Believe in Truth," interview by Marcin Rychter, *Kronos*, March 4, 2011.

aware that Brassier has a personal axe to grind against his former group, and also fully aware that Brassier's primary target (the Object-Oriented Ontologists) are not primarily "online" figures but instead are "pumping out" articles and books by the dozens? Then again, amidst the fog of the introduction and its confusingly contrary hints as to what many cynical people are saying, who's to say that "pumping out" articles and books is any better than having written nothing, but having "several" books "forthcoming" instead of written? So thick is the gloom of insinuation that at times there is no way to parse the meaning of the book without interpreting the numerous tacit digs that lurk in the background.

Gratton does make a number of interesting arguments, and I will consider them, though it would have been preferable to meet them in less alloyed form. His claim that he "wouldn't write at such length [...about] authors [he doesn't] greatly respect" (6) makes a strange fit with the rest of the introduction, which reads like an extended permission slip — written in invisible ink — for mainstream continental philosophers to indulge in sarcastic remarks at Speculative Realism's expense. For instance, "A movement should have to prove its staying power and importance, not just get name-dropped in art catalogues and cloying treatises" (3). Is Gratton one of the many people who are saying this? Presumably not, since he went ahead and "pumped out" a 266-page book on Speculative Realism less than a decade after the movement began. Furthermore, what is wrong with art catalogues? And what on earth is a "cloying treatise"? There is no telling, for we are in the London of *Bleak House*:

> Fog everywhere. Fog up the river, where it flows among green aits and meadows; fog down the river, where it rolls defiled among the tiers of shipping and the waterside pollutions of a great (and dirty) city. Fog on the Essex marshes, fog on the Kentish heights. Fog creeping into the cabooses of collier-brigs; fog lying out on the yards and hovering in the rigging of great ships; fog drooping on the gunwales of barges and

> small boats. Fog in the eyes and throats of ancient Greenwich pensioners, wheezing by the firesides of their wards.[7]

Gratton habitually belittles the originality of the Speculative Realists, claiming that Meillassoux's philosophy was anticipated two years in advance by the analytic philosopher John Nolt (40), despite minuscule similarity between these authors. He claims that Meillassoux stole his theory of God from both Philo of Alexandria (66) and Richard Kearney (75) — or should I say he *insinuates* it, since Gratton rarely comes right out and says anything of the sort. Perhaps most foolishly, he tweaks my nose with a "[sic]" following a typographical verb-tense error in my translation of Meillassoux's *L'Inexistence divine*: "because it cannot be understand [sic] how the lifeless [...]." Such things happen when writing and editing books, but Gratton makes the decision to leave the typo and draw attention to it, rather than quietly fix it or put the correct word in brackets as well-mannered authors generally do. Unfortunately for him, the snark backfires when his own book turns out to be riddled with more typographical mistakes than any other I have seen under the Bloomsbury label. The errors include frequent cases of words missing from sentences, the oddly foreign tourist-like claim that the aforementioned Nolt teaches at the "University of Knoxville" rather than the University of Tennessee (40), the misstatement of my article subtitle "A New Theory of Causation" as "The New Causality" (105), the misspelling of the Polish journal *Kronos* as *Chronos* (217n1), and two different misspellings of Jean-Luc Boltanski's surname just five lines apart (198–99). He also omits Steve Woolgar's name as co-author from Bruno Latour's *Laboratory Life*, while calling the subtitle of that book *The Construction of Scientific Fast* rather than *Facts*[8] (90). In a crowning *bizarrerie*, he even ascribes some words I wrote my-

---

7 Charles Dickens, *Bleak House*, ed. Nicola Bradbury (London: Penguin Books, 2003), 13.
8 Bruno Latour and Steve Woolgar, *Laboratory Life: The Construction of Scientific Facts* (Princeton: Princeton University Press, 2013).

self to Leon Trotsky, though he should have known that "dusky underworld" sounds a lot more like me than like the goateed revolutionary (92). Gratton has what it takes to be a solid, adult critic of Speculative Realism and Object-Oriented Ontology from his holdout Derridean position. But one wastes so much time unravelling his smirky innuendoes that I occasionally find myself longing instead for Wolfendale's open expressions of hatred. Unfortunately, it will be necessary to call out more cases of this kind as we move forward, since there are times when Gratton's arguments are practically soaked in sub-verbal insinuation.

Amidst a surprising occurrence of the phrase "fuck and die" on page ten, the reader finally gains sight of a clear statement of Gratton's own philosophical outlook:

> My hunch is this: speculative realism may stand the test of time, but only if takes the reality of time as a test to pass. [...] My view is that those critiqued by the speculative realists, such as Martin Heidegger, Jacques Derrida, and several others were not "correlationists," but were after a realism of time — Being as time, as Heidegger put it, a claim that made his project and the later deconstruction possible. (10)

This is, in fact, the intended lesson of Gratton's book — philosophy must be grounded in a specific theory of time, and Meillassoux and I both fail this test because we are too close to Plato. Coming from a Derridean like Gratton, the accusation of Platonism is obviously not meant as a compliment. But at least it is a clear thesis, and like all clear theses, it is honorable enough to risk refutation. My response will be as follows: (a) Leaving Meillassoux to defend himself if he wishes, I will show that Gratton is wrong to claim that my philosophy bears any significant resemblance to Plato's, and (b) I will show that Gratton is wrong to link Heidegger's philosophy of time with Derrida's. For in fact, they are completely different.

General Survey of Gratton's Views on SR

Gratton's book covers not only the four original Speculative Realists but also an interesting cross-section of neighboring thinkers — Jane Bennett, Elizabeth Grosz, Adrian Johnston, and Catherine Malabou. Nonetheless, I will focus here exclusively on his treatment of Meillassoux's philosophy and my own. The reason is that the two of us are the primary targets in the closing argument of his book (201–16), as presaged in the introduction:

> Meillassoux could not do his work [...] without the mathematics of set theory. I began to wonder if we weren't returning to Platonism, the view that what is ultimately real is outside time. [...] But Harman argues that objects as they are in themselves are not in time, since time is embedded in appearances, which seems to repeat Plato's account. We will ask if this is a major problem with his work. (8)

But "we" will do considerably more than "ask." "We" will answer that it is a major problem indeed. The book's conclusion will give us Gratton's argument for a "realism of time" (202). He urges that the Speculative Realists follow him down this path, "lest they give themselves over to the idealism of objects, mathematics, and so on" (202). The role played by "and so on" in this passage is unclear. But no matter, since objects and mathematics take the brunt of his criticism.

Before entering into his account of Meillassoux, allow me to point to two passages where Gratton overgeneralizes about the Speculative Realists. The first comes when he says, "it should be said that there has been a longstanding divide between Anglo-American and Continental philosophy, and speculative realists promise a move beyond this divide" (40). Gratton does not back up this claim with citations, and as far as I know, Brassier is the only Speculative Realist who offers such a promise.[9] Badiou also

---

9 Ray Brassier, "Postscript: Speculative Autopsy," in Peter Wolfendale, *Object-Oriented Philosophy* (Falstaff: Urbanomic, 2014), 414. Brassier dismisses the

makes this promise, in the course of boasting about his personal prowess in both mathematics and literature, but I do not recall Meillassoux having said much at all about the analytic/continental divide.[10] For my own part, I wish to *widen* the gap between the two traditions.[11] The second overgeneralization comes when, after quoting a passage from *The Quadruple Object* in which I note that we humans are a relatively minor species orbiting a mediocre sun, Gratton leaps to the assertion that "this apocalyptic affect pervades speculative realism, from Meillassoux's depictions of the end of humanity to Brassier's nihilism" (52). Not really. There is nothing inherently "apocalyptic" about saying that humans are not so important in the universe as a whole, which is all I say on the topic. Meillassoux does speak of the possible coming of a Messiah and then a God who will completely transform existence into a World of Justice, and I suppose this could be called "apocalyptic," though "eschatological" or "soteriological" would seem more to the point.[12] Brassier is really the only Speculative Realist who revels in discussing the end of our species and the universe as a whole, and this remains a fetish of his personal project.[13] Moreover, even the arguments Gratton cites against us on this score—from Adrian Johnston and Slavoj Žižek—are not so much anti-apocalyptic as outright idealist, through their shared claim that it can only be a "fantasy" to imagine gazing upon a world in which humans are no longer present, since we would still have to be there gazing at the fantasy (52). Alain Weisman's bestseller *The World without Us* was based on an interesting concept, a consideration of what would happen to various buildings and facilities if humans were

divide as a mere "sociological fact."
10 Alain Badiou, *Being and Event,* trans. Oliver Feltham (London: Continuum, 2005), xiii–xiv.
11 Graham Harman, "The Enduring Importance of the Analytic/Continental Split," *Gavagai* 3 (2017): 158–60.
12 Quentin Meillassoux, "Appendix: Excerpts from *L'Inexistence divine,*" in Graham Harman, *Quentin Meillassoux: Philosophy in the Making* (Edinburgh: Edinburgh University Press, 2015), 175–238.
13 Ray Brassier, *Nihil Unbound: Enlightenment and Extinction* (New York: Palgrave, 2007).

suddenly to disappear. And it is true that Brassier and Meillassoux both make extensive realist use of the trope of a world devoid of humans. But this is not what OOO is about, since for us the thing-in-itself is not attained by removing humans from the scene, but by stressing that objects remain mysterious even when humans are right there staring at them.

In any case, after "praising" Speculative Realism (with the word "luckily") for having oversimplified a 200-year period of philosophy by dismissing it as anti-realist (14), Gratton eventually gets down to business with an opening-chapter summary of correlationism. That summary is actually quite good, beginning with a brutally anti-realist epigraph from Maurice Merleau-Ponty, a thinker who too often provides cover for phenomenological idealists masquerading as realists (13). Whereas the Speculative Realists themselves tend to explain correlationism by referring to Immanuel Kant, Gratton usefully expands the map by also incorporating the analytic philosopher Michael Dummett (22–26). Late in the chapter, he also reaches a genuine insight about Meillassoux: "What's striking about *After Finitude* is that Meillassoux, frankly, has little to combat idealism as such. He expends a lot of energy on correlationisms but, as we'll see, his method has nothing to say about idealisms that simply *deny* any correlation at all" (37). No one who reads Meillassoux carefully could argue that he is close to naïve realism; in chapter 6 we will see that Christopher Norris makes this claim about the early parts of Meillassoux's first book, though this is merely a product of Norris not reading very carefully. Yet I myself have argued, and Gratton rightly implies, that there is no sufficient remedy for outright idealism in *After Finitude,* a charge that might be extended to Meillassoux's teacher Badiou as well as their fellow traveler Žižek, given his minimal Lacanian sense of the Real as nothing but a traumatic wound to the symbolic order.

Before getting to the most interesting parts of Gratton's reading of Meillassoux, there is no escaping the burden of what he gets wrong, starting from the least important errors and working our way to the more serious lapses. First, there is the following: "This is perhaps why Meillassoux differentiates between 'refutation' and 'disqualification,' [...] though frankly it's impossible to make out" (41), in connection with Meillassoux's presentation at Goldsmiths.[14] In fact, it is very easy to understand this particular distinction. In the passage in question, Meillassoux is looking for a rational argument to "refute" the correlationist, as opposed to a mere "disqualification" such as casting aspersions on the correlationist's psychological motives or calling him boring. Second, Gratton spends a bit too much time dwelling on the "ridiculousness" of Meillassoux's theory of a virtual God who does not now exist but may exist in the future, though he lets Adam Kotsko shoulder the burden of mocking it for him (65). While it is no doubt true that Meillassoux will convert few readers to his strange theology, one should not just admire those philosophies with whose content one happens to agree; this is the dogmatic flaw found in Brassier, Wolfendale, and others, not a good general model for philosophical behavior.

There are other problems with Gratton's account of Meillassoux. As mentioned earlier, he reports that "[i]t so happens that *two years before* the publication of *After Finitude,* John Nolt, a University of Knoxville [sic] philosopher, published a similar argument confronting anti-realism" (40; italics added). This looks very much like a trial balloon for questioning Meillassoux's originality. The real problem with this strategy is that Meillassoux's discussion of ancestrality and the arche-fossil is not meant to be original, and is not even meant as an "argument." Nolt's article is a perfectly lucid piece of analytic philosophy which proceeds through several steps to the conclusion that "the cosmos has structure that is independent of our cognition — i.e., intrinsic structure."[15] While this may sound similar to Meillassoux's discussion of the arche-fossil, the difference is that Nolt is a straightforward scientific realist who considers the existence of an intrinsic structure of the universe to be the final

14 Ray Brassier, Iain Hamilton Grant, Graham Harman, and Quentin Meillassoux, "Speculative Realism," in *Collapse III,* ed. Robin Mackay (Falstaff: Urbanomic, 2007), 429.
15 John Nolt, "An Argument for Metaphysical Realism," *Journal for General Philosophy of Science* 35 (2004): 72.

lesson of the story. Nowhere does Nolt defend the equal rights of the correlationist side of the argument that "the universe has an intrinsic structure — *for us*." Now as always, those who overlook this side of Meillassoux are advised to reread his portion of the Goldsmiths transcript. Those crucial pages are all about how the correlationist *has a point,* and needs to be defeated by oblique means rather than the direct ones used by Nolt, Paul Boghossian, and others.[16]

A more serious difficulty, in which Gratton is not alone and Meillassoux not blameless, stems from the false claim — expressed rather triumphantly, I might add — that Meillassoux is merely confusing epistemology and ontology:

> Is his refutation of the correlationist as knockdown as Meillassoux argues? In a word, no. First Meillassoux is in danger of portraying Kant et al. as particularly daft philosophers who can't distinguish between ontological and epistemological claims. Kant isn't asserting that the in-itself doesn't exist, but rather that what we know can't simply be accounted for by some unmediated access to the in-itself. [... And] as Peter Hallward points out, one can say such and such are the epistemological or linguistic conditions for knowledge [...] without ever believing that the things in the world "depend" on thinking for existence.[17] (46–47)

Along with Hallward, David Golumbia makes a similar point in his article, which claims that correlationism never really existed.[18] But in fact, Meillassoux is guilty of no such conflation

---

16 Ray Brassier et al., "Speculative Realism," 408–49; Paul Boghossian, *Fear of Knowledge: Against Relativism and Constructivism* (Oxford: Oxford University Press, 2006).

17 The reference is to Peter Hallward, "Anything Is Possible: A Reading of Quentin Meillassoux's 'After Finitude,'" in *The Speculative Turn: Continental Materialism and Realism,* eds. Levi R. Bryant, Nick Srnicek, and Graham Harman (Melbourne: re.press, 2011), 130–41.

18 David Golumbia, "'Correlationism': The Dogma That Never Was," *boundary 2* 43, no. 2 (May 2016): 1–25.

between the epistemological and ontological registers. Nowhere does he claim that Kant says the thing-in-itself depends on the human mind for existence. Instead, he draws a distinction between "weak" and "strong" correlationists, with Kant a textbook example of the "weak" type who holds that something does exist outside thought, though we simply cannot know it. Although Meillassoux is not guilty of misreading Kant, he is nonetheless guilty in *After Finitude* of an ambiguous use of the word "correlationism," as he later admitted in his 2012 Berlin lecture.[19] The ambiguity is as follows. On the one hand, Meillassoux usually treats Kant as the shining exemplar of correlationism. But on the other, he defines the "correlational circle" in terms that do not apply to Kant, namely, "to think a thing outside thought is itself a thought, and therefore to think anything outside thought is impossible." This view is of course not held by Kant, but only by the *strong* correlationist, as well as the idealist, and therefore should have been called the "strong correlational circle" instead. We should emphasize once more that, far from being a scientific realist in the manner of Nolt, Meillassoux holds that even Kant makes too many concessions to the thing-in-itself outside thought, and much prefers the strong correlationist to the weak one. He reaches his own philosophical position by radicalizing the strong correlational circle, just as OOO can be interpreted as a radicalization of Kantian weak correlationism beyond the human sphere.

There is a final point on which I am not sure whether Gratton gets Meillassoux right or not, because the textual evidence is murky. In the course of comparing Meillassoux with Philo, Gratton makes the following statement: "Meillassoux is clear that matter was created *ex nihilo*" (67). This was once my view as well, though I no longer think it is so clear. The reason for doubt stems from Meillassoux's argument, in *After Finitude*,

19 Quentin Meillassoux, "Iteration, Reiteration, Repetition: A Speculative Analysis of the Meaningless Sign," trans. Robin Mackay and M. Gansen, in *Genealogies of Speculation: Materialism and Subjectivity Since Structuralism*, eds. Armen Avanessian and Suhail Malik (London: Bloomsbury, 2016), 117–97.

that his "principle of unreason" should be accepted in a strong sense rather than a weak one. The weak sense would be that *if* something exists, then it must be contingent, while insisting that this in no way entails that something *must* exist (73). The strong sense, on the other hand, would say that it is necessary that something exist, because it is necessary that contingent things exist (74). We need not go into Meillassoux's attempted proof of the strong reading here, and only mention in passing that he does support it. But this runs counter to the sense one gets from *The Divine Inexistence* that matter was created *ex nihilo*, just as later happened with life and thought, and as might happen one day with justice and the Virtual God. For if the strong reading of the principle of unreason is correct that something *must* exist, it is hard to see what that could be for Meillassoux other than matter, which provides the indispensable bedrock in his philosophy for the later contingent emergence of life and later thought. But it is time to turn to Gratton's account of OOO.

Gratton deals with me primarily in chapter 4 of his book, though numerous other references are sprinkled throughout, including in the all-important conclusion of the book. Chapter 4 contains a few misleading remarks that need to be dealt with before getting to the substance of Gratton's critique. Unlike Wolfendale, he judges that my work is "clear and schematic" (85), which frankly is the reaction most readers have. We will see that Gratton has plenty of criticisms to make of my philosophy, though he thankfully avoids the affectation of claiming that I am so unclear that he had to work oh so very hard just to make my writings intelligible, a pretense with which Wolfendale's book is irredeemably saturated. Gratton also claims that although I write extensively about my differences from Edmund Husserl and Heidegger, "a better passkey to [Harman's] work is through the writings of Levinas" (85), Naturally, "this is not to say that Harman's account is not original" (85), though in fact there are numerous insinuations throughout the book that it is not original. In any event, Gratton shows insight in pointing to the impact of Levinas on my thinking, which occurred primarily in my early twenties, an age at which influences leave a deeper and more primordial stamp than affinities discovered later. By contrast, I was nearly thirty years old before starting to read Latour, meaning that he helped refine my position rather than shape its basic suppositions.

There are two possible ways in which the link Gratton draws between me and Levinas could be misleading. First, he overstresses the importance of Levinasian "alterity" for my work (87). For one thing, this is historically false. It is true that I was first reading Levinas in 1991, at twenty-three years old, under the guidance of his translator Alphonso Lingis. It was Lingis's critique of my holistic reading of Heidegger, along with my readings of Levinas, which helped set the stage for what is now my decidedly non-holistic interpretation of Heidegger's tool-analysis. Lingis's own version of this critique can be found today in his under-read article on Levinas and substance.[20] But this movement toward substance is already enough to show that absolute alterity was not what interested me about Levinas. In his wonderful short work *Time and the Other* Levinas links alterity with the futuricity of time, as contrasted with what he regards as Heidegger's mere "future of the present," in which the so-called future is merely collapsed into the threefold present of *Dasein*'s "thrown projection." I still admire Levinas's argument about futuricity today, despite the paradox that he seems to draw it from Bergson, who is not a thinker of alterity in Levinas's sense. In any case, what I found interesting in Levinas (and still do today) was not so much his famous notion of alterity as his discussions of the *hither side* of being, referring both to the enjoyment of such entities as cigarettes and apples and the elemental medium in which they occur. My concept of withdrawn real objects dates instead to 1997 and my long summer readings of Xavier Zubíri, whose notion of individuals has a more Aristotelian flavor and which subtracts them from their relations to such a degree that he (wrongly) denies that a knife or a farm can be real, given that they exist only in their "respectivity" to other things. Zubíri also

---

20 Alphonso Lingis, "A Phenomenology of Substances," *American Catholic Philosophical Quarterly* 71, no. 4 (Autumn 1997): 505–22.

strikes a disappointingly naturalist note in locating the reality of things in their "atomic-cortical structure," so reminiscent of Saul Kripke falling back on the number of protons in gold as being the core of its reality.

Second, it is hard to follow Gratton's argument when he identifies my "object in withdrawal" with Levinas's "elemental" (86). Rather, the elemental in Levinas is the sensual, sub-objective medium in which sensual objects first take form. Although I ultimately call this elemental medium "black noise," meaning that it emanates from objects which become objects as soon as we turn our attention to them, there is indeed something to be gained from a phenomenology of the non-objective element. The growing interest in Gernot Böhme's theory of "atmospheres" shows that many others are intrigued by this topic as well.[21] But I cannot endorse Gratton's claim that the interpretation of the elemental by John Sallis is a good fit with my work. Sallis writes as follows: "the recession of the elemental, its *withdrawal into fathomless depth*, its withdrawal that is neither simply revelation nor concealment."[22] When I speak of withdrawal in a OOO context, I do not mean a withdrawal "that is neither simply revelation nor concealment" (the old Derridean tap dance of neither/nor), but a withdrawal that is simply concealment. But this is clearly not what Levinas means by the element, and the discrepancy is explained simply by the fact that Sallis uses the word "withdrawal" in a less hardcore sense than my own.

Next Gratton gives, as an example of my term "undermining," the philosophy of British Empiricism and its bundles of qualities (89). But for me this is a textbook case of *overmining*—the empiricists hold that a bundle of qualities is all we need, and any notion of a distinct object holding them all together is a needless fiction. In short, they think the "object" is simply the sum total of content to which we have access in

---

21 Gernot Böhme, *The Aesthetics of Atmospheres*, ed. Jean-Paul Thibaud (New York: Routledge, 2017).
22 John Sallis, "Levinas and the Elemental," *Research in Phenomenology* 28 (1998): 158.

sense-experience, not something that remains unified despite its shifting, kaleidoscopic figures, as phenomenology holds. On a related note, Gratton glosses my rejection of materialism as a *duomining* move with the following sentence: "For Harman, scientific materialism 'jeers' objects from below, while a 'German Idealist' 'dialectical materialism' 'jeers' from above" (92). This may be the least felicitous use of scare-quotes I have ever seen; they are so numerous and disjunct that I lose track of which are direct quotes and which are intended as sarcastic putdowns of my argument. Accordingly, I cannot begin to respond. Surprisingly, however, there is another point on which Gratton does me *too much* credit:

> Spinoza's point [when he claims that thought and extension are just two of infinitely many modes] is that there is no reason there wouldn't be infinite modes or means of accessing this world. Harman's description of sensuous objects is similar: there may be indeed many ways objects, animals, and so on, have of relating or accessing the things of this world beyond the three noted [by Levinas]. (95)

This is a beautiful idea expressed in lovely prose, and one I agree with in principle. But most of my writing on this topic has been about the difference between real objects and *any* form of sensuousness, and I have not done enough as of yet to explore the variety of possible sensual worlds. It is Shaviro in *Discognition* who has gone some way towards opening up this topic, and even Metzinger with his account of various neuropathologies in *Being No One*.

We shift now to a topic where Gratton typically gives me *too little* credit instead, when he refers to the discussion of the "tension" between objects and qualities as "doing much of the conceptual heavy lifting in Harman's accounts" (102). Given that "term X is doing a lot of heavy lifting for you" is established continentalese for "you're just throwing that term around without even knowing what it means," this is an especially ungenerous moment in his account. It would be more accurate to say that the word "tension" is the *result* of a lot of heavy lifting. Years of work were needed to reach a simple understanding of how time and space can both be understood as different forms of the object–quality tension, and more years needed before it became clear that the two other forms of such tension (RO–RQ and SO–RQ) could be identified as "essence" and "eidos." I daresay this is one of the most original and productive results of OOO so far. Traditionally, philosophers have speculated on space and time as two peerless aspects of the cosmos, sitting on a pedestal by themselves, with discussion mostly limited as to whether or not they should be collapsed (as with Hermann Minkowski and sometimes Heidegger) into a single space-time. I am not aware of other efforts to expand the spatio-temporal schema to show that essence, eidos, or anything else belongs there as well. The fact that there is more to be said about the underlying "tensions" than I have said so far is simply how things go in philosophy. A placeholder term is never the final stage of an insight, but it does help make the ultimate insight possible.

A related deficit of generosity occurs when Gratton quotes a passage from *The Quadruple Object* which says that real objects *must somehow* be translated into sensual caricatures of themselves, *must* serve as the fuel that makes causal relations possible, and so forth. The italics are Gratton's own, and he hammers them repeatedly into the citation, as if to suggest that I am taking undue liberties in merely waving my arms and asserting something I cannot explain: though we will see later that his sainted Derrida does this himself at a key moment (103). Gratton continues to hammer this point for several pages, eventually concluding as follows: "His use of 'somehow' and 'must' covers over an argument for causality, and previous antecedents in the history of philosophy using occasionalism could only offer mysticism in place of explanation" (105). Here, like Norris who is discussed in chapter 6 below, Gratton openly invites the reader to imagine that I am mystically appealing to God as the universal causal agent. There is no trace here of my frequent emphasis that both my model of indirect causation and Latour's differ not only from occasionalism but also from Hume and Kant, by refusing to permit any privileged super-entity (whether God or the mind) to be the sole locus of causation. Furthermore, OOO has nothing to do with "mysticism," which claims direct access to the truth just like rationalism, though by different means, while the object-oriented position is that any such access must be indirect. In short, the case here is the same as with "tension." The "musts" and the "somehows" are not invoked from thin air as an excuse for nothing to say, but are the provisional result of a process of narrowing down the place where causation must occur. We are not left with mere guesses about causation, but are partway down the path to a solution. In the famous words of Sherlock Holmes, "eliminate all other factors, and the one which remains must be the truth."[23] The passage above that Gratton mocks with extensive italics represents the stage of having eliminated the impossible, which, for me, is direct causation. The improbable option that remains is vicarious causation, in which real objects are mediated by sensual ones and sensual objects by real ones, and even Sherlock Holmes needs time to progress from one step to the next. This could certainly lead to what is called "the Holmesian Fallacy," in which someone prematurely eliminates an option as impossible that is actually quite possible. But in that case, Gratton would need to show that direct causation is possible, or at least refute my argument that it is not. He does neither of these things.

There are a few more matters to deal with before getting to the core of Gratton's temporal argument against OOO. One is his implication that, with the advent of the Anthropocene Era — in which human impact on the non-human world is more obvious than ever — it is somehow an irresponsible or shifty maneuver to switch to a discussion of inanimate things. He actually puts it in even less flattering terms, "To describe, then, the power of things at precisely *this* time could have the feel of an alibi for [avoiding] the human responsibility in the ecological strife in and around us — like an only child suddenly talking about the

---

23 Arthur Conan Doyle, *The Sign of Four* (Scotts Valley: CreateSpace Independent Publishing Platform, 2018), 6.

powers of an imaginary friend when caught with a mess" (110). We cannot allow Gratton to get away with the word "could." He must take full ownership of this passage: not only of its insulting comparison of OOO to a lying or deluded child, but more importantly of the implied — and bizarre — thesis that the Anthropocene gives us *even more* reason to continue the human-centered emphasis of post-Kantian theory. This argument rests on a simple equivocation. The fact that humans have *a very strong causal role* in giving rise to the Anthropocene does not mean that the *appearance of the Anthropocene to human thought* must be our theoretical starting point now more than ever. It is the same equivocation noted by Manuel DeLanda on the first page of his book *A New Philosophy of Society*: the fact that humans are necessary ingredients of human society does not entail that human society is equivalent to how it appears to humans.[24] Instead, we are dealing with real causal forces — in the cases of both human society and the Anthropocene — that resist any precise thematization by human theories. In *Art and Objects* I make a similar criticism of the modern formalist theories with which I otherwise agree, namely, those of Clement Greenberg and Michael Fried.[25] For art to be independent of the human beholder does not also require that art be devoid of a human *ingredient,* which is wrongly assumed in the Greenberg/Fried critique of much "postmodern" art.

In the next passage I have in mind, Gratton refers to "Harman's rhetoric on undermining and overmining" (116). Although I personally view rhetoric in a positive sense, as the branch of philosophy that studies the power of *unspoken* syllogisms (see Marshall McLuhan's treatment of media) it is clear that Gratton means "rhetoric" in the more recent, dismissive sense of the term.[26] He could have just said I was wrong, but he chooses instead to farm out this task to my fellow Specu-

24 Manuel DeLanda, *A New Philosophy of Society: Assemblage Theory and Social Complexity* (London: Continuum, 2006), 1.
25 Graham Harman, *Art and Objects* (Cambridge: Polity, 2020).
26 Marshall McLuhan, *Understanding Media: The Extensions of Man* (Cambridge: MIT Press, 1994).

lative Realist and all-around good guy Iain Hamilton Grant. The occasion for my debate with Grant was his response to my essay faulting his anti-object-oriented theory for a form of "undermining."[27] He responded in his usual warm and friendly way, in an accompanying piece entitled "Mining Conditions: A Response to Harman."[28] Gratton captures the gist of that article when he writes,

> Grant is arguing that his Idealism, contrary to the normal uses of that term, concerns horizontal formations of powers that would both produce and undo any particular being, and thus, unlike Harman, is fully temporal. One cannot discuss any given object without discussing its history and its becoming. This is what links all forms of Spinozism from (early) Schelling to Deleuze. (116)

Gilbert Simondon would be another name to throw into the mix. Yet there are at least two problems with this aspect of Grant's position. The first, as Brassier and I both noted at Goldsmiths, is that as much as Grant wants to stress the *productivity* of nature in his position and downplay its status as a *one*, individual objects are accounted for in his position only as the result of "retardations" of a more primordial productive force.[29] It is hard to see where such retardations could come from if there are no preexistent obstacles to the free flow of production. And without such obstacles, one is left with vague talk about "tendencies" or "virtual powers" that might exist quasi-independently of each other in nature without quite being fully-formed objects.

---

27 Graham Harman, "On the Undermining of Objects: Grant, Bruno, and Radical Philosophy," in *The Speculative Turn: Continental Materialism and Realism*, eds. Levi Bryant, Nick Srnicek, and Graham Harman (Melbourne: re.press, 2011), 21–40.
28 Iain Hamilton Grant, "Mining Conditions: A Response to Harman," in *The Speculative Turn: Continental Materialism and Realism*, eds. Levi R. Bryant, Nick Srnicek, and Graham Harman (Melbourne: re.press, 2011), 41–46.
29 Brassier et al., "Speculative Realism," 315, 352–53.

The next problem comes in the following statement by Gratton, one with which Grant would presumably agree: "One cannot discuss any given object without discussing its history and its becoming." This is a statement that poses as a truism while barely concealing a falsity in its breast. It is similar in form to the argument that artworks cannot be understood apart from their socio-political contexts, or that all architecture must be "site-specific." These arguments are fundamentally deceitful insofar as they give themselves a low hurdle to clear and their opponents a very high one. The low hurdle is cleared in approximately the following fahion: "obviously everything must be understood in relation to its context, and therefore everything is defined by its context." But there is a *non sequitur* after the comma, since there is no good reason to hold that *all* aspects of a thing's context are relevant. By contrast, the high hurdle looks something like this: "our opponents say that things are completely unaffected by their context, which is obviously ridiculous." I have repeatedly faced some form of this objection over the years, usually from people who play the Simondon card and claim that I am dealing only with fully-formed individuals rather than the deeper process of individuation. But this Game of Hurdles deceives for the following reason. The more plausible solution is that every object is affected by *some* aspects of its context but not others; a "site-specific" building may respond to the river nearby, to the specific type of sunlight found at the site, to the area's rich Native American history, to the buildings currently located across the street, or to all these factors — and much more — simultaneously. But no building can possibly relate to *all* aspects of its context. Certain selections are always made as to the inclusion and exclusion of what belongs to the "site." The same holds for the individuating history of an object. Some incidents in my life, as in Gratton's no doubt, have had a powerful or even transformative impact on who I am today. But by no means does *everything* that happens leave a trace, unless we beg the question by positing some sort of universal cosmic memory that preserves everything at a level too minute for the human sensorium. In short, objects have firewalls and do not reflect the sum total of everything that has happened to them. Even the evolution of animal species responds to certain specific environmental pressures, not to all of them. The only theory capable of addressing both the effectual and ineffectual aspects of history or environment is one that allows for things to be cut off from each other to some extent. The "everything is continuous" option, such as Grant's "retardation" model of individuals, leaves us with no explanation of why retardation should ever occur. As Brassier put it at Goldsmiths, "If you privilege productivity, if these ideal generative dynamisms that structure and constitute material reality can be characterized in terms of the primacy of production over product, then the question is, how do we account for the interruption of the process? How do we account for discontinuity in the continuum of production?"[30]

Gratton pulls out a different knife in the ensuing passage: "But Grant implicitly, I think, is making another suggestion: it is Harman who is a reductionist in his object-oriented ontology, reducing being from its utter contingency and creativity to an order of given objects" (116). If so, this would be reminiscent of Brassier's objections to Latour, which I considered in *Speculative Realism: An Introduction,* to the effect that Latour claims to oppose reduction but then reduces everything to actants.[31] This is actually a legitimate point, and not just a product of Brassier's well-known *animus* against Latour, as can be seen from the fact that the same question was once put to me by the prominent Dutch Latourian Gerard de Vries. I have had different thoughts about this question over the years, and will simply explain how I see the issue now. The grain of truth in Gratton's and Brassier's objections is that no philosophy can place equal valuation on everything. Latour's theory entails that local actors are the ultimate reality, and there are losers in his theory as in any other. "Economy," "society," and "capitalism" cut a rather

---

30 Ibid., 315.
31 Ray Brassier, "Concepts and Object," in *The Speculative Turn: Continental Materialism and Realism,* eds. Levi R. Bryant, Nick Srnicek, and Graham Harman (Melbourne: re.press, 2011), 51; Graham Harman, *Speculative Realism* (Winchester: Zero Books, 2013), 46.

sorry figure in the eyes of the Latourian, since all of these look like massive reifications that fail to account for the details. And speaking of capitalism, in Marx's thinking most cultural forms are losers, since they look like mere ideological superstructure by comparison with the true, underlying economic forces. In Gratton's work, we will see, time is the winner and enduring individual entities the big loser. Whatever your philosophy, there is no escaping this sort of result, though there are always ways of arguing for the primacy of one sort of reality over another. I do not think "reduction" is a good name for this process. Another name is needed, and that name would also describe what OOO — much like Latour and Whitehead — does when giving arguments that individual entities are the only game in town.

So, what does "reduction" mean? It already has an established sense in much analytic philosophy, in distinction from the harsher activity known as "elimination." But this is not quite the sense of reduction I use. For me, it means "wrongly ridding the world of things that actually exist." The argument for a third term existing between the undermined and overmined versions of an object is as follows: (a) undermining cannot explain emergence, and (b) overmining cannot explain change. This is not the place to repeat that argument, which can be found in literally any of my published accounts of mining.[32] The anti-reductionist justification in this case is that the third term must exist in order to be able to explain emergence and change. Therefore, to remove the elusive real object from existence is to get rid of something that we know full well is an inhabitant of the world. Usually it is easy to spot the reducers in any quarrel, because they are the ones who want to move most quickly in removing as many things from existence as possible (as with Brassier's disturbing crusade against Santa Claus and the Tooth Fairy) while the non-reducer is the one who proceeds more cautiously. Well then, Gratton might ask, is OOO not the overly hasty party in

---

32 Graham Harman, "Undermining, Overmining, and Duomining: A Critique," in *ADD Metaphysics*, ed. Jenna Sutela (Aalto: Aalto University Design Research Laboratory, 2013), 40–51.

"reducing being in its utter contingency and creativity" to a set of fully formed objects? No, because I see no argument for the existence of any such thing as "being in its utter contingency and creativity," and do not think Grant's account of individuals as produced through the "retardation" of a primal productive force is a workable model. More than this, despite Grant's argument against my reasoning in his "Mining Conditions," I still see him as a champion of the One in the manner of Giordano Bruno, and am unaware of a way to get from that starting point to a theory that resembles anything like the world we know.[33]

Before giving an exposition of Gratton's main argument against me, it can be said that it goes wrong in three basic ways, two of them the result of his grossly exaggerating my similarities with Plato, despite the far more obvious similarities between OOO and Aristotle. The first is his false claim that I consider time to be "illusory," and the second is his ascription to me of a "two-world theory" that I simply do not endorse. As for the first of these, Gratton says "If time is but the sensuous, it cannot touch the reality of the thing itself, and [Harman] himself notes there is *no correspondence* between the thing itself and its sensuous objecthood or qualities. Time would be, in the strictest sense, 'illusory'" (99, italics added). I have italicized "no correspondence" because it does not mean the same thing as "no connection." True enough, I do not uphold a correspondence theory of truth between sensual and real objects, because there is no identity of form between the two: as if the real object were simply the same thing as the sensual one but "inhering in matter," or something else of that sort. At the heart of OOO is the idea that the real object undergoes *translation* into a sensual one, so that there is no isomorphy between the two; the form itself changes between one place and another. But this does not mean that the sensual interplay between object and qualities has no effect at all on reality. Unlike Plato, I have no theory of *eternal* forms. For me, forms can always be transmuted or utterly destroyed. More

---

33 Giordano Bruno, *Cause, Principle, and Unity*, ed. and trans. Robert de Lucca (Cambridge: Cambridge University Press, 1998).

importantly, real objects are only transformable or destructible by way of something that happens on the sensual level, which distinguishes this theory from Deleuze's treatment of "sterile surface effects" atop a vibrant virtual realm where the real action occurs. The real object does remain buried beneath the play of surfaces, but it remains perfectly vulnerable to happenings on the surface. A collision of cars, for example, can destroy the *real* cars, not just their appearances. By contrast, if Plato had ever allowed for the form of a car in his dialogues, he would have had to treat it as being just as indestructible as the others. Gratton, who is overly committed to a Derridean notion of difference and more difference everywhere, sets an impossibly high bar for the avoidance of stasis. In this respect he bears some resemblance to Shaviro. It is not enough for either of them that my real objects are mortal and perishable. They demand in addition that these objects must not remain what they are for even the smallest fraction of an instant. Granted, in Shaviro's case there is a Whiteheadian allowance for the momentary "privacy" of an individual, but for Gratton as for Derrida, any trace of identity whatsoever is a grave signal of "Platonism." It is another case of the Game of Hurdles, a low hurdle for oneself to clear and an impossibly high hurdle for one's opponent.

As for the second point, after quoting a passage from *The Quadruple Object* in which I explain that interaction only occurs on the sensual level, Gratton writes as follows:

> Pausing for [a] moment in this account, we are in danger of another Platonism. Recall that the vulgarized Plato posits a two-world theory — Harman argues that his is not "two worlds," but "two faces" of objects — in which there was the world of becoming where time takes place, and an eternal realm in which the "form" of things is accessible only to thought. (102)

Gratton does go on to admit that I differ from Plato in certain respects, but none of them touch on the three major differences he elides in the passage above. First, there is no "eternal" realm in OOO, and this is a difficult barrier indeed to any attempt to characterize it as Platonism. Second, I do not hold that the "form" of things is accessible only to thought, a point on which I explicitly criticize Husserl, given my view that both thought and sensation belong to one and the same *sensual* level. Third and finally, the phrase "Harman argues" implies that I make some sort of hair-splitting verbal distinction to distance myself from Plato. But the difference is perfectly obvious. There are not two worlds in OOO, but trillions of them. The interior of every object is a sensual world, or what Lingis calls a "level," and there is no special, insuperable barrier between a unified world of forms and another of appearances.[34] The OOO theory of real and sensual is as different from Platonic doctrine as it is from Kant's own two-world theory. The real and the sensual are everywhere intertwined, and the barriers between them are local and provisional. This leads us to the heart of Gratton's argument, which pertains to the supposed incoherence of the model of vicarious causation. My general sense while reading along is that he makes my theory more complicated than it is, and that the supposed errors he highlights are the result of his misreading how certain key terms are used. Let's go through his argument and see what he gets right and what he gets wrong. There are some of both in his account.

For the most part, Gratton is right that I am closer to Husserl than to Levinas on time. We have seen that for Levinas, alterity gives us a real future of surprising otherness that is foreclosed by Heidegger's theory of temporality (and I agree more with this critique of Heidegger than does Gratton himself). There is nothing like alterity in Heideggerian temporality, and in *Tool-Being* I made an argument to this effect, to be reprised in a moment when Gratton tries to wield Heidegger against me. But it is true that *The Quadruple Object*, in treating time as a tension purely between sensual objects and sensual qualities, puts alterity to the side. This does make me closer to Husserl, insofar as no in-

---

34 Alphonso Lingis, "The Levels," in *The Imperative* (Bloomington: Indiana University Press, 1998), 25–38.

itself plays a role in either of our accounts of time — the difference being that Husserl does not accept even the existence of a withdrawn in-itself, while for me the in-itself does exist, though at a level submerged between the sensual-temporal play of surfaces. But immediately after linking me with Husserl, Gratton claims that I have nonetheless misread that philosopher's theory of time: "for Husserl, there is no such thing in intentionality as a static entity," he claims (98). At first it is unclear how to read this statement, since obviously *there are* static entities in Husserl; the adumbrations of an intentional object shift constantly, but if the object itself did not remain constant during this process, we would be back in the world of British Empiricism that Husserl refutes. Instead of a "static" apple remaining the same beneath its shifting sensory profiles, we would have a series of loosely related apple-manifestations. But I sense that this is not Gratton's central point. Instead, he immediately shifts to Husserl's phenomenology of internal time-consciousness and says that "Harman, to his loss, makes little use of Husserl's discussions of time, though they bear directly on the discussion of adumbrations in all of Husserl's texts"[35] (98). Later in this chapter, I will consider what Husserl actually says about time. But it is hardly to the point when Gratton adds that time itself is needed for the construction of immanent objectivity, since without it we would have nothing but "a frozen moment attached to one adumbration or another" (98). Yes, but this is precisely how I define time: as the tension between an enduring (not eternal) immanent object and its shifting adumbrations. It does not follow, as Gratton seems to argue, that "time" is an overarching category that subsumes *both* the stable immanence of an object *and* its adumbrations. My argument, rather, is that the experience of time is itself generated by this duality. For his part, Gratton wants to posit time as some sort of non-momentary force that makes the duality possible in the first place. But there is a genuine tension

---

35 Edmund Husserl, *The Phenomenology of Internal Time-Consciousness*, ed. Martin Heidegger, trans. James S. Churchill (Bloomington: Indiana University Press, 2019).

between objects and qualities in Husserl, and no reason to claim that change is more primordial than stasis in his work.

Drawing on my essay "The Road to Objects," Gratton italicizes a number of phrases in order to emphasize my purported but non-existent Platonism: for me "*only the present exists,*" "*time does not exist because only the present exists,*" "*seem* to *feel,*" *apparent* endurance"[36] (99). Yet he quotes enough from my essay that its meaning should be clear enough. The point is to strike a balance between our lived experience of time, the endurance of sensual objects within the flow of time we do experience, and the further endurance of real objects that are affected by shifting adumbrations even less than sensual objects are. What Gratton is really trying to do is argue against any possible *identity* of anything over any stretch of time at all. But this is merely a product of his own Derridean anti-identity agenda. Indeed, a typical Derridean accusation is not long in coming down the pipe:

> [Harman's theory] is precisely what Heidegger and Derrida critique as the "metaphysics of presence"—the view that there is an eternal present beyond or behind the appearance of things, whether the forms in Plato, the *cogito* in Descartes, the transcendental ego in Husserl, or indeed, the non-material, transcendental objects in Harman. (99)

This passage suffers from two small problems and two big ones. Small Problem 1: my real objects are not "transcendental" but closer to what he should have called "transcendent," while keeping in mind that they do not transcend in some perfect, eternal world but just slightly beyond the temporal interplay of sensual objects and sensual qualities. Small Problem 2: OOO upholds neither eternal forms like Plato, nor an idealist *cogito* like Descartes, nor a transcendental ego like Husserl. Big Problem 1: Gratton blurs the distinction between the relational and temporal senses of "presence." Big Problem 2: Gratton blurs the distinction between Heidegger's and Derrida's very different senses

---

36 Graham Harman, "The Road to Objects," *continent* 1, no. 3 (2011): 176.

of the "metaphysics of presence." Let's ignore the small problems and turn immediately to the big ones.

Heidegger's concept of the metaphysics of presence is best understood through his hundred-page critique of Husserl at the opening of his brilliant Marburg Lecture Course, *History of the Concept of Time*.[37] The problem with "presence," Heidegger tells us there, is that phenomenology ultimately thinks that whatever is real can be made present to consciousness. It is on this basis that Heidegger accuses Husserl — rightly — of missing out on the *Seinsfrage*, with its implication that being is what *withdraws* from any direct presence. It is the most basic of Heidegger's characteristic insights, and one that will be linked with his name forever. In the context of OOO, this is incorporated explicitly into the notion of real objects, which cannot be made present to consciousness or indeed to anything else whatsoever. When Gratton claims that the metaphysics of presence means belief in "an eternal present beyond or behind the appearance of things," he misses the point in a couple of ways. First, we have seen that there is nothing "eternal" in object-oriented philosophy, which is a thoroughly earthly theory of the creation, endurance, and destruction of individual things. Second, "beyond or behind the appearance of things" is a phrase that refers not to the metaphysics of presence but to Heidegger's *remedy* for it. Among other things, Being is not identical with appearance — that would be Husserl — but "beyond or behind it."

Gratton has little choice but to agree with me on this point: there is no feasible sense in which we can say that Heidegger thinks everything must be present to the mind, unless one wishes to make the claim — as some Husserlians and even Wolfendale do — that Heidegger's *Sein* is really just another Husserlian "horizon," still present to conscious thought as a tacit background rather than as something explicitly present.[38] Yet I doubt

---

37 Martin Heidegger, *History of the Concept of Time: Prolegomena*, trans. Theodore Kisiel (Bloomington: Indiana University Press, 1985).

38 One such case is Burt Hopkins, *Intentionality in Husserl and Heidegger: The Problem of the Original Method and Phenomenon of Phenomenology* (Dordrecht: Kluwer Academic Publishers, 1993).

Gratton would do this, given his own tendency to put Heidegger and Derrida on the same side *against* Husserl's idealism. What makes the situation more perilous is that Gratton — like Derrida — blurs "present" in the sense of "presence before the mind" with the temporal sense of "present" as "a single instantaneous now." If we assume that Gratton concedes my point that Heideggerian *Sein* is not something that can be present to the mind, he can still shift equivocally to the second sense of time as a present instant. Here, he has backing from most mainstream readings of Heidegger, which treat the philosopher as an enemy of "isolated now-points." Since Gratton has read *Tool-Being*, he knows that I reverse this usual understanding of the issue. As I have argued, the reason Heidegger opposes now-points is not because — in the manner of Bergson — he thinks of time as a continuous flux without isolated nows, but because he argues that even in any "now," there is already a threefold structure of thrown projection. This structure is a hybrid mixture of the situation in which I find myself, the possibilities I project upon it, and the unification of these in a single moment, which, when confronted "authentically," becomes the *Augenblick* or moment of vision. It is Bergson rather than Heidegger who argues that time is a continuum that cannot possibly be thought as composed of isolated cinematic frames. Far from making a Bergsonian critique, Heidegger conceives of temporality in a way that can easily be confined to a single instant. In fact, this is the very critique made by Levinas when he says that Heidegger's future is just a "future of the now," one that must be complemented by the radical future of surprising alterity.

In a word, Heidegger has much in common with the occasionalist tradition of time as a series of vanishing instants, whereas this is the polar opposite of Bergson. Gratton's depiction is different. He claims — rightly — that Heidegger was opposed to "vulgar clock-time" and also holds — wrongly — that this opposition is eventually consummated in the move from the *Zeitlichkeit* of *Dasein* to the *Temporalität* of being itself, as in *The Basic Problems of Phenomenology*[39] (100). While mainstream enough, this view is incorrect. *Dasein*'s temporality is only comparable to vulgar clock-time in what Heidegger calls the mode of inauthentic everydayness. And even there, the structure of thrown projection is already visible, meaning that *Dasein* in any instant already finds itself in a situation and projects possibilities upon it. Awareness of this is heightened in the authentic moments Heidegger calls "anticipatory resoluteness," and we need no supposed transition to the *Temporalität* of Being. This is just Gratton's back-door way of claiming that Heidegger joins Derrida in a joint rejection of any present instant of time, though this merely reflects Derrida's own obsession with getting rid of anything like identity. In Heidegger's own philosophy there is no hostility to the present instant, but simply a brilliant analysis of how any present moment is already more textured and layered than we realize. The fact that he calls certain dimensions of a moment "past" and "future" has nothing to do with any view of time as a continuous and non-identical flux, though admittedly most readers of *Being and Time* do jump to that conclusion. When Gratton asserts that "Heidegger argues for the reality of time implicit and prior to any correlation of *Dasein* and *Sein*, humans and world; it is the condition of possibility for our 'thrownness' towards the future itself" (99–100), this is simply another instance of the mistake seen above, when he claimed that time must be prior to Husserl's distinction between enduring intentional objects and their adumbrations. Time in Heidegger is not some disembodied condition of possibility for the thrown projection of *Dasein*, but first emerges from this structure itself. The great German thinker never really gets beyond this brilliant analysis to account for what we might call the "flow" of time.

As mentioned, Gratton also blurs the line between Heidegger and Derrida. We have seen that for Heidegger, the metaphysics of presence is avoided primarily through the withdrawal of Be-

---

39 Martin Heidegger, *The Basic Problems of Phenomenology*, trans. Albert Hofstadter (Bloomington: Indiana University Press, 1988).

ing from any presence to consciousness, a withdrawal that is not incompatible with the identity of Being. There is a further *apeironish* tendency in Heidegger to allow only Being to withdraw, while individual beings tend to be stranded in the realm of presence. The partial exceptions we find in works like "The Thing" remain only partial because *Dasein* always stays on the scene as the user of jugs and temples, and thus we never really catch sight of object–object relations with no *Dasein* in the vicinity (this is Heidegger's strong correlationist side).[40] In *Tool-Being* I tried to show how a theory of individuals can be drawn from Heidegger, despite his likely reluctance to go along with it were he alive today. But more importantly, withdrawal of an identical Being is unacceptable to Derrida, because he thinks the rejection of presence must also extend to cases of "self-presence." By this he means what we usually call "identity," since "the thing itself is a collection of things or a chain of differences" or "an economic concept designating the production of differing/deferring."[41] This is why difference is an important positive resource for Derrida in a way that identity simply is not, whereas for Heidegger both concepts are very much still in play.[42] Yet it must be asked by what right Derrida — and with him, Gratton — redefines identity as "self-presence," thereby automatically exposing it to the blows that he and Heidegger direct against the metaphysics of presence. The most flagrant case of this sort comes when Derrida praises, without evidence, "Heidegger's insistence on noting that being is produced as history only through the logos, and is *nothing* outside of it."[43] But this is his own agenda, not Heidegger's, and it will not do to invent — as Gratton does — a

---

40 Martin Heidegger, "The Thing," in *Poetry, Language, Thought*, trans. Albert Hofstadter (New York: Harper & Row, 1971); Martin Heidegger, "Insight into That Which Is," in *Bremen and Freiburg Lectures: Insight into That Which Is and Basic Principles of Thinking*, trans. Andrew J. Mitchell (Bloomington: Indiana University Press, 2012).
41 Jacques Derrida, *Of Grammatology*, trans. Gayatri Chakravorty Spivak (Baltimore: Johns Hopkins University Press, 2016), 90.
42 Martin Heidegger, *Identity and Difference*, trans. Joan Stambaugh (Chicago: University of Chicago Press, 2002).
43 Derrida, *Of Grammatology*, 22. Italics added.

doctrine that falsely places time *prior* to its actual emergence from either the duel between an intentional object and its adumbrations (Husserl) or *Dasein*'s thrownness into a situation and its projection of possibilities upon it (Heidegger). Such a dogma derives solely from an anti-identity research program that today is still a hip academic position, though it lacks philosophical grounding and impoverishes our ability to explore the workings of time, since it decides them by fiat in advance.

There are only a few more points to consider in Gratton's reading of my theory. After misreading OOO space as being "inside" an object, he adds the Derridean warning that "we should be wary of the metaphor of 'inside'" (100), and claims that I am unable to think the space *between* different objects. But my theory of space inteprets it as the tension between real objects and *sensual* qualities, and Gratton forgets that this a case of "fusion," meaning that the real object has no sensual qualities until it receives them in cases of allure. Strictly speaking, the only thing that exists inside an object for me is the interplay of sensual objects and sensual qualities, though there are also the real qualities that belong (as OOO learned from Husserl) to a sensual object as its *eidos*. The real object plays no role except as an observer of all this, and that is why no real object can ever be said to exist inside another real one. More to the point, space is nothing but the space between different objects. When allure builds a bridge to the real, it is a real that is not part of the current sensual interior. Thus, the whole OOO theory of space — and of vicarious causation — is about how the inside of one object bonds with a different object, despite Gratton's claim that it occurs only "inside" a single one. For this reason, he is also wrong to claim that "tensions are hidden or invisible" (100), since the aesthetic cases covered by allure are just one example of a highly visible tension. Among other things, this marks an absolute difference between metaphorical and literal language of the sort that Derrida forbids, given his disallowance of real objects (the core of all metaphor) in the first place. For similar reasons, Gratton is wrong to link OOO's allure with Husserl's eidetic variation, since the latter can occur within a purely sensual framework, which is all Husserl has, after all, while allure, by definition, cannot. In OOO terminology, allure is RO–SQ and eidetic variation leads to SO–RQ, so that they actually have nothing in common. Later, we will see Wolfendale repeat this mistake.

This touches on Gratton's further rejection of my claim that OOO can be understand in mereological (i.e., part/whole) terms. As he puts it,

> I'm skeptical there can be a mereology of objects in Harman, for the simple fact that objects (even great and smaller ones, even "parts" and wholes) only gets as far as the *sensuous,* that is, can't be a part of anything. (What would it mean to think that a part that is not really, but only "sensuously" a part of something?) And if the "interior" of one object is the "sensuous" one of another — the obvious way out of this whole maze — then the "interior" is not in the depths but surfing along the surface, which means it was never interior in the first place. (106)

Here I appreciate Gratton's efforts to work through the technical details of OOO, and I can see why he is puzzled. But the root of the problem is that he is reading "interior" in two different senses while supposing that I am the confused party. It is certainly true that for me, an object is cut off not only from external objects but even from its own parts: which are themselves objects, after all, and thus are not exempted from the global problem of real object–real object interaction. An object has indirect relations with its own parts too, but these parts are *real* objects, not sensual ones, which Gratton rightly notes would be ridiculous. The real parts of an object do need sensual mediation in order to combine into the larger real object — real water is made of real hydrogen and real oxygen, but these atoms in turn make contact only through sensual mediation. But the parts of an object are not "inside it"; remember, only sensual objects and sensual qualities — plus the real qualities of the sensual object's own eidos — are "inside" another object. The term "inside" does not pertain to the part/whole relationships that create a real object in the first place. Ian Bogost expresses this nicely, in words cited by Gratton himself,

> The thing that needs to be remembered here is that Harman's sensual object only exists in the experience of another object in the first place; it's not some persistent abstraction. […] [W]e must remind ourselves that objects have different senses of presence, both in themselves and in relation to other units. Time is on the inside of objects.[44] (106)

Gratton responds, "But this is not Harman's model" (106). Yes, it is! Bogost knows my thinking well. Even so, Gratton sees an additional difficulty, "this [just] inverts the problem: if time is on the *inside* of an object, then the sensuous part would be forever frozen in the present, which at least to this object that I am appears not to be the case — things in the world appear to be very much in motion and changing, which is generally taken to be an index of time" (106). I am not entirely sure that I understand Gratton's objection, but there is nothing "frozen" about the interior of an object, since it is precisely here that the tension between sensual object and sensual qualities occurs, and this — as Gratton knows — is the tension I call time. "Finally," he tells us, "if time is only at the layer of the sensuous, even for its parts, there can be no change, since they are 'ever in the present'– the true dictum of Harman's view of objects" (106). But there can be change, because what happens on the interior of objects occasionally leads to *allure,* in which the interior of one real object makes contact with another real object external to it, and this is the root of change in my model. To draw an analogy from evolutionary theory, there is neither eternal stasis nor constant flux, but something closer to what Niles Eldredge and Stephen Jay Gould call "punctuated equilibrium."[45] Most of

---

44 Ian Bogost, "Time, Relation, Ethics, Experience: Some Responses to the Alien Phenomenology Reading Group," July 4, 2012, http://bogost.com/blog/time_relation_ethics_experienc/.

45 Niles Eldredge and Stephen Jay Gould, "Punctuated Equilibria: An Alternative to Phyletic Gradualism," in *Models in Paleobiology,* ed. Thomas J.M.

the sensual interplay between objects and qualities has no effect on the outside world at all, but once in a while: boom! On this basis, I reject Gratton's conclusion that "object-oriented ontology [...] has hit an impasse" (106). He has not shown this by any means, and thus I reject his view that his own "realism of time" (202) is needed to escape the supposed but non-existent impasse of OOO.

One other issue is worth mentioning. Gratton claims in passing that my theory is simply arbitrary, no more justified than any other. After claiming that "each philosopher has a depiction of the absolute, or a method that begins with a given starting point" (100), he goes on to list a number of historical examples. It seems at first as if he were about to assert that all philosophical theories are equally right and wrong and there is no way to choose between them. But that is not what he does. Using the example of Levinas, he says that (unlike OOO)

> Levinas had a method, which was to take phenomenology to its limits, as he lays out in *Totality and Infinity* and *Otherwise than Being*. [... A]t the least Levinas uses a well-known method to show where that method would fail, namely in trying to make the Other correlate back to the ego of transcendental phenomenology. (101).

Though he never quite says so, Gratton's point seems to be that OOO has no method justifying its conclusions. Yet I do not see that Levinas is any more methodical than I am, even if Gratton prefers his philosophy to mine. As is clear from many publications, the OOO method is to interpret Heidegger's tool-analysis, which I take to be the most insightful moment of twentieth-century philosophy, and show that it cannot work on its own terms. Heidegger counters the presence-at-hand of entities with a ready-to-hand system of equipment, reading the former as falsely non-relational and the latter as the true relational root from which present-at-hand beings emerge. My method is to

Scopf (New York: Doubleday, 1972), 82–115.

show that this opposition cannot account for another key Heidegger insight: the *broken* tool. If an entity were purely relational, then it would hold no surplus in reserve that would enable it to be out of joint with the tool-system in any way, let alone break. On this basis, I argue that the usual distinction readers draw from Heidegger — implicit practical dealings with things vs. explicit encounters with them — is superficial, since both must be read in relational terms. In order to account for the broken tool, we need a submerged entity that is never fully expressed in any of its practical *or* theoretical appearances and is ultimately unexpressed even in its brute causal relations with non-human things.

Although controversy has surrounded this reading from the start, it would be hard to argue that I have not even attempted to ground OOO by working through the failings of a well-known method — namely, Heidegger's own. Gratton takes a more specific stab at claiming some arbitrariness in the theory, one that Wolfendale also attempts: how do we know that there is not just one object behind everything (101)? How do we know that there is not just one Platonic form (103)? Interesting questions, but it cannot be claimed that I have not tried to answer them. For example, in my critique of James Ladyman and Don Ross, I offered an argument against their view that there is really just a single mathematical structure behind everything, while what we call "objects" are simply the correlate of the humans who try to come to grips with them scientifically, whether it be quarks, chemicals, or even traffic jams.[46] In the first place, Ladyman and Ross have to assume the existence of an observer who is sufficiently distinct from the underlying mathematical structure to be able to encounter derivative objects that are less real than their hypothesized structure. So, their ontology already contains at least three terms: mathematical structure, apparent entities, and an observer who correlates with them. Why not just remain content

---

46 Graham Harman, "I Am Also of the Opinion that Materialism Must Be Destroyed," *Environment and Planning D: Society and Space* 28, no. 5 (2010): 772–90.

with this situation, then? Because in that case we are left with a theory like that of Parmenides, in which reason tells us that everything is one, while the senses deceive us with apparent multiplicity. Deleuze improves considerably on this model by populating his "virtual" with varying intensities along a continuum, but in either case it is unclear why the primordial continuum should bother erupting into local appearances in the first place. If you say that this is merely an artifact of sensing or thinking subjects — as Shaviro and Bryant seem to do — it is still unclear why such subjects would ever emerge from the continuum. We can always be wrong about the specific links between sensual objects and their supposed substrata in real ones — that's what fallibilism in science is all about. But there are no grounds for holding that multiplicity as such is a mere surface effect generated by a specific entity — the subject — whose very existence already proves a real multiplicity. Object to this argument all you like, but please stop pretending I have never made it.

Before his concluding remarks on his own philosophy, Gratton sees fit to take a few more digs at Speculative Realism. For instance, "[Speculative Realism's] turn to realism often means stomping at times inelegantly across subfields long covered in analytic philosophy" (201). There is much to celebrate in recent analytic metaphysics, and I look forward to more interaction between that tradition and ours. But on what grounds does Gratton claim that we are "stomping inelegantly" in our progress toward that goal? I do not recall him attempting to link OOO with analytic philosophy at all. His primary effort is to claim that Meillassoux was beaten to the punch two years in advance by Nolt, though we have seen that the latter is a straightforward scientific realist and Meillassoux is not. This argument is certainly not Gratton at his most "elegant." It is also strange, to say the least, for a Derridean to call upon analytic philosophers to beat up Speculative Realists as copycats; it would be an understatement to say that Derrida is not part of the canon of great thinkers recognized by analytic philosophy, so perhaps Gratton ought to have sided with us. Instead, he sends mixed messages about his own future intentions, saying in the same sentence "such a movement as I call for here" *and* "we declare no new brands or movements here" (202). Brands, schmands. The reference to "brands" is just a decaffeinated version of the same insult — directed primarily at OOO — that we will see is cherished by Wolfendale and Brassier. Gratton accuses me of "dismissing" Heidegger just because I say he has "'nothing to teach' us about time" (202). But it would be hard to look at my career and characterize my attitude toward Heidegger as "dismissal," and equally hard to claim there is anything contemptuous about interpreting his theory of time as a theory of the collapsed threefold instant rather than one of time in the usual sense. Such sentiments are not limited to Gratton's conclusion. Elsewhere, he sees fit to lecture Speculative Realism about proper humility before the history of philosophy:

> The speculative realists hold [...] that there is something outdated about [Heidegger, Derrida, and Irigaray], trapped constantly spinning yarns about a tradition now being surpassed. [...] But while I think Heidegger's grip on the history of philosophy is a grip that almost strangles it, the insistence that movements are wholly new and the word "tradition" is a synonym for "naïve" leads me to speak up to point out the repetitions of a past we can't easily escape. (202)

Since to my knowledge none of the original Speculative Realists has written about Luce Irigaray, I am not sure why she was listed among the offended parties. More importantly, the passage above is a field filled with straw men. What Speculative Realist has ever referred to the "tradition" as "naïve"? Gratton well knows that I spent years of work developing my reading of Heidegger, that I constantly credit Aristotle and Leibniz as inspirations for my position, and always do my best to give historical precedents for any idea I introduce. His insinuation that he is somehow more respectful of the "tradition" than OOO is an injustice not supported by even a cursory examination of our respective writings. Worse yet, it is a form of what magicians call "misdirection." After all, Gratton does not really believe that the

Speculative Realists are disrespectful to "the tradition." What bothers him is our collective lack of reverence for continental philosophy as it was up through the mid-1990s, in which Derrida ruled the roost. This was no doubt a world in which Gratton would have felt more at home, and he is perfectly free to fight for its return using whatever arguments he can muster. Yet in doing so, he need not pretend that he is fighting for the "tradition" in some more general sense. What he champions is simply a further extension of the priorities of early 1990s Anglophone continental thought, which was as limited a period as any other, and one that simply left no room for either the "speculative" or "realist" aspects of Speculative Realism, as Gratton also knows. The issue is one to be settled on the intellectual battlefield, not by insinuations of arrogant disregard for precedent by those with whom he happens to disagree. After declaring his "humility" in the book's final paragraph, Gratton expresses his humble sentiments by ending as follows: "This is my speculative gambit, and unlike speculative realists returning to a certain Platonism, time is on my side" (216). But the supposed Platonism has not been demonstrated, nor has a convincing case been made that "time is on his side," except in a punning sense of the phrase.

The Role of Levinas

A good rule of thumb: whenever a Derridean links you with Levinas, you had best be on your guard. You may find yourself dragged to the swamp and beaten by thugs driving a pickup truck with the words "Violence and Metaphysics" stenciled on the side.[47] This is not to say that Derrida does nothing interesting with Levinas, only that the latter has too often been treated in recent decades as if he were a wholly owned subsidiary of deconstruction. My view is different. I see Levinas as the more redoubtable figure in the long term, and as the post-war figure

---

47 Jacques Derrida, "Violence and Metaphysics: An Essay on the Thought of Emmanuel Levinas," in *Writing and Difference*, trans. Alan Bass (Chicago: University of Chicago Press, 1978), 79–158.

who pushed Heidegger further than anyone else. To show why, we need to explore what Derrida misses in his often powerful critique.

I am not among those who consider Derrida a sophist or charlatan, a view found among many analytic philosophers and even some continentals. But yes, I do experience considerable frustration with his prose style, which even Gratton concedes can be "infuriating."[48] To see what I mean, one need only read the first sentence of his "Violence and Metaphysics," which takes up sixteen lines of text and bears no resemblance to the ways that James Joyce or Marcel Proust make such outbursts work effectively.[49] Above all, these lines are nowhere near the point of Derrida's essay; as too often happens in his work, an argument meriting ten or so pages is encrusted with uncouth pirouettes for dozens more. Thus I will be forgiven for not giving a blow-by-blow account of this piece, which contains too many passages like the following: "A community of the question, therefore, within that fragile moment when the question is not yet determined enough for the hypocrisy of an answer to have already initiated itself beneath the mask of the question, and not yet determined enough for its voice to have been already and fraudulently articulated within the very syntax of the question" (VM 80). We are too quick to blame "Derrida's second-rate imitators" for crimes against good prose, when the philosopher himself deserves significant blame. After reading seventy-three pages of this sort of river sludge, any commentator deserves an iced tea and a recliner.

Yet there is another sense in which Derrida's prose has a style to which one grows perfectly well accustomed, one that does not hide the sheer emptiness that many of his foes imagine. In *Guerrilla Metaphysics,* I complained about his essay "White Mythology" that "as in many other cases [in Derrida], we find a hard-hitting ten-page core surrounded by an additional fifty

---

48 Gratton, *Speculative Realism,* 215.
49 Derrida, "Violence and Metaphysics," 79. Subsequent page references are given between parentheses in the main text, preceded by VM.

pages of highly mannered intellectual collage."[50] But I would say that "Violence and Metaphysics" is considerably less annoying than "White Mythology." In the present case a more apt metaphor would be that of a foam mattress standing eight inches tall, but compressible — with some work — to its true height of two inches of material. In the essay now to be discussed, it only takes Derrida three pages to get to the point, and he then stays on topic all the way to the end, though without being very economical in arriving there.

In a sense, the whole point of "Violence and Metaphysics" can be grasped from its final words, drawn from Joyce's *Ulysses,* "Jewgreek is greekjew. Extremes meet."[51] After all, it would be perfectly fair to say that Levinas opposes Greek philosophy with the Judaic ethical and prophetic tradition, largely to the disadvantage of the former. Amidst a spirited defense of Husserl, Heidegger, and the Western philosophical tradition against the Levinasian claim that they are "violent," Derrida shows, among other things, that there is no simple way to read "violence" and "nonviolence" such that the first would belong to philosophy and the second to ethics or religion. This is what he means by "Jewgreek is greekjew." Many of his points are good ones, though I will also say that Derrida misses something important in Levinas. Gratton's presumed point in linking me with the notion of "alterity" is to imply that OOO becomes committed to the same impossible pure otherness that Derrida exposes in Levinas. This, I will show, is not quite right.

Derrida begins by setting the parameters for his analysis of Levinas, whose work he clearly knows well: "The entirety of philosophy is conceived on the basis of its Greek source. As is well known, this amounts neither to an occidentalism, nor to a historicism. It is simply that the founding concepts of philosophy

---

50 Harman, *Guerrilla Metaphysics: Phenomenology and the Carpentry of Things* (Chicago: Open Court, 2005), 111; Jacques Derrida, "White Mythology: Metaphor in the Text of Philosophy," in *Margins of Philosophy,* trans. Alan Bass (Chicago: University of Chicago Press, 1982), 207–71.
51 James Joyce, *Ulysses* (Scotts Valley: CreateSpace Independent Publishing Platform, 2017), 279.

are primarily Greek" (VM 81). He will soon make the important point that Levinas himself is also a philosopher working within the Greek tradition, not some sort of Jewish mystic: "In the last analysis, [Levinas'] work] never bases its authority on Hebraic theses or texts. It seeks to be understood from within a *recourse to experience itself*" (VM 83). In other words, Levinas is primarily a phenomenologist, despite his religious-sounding way of turning against this tradition. Nonetheless, "the category of the *ethical* is not only dissociated from metaphysics but coordinated with something other than itself, a previous and more radical function" (VM 81). And indeed, "it is at this level that the thought of Emmanuel Levinas can make us tremble" (VM 82). Despite its phenomenological underpinnings Levinas's thinking "seeks to liberate itself from the Greek domination of the Same and the One [...] as if from oppression itself—an oppression certainly comparable to none other in the world, an ontological or transcendental oppression, but also the origin or alibi of all oppression in the world" (VM 83). And further, "this thought calls upon the ethical relationship—a nonviolent relationship to the infinite as infinitely other, to the Other—as the only one capable of opening the space of transcendence and of liberating metaphysics" (VM 83). As for Derrida's own stance on these matters, he claims a certain neutrality: "We will not choose between the opening and the totality" (VM 84). While this is arguably true of Derrida's career as a whole, it is fair to say that his "Violence and Metaphysics" falls more on the side of Greek philosophy than on that of the ethical opening proposed by Levinas, who comes off primarily as an unfair critic of Husserl and Heidegger. Bear in mind that this is also what Gratton wants to say about OOO—that it unfairly critiques Husserl and Heidegger despite taking these figures as its basis.

The first signs of Derrida's preference for phenomenology now begin to appear: "it is difficult to overlook the fact that Husserl so little predetermined Being as an object that in *Ideas I* absolute existence is accorded only to consciousness" (VM 85), though he nearly concedes that Levinas has a point about Husserl's confinement to the subject–object correlate. Derrida is far from accusing him of being a sloppy interpreter of phenomenology, since "Levinas is certainly quite attentive to everything in Husserl's analyses which tempers or complicates the primordiality of consciousness" (VM 86). Nonetheless, "despite all these precautions, despite a constant oscillation between the letter and the spirit of Husserlianism [...], a break not to be reconsidered is signified" (VM 86). Namely, in Levinas's eyes, "one cannot simultaneously maintain the primacy of the objectifying act and the irreducible originality of nontheoretical consciousness" (VM 86). This seems to push Levinas more in the direction of Heidegger, with his greater awareness of pre-theoretical comportment and the historical situatedness of Dasein, far from any theoretical mastery. But the same charge Levinas makes against Husserl will also be made against Heidegger, "and made with a violence that will not cease to grow" (VM 88). Despite Heidegger's apparent overcoming of the Western priority of theory and light, "Heidegger still would have questioned and reduced theoretism from within, and in the name of, the Greco-Platonic tradition" (VM 88). One example is his concept of *Mitsein,* being-with. This might look at first like an anticipatory Levinasian moment in *Being and Time,* but "the structure of *Mitsein* itself will be interpreted [by Levinas] as a Platonic inheritance, belonging to the world of light" (VM 89). By contrast with this, Levinas seeks "only the other, the totally other, [which] can be manifested as what it is before the shared truth, within a certain nonmanifestation and a certain absence" (VM 91). For, "incapable of respecting the Being and meaning of the other, phenomenology and [Heideggerian] ontology would be philosophies of violence" (VM 91).

The only possible escape from this situation is an encounter with the absolutely other, that textbook Levinasian theme: "there is no way to conceptualize [this] encounter: it is made possible by the other, the unforeseeable, 'resistant to all categories.' [...] The infinitely other cannot be bound by a concept, cannot be thought on the basis of a horizon; for a horizon is always the horizon of the same, the elementary unity within which eruptions and surprises are always welcomed by understanding and recognized" (VM 95). This is why for Levinas ethics is first philosophy, and he also speaks of *metaphysics* in opposition to ontology. Yet Derrida is suspicious as to whether Levinas really escapes totality in this way: "Levinas is very close to Hegel [...] at the very moment when he is apparently opposed to Hegel in the most radical fashion. This is a situation he must share with *all* anti-Hegelian thinkers" (VM 99; italics added). The Hegelian path, of course, would be to say that the other is the negation of the same, thereby drawing it into a dialectical process, with the accessible always recuperating the inaccessible in the manner of Meillassoux's correlational circle. After all, the infinitely other does appear in the form of a *face*. And "Levinas also often says *kath'auto* and 'substance' in speaking of the other as face. The face is presence, *ousia*" (VM 101). And furthermore, "for the Other not to be overlooked, He must present himself as absence, and must appear as nonphenomenal" (VM 103). A nonphenomenality that appears is not the only paradox in play, since the Other is simultaneously both the only being I can wish to murder and the one I am forbidden to murder (VM 104). This leads to the surprising realization that "asymmetry, non-light, and commandment then would be violence and injustice themselves" (VM 106), even though "infinity [... supposedly] cannot be violent as totality is" (VM 107). Similarly, God is both the infinity that speaks against war *and* the very possibility of the offending otherness that summons us to war. "God, therefore, is implicated in war," but as linked with ethical infinity He is its opposite, so that "war [both] supposes and excludes God" (VM 107). And speaking of God, since He hides his face from Moses in Exodus 33, it is "at once more and less a face than other faces" (VM 108).

A related paradox is that Levinasian ethics is beyond any ethics in the sense of a specific set of rules: "Ethics, in Levinas' sense, is an Ethics without law and without concept, which maintains its non-violent purity only before being determined as concepts and laws [... I]t is perhaps serious that this Ethics of Ethics can occasion neither a determined ethics nor determined laws without negating and forgetting itself" (VM 111). Levinas thus finds himself trapped in "the necessity of lodging oneself within traditional conceptuality in order to destroy it" (VM 111). Even as he claims that "true" exteriority is not spatial, he is nonetheless forced to have recourse to the spatial sense of the term (VM 112). Anticipating one of OOO's own criticisms, Derrida notes that despite the infinite taking shape in the face, "the infinitely Other would not be what it is, other, if it was a positive infinity, and if it did not maintain within itself the negativity of the indefinite, of the apeiron" (VM 114). There is a related problem with language, for although Levinas is faced with the "problems [of speaking positively] which were equally the problems of negative theology and [intuition-based] Bergsonism, he does not give himself the right to speak, as they did, in a language resigned to its own failure" VM (116). Namely, both negative theology and Bergson permit themselves "to travel through philosophical discourse as through a foreign medium" (VM 116), but Levinas cannot do this because of his view that "only discourse (and not intuitive contact) is righteous" (VM 116), even though discourse is also the very possibility of violence. Finally, the same fate befalls history; for Levinas "history [is] the very movement of transcendence, of the excess over the totality without which no totality would appear as such," but at the same time, "history is violence." Thus, Levinasian metaphysics is itself "violence against violence, light against light" (VM 117).

Derrida follows up with a lengthy defense of Husserl, a defense relevant to us here because OOO mostly takes Levinas's side against the founder of phenomenology. First there is the familiar critique that "[Levinasian] metaphysics [...] always supposes a phenomenology in its very critique of phenomenology" (VM 118). Whereas Levinas accuses intentionality of being governed by the model of adequation between thought and object, Derrida claims that Husserl was already beyond this, "by demonstrating the irreducibility of intentional incompleteness, and therefore of alterity" (VM 120). He asks rhetorically whether there is "a more rigorously and, especially, a more literally Husserlian theme than the theme of inadequation" (VM 120)? Another rhetorical question follows, when Derrida asks "whether Husserl finally *summarized* inadequation, and reduced the infinite horizons of experience to the condition of available objects" (VM 120). Like contemporary Husserlians when they challenge Heidegger's supposed step beyond his teacher, Derrida seems to think the "horizon" in phenomenology is already enough to overflow totality: "The horizon itself cannot become an object because it is the unobjectifiable wellspring of every object in general. [...] The importance of the concept of horizon lies precisely in its ability to *make* any constitutive act *into* an object, and in that it opens the work of objectification to infinity" (VM 120). This is enough, Derrida holds, to show that Husserl respected infinity and exteriority perfectly well. Indeed, "phenomenology is respect itself, the developing and becoming-language of respect itself" (VM 121). In this sense, phenomenology *is* ethics, however phenomenal it remains, since "ethics [...] must have a meaning for concrete consciousness in general, or no discourse and no thought would be possible" (VM 121–22). Against Levinas's complaint that in the *Cartesian Meditations* Husserl only allows the other to be an *alter ego,* another me, Derrida states bluntly that "this is exactly what Husserl does not do" (VM 125). And anyway, the only means to avoid violence is to see the other as an ego; this is "the most peaceful gesture possible" (VM 128). Even God "has *meaning* only for an ego in general. Which means that before all atheism or all faith, before all theology, before all language about God or with God, God's divinity (the infinite alterity of the infinite other, for example) must have a meaning for an ego in general" (VM 132).

From here Derrida turns to a similar defense of Heidegger, who is also criticized by Levinas despite his evidently greater departure from totality thanks to his ever-withdrawn *Sein*: "If the meaning of Being always has been determined by presence, then the *question* of Being, posed on the basis of the transcendental horizon of time [...] is the first tremor of philosophical security, as it is of self-confident presence" (VM 134). Nonetheless, Levinas is quoted as accusing Heidegger of subordinating the relation to the other to the ontological difference between a being and its being (VM 135). Derrida defends Heidegger from this charge in two different ways. The first is to deny that Being "precedes" beings in the ontological difference: "Being, since *it is nothing* outside the existent […] could in no way *precede* the existent, whether in time, or in dignity, etc. […] Being is not a principle, is not a principial existent, an *archia* which would permit Levinas to insert the face of a faceless tyrant under the name of Being" (VM 136). This eventually leads Derrida to one of my least favorite Derridean themes, the misleading claim that "since Being is nothing (determinate), it is necessarily produced in difference (*as* difference)" (VM 150). The other way he defends Heidegger from Levinas is by invoking the classic late Heideggerian theme of *sein lassen* or "letting-be." Letting-be turns out to be the condition of possibility for ethics itself, since without it, "violence would reign to such a degree that it would no longer even be able to appear and to be named" (VM 138). Thus, Levinas cannot be right that anyone's relation with a person could be "dominated" by Being (VM 139). While Levinas holds that all violence is a violence of the concept, Heidegger bans from the outset any notion that Being is equivalent to the concept of Being. As for Levinas's beloved Greek phrase *epekeina tēs ousias*, referring to the Platonic Good beyond Being, Derrida does not interpret this *epekeina* as beyond Heidegger's Being, but rather as "beyond ontic history," which pertains only to specific beings (VM 141–42). In defending Heidegger's ontological difference from Levinas's critique, Derrida makes the somewhat alarming statement that "the difference between the implicit and the explicit is the entirety of thought" (VM 142), a statement less harmless than it looks, since it implies — like hermeneutics itself — that thought is primarily about what is implicit or explicit *for humans*. Another alarming moment comes when Derrida tries to affirm that Heidegger is beyond Levinas's critique insofar as he already beyond all "humanism" (VM 143). But just as Hegelians like to attack "subjectivism" to distract readers from their own idealism, Heideggerians attack "humanism" in order to distract us from their own inability to think relations not involving humans — and please do not tell me that *Dasein* is not human. Derrida is another such Heideggerian, though at bottom he is really more of a Husserlian.

So goes the most influential interpretation of Levinas ever written, so influential that in certain quarters Levinas has never recovered. Although "Violence and Metaphysics" surpasses its self-imposed stylistic burdens to become yet another intelligent reading by Derrida of a contemporary, we should not overlook the *narrowness* of his concerns. For as we will see shortly, there are actually *three* central themes in Levinasian philosophy, of which ethics and its non-totalizable infinity is merely the most famous. The second, barely mentioned by Derrida, is the enjoyment that occurs on the *hither* side of being, which always deals with specific things even as it bathes in an amorphous "elemental" realm. Derrida could and should have paid more attention to this aspect of Levinas. The same may not be true of the third aspect of Levinas, since perhaps only Alphonso Lingis has paid it sufficient attention: the Levinasian philosophy of individual substance.[52] We will see that Levinas sometimes verges on abandoning this theory, ascribing the inexhaustible depth of things to their "matter" alone. But eventually he is unable to escape substantiality, though this is not an issue Derrida can touch, given his obsession with the idea that nothing is produced except as difference. Substance, after all, is always a positive term its own right, not something primarily differential or relational. But let's return briefly to the one aspect of Levinas that Derrida does discuss: metaphysics, infinity, ethics, non-violence. What does Derrida give us here, if anything? I would say that he gives us little more than a return to the old correlational circle; the inapparent must somehow appear, and therefore alterity fails to be a pure alterity, since it must always have a face. Let's return to this issue later, since I first need to counter Gratton's suspiciously Derridean link between OOO and alterity by showing that otherness is just one part of my interpretation of Levinas.

If memory serves, there are four places where I have written extensively about Levinas, all of them more than a decade old. It had been years since I reread any of them, and the greatest pleasure of responding to Gratton's book was the spur it pro-

52 Lingis, "A Phenomenology of Substances."

vided to revisiting my earlier thoughts on this crucial French thinker. The first passage is §21 of *Tool-Being*, "Contributions of Levinas" (2002).⁵³ The second is the whole of chapter 3 of *Guerrilla Metaphysics*, entitled "Bathing in the Ether" (2005). The third is an article published in the British cultural magazine *Naked Punch*, entitled "Aesthetics as First Philosophy: Levinas and the Non-Human," which focused on *Otherwise Than Being* (2007).⁵⁴ The fourth is my article on *Totality and Infinity*, published in *Philosophy Today* under the title "Levinas and the Triple Critique of Heidegger" (2009). In its original form, this article was delivered as a 2006 conference paper in Sofia, Bulgaria under the title "Bread, Tobacco, and Silk: Levinas on Individual Substance."⁵⁵ Let's revisit these publications briefly, so as to contrast the main points of my own interest in Levinas with Derrida's and Gratton's.

The pages on Levinas from *Tool-Being* make it immediately clear that they are not very concerned with otherness: "Most discussions of Levinasian philosophy quickly zero in on his notion of 'the Other'; it is here that both his friends and his enemies reach a final verdict as to his legacy. But for the moment, I ask readers to forget all of the ongoing disputes over 'alterity.'"⁵⁶ I suggest there instead that we focus on the reading of Heidegger found in Levinas's important early works *Existence and Existents* and *Time and the Other*, the first of them written in a prisoner of war camp near Hannover during World War II. The phrase "existence and existents" is the Levinasian way of writing "being and beings," Heidegger's famous ontological difference. As Levinas puts it, "Heidegger distinguishes subjects and objects — the beings that are, existents — from their very work of being [...]

---

53 Harman, *Tool-Being*, 235–43.
54 Graham Harman, "Aesthetics as First Philosophy: Levinas and the Non-Human," *Naked Punch* 9 (Summer/Fall 2007): 21–30.
55 Graham Harman, "Levinas and the Triple Critique of Heidegger," *Philosophy Today* 53, no. 4 (Winter 2009): 407–13. The fascinating conference in Sofia, Bulgaria, entitled "Levinas' Metaphysics: Right of the Other," was held on October 27, 2006.
56 Harman, *Tool-Being*, 235.

The most profound thing about *Being and Time* for me is this Heideggerian distinction."[57] And further, "a thing is always a volume whose exterior surfaces hold back a depth and make it appear."[58] Against Gratton's constant refrain that time must be presupposed for any analysis of specific beings to be possible, in *Tool-Being* I agree with Levinas that the opposite is the case. As that great master puts it, in one of his finest passages, "Is [the relation of being and beings] not rather accomplished by the very *stance* of an instant? [...] An instant is not one lump; it is articulated" (EE 17–18). Here I wonder why Gratton does not explicitly address this point. Instead, he immediately changes the subject to alterity, which I openly downplay as an issue of much importance to my work. According to my reading of Levinas, he acknowledges Heidegger's analysis of the articulated single instant; only then does he break free of it by recourse to Bergson and the surprises of novelty, and eventually through an appeal to alterity itself. But I also cite an important difference between Heidegger and Levinas in their respective views of the ontological difference: "while Heidegger situates this duel [of a being and its work of existing] *between* being and beings [...] Levinas says that beings *are* the between. The philosophical implications of this delicate shift are enormous [...] The famous ontological *Zwischen* [between] now occurs *within* the things rather than above or beneath them; the difference between almonds and rivers is no longer simply 'ontic.'"[59] I add later that "[Heideggerians] remain so fixated on the step beyond present-at-hand entities [...] that they assume that entities can be interpreted *in no other way* than ontically [... But] the reality of objects does not unfold in some sort of ontic junkyard."[60] In fact, despite Levinas's step beyond Heidegger in elevating the status of specific beings, there is a sense in which he continues to dismiss them as "ontic" too. As discussed in *Tool-Being,* the Levinas of *Exist-*

57 Levinas, *Time and the Other*, 44–45.
58 Emmanuel Levinas, *Existence and Existents*, trans. Alphonso Lingis (Pittsburgh: Duquesne University Press, 2001), 47.
59 Harman, *Tool-Being*, 237.
60 Ibid., 238.

ence and Existents is too devoted to the notion of a formless *il y a* or "there is," encountered in insomnia just as Heidegger's formless Being is said to be met with in *Angst*. For Levinas, it is only through a *hypostasis* performed by the human mind that individual beings first take form.[61] Nonetheless, individuals play a central role for Levinas in a way they normally do not for Heidegger. As Levinas says, "We breathe for the sake of breathing, eat and drink for the sake of eating and drinking, we take shelter for the sake of taking shelter, we study to satisfy our curiosity, we take a walk for the walk. All that is not for the sake of living; it is living. Life is a sincerity."[62] In chapter 7 below we will encounter Dan Zahavi's mockery of the term "sincerity," which suggests a surprising lack of familiarity on his part with the importance of this term for Levinas. At the moment we are more concerned with Gratton, who fails to mention any of these central aspects of my interpretation. His apparent goal, as suggested earlier, is simply to maneuver me into the usual Derridean Kill Box for Levinasians that is set up by "Violence and Metaphysics."

In *Guerrilla Metaphysics,* I am once again not concerned with Levinas as a thinker of "alterity," and thus escape the Derridean death zone once more. Levinas, like Merleau-Ponty and Lingis, is treated instead as a "carnal phenomenologist" concerned with "the translucent mist of qualities and signals in which our lives are stationed."[63] Here I openly assert that phenomenology still has much to teach us, though we will see that Zahavi is in such a rush to deny that I know what phenomenology is about that he never pauses long enough to see that we agree. I cite Levinas as saying that "I eat bread, listen to music, follow the course of my ideas."[64] But I also defend Husserl against Levinas in one important respect. Levinas holds that "the thesis that every intentionality is either a representation or founded on a representation or is founded on a representation dominates the [*Logical Investiga-*

61 Ibid., 239–40.
62 Levinas, *Existence and Existents*, 44.
63 Harman, *Guerrilla Metaphysics*, 34.
64 Emmanuel Levinas, *Totality and Infinity: An Essay on Exteriority,* trans. Alphonso Lingis (Pittsburgh: Duquesne University Press, 1969), 122.

tions] and returns as an obsession in all of Husserl's subsequent work."[65] We have seen that this is a half-truth, and that it applies more to Brentano than to Husserl; in the fifth of the *Logical Investigations,* Husserl makes it perfectly clear that he views intentionality as primarily *object-giving* rather than representational, due to the rift he discerns between the intentional object and its adumbrations. In this respect, Levinas is wrong to say that Husserlian intentionality is merely a luminous presence of the given. For Husserl, it takes a great deal of phenomenological labor to perform the eidetic reduction that gives us the object in its own right, rather than the object as encrusted with superfluous sensory detail.[66] But Levinas misses this side of Husserl, and sees an escape route only in an immediate turn to alterity in the form of *passivity*: "to assume exteriority is to enter into a relation in which the same determines the other while [also] being determined by it."[67] Such passivity is not enough as long as the Other is treated as a place foreign to all individuality (as in the Levinasian *il y a* and his formless alterity), instead of allowing it a home in advance. Much like Gratton and Sallis, Levinas sometimes equivocates between an alterity beyond experience and a medium within it, their common feature being that neither is made up of specific things: "In enjoyment the things are not absorbed in the technical finality that organizes them into a system."[68] Yet we must not lose sight of the fact that enjoyment is beyond and alterity is on the hither side; the first is on the near side of being while the latter is beyond it. But true enough, Levinas sometimes mixes these two registers: "In enjoyment, the things revert to their elemental qualities [... O]ne is steeped in it; I am always within the element [... T]he adequate relation with the element is always *bathing* [... A]s though we were in the bowels of being."[69] Yet for Levinas the bowels of being must surely be found in alterity, while enjoyment takes place not in its

---

65 Ibid., 122.
66 Harman, *Guerrilla Metaphysics*, 34–35.
67 Levinas, *Totality and Infinity*, 128. Punctuation and italics modified.
68 Ibid., 130.
69 Ibid., 134, 131, 132 (italics modified), 132.

bowels but on its outermost layer. These are two completely different places — I certainly do not "enjoy" the Other in the sense of immediate bathing. The only point in common between the beyond and the hither side of being is that together these dimensions sandwich the Heideggerian tool-system. As Levinas writes, "The element has no forms containing it; it is content without form [...] The pure quality of the element does not cling to a substance that would support it [...] Quality manifests itself in the element as determining nothing."[70] It follows that whether we enjoy bread, cigarettes, or something else entirely, the role of the element in both cases is the same. It is a flowing liquid, so that there is no elemental bread or elemental cigarette, but simply a disembodied element that flows on the hither side of both.

There are other passages where Levinas seems to register the opposite intuition: "in fact the sensible quality already clings to a substance. And we shall have to analyze further the signification of the sensible object qua thing."[71] It is a contradiction he never quite resolves, given his tendency to distinguish — more sharply than Husserl — between an elemental sensibility on one side and a praxis and thought that carve up the element — and the *il y a* and "mythical" realm of alterity — into pieces on the other. It is here that I depart from the Levinasian element by calling it "black noise," by analogy with the cybernetic term "black boxes," since the supposedly shapeless element is really made of objectified units that come into focus as soon as we pay attention to them. Even the wind and waves have definite contours if we take care to notice, and are not some sort of sensible apeiron. But neither is the realm beyond being just an ethical apeiron, a view Levinas unfortunately seems to hold when, replacing the *il y a* of the early works with the "mythical" in *Totality and Infinity*, he tells us that the mythical is "an existence without existents, the impersonal par excellence."[72] In OOO terms, Levinas *undermines* at two different levels, that of alterity and that of the element. He

70 Ibid., 131, 132.
71 Ibid., 137.
72 Ibid., 142.

makes this point easy for us when he openly admits it: "the element extends into the *il y a*."⁷³ This line of thought concludes in Levinas's passage about the Kantian *Ding an sich,* which is simply a projection of his own anti-realist side onto Kant himself: "in postulating things in themselves so as to avoid the absurdity of apparitions without there being anything that appears, Kant does indeed go beyond the phenomenology of the sensible. But at least he does recognize thereby that of itself the sensible is an apparition without there being anything that appears."⁷⁴ In closing, I suggest that this disallowance of real individual objects leads Levinas in the wrong direction when it comes to aesthetic phenomena. In his own words: "The aesthetic orientation man gives to the whole of his world represents a return to enjoyment and to the elemental on a higher plane. The world of things calls for art, in which intellectual accession to being moves into enjoyment, in which the Infinity of the idea is idolized in the finite, but sufficient, image."⁷⁵ But this movement from the idea to the aesthetic is not the same thing as the one from the objective to the non-objective, as Levinas wrongly holds. Just as every enjoyment is a *specific* enjoyment, every artwork has a *specific* effect, and is neither an ethical nor a sensible *apeiron*. Here again we see that Gratton misses my rejection of the formlessness of Levinasian alterity, which is so reminiscent of Kant's own formless sublime.

In "Aesthetics as First Philosophy" I lay out my full critique of Levinas, which treats him as overcoming the oppressive "totality" of things not through the sole avenue of "alterity," as Gratton wrongly implies. Instead, there is a threefold overcoming, of which alterity is only one of the folds. We have seen that the second occurs through the *elemental,* which Levinas mistreats as formless in the same way he mistreats alterity. The third way, whose recognition I owe to Lingis, is through the treatment of entities as individual substances. As I put it in my 2007 article, "What best resists the sleek power struggle of totality is the iden-

---

73 Ibid., 142. Translation modified.
74 Ibid., 136.
75 Ibid., 140.

tity of individual things. The world is filled with concrete realities never fully grasped by any handling, bathing, or biting."[76] Hence my claim that, contra Levinas, "ethics cannot be first philosophy."[77] Instead, aesthetics is first philosophy. Totality, being, and war are different names Levinas gives to the oppressive system of being that—like Heidegger when crusading against the "ontic"—he too often identifies with the realm of *specific* beings. These three terms are interchangeable for Levinas, but cannot be taken in their literal meaning. To give just one example, what Levinas means by "war" is not the opposite of "peace." As he tells us, "rational peace [...] is calculation, mediation, and politics. The struggle of each against all becomes [...] reciprocal determination and limitation, like that of matter."[78] In this respect, Derrida's supposedly liberating claim that "the thing itself is a collection of things or a chain of differences" is really just a reprisal of the Levinasian model of war, despite the typically ineffectual Derridean proviso that "in this play of representation, the point of origin becomes ungraspable."[79] Such a play of inter-relationality is another name for totality, and Levinas aims to go beyond it, though we must criticize his way of doing so. Unfortunately, he identifies what is beyond relationality as both the "One" of Plotinus and as a rather un-Cantorian unified "infinity," both of them simply latter-day forms of the shapeless pre-Socratic *apeiron*.[80] To make matters worse, by also calling it the Good he denies that it has any "quiddity," any specific character that an individual object would have.[81] As I put it in the article, "Just as Levinas exaggerates the Infinite Other into a single rumbling mass of Goodness, he exaggerates the realm of enjoyment into a flickering chaos of nonsense."[82]

76 Harman, "Aesthetics as First Philosophy," 21.
77 Ibid. Italics removed.
78 Emmanuel Levinas, *Otherwise Than Being, or Beyond Essence,* trans. Alphonso Lingis (Pittsburgh: Duquesne University Press, 1998), 2.
79 Derrida, *Of Grammatology,* 90, 36.
80 Levinas, *Otherwise Than Being,* 95, 147.
81 Ibid., 182.
82 Harman, "Aesthetics as First Philosophy," 23.

In what follows, I go on to show that *sincerity* is the term that unifies all three aspects of his philosophy: the ethical, the elemental, and the substantial. And ultimately, the substantiality of individual things is the place where sincerity is best understood, "Nails, screwdrivers, cages, and drums are not merely devices enslaved to a wider system of tools: each reposes in itself, busy being itself and not just passing into relation with the others."[83] In other words, "sincerity is the Levinasian version of the classical principle of identity," though we know that identity is dismissed by Derrideans as belonging to a naïve and oppressive metaphysics of presence.[84] It is what Levinas famously calls *illeity*, which "indicates a way of concerning me without entering into conjunction with me."[85] Levinas treats language as one important way of touching things without fusing into them, though language in his view "remains a localized power belong to humans, or at most to sentient creatures more generally."[86] Most importantly, he distinguishes in language between the said and the saying. Whereas the said is a literal content of communication, saying "signifies to the other [...] with a signification that has to be distinguished from that borne by words in the said. The signification to the other occurs in proximity. Proximity is quite distinct from every other relationship."[87] While this might seem to link ethical proximity to language, we should remember that proximity is a broader category referring to contact without fusion, including such cases as the enjoyment of bread or tobacco, and that human ethics therefore cannot take the lead. Instead, proximity — also known as sincerity and illeity — occurs whenever two things are closed off from each other but still make contact, which is precisely what is meant by the OOO idea of vicarious causation. For "sincerity is everywhere: in surface, in depth, and in the substance that straddles them both."[88] But

83 Ibid., 24.
84 Harman, "Aesthetics as First Philosophy," 24.
85 Levinas, *Otherwise Than Being*, 12.
86 Harman, "Aesthetics as First Philosophy," 25.
87 Ibid.
88 Ibid.

Levinas falls into the usual modern error that Whitehead was the first to challenge openly, by placing sincerity primarily in the human subject: "the subject is [...] too tight for its skin. Cutting across every relation, it is an individual unlike an entity that can be designated as *tode ti* [...] The ego is an incomparable unicity."[89] Here we are too close to Badiou and Žižek, with their shared neo-modernist notion of a unique thinking subject alone in its placement outside the world, even if Žižek grants this ability to all humans while Badiou is highly restrictive as to who counts as a genuine subject.[90]

Like all phenomenologists, Levinas plays a double game, claiming that his concept of language is neither subjective nor objective but combines the best aspects of both: "the implication of the subject in signification [...] is equivalent *neither* to the shifting of signification over to the objective side [...] *nor* to its reduction to a subjective lived experience," though we have seen that this game — in Merleau-Ponty as well — ultimately collapses into idealism with a realist alibi.[91] This is nothing but correlationism, although correlationism is a specific form of *relationism*, and relation is precisely the totality or war that Levinas needs to escape. But in attempting to do so, he focuses too intensely on human ethics, despite the wider sense of proximity he has established, and thus falls back into the Cartesian rift between what I call "full-fledged humans and robotic causal pawns."[92] After considering Levinas's marvelous analysis of the "fission" of the subject, in which the asymmetrical relation between me and the other leads me to "substitute" myself for the other and take responsibility for them, I argue that his conception of aesthetics leads in a direction far broader than this narrowly human one, before concluding that "Levinas is the accidental mentor of a new theory of causation."[93] Once again, it is clear that my inter-

---

89 Levinas, *Otherwise Than Being*, 106, 8.
90 Badiou, *Being and Event*; Slavoj Žižek, *Less Than Nothing: Hegel and the Shadow of Dialectical Materialism* (London: Verso, 2012).
91 Levinas, *Otherwise Than Being*, 131.
92 Harman, "Aesthetics as First Philosophy," 28.
93 Ibid., 30.

est in Levinas has nothing to do with the "alterity" that Gratton highlights, since I dispense with both the anthropocentric and *apeiron*-like aspects of the Levinasian other.

That brings us to my final extended piece of work on Levinas, the Sofia lecture that eventually became "Levinas and the Triple Critique of Heidegger" in the pages of *Philosophy Today*. As the title suggests, this article reprises the threefold consideration in "Aesthetics as First Philosophy," and again draws on Lingis's important inquiry into the Levinasian conception of individual substance. Here I will simply draw out a few complementary topics that this article handles better than the publications already covered. My case is that Heidegger misses not one but *three* aspects of reality that Levinas highlights like never before: the alterity of ethics, the enjoyment of the elemental, and the closed-off character of individual things against the Heideggerian tool-system with its global and mutual referentiality. Yet as we have just seen, there is still a major problem with how Levinas does this, one resulting from his ingrained modernism: "While Heidegger is quick to dismiss drums, houses, and tea plantations as 'ontic,' Levinas glimpses the metaphysical dimension of particular things. My one criticism of the Levinasian approach is that it remains too human-centered, too much in the shadow of Kant's Copernican Revolution," though here Descartes deserves blame as well.[94] As I add, "only in this way do we make a clean break with the Heideggerian climate, where being and *Dasein* always come as a pair."[95] Much like Chalmers and Strawson in recent philosophy of mind, Levinas sees first-person experience as the one place where the global war of relations is halted. This was already clear in *Existence and Existents*, when only human thought was allowed to "hypostatize" a rumbling unified being into pieces, and this notion remains operative in *Totality and Infinity*: "The separation of the Same is produced in the form of an inner life, a psychism. The psychism constitutes an event in

---

94 Harman, "Levinas and the Triple Critique of Heidegger," 407.
95 Ibid., 408.

being [...] it is already a way of being, resistance to the totality."[96] Yet it is not only a way of resistance, as if there were others. For Levinas it is the only one.

Here he makes two different errors. The first is the sort opposed — perhaps excessively — by panpsychists when they claim that "psychism" is found not only in humans. We have seen that Chalmers extends it as far as thermostats, while Strawson (like Shaviro and Whitehead) finds it absolutely everywhere. A bigger issue is that, even if we were to uphold the existence of full-blown panpsychism extended to every existing entity, we are still left with the old distinction between direct first-person experience and third-person scientific description, although both involve a view from the outside. My experience of myself does not exhaust myself, which is why the deeper, zero-person reality of the self must be taken into account, despite its withdrawal from direct access by introspection and science alike. In short, the self is also a substance, and thus it sets up shop in the world in a way that neither the psychologist nor the neuroscientist can master. Levinas is aware, perhaps too aware — given his aforementioned tendency to conflate them — that even the things of enjoyment are saturated with something of the beyond. Speaking of our enjoyment of the sensuous, he states that "what is essential to created existence is its separation with regard to the Infinite [which is why he describes enjoyment as an "atheism" (GH)]. This separation is not simply a negation [... but] precisely opens upon the idea of infinity."[97] Lingis has argued further, in *The Imperative,* that this penetration of the sensual by ethical considerations also holds for individual things, each of which generates the rules for perceiving or enjoying it properly.[98] This takes Lingis some way beyond Levinas, given that for the latter, both ethics and the elemental are meant to resist the particularity of individuals, while for Lingis it is individuals themselves that simultaneously incarnate our specific enjoy-

---

96 Levinas, *Totality and Infinity,* 54.
97 Ibid., 150.
98 Lingis, *The Imperative.*

ment of them and a specific secular form of the moral law; it is ethically wrong, Lingis holds, to listen to recorded music on a snowy day in a temple in Kyoto.[99] By contrast, Levinas seems to think that infinity itself is produced by the human psyche: "Infinity does not first exist, and then reveal itself. Its infinition is produced as revelation, as a positing of its idea in me."[100] This is every bit as correlationist as Heidegger's positing of the *Sein/Dasein* couple, and his adoption of it from Heidegger shows why Levinas remains subsumed by it, even if he partly succeeds in leaving the "climate" of Heidegger's philosophy. If there is one way that Levinas truly gets us beyond Heidegger, it is neither in his alterity of the infinitely other nor in his enjoyment of the elemental but through the combination of the two in his theory of substance, though he never fully rises to the level of his insight.

Nonetheless, against Heidegger's tool-analysis, he tells us that things "are not entirely absorbed in their form; they [...] stand out in themselves, breaking through, rending their forms, are not resolved in the relations that link them up to the totality [...] The thing is always an opacity, a resistance, an ugliness."[101] This is not only the object-oriented side of Levinas; it is Levinas at his best, freed from his *apeironish* commitments to a shapeless other and equally shapeless element. Even as he discovers the innate substantiality of things in the selfsame palace of Versailles, the stone that remains the same stone even as it crumbles, the same pen and armchair to which I return each day, he shrinks back from this insight by ascribing it to the realm of human experience alone: "the world of *perception* is thus a world where things have identity," and "an earth inhabited by men endowed with *language* is peopled with stable things."[102] Though he shifts back quickly to the intuition that things have a depth in their own right, he ascribes this to "matter," implying that form is produced by humans alone.[103] Even so, he joins OOO

99 Ibid., 21.
100 Levinas, *Totality and Infinity*, 26.
101 Ibid., 74.
102 Ibid., 139. Italics added.
103 Ibid., 192–93.

in rejecting a two-world theory of shapeless matter and visible form, when he offers the following wonderful gesture towards a mereology of things: "But a part of a thing is in turn a thing: the back, the leg of a chair, for example. But also any fragment of the leg is a thing, even if it does not constitute one of its articulations — everything one can detach and remove from it."[104] This is actually closer to Tristan Garcia than to OOO, since Garcia's ontology is much flatter than mine. He allows for any fragment of anything to be equally a thing, while OOO places some restrictions on this.[105] But unlike Garcia, Levinas seems to imagine that a fragment of the leg must actually be broken off by a human to become a thing, which treats the reality of parts as nothing more than a correlate of human action. What Levinas fails to consider is the crumbling of an abandoned chair in the absence of any human witness, or even after the outright extinction of our species. In the end, he is too much a phenomenologist to take such a possibility seriously. In any case, we see for a final time that Gratton's manner of linking me to Levinas through alterity is a gross misreading, and primarily the symptom of a Derridean wish to maneuver me into the ambush site of "Violence and Metaphysics." But I was never there, and it is not clear that Levinas was ever there.

Let's summarize what we have seen in this chapter about Levinas, his flaws according to Derrida, and the link Gratton implies between those flaws and OOO's own. Despite being a phenomenologist himself, Levinas critiques Western philosophy for its over-reliance on "light," its bias in favor of the given. Derrida essentially makes a twofold response to this critique, (a) there is no way to deal with non-light in a philosophical register, since the hidden must somehow appear in a face, and (b) Husserl and Heidegger already do a fine job of getting as close to the hidden darkness as a philosopher can, and in this respect Levinas is unfair.

---

104 Levinas, *Totality and Infinity*, 160.
105 Tristan Garcia, *Form and Object: A Treatise on Things*, trans. Mark Allan Ohm and Jon Cogburn (Edinburgh: Edinburgh University Press, 2014).

We begin with the second point. Derrida's strategy for defending Husserl against Levinas is roughly threefold. First, despite Levinas's claim to the contrary, Husserl is the great theorist of *inadequation*, given that the fulfillment of intentionality always remains an unreachable ideal. Second, Husserl's concept of "horizon" is as "other" as we will ever need, since the horizon is not an object but the permanent wellspring of any new objectification that might occur. Third, even Husserl's supposed idealism is not as bad as it seems, since — we have seen — even the inapparent must first have *meaning* for an ego in order to strike us as inapparent in the first place. What is remarkable about all these points is that they are the same things a conservative phenomenologist would say, thereby causing a clash with Derrida's image as a cutting-edge innovator. Inadequation is certainly an interesting theme in Husserl, but it merely concerns the difficulty of overlap between sensual and intellectual access to things. Try as we might to intuit the essence of a pineapple, it is impossible not to be waylaid by its numerous adumbrations. Yet for Husserl both the essence and the adumbrations are still correlates of a possible intentional act, even if that act remains elusive. And for all his calls for a return to "the things themselves," this phrase is the very opposite of "the thing-in-itself," an object not only beyond adequation but beyond correlation altogether, which is what Levinas rather than Husserl seeks. The same holds for the supposed wonders of the "horizon," which Husserlians often claim beats Heidegger to the punch on *Sein*. But there is a difference between the two. The fact that the horizon is a pre-objective wellspring for objects does not mean that it is not the vague correlate of an intentional act, which of course it always is for classical phenomenology. Heidegger's Being, by contrast, is supposed to be that which withdraws from any presence, even though in practice he treats it as always the correlate of *Dasein*. Finally, the notion that the other must first "mean" something and thereby appear to the ego is flat-out correlationism, and we will address it shortly. Those like Gratton who contrast Speculative Realism badly with Derrida should at least concede that Derrida never really argued this point thoroughly, and that he would have been forced to sharpen his arguments had he been with us at Goldsmiths and in the years that followed.

What about Heidegger's supposed pre-emptings of the Levinasian critique? One would expect these to be stronger challenges, given Heidegger's own frequently expressed worries about presence. But Derrida cannot quite say this, given his commitment to the notion that Husserl already had sufficient resources — with inadequation and horizon — to address the alterity with which Levinas reproaches him. While I largely agree with Derrida that Heidegger was well on his way to something like what Levinas wanted, Levinas already knows this. He is second to none in his admiration for what Heidegger brings to philosophy. Derrida also rightly notes that Heidegger put the meaning of being *in question,* thereby showing that all philosophical light is haunted by shadow. Finally, I would also side with Derrida in saying that Heidegger's ontological difference cannot "subordinate" my relationship with the other, since ungraspable otherness is already entailed by the "Being" side of the difference. There is also something to be said for Heidegger's "letting-be," though I do not follow Late Heidegger Exceptionalism in taking this to be some sort of clean break with the early concept of resoluteness. I also suspect that Heidegger's Being is in fact already *epekeina tēs ousias,* and that Derrida is right in thinking it is primarily beyond the present-at-hand beings of the ontic realm. To summarize, I think that Heidegger (but not Husserl) has much to say in advance about what Levinas calls alterity, and that is why alterity is not the most interesting part of Levinas. What can be found in Zubíri but never found in either Heidegger or Levinas was the notion of the *specific* alterity of individual things; the latter two thinkers are too beholden to the conception of Being or Infinity as something like a formless *apeiron,* as Derrida notes himself.

What I love about Levinas that Derrida does not even see is the former's shift to a new conception of individual substance. We enjoy this bread, this cigarette, this car, the ideas playing in our minds right now. Unlike for Husserl, these entities are not just the correlates of an intentional act, but objects closed off in themselves and not amenable to presence, not even as a *telos* somewhere down the road. And unlike for Heidegger, they do not simply fuse into a holistic tool-system, since each forms an end in itself. Finally, unlike for Derrida, these individual substances are perfectly determinate — this bread is this bread and nothing else — and hence it is untrue that bread "is necessarily produced in difference (*as* difference)."[106] To say that the bread is produced in difference is the same as to hold that it is nothing outside its context (i.e., outside the text) but simply emerges *from* its context via differentiation from it. What this shows is that Derrida had more to learn from both Levinasian alterity and Heideggerian *Sein* than he realized. What Derrida misses, and what is missed by the correlational circle he affirms no less than Meillassoux, is the specific non-*apeironish* alterity of things that exist before entering into the drama of mutual differentiation, which happens only on the relational level.

How Gratton Is Wrong about Time

We have seen that Gratton is critical of me for saying that only the "now" exists. For this reason he sends me to the library to consult Husserl's *Phenomenology of Internal Time-Consciousness,* which in his view establishes that everything is immersed in time, leading to a refutation of my supposedly "static" sensual entities. That is not actually what Husserl shows in the work in question, and we will get to that shortly. But I want to begin with two points about the use of Husserl by OOO. One is that Husserl's intentional object enables him to differentiate his own position from two distinct and even opposite competitors. The one closer in age was Kazimierz Twardowski, whose theory of an object "outside" the mind struck Husserl as a road to skepticism; this is why he kept his own intentional objects immanent enough that they could always be, in principle, the correlate of some intentional act. In OOO terminology, this enables Husserl to distinguish SO from RO, and he also made the explicit deci-

---

106 Derrida, "Violence and Metaphysics," 150.

sion to reject the very existence of RO. The other, much older competitor was his teacher Franz Brentano. For Brentano, as we learn again in Husserl's writings on time, experience is all about *content*.[107] Yet for Husserl the content of an experience is never enough, since an intentional object — like the act that correlates with it — can remain the same despite shifting content, as when an apple remains the same apple despite oscillating surface-features (PIT 36). Again resorting to OOO terminology, this is enough for Husserl to be able to distinguish SO from SQ, while for Brentano — as for the empiricists — there is only SQ with no underlying SO. Insofar as Husserl *does* utilize SO as the very core of his philosophy, he is in fact committed to the identity of stable intentional objects, which does not mean eternal ones.

The second point is one where Gratton misreads my intentions, though it is probably my own fault since I have not written very much about this topic. The fact that I say only the "now" exists does not mean I think that the now is a single *point* of time; quite the contrary. Here is what I really mean. Every reader of OOO knows of my fondness for the Islamic and later the European occasionalists, who posed the important problem of how two things can interact at all. I reject their solution that God is the universal mediator, and for the same reason reject the related Hume/Kant solution that the mind is the mediator of all causation. Like Latour, I hold that the mediator must always be a secularized and local one, though unlike Latour I approach the problem with a duality of real and sensual objects, each able to touch the *opposite* kind directly. Yet there is another point to consider about the occasionalists, which is that they come in two basic forms that are often combined.[108] Namely, we can speak here, as in the chapter on Shaviro, of "spatial" and "temporal" occasionalisms. Spatial occasionalists are those who raise the problem about causal interaction between separate beings.

---

107 Husserl, *The Phenomenology of Internal Time-Consciousness,* 29ff. Subsequent page references are given between parentheses in the main text, preceded by PIT.

108 Graham Harman, "A New Occasionalism?" in *Reset Modernity!,* eds. Bruno Latour and Christophe Leclercq (Cambridge: MIT Press, 2016), 129–38.

Temporal occasionalists, who push things further, are those who hold that even the present moment cannot endure by itself, but is constantly annihilated and therefore in need of a continuous creation. (Note that this is not the same thing as holding that God "sustains" the world, as in Philo of Alexandria and Thomas Aquinas, since in this model things can still touch each other directly. God is simply a background energy source on which they rely when making contact.) Now, I am on record as supporting "spatial" occasionalism, since I hold that real objects cannot make direct contact. But in no way do I support "temporal" occasionalism. Here I am with Aristotle as viewing time (in the SO–SQ sense) as a continuum, not a sequence of distinct instants. At times Gratton seems to think that when I say only the "now" exists, what I mean is that it exists only in punctiform fashion, with no bridge to previous or upcoming instants. But that is not my position.

Let's begin by showing that Husserl's analysis of time is by no means incompatible with the treatment of this topic in OOO. He begins his discussion in the most Husserlian possible fashion: "Involved in this [analysis …] is the complete exclusion, stipulation, or conviction concerning Objective time (of all transcendent presuppositions concerning existents)" (PIT 23). He then adds that "one cannot discover the least trace of Objective time through phenomenological analysis" (PIT 23). In a word, he is bracketing the existence of any real time outside its presence to us. Normally OOO has a bone to pick with phenomenological bracketing, since it leads directly to idealism. But in the present case that hardly matters; for OOO, time arises from the SO–SQ rift, which unfolds entirely within the sensual realm and has nothing to do with withdrawn reality. Thus, if there is any topic on which Husserl and OOO are likely to agree most, it is time. Although Gratton wants to imply that Husserl is more oriented toward flux and alteration than is static old OOO, we will see that this complaint is hollow. The reason is that Husserl is the absolute champion of objects capable of enduring through time. After all, this is the whole point of his disagreement with Brentano's theory of it. As Husserl puts it,

> Let us look at a piece of chalk. We close and open our eyes. We have two perceptions, but we say of them that we see the same piece of chalk twice. We have, thereby, contents which are separated temporally [...] The object, however, is not merely the sum or complexion of this "content" [that we perceive in it], which does not enter into the object at all. The Object is more than the content and other than it. [...] Phenomenologically speaking, Objectivity is not even constituted through "primary" content but through characters of apprehension and the regularities which pertain to the essence of these characters. (PIT 27)

The regularities of intentional objects are not just a primordial fact for Husserlian phenomenology, but are the central fact that differentiates phenomenology from empiricism and its bundles of qualities, as well as from Brentano. To claim that such objects are rooted in a priority of temporal change gets it backwards: instead, we notice change only because all the changing apples and blackbirds remain the same objects. And furthermore, "we are concerned with reality only insofar as it is intended, represented, intuited, or conceptually thought. With reference to the problem of time, this implies that we are interested in *lived experiences* of time" (PIT 28). As for Gratton's complaint about OOO confining itself to the "now," I should note that Husserl deliberately confines himself in just the same way, as when he speaks of such "self-evident laws" as these: "that two different times can never be conjoint; that their relation is a non-simultaneous one" (PIT 29). In short, OOO and Husserl agree on the following basic principles when it comes to time, despite Gratton's stated wish to drive a wedge between us: (a) There is a now that is not simultaneous with other nows; (b) The now is not punctiform, meaning that it does not occur in a single temporal instant; (c) The intentional/sensual object remains undivided despite its wildly fluctuating surface-qualities.

It is Brentano rather than OOO who can be criticized for thinking of time in terms of an excessively narrow "now," and Husserl does precisely this. He tells us that Brentano developed his theory of time in lectures, and that it was only partially reported in the writings of his prominent students Anton Marty (1847–1914) and Carl Stumpf (1848–1936) (PIT 22). For Brentano, when we hear the sounding of a musical note, it neither disappears nor remains when the stimulus to the ear is gone. If it disappeared, we would simply experience a sequence of isolated notes with no connection between them; if it remained, the opposite problem would occur, "a chord of simultaneous notes or rather a disharmonious jumble of sounds" (PIT 30). The solution is obviously somewhere between these two extremes. But Husserl does not accept Brentano's own solution; quite apart from his dislike for Brentano's mixing of physical and psychological elements in his discussion of time, he rejects even the phenomenological core of his teacher's theory. According to that theory, the sound *does* cease once the stimulus is gone, but the present moment is filled with what Brentano calls "primordial associations" with notes now past and even the anticipated notes of the future (PIT 33). The real present is always the present of whatever the current physical stimuli to the sense-organs may be. Thus, for Brentano, our lived experience of time is really just the product of phantasy. Husserl notes that "as a consequence of this theory, Brentano came to disavow the perception of succession and alteration. We believe that we hear a melody, that we still hear something that is certainly past. However, [for Brentano] this is only an illusion which proceeds from the vivacity of primordial presentation" (PIT 32). A strange side-effect of this fixation on the present is that our real intuition of the present is combined with non-real "primordial associations" with absent past and possible future experiences. As Husserl comments, "This involves something remarkable, namely, that non-real temporal determinations can belong in a continuous series with a unique, actual, real determinateness to which they are joined by infinitesimal differences [... T]emporal determinations of every kind are joined in a certain way as necessary consequences to every instance of coming to be and passing away that takes place in the present" (PIT 34). A few pages later, he speaks even more harshly: "This implies [...] that the past [...] must also be present, and that the temporal moment 'past' must, in the same sense as the element 'red' that we actually experience, be a present moment of lived experience — which, of course, is an obvious absurdity" (PIT 38).

Something decisive occurs as Husserl critically sifts through the problems with Brentano's theory of time. He notes that what leads Brentano to append "primordial associations" to time is his prejudice that all intentionality consists of represented content, and thus the only way to make room for the past is through modifying such present content. Thus, "to the primary content of perception are joined phantasms and more phantasms, qualitatively alike and differing, let us say, only in decreasing richness and intensity of content" (PIT 37). For Husserl, whose initial break with Brentano hinged largely on his emphasis of intentional objects over experienced content, this sounds like a repetition of the same problem as before. For "we do not encounter temporal characters such as succession and duration merely in the primary content, but also in the Object apprehended and in the acts of apprehension" (PIT 37). And "Brentano [...] also [falls] into the error of reducing everything, in the manner of sensualism, to mere primary content" (PIT 38), which is precisely Husserl's basis for rejecting empiricism no less than "sensualism," assuming they are different in the first place. This is a serious problem for Gratton's critique of OOO on time. For if Husserl's theory of time — like his phenomenology more generally — is based on a shift from the content to the objects and acts of experience, this is a point on which the OOO theory of time closely resembles him. In short, our theory of the present is like Husserl's, not like Brentano's, and thus it cannot be claimed that we fail to live up to what Husserl has seen in these matters. What he has seen is that our relation to the past and future cannot be explained in terms of present *content*.

Husserl traces Brentano's now-centric model to an idea found in Johann Friedrich Herbart (1776–1841) and Hermann Lotze (1817–81) to the effect that everything must be in the present, since even a temporal succession of instants must be understood as such by a single momentary consciousness. On this basis, Brentano would be justified in reducing the past to phantasmal inscriptions in the present. But Husserl notes an objection to this idea by William Stern (1871–1938) who termed it the "dogma of the momentariness of [the] whole of consciousness."[109] What Stern defends by contrast is a model according to which, in Husserl's words, "we do not have the sounds all at once, as it were, and we do not hear the melody by virtue of the circumstance that the earlier tones endure with the last. Rather, the tones build up a successive unity with a common effect, the form of apprehension" (PIT 41). In other words, there is something like a "specious present" in which we perceive a series of temporal nows without having to shove them all into the current one. While this is a good step forward, Husserl remains unsatisfied with Stern's model, and asks as follows: "The question still remains how the apprehension of transcendent temporal Objects which extend over a duration is to be understood. Are the Objects realized in terms of a continuous similarity (like unaltered things) or as constantly changing (like material processes, motion, or alteration, for example)" (PIT 42)? Both Gratton and Shaviro are no doubt cheering for the latter option, but Husserl — and I with him — will choose the former. As he puts it in a crucial passage, "a phenomenological analysis of time cannot explain the constitution of time without reference to the constitution of the temporal Object. By *temporal Objects*, in this particular sense, we mean objects which not only are unities in time *but* also include temporal extension in themselves" (PIT 43). Thus for Husserl there is no kaleidoscopic flux-o-rama acid trip in which change is primordial and unified objects a mere byproduct, as if opposed to a stodgy, middle-aged cigar party that affirms the stasis of enduring things. In this case, the middle-aged cigar smokers are not just closer to what Husserl and OOO think, but closer to the philosophical avant garde.

In §8, Husserl begins to develop his own theory, beginning with a familiar Husserlian gesture: "We now exclude all trans-

---

109 William Stern, "Psychische Präsenzzeit," *New Yearbook for Phenomenology and Phenomenological Research* 5 (2007): 310–51.

cendent apprehension and positing and take the sound purely as a hyletic datum" (PIT 44). The sound "begins and stops, and the whole unity of its duration, the unity of the whole process in which it begins and ends, 'proceeds' to the end in the ever more distant past. In this sinking back, I still 'hold' it fast, have it in a 'retention,' and as long as the retention persists the sound has its own temporality. *It is the same and its duration is the same*" (PIT 44; italics added). I added italics to the final sentence in order to emphasize that, contra Gratton, there is an abiding *identity* here that precedes any discussion of change. Only in the shift to the "modes" of this experience can we speak of a "continuous flux" (PIT 44). There is a specific phase in which I become conscious of the sound beginning, and I remain "conscious of it as now" for as long as "I am conscious of any of its phases as now" (PIT 44). But I am also "conscious of a continuity of phases as 'before,' and I am conscious of the whole interval of the temporal duration from the beginning-point to the now-point as an expired duration. I am not yet conscious, however, of the remaining interval of the duration" (PIT 44). Once the sound ends, "I am conscious of this point itself as a now-point and of the whole duration as expired […] the end-point is the beginning of a new interval of time which is no longer an interval of sound" (PIT 44). The whole interval of sound is now "something dead […] a no longer living production, a structure animated by the now productive point of the now. This structure, however, is continually modified and sinks back into emptiness" (PIT 45). In other words, "the sound vanishes into the remoteness of consciousness" (PIT 45). And furthermore, "The sound itself is the same, but 'in the way that it appears,' the sound is continually different" (PIT 45). Brentano gets into trouble by thinking that experience is only of the present, so that therefore anything past must be inscribed into the present through indirect "primordial associations." It is an analysis of time based on "content," whereas Husserl insists that the content remains the same and the sound changes only in the "way" it appears. This way or modality belongs not to the content of the sound-experience, but only to the changed status of the act that intends it. In short, Husserl deals with past sound as a modification of the structure of the intentional act rather than of its content. Only the current sound is truly "perceived," whereas the expired moments of the sound are something of which "we are conscious [...] in retentions, specifically, that we are conscious of those parts of those parts or phases of the duration, not sharply to be differentiated, which lie closest to the actual now-point with diminishing clarity, while those parts lying further back in the past are wholly unclear; we are conscious of them only as empty" (PIT 46). And further, "that part of the duration which lies closest still has perhaps a little clarity; the whole disappears in obscurity, in a void retentional consciousness, and finally disappears completely [...] as soon as retention ceases" (PIT 46). The closer we are in time to the present sound the more distinction there is, while the further we go the more blending there is (PIT 46).

Even though the sound-object or musical object continues, it remains one and the same thing, but its past phases become modally cloudier and more obscure. To repeat, Husserl treats the past not as an inscription in the present, but as an emptier intention than the perfectly fulfilled one of the current phase of sound or music. These emptier intentions that pass away are called "running-off phenomena" (PIT 48). There is a "continuous line of advance" that is "constantly expanding, a continuous line of pasts" (PIT 48). This is a continuum, even though no moment in it is ever repeated. "Since a new now is always presenting itself, each now is changed into a past, and thus the entire continuity of the running-off of the pasts of the preceding points moves uniformly 'downward' into the depths of the past" (PIT 49). Impressional consciousness passes into retentional consciousness (PIT 50). Each retention "bears in itself the heritage of the past in the form of a series of shadings" (PIT 51). The now is "the nucleus of a comet's tail of retentions referring to the earlier now-points of the motion" (PIT 51). Once the sound ends, "we have a mere fresh phase of memory, to this is again joined another such, and so on" (PIT 52). Retentional sound "is not actually present but 'primarily remembered' precisely in the now" (PIT 53). There are always reverberating echoes as well, immediately following the "now" of a sound, but these are directly perceptual rather than retentional. As Husserl puts it, "The reverberation of a violin tone is a very weak violin tone and is completely different from the retention of loud sounds which have just been" (PIT 53). Brentano failed to recognize that there is a difference between the phantasy of a sound and the present of that sound. "'Past' and 'now' exclude each other. Something past and something now can indeed be identically the same, but only because it has endured between the past and now" (PIT 56).

Husserl goes on to draw even more insights for another seventy pages or more. But since we are concerned primarily with Gratton's critique, what we have already cited is enough to establish the following points. First, the OOO conception of time as SO–SQ is no more confined to a timeless now-point than in Husserl's conception, since the two conceptions are one and the same. Time is concerned primarily with the identity of an object that persists over a duration, even though different phases of that duration pass further and further into the depths of retentional consciousness. In other words, there is no contradiction between identity and time. Quite the opposite. Second, and related to this, there is no question of a wider category called "time" that must be drawn upon as if it were *prior* to the difference between an intentional object and its adumbrations. If there were just one adumbration after another, as in Brentano's theory of one momentary set of present content after another, then we would not experience time at all, and would live our lives in the manner of disconnected instants of consciousness. The only reason Husserl can account for anything like time is because he *rejects* Brentano's model of consciousness as a specific experienced content and shifts to his own model of intentional objects that are deeper than any such content. The *same* violin-sound rings out for five or six seconds with a subtly wavering vibrato; it is the same because it is the vibrato *of one and the same violin-sound*. Far from identity being excluded from the analysis of time, time is always the time of identities. Third and finally, and again contra Gratton, this model of present immediacy fading ever further into the depths of the past is not at all what is going on in Heidegger's threefold temporal structure, which would still be found even if we *could* condense time into a single punctiform instant.

Stated differently, I am saying that Husserl has a philosophy of time but Heidegger most certainly does not. Any claim that Heidegger passes from vulgar clock-time to *Dasein*'s authentic temporality to the *Temporalität* of Being itself does not even address the issue of whether he has any theory of time at all. Indeed, the shift from the vulgar flow of clock-time to *Dasein*'s authentic temporality is an explicit effort to get rid of the Husserlian notion of time as a flow, which is precisely why *Augenblick* (moment of vision) is a key term for Heidegger but not for his teacher. In other words, there is no "phenomenology of internal time-consciousness" anywhere in Heidegger's philosophy, despite the fact that he was the editor of Husserl's own treatise on the subject (though rather reluctantly so, I might add). As for the supposed shift from *Dasein*'s temporality to the *Temporalität* of Being itself, this is no switch back to the moving flow of time, but simply another aspect of Heidegger's movement from an activist conception of resolute *Dasein* to the passive model of letting-be, eventually completed at some point in the 1930s. But the active/passive distinction has nothing to do with the instant/flux distinction. Heidegger belongs, I have said, to the occasionalist tradition of time: much like Whitehead, which is one of their most striking points in common. Husserl, idealist though he is, belongs instead to the tradition of time as an unbroken continuum found not only in Bergson and Deleuze, but much further back in Aristotle's *Physics*. On this point I side with Husserl and his confederates, not with the Heidegger/Whitehead model of occasionalist time, though I do accept the "spatial occasionalist" problem of the difficulty of causal relations.

Given that Husserlian time is so far from refuting the OOO model of SO–SQ that it practically coincides with it, one has to wonder why Gratton was so confident in the lethality of his appeal to Husserl. There must be another influence. I smell Derrida nearby, and in particular, I smell the Derrida of "*Ousia* and

Grammē.[110] In this article Derrida deals not with Husserl's theory of time as just discussed, but with Aristotle, Hegel, Heidegger, and — to a lesser extent — Kant. It contains Derrida's usual wordy historical analyses, culminating in a four-page summary of the general ideas of his piece. Two in particular jump out. The first is his claim that "presence" in the sense of presence-at-hand and "presence" in the temporal sense of the now are so closely related as to be indistinguishable. For this reason Derrida will oppose both, and Heidegger understands himself to be doing much the same thing, though here I think he misreads the tendency of his own philosophy. As Derrida writes, at the bottom of his first page,

> In what way has a certain determination of time implicitly governed the determination of the meaning of Being as presence in the history of philosophy? Heidegger announces the question [...] only, and does so on the basis of what he still considers a sign, a point of reference, an "outward evidence." This outward evidence is the treatment of the meaning of Being as parousia or ousia, which signifies, in ontologico-Temporal terms, 'presence' (*Anwesenheit*). Beings are grasped in their Being as 'presence' (*Anwesenheit*); this means they are understood with regard to a definite mode of time — the 'Present' (*Gegenwart*).[111]

The point is repeated near the end of the article: "In *Being and Time* and *Kant and the Problem of Metaphysics* it is difficult — we are tempted to say impossible — to distinguish rigorously between presence as *Anwesenheit* and presence as *Gegenwärtigkeit* (presence in the temporal sense of newness)."[112] Note that Derrida is not just "tempted" to call it impossible but *does*

---

110 Jacques Derrida, "*Ousia* and *Grammē*: A Note on a Note from B*eing and Time*," in *Margins of Philosophy*, trans. Alan Bass (Chicago: University of Chicago Press, 1982), 29–67.
111 Ibid., 31. Both of the Heidegger passages cited here are from *Being and Time*, 47.
112 Derrida, "*Ousia* and *Grammē*," 64.

call it that, despite his usual mannerism of quickly half-revoking whatever he says in order to escape possible charges of being too simple-minded. It follows for Derrida — as for Gratton — that if we are to break free of the ontotheology of the metaphysics of presence, we must escape *both* the immediate presence-at-hand of anything to the mind *and* the idea that there is any "now" in time. Here I disagree with Husserl on one side, with Heidegger on the other, and with Derrida altogether.

In the case of Husserl, I agree with both Heidegger and Levinas that his phenomenology is utterly saturated with the presence of *Anwesenheit*. We have seen that Heidegger makes this case brilliantly in the first one hundred pages of *History of the Concept of Time*. For Husserl, the being of anything consists in its presence before the mind, and he never questions the being of intentionality as such, which is why he missed, perhaps narrowly, posing the question of Being himself rather than letting Heidegger do it later. Levinas makes the same objection by arguing that intentionality closes off alterity, though he is also unsatisfied with Heidegger's solution, since Being belongs to the circle of the Same and is therefore not enough. We must go further and seek out that which is *epekeina tēs ousias,* the Good beyond Being. We are now familiar with Derrida's argument that Levinas is unfair to both Husserl and Heidegger, given his claim that Husserl knew about the ultimate unfulfillability of intentional acts and the non-objectifiability of the horizonal wellspring of all intentional objects, and his further claim that Heidegger's ontological difference already does the work of alterity that Levinas thinks ethics alone can perform. As a reminder, I reached a mixed verdict on Derrida's assessment here. For there is no sense in which unfulfillment and the horizon can do the work of Heideggerian Being, given that Husserl cannot accept either an object or a horizon that would not, in principle, be there implicitly for consciousness, and also — contra Derrida — no sense in which the implicit/explicit pair exhausts the theme of philosophy. The implicit is still found only in intentional acts, and the being that withdraws is what is inaccessible to *any* intentional act, and therefore nonexistent in Husserl's eyes. In Heidegger's case I largely agree with Derrida that the ontological difference is good enough to resist the reign of presence, and thus I think that Levinas has a better case against Heidegger in the other direction — on the side of immediate enjoyment and the elemental ether in which such enjoyment takes place.

In the case of Heidegger, I do not agree with Derrida's view that *Anwesenheit* and *Gegenwärtigkeit* are one and the same. The reason is that Heidegger easily overcomes *Anwesenheit* with his relentless assault on presence-at-hand as accounting for the Being of beings. Indeed, this is his most singular philosophical achievement. But in no way does he overcome the *Gegenwärtigkeit* of the temporal now. No matter how hard Derrida tries to show that Heidegger and Bergson are both stuck in the Aristotelian tradition of thinking about time, Bergson and Aristotle (like Husserl) are deeply aware that time is a continuum. Indeed, this is the central insight of all three thinkers when it comes to time. Presumably, Heidegger as a human being was also aware of the continuous aspect of time, but this does not mean that Heidegger's *philosophy* accounts for it. To the contrary, Heidegger is unable to reach any continuum through his threefold analysis of *Dasein*'s authentic temporality (or even of the *Temporalität* of Being itself). When Heidegger analyzes the threefold structure of thrown projection, this merely gives us another critique of *Anwesenheit*, since thrownness means we are always thrown into a situation whose exact character can never be directly present to the mind. But it is not also a critique of the *Gegenwärtigkeit* of the now, even though most readers assume he has also accomplished this very different step. By treating time as a continuum, Aristotle, Bergson, and Husserl all reject the notion of an isolated now-point from the start. But Heidegger merely shows that in any given instant, much more is going on than meets the eye, so that even *Gegenwärtigkeit* automatically excludes *Anwesenheit*, despite Derrida's assumption that the two concepts are indistinguishable.

I argued as early as *Tool-Being* that if we attempt the thought experiment of asking what a single, isolated instant of time would be like, we immediately find that this experiment cannot even be attempted in the continuum model of time found in Aristotle, Bergson, and Husserl (not to mention William James and Deleuze). But it can easily be carried out in Heidegger's philosophy, since any isolated "now" can be analyzed perfectly well in terms of thrown projection. There is nothing, absolutely nothing in Heidegger that requires him to refuse the theory that time is made up of individual "frames" in the cinematic manner. Stated differently, there is no easy passage from thrown projection to any "flow" of time. This is a passage that Heidegger simply never illuminates for us; in fact, this is already the thrust of his critique of vulgar clock-time: the fact that such a vulgar conception merely treats time as "passing" without pausing to understand how complex the "now" already is. Heidegger, like Whitehead and Latour, belongs to the occasionalist tradition of time rather than the continuist tradition, even if he never calls upon God or anything else to explain how one moment gives way to the next. To summarize, Derrida gets it wrong in both cases. There is no infinity beyond representations in Husserl, and no effective critique of the "now" in Heidegger, even if Heidegger himself seems to think so. Contra Gratton, to say such a thing is not insulting to Heidegger, but simply the natural result of considering what Heidegger did and did not actually accomplish. No commentator should aspire to flattery at the expense of precision. There are plenty of insights of which Heidegger can be proud, without our having to credit him with non-existent ones.

Earlier I mentioned that there is a second key idea that jumps out from "*Ousia* and *Grammē*," and it is one we have seen before. Midway through his article, Derrida says the following about Hegel: "The transformation of Parousia into *self*-presence, and the transformation of the supreme being into a subject thinking itself, and assembling itself near itself in knowledge, does not interrupt the fundamental tradition of Aristotelianism."[113] Forgetting about Aristotle for a moment, the critique of Hegel's concept of the subject thinking itself in knowledge as a form of "self-presence" looks fair enough. Hegel does tend to treat

---

113 Ibid., 52.

thinking as self-transparent, though we need not accept this idea, which is precisely why I rejected the Shaviro/Strawson/Chalmers priority of first-person introspective experience. In this limited respect, I am happy to agree with Derrida's rejection of self-presence. But he also means self-presence in what he takes to be a more damaging sense — namely, in the sense of identity. This is the same reason why, in *Of Grammatology*, he rejects the idea of Being as anything *apart* from its manifestation in individual beings, and in "White Mythology" conflates his own critique of the literal *meaning* of words with the individual *being* of substances. This leads him to misread Aristotle's theory of substance as a police-like attempt to govern our use of language, though it is clear that Aristotle values ambiguous poetic language to a degree matched by few other philosophers. To summarize, Derrida not only thinks that the now of *Gegenwärtigkeit* is illusory, but also thinks that we cannot critique the *Anwesenheit* of onto-theology without also denying that a thing can be one and the same as itself. Remember that I am no Hegelian, and do not accept that there is a subject viewing itself in utter transparency, which would be the only valid meaning of the phrase "self-presence." The mere fact that a substance is itself and not another — as Aristotle argues, to Derrida's chagrin — does not entail that any substance is "self-present." A substance is zero-person, not a transparent first-person.

This is what makes the closing pages of "*Ousia* and *Grammē*" so unsatisfactory. In the first place, Derrida's opening thesis is wrong: "Therefore we can only conclude that the entire system of metaphysical concepts, throughout its history, develops the so-called 'vulgarity' of the concept of time [...] but also that an *other* concept of time cannot be opposed to it, since time in general belongs to metaphysical conceptuality."[114] The first part of this statement is correct in a sense — insofar as the vulgar concept of time sees it as consisting of a series of transient "nows," it is tied to the metaphysical conception of a present now, although one that Husserl's critique of Brentano already over-

---

114 Ibid., 63.

comes. But to assert further that Heidegger's own conception of time cannot overcome this vulgarity neglects the fact that he actually does so. Dasein is thrown into an absence, and even if we view Dasein as existing in a single instant (which nothing in Heidegger forbids), that instant of time is not constituted by vulgar presence. The whole point is that we are thrown into something fundamentally absent. As if anticipating this objection, Derrida soon adds the following complaint: "that which gives us to think beyond the [Greek] closure [of presence] cannot be simply absent."[115] This statement has a mixed relation to Derrida's reflections in "Violence and Metaphysics." On the one hand, Derrida in that essay does credit Heidegger's ontological difference with already doing the work of otherness that Levinas found missing in the German philosopher. But on the other hand, we recall that Derrida immediately recuperated the otherness of Being into presence by claiming that the inapparent must somehow appear, and that this is an unsurpassable limitation of philosophy. The latter sentiment enables him to turn now against the same otherness of Being in Heidegger that he had used against Levinas and to offer, in contradictory fashion, something that sounds like a Levinasian objection to Heidegger. Derrida adds, with a typically modern European note, that "absent, [absence] would either give us nothing to think or it would still be a negative mode of *presence*."[116]

Essentially, Derrida paints himself into the corner of Meno's Paradox several decades before Meillassoux does the same. That ancient Paradox, we recall, says that we either know something or we do not, which Socrates opposes with *philosophia,* the idea that we can look for something that we do not have and will never have. The modern-day Meno counters, like Derrida, with the claim that we are then left either with negative theology or with good old presence, albeit it in scare-quotes, and no other option in sight. Derrida's philosophy is thus a classic case of Modern Onto-Taxonomy. He calls for a "sign of […] excess [that] must

115 Ibid., 65.
116 Ibid.

be absolutely excessive as concerns presence-absence, all possible production or disappearance of beings in general, and yet, *in some manner* it must still signify it, in a manner unthinkable by metaphysics as such."[117] Where is Gratton when you need him? For all the hard knocks he dealt me for saying "somehow it must" and using the term "tension" before having a completely worked-out theory of all its details, he apparently gives Derrida a pass on saying that "in some manner" there must be an excess that signifies without signifying. But this is hardly a surprise. Derrideans always grant Derrida the license that they permit no one else, though this is perhaps "a merely sociological" fact, as Brassier might say.

Yet that is less interesting than Derrida's coincidence with Meillassoux on this point. Readers of my book on the latter will recall my criticism of his argument that strong correlationism, which he attempts to radicalize into his own position, is not a form of idealism. He begins by deploying the correlational circle against both naïve realists and Kantian weak correlationists, using the familiar German Idealist argument — to think a thing outside thought is to turn it into a thought, and thus the circle of thought closes on itself. Nonetheless, Meillassoux adds, the fact that we cannot *think* the in-itself does not mean that *there is* none, and — *presto!* — the strong correlationist is not an idealist, because at least the former knows that thought and reality need not coincide. But nothing comes of this, because "reality" as anything different from thought has already been disqualified in the first step. Thus, there is only a choice between realism, weak correlationism, and outright idealism, and Meillassoux is stuck with idealism. See also Derrida, who accepts a version of the correlational circle ("there is no absence that does not also appear") while adding that there must be *another* kind of excess that is somehow beyond the unified presence-absence of the circle that "must still signify, in a manner unthinkable by metaphysics as such."[118] But in for a dime, in for a dollar. If you

---

117 Ibid.
118 Ibid.

accept the correlational argument, you can never emerge from it, no matter how sophisticated a word-trick you produce, since any possibility of "excess" has already been foreclosed in the first step of your argument. This is why I opt instead for a radicalization of weak correlationism, which avoids the impossibility of direct access as called for by mainstream realism, and the equal impossibility of an idealism that reduces things to their appearance, however sophisticated the dialectics that turn it into an "objective" idealism that at least avoids "subjectivism." Eliminate the two impossibilities as Sherlock Holmes would do, and radicalized weak correlationism, however improbable, becomes the only place to look.

But perhaps Derrida is not so incompatible with the object-oriented approach after all. This is the verdict of Levi Bryant in his important article "The Time of the Object." Bryant has a great deal to say about "*Ousia* and *Grammē*," and he is more positive about it than I am. As usual, he shows considerable generosity to my position:

> [In "*Ousia* and *Grammē*,"] Derrida immediately assimilates substances, things, to presence. Henceforth substance will be treated as a *synonym* for presence, such that to speak of substance is to speak of presence and to speak of presence is to speak of substance [… Yet] far from being characterized by presence, substance seems to be that which withdraws from presence, or that which is nowhere and never present. It is for this reason that Graham Harman argues that the very being of the substance of objects lies in *withdrawal*.[119]

At the end of his article, Bryant speaks in the same spirit, "Harman's concept of substance as withdrawal therefore renders legible a whole series of ontological *aporias*" (TO 89). But a great

---

119 Levi Bryant, "The Time of the Object: Derrida, Luhmann, and the Processual Nature of Objects," in *The Allure of Things: Process and Object in Contemporary Philosophy*, eds. Roland Faber and Andrew Goffey (London: Bloomsbury Academic, 2014), 71–72. Subsequent page references are given between parentheses in the main text, preceded by TO.

deal happens between these two passages. Even while seeming to endorse my conception of withdrawn substance, Bryant adopts in the meantime a number of elements from Derrida, Maturana/Varela, and Luhmann that he thinks will help us gain a better conception of substance than my own. In doing so, he repeats Shaviro's claim that my substances are too "static" and need to be invested with greater dynamism.

Early in the article, Bryant quickly says something that I would never say myself, "if substances are necessarily withdrawn, if they cannot be treated as synonymous with presence, then this is precisely because they are fissured from within by time" (TO 74). In other words, Bryant wants a more dynamic theory of substance than the one I provide. We recall that for him, local manifestations are produced by various "regimes of attraction" or contexts of relation in which they occur. In a pair of fine examples, Bryant notes the different behavior of flames on earth and in a space station, and the different effects on human skin of different weather conditions (TO 75). Yet Bryant is still basically object-oriented in his approach, and thus he still holds that entities must have a certain independence from the various regimes of attraction in which they find themselves. Yes, a mouse will die if placed inside one of Robert Boyle's vacuum pumps, but it is *the mouse* that dies rather than the entire context — death is a local manifestation of the mouse rather than the mouse itself, and rather than the experimental apparatus as a whole (TO 75–76). For Bryant, what entities possess apart from their various manifestations are *powers*. By contrast, qualities are simply manifestations of these powers. Furthermore, powers are "fluctuating [...] because they can gain and lose powers, and because the power of a substance's powers can diminish and intensify in their strength" (TO 77). Thus, the withdrawn powers of virtual proper being are not static, but constantly shift through variable intensities and even by adding or losing specific powers, "The affects of a substance are not fixed, but fluctuate in all sorts of ways as a result of processes within the substance and encounters with other substances" (TO 77). Thus, actualization is a *temporal* process — unlike in my theory of substance, which treats process as belonging only to the sensual realm—and this leads Bryant to Derrida's infamous notion of *différance*. Although *différance* has at least two main senses (differing, deferral), Bryant says that "Derrida seems to prefer the sense of difference as a *verb,* seeing 'difference between' as an *effect* of the activity of *différance*" (TO 78). Bryant makes a surprising link between Derrida and Whitehead when he adds that "substances and their differences […] are therefore like blooming flowers. Their extended nature is something that must be produced in an extending or extensionalizing activity akin to that described by Whitehead in *Process and Reality* in his theory of extension" (TO 79). Although Bryant wrote his article on the occasion of a Whitehead conference, there is more to his invocation of the British philosopher than this. We recall that Bryant is primarily a Deleuzean, and bridges between Deleuze and Whitehead have long since been built (as by Shaviro and Stengers) despite my aforementioned objections to this link.

Further distinguishing his OOO position from my own, which is sometimes abbreviated OOP (for Object-Oriented Philosophy), Bryant employs Derrida to argue that "the powers or potentials of an object themselves never become present, nor are they ever static, but rather they fluctuate in terms of the degree of their power and the power they possess" (TO 79–80). This brings us to the part of Bryant's article influenced by autopoietic systems theory. From his previous arguments, he states, "it follows that the *identity* of a substance is not a fixed and abiding given that persists beneath change, but a perpetual *activity* on the part of substance" (TO 82). And further, "because objects are structured by *différance,* it follows that the identity of an object is not an abiding sameness, but a perpetual activity or process wherein the object constitutes itself as that object across time and space. Identity is a perpetual work objects must do in order to maintain themselves as that object" (TO 82). This having been established, it is easy for Bryant to turn to autopoiesis. As is well known, Maturana and Varela distinguish between "allopoietic" and "autopoietic" machines. The former are produced from the outside, with Bryant's example being an asteroid formed from the compression of numerous colliding rocks. A good example of an autopoietic machine, by contrast, would be a living organism such as a cell. The cell's unity is not given once and for all, like the asteroid until it is destroyed, but must be constantly produced by labor on the cell's interior. As Bryant puts it, "where allopoietic machines are largely indifferent to maintaining their unity across time, autopoietic machines both strive to maintain a particular sort of unity and are perpetually producing that unity through the interaction of their components" (TO 83). Autopoietic machines are also *negentropic,* in the sense that by producing their own unity, they work to decrease their own entropy. In this respect, transferring the terminology beyond its biological roots, "substances or objects are negentropic systems" (TO 83). The social systems theorist Niklas Luhmann, whose work Bryant knows well, draws on these ideas heavily. In Luhmann's own words, "All elements pass away. They cannot endure as elements in time, and thus they must be constantly produced on the basis of whatever constellation of elements is actual at any given moment. Reproduction thus does not mean repeatedly producing the same, but rather reflexive production, production out of products."[120] Bryant glosses this nicely by saying that "identity is not something in *addition* to the changing qualities of that substance but is rather the activity of the substance itself" (TO 84). But despite this "structural" openness, there is "operational" closure, to use Luhmann's terminology. Bryant cites the case of electric eels detecting other creatures in a river by means of electromagnetic fields, a type of perception closed to humans in our current evolutionary form (TO 84).

Nonetheless, *différance* would still seem to be incompatible with substance. As Bryant notes, "the local manifestations of substance are a product of deferral that is generally produced as a result of the exo-relations the substance enters into with other substances […] leading to the suspicion that substances are *constituted* by their relations, such that they have no autono-

---

[120] Niklas Luhmann, *Social Systems,* trans. John Bednarz Jr. with Dirk Baecker (Stanford: Stanford University Press, 1996), 49.

mous existence [apart] *from* their relations" (TO 86–87). Yet he also reminds us of the other sense of *différance* as "spacing," through which "entities are differentiated from one another" (TO 87). It follows that difference is not just about the process of becoming-other, but also about the "scissions and divisions between entities whereby they become independent entities [...] in the form of *polemos*" (TO 87). Turning to Derrida's "Signature Event Context," Bryant highlights his awareness of "the possibility of [a sign] breaking with the context in which it emerged, such that it can fall into other and different contexts" (TO 88), something we would never catch Ferdinand de Saussure saying about signs, given his purely differential conception of how they work.[121] Derrida refers to this as the "iterability" of signs in places other than their originating contexts, and Bryant wonders why Derrida restricts iterability to signs rather than naturally extending them to allow for "iterable" substances that can be the same thing in multiple times and places (TO 89–90). In *Voice and Phenomenon* Derrida sounds a lot like David Hume (and Gratton) when claiming, in Bryant's words, that "we must abandon the thesis that the synthesis of time is accomplished by a pre-existent transcendental identity or unity that affects the synthesis of traces of the past"[122] (TO 90). It is the intentional object as a "bundle of traces" rather than a bundle of qualities, though to me this seems like needless forfeiture of what makes Husserl the thinker he is. Bryant challenges Derrida by saying that substances are real precisely as *produced* by "the interplay of these traces and differences themselves" (TO 90). There is no identity *preceding* the synthesis of time, since identity is the result of this synthesis itself (TO 90).

---

121 Jacques Derrida, "Signature Event Context," in *Margins of Philosophy*, trans. Alan Bass (Chicago: University of Chicago Press, 1982), 307–30; Ferdinand de Saussure, *Course in General Linguistics*, trans. Wade Baskin (New York: Columbia University Press, 1994).
122 Jacques Derrida, *Voice and Phenomenon: Introduction to the Problem of the Sign in Husserl's Phenomenology*, trans. Leonard Lawlor (Evanston: Northwestern University Press, 2010).

Bryant's article has a number of points in its favor. First, it makes an ingenious attempt to synthesize the ideas of OOO with those of Derrida: a union that many find impossible, and that I for one prefer to downplay, given what I regard as Derrida's excessive anti-realist baggage. Bryant also offers a vision of OOO as a dynamic theory opposed to the "static" model of reality that many readers see and reject in my version. As usual, he also does fine interdisciplinary work in linking these ideas with the autopoietic systems theories of Maturana, Varela, and Luhmann, which he already did in memorable form in his widely read book *The Democracy of Objects*.[123] To explain why I cannot follow Bryant in all of this will require several steps.

Let's start with his "virtual proper being," which is made up of powers, but powers which shift in intensity and even increase and decrease in number. The problem here, as I see it, is that Bryant thereby joins Derrida in a retreat from Husserl to Hume, though we should note that Bryant has far less at stake in Husserl than does Derrida himself. Essentially, Bryant is saying that virtual proper being does not stay the same over time but is a "bundle" of altering powers with no inherent identity, even if it is "operationally closed" from its environment. He makes this clear at the end of the article when he proposes alliance with Derrida in holding that identities are not non-existent, but are *produced* through a bundle of traces synthesized in time. I imagine that Derrida would be happy to go along with this, because it cedes the central point that identity is a derivative product of the non-identical, though the French thinker would surely add the distracting proviso that the primary/derivative distinction "remains within the language of metaphysics," thereby "erasing" this claim in the same moment as uttering it. But more importantly, such an alliance would leave Bryant with no way to account for the identity of a thing over time — given that its powers are constantly shifting — other than through a historical trajectory that links all the shifting powers as connected to

---

123 Levi R. Bryant, *The Democracy of Objects* (Ann Arbor: Open Humanities Press, 2011).

some original virtual proper being at some unknown point in the past. Something similar is attempted by both DeLanda and Latour, though I do not think that either has much success with the maneuver. The problem is that it is far too permissive about what constitutes the identity of an object in its assumption that *all* the details of the history of a thing must be inscribed in its present state. In this way, it becomes impossible to distinguish between the essential and accidental "powers" of a thing, except by means of some arbitrary external criterion.

As an example, imagine a precocious four-year-old child who watches a chess program on television, becomes intrigued by the game, and receives a small chess set as a gift. It is easy to imagine such a child introducing the game to a growing circle of friends and easily defeating them in match after match. Let's now imagine that this child does not continue with chess, forms entirely different mental interests within a few years, and by midlife is a rusty and barely competent chess player. Perhaps the grown-up child has become a world-renowned cellist, one so remarkably gifted that critics frequently say they were "born" to be a cellist. Now, we can say that this musician's former chess-playing powers have atrophied to the point that they barely exist any longer. Even so, a good number of their other four-year-old traits still persist as enduring aspects of their character. If we are devotees of Bryant's philosophy, we will say that chess-playing power belonged to the musician for a while at ages four to five before "de-intensifying" or perhaps disappearing. Yet given that Bryant wishes to speak of virtual proper being solely as a "bundle of powers," it is not clear how the chess-playing future cellist can be the same person as the post-chess-playing child. One could always push things to the limit and say that they were not the same child, that the child is "many," an adventure across time: that we can only speak of the "lives" of the cellist in the plural (there are still intellectual circles today where pluralizing any noun is taken as a sign of superior insight). But in that case, it is not clear why the fifty-year-old cellist would have any closer relation to their four-year-old, chess-playing self than they would with other present-day cellist friends of similar lifestyles, political views, taste in literature, and so forth. More generally, to say that identity is produced only from the outside is to sacrifice both the phenomenological fact that entities *are recognized* as the same despite changing features, and the ontological principle that the same object can simultaneously be seen in different ways from different vantage points without being more than one object. After all, the latter claim would soon lead us to Merleau-Ponty's impossible view that a house is "the house seen from everywhere," as if it were a sum of views rather than being what makes views of the house possible in the first place.[124] Such a procedure treats everything as primarily a surface-effect or bundle-effect so that identities come second, as derivative products of those surfaces and bundles. But in that case, I am not sure why Bryant would still want to call his position object-oriented. It would be more accurate instead if he were to call himself "difference-oriented," while adopting a Derridean position that iterability is all the identity we need.

Second, I do not think the references to autopoietic systems theory do the work Bryant wants them to do. According to systems theory, a system *does* maintain a certain identity across time from a standpoint outside it, which is precisely why it has often been accused of a bias toward political conservatism. I mentioned earlier that Luhmann is famous for holding that systems are extremely difficult to change, since they tend to interpret outside influences in their own terms; his contempt for political protests is just one result of this view. In short, it is not even clear that autopoiesis is more committed to change than to stasis, which is why Luhmann's ontology is nowhere near as relational as Latour's.

It is true that as soon as we look inside any system, we will see that a lot of work goes into maintaining it. My former employer, the American University in Cairo, is still there in basically the same form as I left it, but there has been such turnover from my time in administration that I count only three people still in

---

124 Maurice Merleau-Ponty, *Phenomenology of Perception,* trans. Colin Smith (London: Routledge, 2002), 79.

place of the dozen or more colleagues I had in the Provost's Office. Eventually, those three will also be gone, no doubt replaced by competent successors. Any living or quasi-living system will experience abundant changes in its parts. But all this means is that the parts of a university administration, or of any system, have a limited time on the job. It does not follow that everything is in constant flux, so that identity is only a second-hand product. It was not through some change in my identity that I decided to leave university administration; my position involved relatively stable tasks over the course of four years, and this did not change even though the Provost, my boss, changed two or three times in rapid succession while I was there. In order to leave Cairo, I needed my wife to prefer to live elsewhere, then needed to cut down on commuting by accepting a new job closer to her own. In short, the notion of constant flux is a continuist solution to what is often a punctuated problem, as in the Eldredge/Gould or Margulis challenges to Darwinian gradualism in evolutionary theory. The parts of a cell seem to us to change constantly, but that is mostly because they die quickly by the standards of the human lifespan, which is not the same thing as saying that they have no identity but are immersed in Heraclitean flux. In my book *Immaterialism,* I criticized the actor-network approach to history on analogous grounds. Whereas ANT could treat the Dutch East India Company only as a flux or trajectory across time, characterized by constantly changing powers and personae, I argued that historical objects are best seen through a *discrete* series of initial symbioses — half a dozen or so, not infinite in number — that fix the nature of an entity early on, thus leading it into a long period of relative stability marked by a phase of ripening and a phase of decline, ending ultimately in destruction as it falls out of phase with its environment. By contrast, the "flux" model of history cannot explain why entities do remain relatively stable. When autopoiesis theory is successful, as in Luhmann's best work, this is generally because it emphasizes the *stability* of a system over its many vacillations. Yes, every system is swarming with internal parts, but once we regard these parts as systems, we see that they too are marked by relative stability, however short-lived by comparison with the solar system or even the Roman Empire.[125]

Everyone knows that the world is marked by both stability and change, by the discrete and the continuous. The only question is how we account for both of these in our thinking. Aristotle does this with a division of labor, placing endurance and discreteness on the side of substance, and perishing and continuity on the side of accidents, time, space, and number. We have seen that the occasionalists opt instead for radical discreteness, and philosophers of difference for radical continuity, even when they add the last-minute epicycles of "folds" and "spacings." The problem with both groups of extremists (the Bryant of "The Time of the Object" belongs with Derrida in the second group) is that they must treat the opposite term as a byproduct rather than as something real in its own right. ooo in my version follows a more Aristotelian model, treating the real as discrete and the sensual as the continuous, with ruptures on one level or the other intermittently rearranging the map. Note that I say intermittently, not constantly. Those who hold that flux and becoming must be *constant* are simply reducing all stasis to flux, and when everything is flux, then no flux is significant. The difference between stability and change becomes trivial.

---

125 See also Graham Harman, "Conclusions: Assemblage Theory and Its Future," in *Reassembling International Theory*, eds. Michele Acuto and Simon Curtis (New York: Palgrave Macmillan, 2014), 118–31.

4

PETER WOLFENDALE

Object-Oriented Philosophy

Wolfendale's book is very long, much longer than it needed to be. But in some respects the length is deceptive, since much of the philosophical work is done in the sections on withdrawal in Heidegger and OOO.[1] Most of the rest of the book consists either of repetitive announcements of the supposed mistakes found in these pages, or in celebratory instances of the author high-fiving himself for having uncovered what he takes to be a gross pattern of errors and manipulations. Here as elsewhere, Wolfendale adopts a style of critical carpet-bombing, in the sense that nearly every paragraph finds something wrong or stumbles across some supposed new blunder. At times this makes it difficult to understand the chief premises from which he is operating, so that much reconstruction was needed in the form of outlines to identify his most important points. He also tends to present his own assumptions about philosophy as obvious truths, even while accusing me of the same vice repeatedly. Finally, he relies more heavily than he admits on the philosophy of Robert Brandom, and in many instances I would rather have responded to Brandom than to Wolfendale himself.

---

1   Peter Wolfendale, *Object-Oriented Philosophy: The Noumenon's New Clothes* (Falmouth: Urbanomic, 2014), 39–78. Subsequent page references are given between parentheses in the main text.

A few disagreements of fact must also be recorded. I deny the accuracy of Wolfendale's account of the state of the Speculative Realist blogosphere in the summer of 2010, which he depicts as if Levi Bryant and I strangled a thriving egalitarian ecosystem by merely asserting our own pre-eminence (xiv). Blog readers are free to travel where they will, and they gravitate naturally to the most active and interesting blogs available. Bryant is surely the greatest philosophy blogger in the history of the medium, and my own blog was visited frequently in those days by my increasing number of readers.[2] There was no assertion of supremacy over and above these basic facts, nor am I even sure what such assertion would entail. As with most social media, since Bryant and I were the two most visible bloggers, we also faced nearly constant attacks from trolls and other aggressors, some of them sending hate mail to our personal accounts. Wolfendale was nowhere near the worst of our blogosphere opponents, though it is true that Bryant and I were consistently annoyed at the time by what we saw as his pretense of superior rationality. I am afraid there is still too much of this attitude visible in his book.

Finally, Wolfendale seems to have misunderstood what happened in our email correspondence of June 2010. Thus a book, which by his own admission was motivated largely by revenge, was written in answer to a slight that never really occurred (xi–xii). As I reread our 2010 correspondence now, I am struck by how *polite* it is on both sides. As Wolfendale accurately reports, I wrote to him on June 21 of that year and offered two options for dealing with his increasing number of blog posts written against me — either condense all of his objections into a single post that I would then answer, or publish an article so that I would then feel obliged to respond. The next day, June 22, Wolfendale responded at length, saying among other things that he would choose the blog post option. Now, he is perfectly correct that I

2   Levi R. Bryant's blog is entitled *Larval Subjects,* https://larvalsubjects.wordpress.com/, and has not been very active for the past few years. My own, *Object-Oriented Philosophy,* https://doctorzamalek2.wordpress.com/, is still active, but now functions mainly as a bulletin board for philosophy news.

responded on the same day in a message that included the following words: "However, I can't be engaging in long responses to long blog posts at this stage of my activities; too little payoff for an awful lot of work. If you ever publish a critique somewhere so that our necks are equally on the chopping block, I'll be delighted to write a response." He summarizes this email by saying that I "revoked" the previously extended option of responding to a single long blog post. While I can see why he might have interpreted my email in this way, it is a simple misunderstanding. Nowhere in the email just quoted was my earlier offer *revoked*; that is Wolfendale's own interpretation of my saying, "I can't be engaging in long responses to long blog posts at this stage of my activities." All the facts show is that I had written two consecutive emails, a day apart, that seemed to contradict each other on a single point. Since I said nothing to explain this contradiction, I wonder why Wolfendale simply didn't ask me about it. The probable explanation of what happened is that I was buried in emails during that period, highly distracted by preparations for my upcoming administrative post, and simply forgot what I told him from one day to the next. Although he tells us that this incident "irked [him] a little" (xii), I see no evidence of annoyance in the emails that followed. His initial response was simply "I entirely understand," and his next message on June 24 turned to asking for advice about applying for a specific postdoctoral position, which I quickly provided. Thus I was surprised by Wolfendale's consistent rudeness to me on our next meeting, at Markus Gabriel's two-week Bonn Summer School in 2012, where Wolfendale was a student and I was on the faculty. When my attempts to joke with him at the refreshment table in Bonn were met with stone-faced silence, I realized he must be very angry about something and simply gave up trying to break the ice. Two years later, his book appeared.

Teamwork

Wolfendale's book, however, did not appear in isolation. There is a back-cover endorsement from Slavoj Žižek that speaks in his favor against me. This came as a surprise, given that Žižek and I are on reasonably friendly terms, and given as well that his endorsement makes little intellectual sense. There was also the afterword to Wolfendale's book by my longtime friend-turned-enemy Ray Brassier, ghoulishly entitled "Speculative Autopsy."[3] I will speak briefly to each of these peripheral factors before moving to deal with Wolfendale himself.

Initially, Žižek's words on the back cover of the book disappointed me. When it was published in 2014 I had still only met Žižek once in person, also at the Bonn Summer School two years earlier. But we had long engaged in warm correspondence linked with my ultimately failed efforts to bring him to lecture in Egypt. I should clarify that the first paragraph of Žižek's endorsement was neither a surprise nor an annoyance, but simply an accurate expression of his well-known differences from OOO. The surprise came in the second paragraph, where the Slovenian thinker is quoted as saying "what Peter Wolfendale does in his detailed and forceful book is what Kant did to Swedenborg." The reference, of course, is to Kant's "Dreams of a Spirit-Seer."[4] What puzzled me here is that Emmanuel Swedenborg (1688–1772) was a full-blown mystic who claimed to have seen dead spirits in dreams. This has nothing at all to do with OOO, which critiques both mysticism and rationalism for the same reason — their shared claim to know reality *directly*, whether by spiritual or intellectual means. I eventually wrote to Žižek about the matter, and though I will keep his exact response private, suffice it to say that I no longer take his endorsement of the book seriously.[5] More recently, we have done events together in Los Angeles and Munich, videos of which can easily be found on YouTube.[6]

---

3   Ray Brassier, "Postscript: Speculative Autopsy," in Peter Wolfendale, *Object-Oriented Philosophy* (Falstaff: Urbanomic, 2014), 407–21.
4   Immanuel Kant, *Dreams of a Spirit-Seer: Illustrated by Dreams of Metaphysics*, ed. Frank Sewall, trans. Emanuel F. Goerwitz (London: Forgotten Books, 2012)
5   Slavoj Žižek, personal communication, November 5, 2016.
6   For our Los Angeles discussion in March 2017, see Ippolit Belinski, "Slavoj Žižek & Graham Harman Duel + Duet (Mar. 2017)," *YouTube*, March

As for Brassier's postscript, it continues the unfortunate pattern of intellectual dishonesty found in all of his remarks on Speculative Realism since 2009. The interested reader can find my account of the history of that movement in at least three different publications, and Brassier has never dared deny any of it.[7] Instead, he has chosen to muddy the waters with a series of public insults aimed at me and my colleagues rather than engaging in the interesting philosophical debate that could be had, often under the pretense that we are not even worth debating. In what follows, I will limit myself to correcting two factual errors and one badly misleading statement in his Postscript.

The two errors are both found, strangely enough, in Brassier's first paragraph: "Has Speculative Realism passed the existence test? Graham Harman has certainly served as its indefatigable midwife. No doubt modesty forbade him from mentioning that he is commissioning editor of the 'thriving book series' he cites, and the self-volunteered editor of the new Speculative Realism section of the popular *PhilPapers* website."[8] There is some real venom to this passage, and it is baffling that Brassier is so bothered by my routine editorial work; I scarcely need mention the foolish own goal of calling one's opponent in philosophical debate a "midwife." Let's start with the second error, which is refuted more quickly. I am not the "self-volunteered" editor of the Speculative Realism section of the *PhilPapers* website, but was invited to become editor by no less a figure than David Chalmers. I had never met or corresponded with Chalmers prior to this invitation, though he did mention having liked my article

---

2, 2017, https://www.youtube.com/watch?v=r1PJo_-n2vI. For our Munich discussion of December 2018, see Lagebesprechungen, "Graham Harman and Slavoj Zizek: talk and debate: On Object Oriented Ontology," *YouTube*, December 6, 2018, https://www.youtube.com/watch?v=6GHiV4tuRt8.

7   Graham Harman, *Quentin Meillassoux: Philosophy in the Making*, 2nd edn. (Edinburgh: Edinburgh University Press, 2015), 77–80; Graham Harman, "The Current State of Speculative Realism," in *Speculations IV*, eds. Michael Austin et al. (Earth: punctum books, 2013), 22–28; Graham Harman, *Speculative Realism: An Introduction* (Cambridge: Polity, 2018), 2–4.

8   Brassier, "Postscript," 409.

"Zero-Person and the Psyche," which, ironically enough, Brassier also liked very much at the time of its completion.[9] Other than that, I am not sure why Chalmers invited me to do the job rather than Brassier or one of his allies. It might be because I write a lot and generally try to say "yes" to everything I am asked to do. Given that so many academics refuse to take on additional work, those who habitually accept it tend to acquire reputations and are "rewarded" with more work. As Vice Provost Ali Hadi of the American University in Cairo once told me, "If you want something done, ask a busy person." If nothing else, I have been busy. As for not mentioning that I am the editor of the thriving Speculative Realism series at Edinburgh University Press, no, this was not due to "modesty" as Brassier sardonically remarks, but to the fact that I cannot legitimately claim credit for the success of the series. Here again I was recruited to the job, this time by Carol MacDonald at EUP, who asked me to write up a series proposal for referees to examine; it has been a rare pleasure to work closely with Carol for the past decade. The Speculative Realism series is, in fact, one of the best-selling at EUP, and if Brassier thinks I could make this happen with personal marketing and branding efforts rather than an interested readership and outstanding authors, he is overestimating my degree of evil charisma.

Otherwise, Brassier's postscript juggles affirmation *and* rejection of the relevance of correlationism, along with recurrent digs at me for deliberately referring to Speculative Realism as a "brand," coupled with his own transparent efforts to rebrand it as the product of personal collaboration between him and his longtime friend Albert Toscano.[10] Although he reports that

---

9   Graham Harman, "Zero-Person and the Psyche," in *Mind That Abides: Panpsychism in the New Millennium*, ed. David Skrbina (Amsterdam: John Benjamins, 2009), 253–82.
10 Brassier, "Postscript," 414n6. As for my use of the term "brand," it occurs in the first paragraph of Graham Harman, "On the Undermining of Objects: Grant, Bruno, and Radical Philosophy," in *The Speculative Turn: Continental Materialism and Realism,* eds. Levi R. Bryant, Nick Srnicek, and Graham Harman (Melbourne: re.press, 2011), 21–40.

Toscano is "annoyed" to be associated with it, his remarkable response to this annoyance is to link his friend to Speculative Realism more closely than even before. I and others owe Toscano gratitude for organizing the 2007 Goldsmiths workshop, and for capably replacing the absent Quentin Meillassoux at the follow-up event two years later in Bristol. But it is a matter of record that Speculative Realism is primarily something Brassier cooked up with me, during April 2006, and it is pointless to attempt a revisionist history at this stage.

But the tricky central matter is responding to Wolfendale's book itself. As mentioned, my method in what follows will be to focus on a small set of important issues raised in his book, while trying to keep everything as impersonal as I can. On some points that arise I will invoke the right of self-defense, though I will try to exercise it in a non-inflammatory way; in any case, I will try to keep my tone less insulting than Wolfendale's own. I will first address the subtitle of the book, *The Noumenon's New Clothes*. This was apparently meant to have a bite to it. The source of this well-known image is the famous 1837 tale by Hans Christian Andersen, in which a small child is the only one with courage enough to say that the emperor is wearing nothing at all, even as others obsequiously praise his non-existent clothing.[11] Since then, the phrase "the emperor has no clothes" has been used and overused by sceptics to refer to the supposed nullity of otherwise popular phenomena. Over the decades, critics have often been proud to refer to such figures as Jacques Derrida or Jackson Pollock as "having no clothes," though the Irish art critic Declan Long once remarked on social media that those who use this metaphor "are dead to [him]," and I too am suspicious of those who resort to the phrase too quickly. Why exaggerate by claiming that a public personality is not just less important than other people think, but *utterly naked*? In the words of Raymond Chandler's detective Philip Marlowe, "All tough guys are mo-

---

11 Hans Christian Andersen, "The Emperor's New Clothes," in *Stories and Tales,* trans. H.W. Dulcken (London: Routledge, 2002), 81–84.

notonous. Like playing cards with a deck that's all aces. You've got everything and you've got nothing."[12]

What I mean to say is that "The Emperor's New Clothes" was not a good model for the subtitle of Wolfendale's book, and for two reasons. First, we should remember that the naked man in the story was the *emperor* and that people feared to tell him the truth because of his immense political power over them. (Incidentally, he is not an entirely unsympathetic character in the story, given his initial honest insistence that he does not see any of the supposed clothes.) In what sense do I enjoy a mighty imperial power that terrified critics are afraid to debunk? This is the first respect in which Wolfendale's subtitle misses the mark. The next problem is the one-word substitution in the subtitle, which speaks not of the emperor's, but the *noumenon*'s new clothes. It is noteworthy that Wolfendale did not choose *Kant's New Clothes* as his subtitle, presumably because he agrees with me that Kant is a legitimate great philosopher and by no means naked. But of all Kant's major concepts, surely the noumenon is the least comparable to an emperor. Although most philosophers since Kant are profoundly in his debt, how many of them have defended the inaccessible noumenon rather than attacking it as a residual piece of dogmatism? Obviously, the latter take is far more common. The defense of the noumenon made by me — and very few others — is a risky position that has to set up shop far indeed from any emperor's palace.

The proverbial subtitle Wolfendale needed instead was this one: *Old Wine in New Bottles*. It would have made more sense and struck closer to the bone. This alternate subtitle would have implied that OOO was merely recycling a moment in the history of philosophy that had been widely discredited since Kant's time. I have counterarguments against this claim too, but it would have been much closer to the target than charging that I am a very powerful person who is really completely naked.

---

12 Raymond J. Chandler, *The Long Goodbye*, in *Later Novels and Other Writings* (New York: Library of America, 1995), 483.

Let's see now if I can distill Wolfendale's book into a manageable number of key points.

His lengthy work covers many different topics. The impression he apparently wants to give is that of a total demolition of my work, as if he were exposing an utterly empty and fraudulent project. But that is not what actually happens over the course of his many pages. Instead, Wolfendale begins with a set of personal suppositions (often left unstated) about what philosophy ought to be, notes my divergence from them, and hints that this is evidence of a systematically irrational and incompetent approach. Strangely central to his enterprise is a point-by-point "refutation" of the interpretation of Heidegger with which my authorial career began. Since relatively few readers of Wolfendale's book will have sufficient background — or even interest — in Heidegger to judge his supposed refutation, he effectively capitalizes on the ignorance of those who merely share his wish to throw stones at me and my colleagues, often for reasons that are less than admirable. To show the arbitrary character of both his philosophical presuppositions and his interpretation of Heidegger will go a long way toward showing that the book's hundreds of pages are built on soft soil.

Wolfendale's introduction (3–25) gives a surprisingly good summary of OOO, and even shows a sense of humor and an engaging prose style, despite the already malicious undercurrent of these early pages. It is not true, as Wolfendale likes to claim (29), that my writings are such a mess that he had to labor as if in a salt mine simply to reconstruct the arguments contained therein. The unbiased reader — meaning one who is not reading the book primarily in order to bask in its negative affect — will no doubt find that my own expositions of OOO are clearer and more to the point. He divides his subject matter into three parts, and I have no objection to this manner of division: 1. Withdrawal, 2. The Fourfold, and 3. Vicarious Causation. Since Wolfendale follows this schema in the expository sections of chapter 2, I will adopt it for my response as well.

The opening section of Wolfendale's chapter 2 (30–37) also has an introductory feel to it, and thus I will consider it here as well. Here we see an aspect of the book that is foreign to Brassier's own interests. Namely, along with his own rationalist proclivities, Wolfendale reports that he has ambitions to be recognized as an insightful Heidegger scholar in his own right. This is mostly visible in the footnotes. In one such note, he reports that while his own Ph.D. dissertation on Heidegger diverges "from the standard analytic and Continental readings, much as Harman's does, [it] comes to conclusions radically different (and, I would argue, *far more nuanced*) than Harman's" (31n20; italics added). In another note a few pages later, he falsely claims that "Harman never provides any generic definition or analysis of the term [Being] that goes beyond his own metaphysical account of it" (33n23). It is hard to respond to this claim, given that the entirety of *Tool-Being* provides just such an account. Whereas most books on Heidegger merely repeat his presentation of Being as a *question*, my debut book takes the risk of claiming that Heidegger already gives us a provisional answer to the *Seinsfrage*, and the same holds of my introductory book *Heidegger Explained* published five years later. Incidentally, since Heidegger scholars seem to enjoy cackling at the supposed arrogance of the title *Heidegger Explained*, I should mention in passing that the title was chosen for me: all books in that particular Open Court series consist of a philosopher's name followed by *Explained*.

Wolfendale also complains that I speak of being only in opposition to "seeming," whereas Heidegger — in his celebrated *Introduction to Metaphysics* — devotes whole sections to four separate oppositions. Although the author does not mention them by name in his note, they are as follows: 1. Being and Becoming; 2. Being and Seeming; 3. Being and Thinking; and 4. Being and the Ought.[13] Does *Tool-Being* really limit itself to the second item on this list, as Wolfendale claims? Not at all. For one thing, the real/sensual pair in my work is relevant to "Being and Thinking" no less than to "Being and Seeming." As for

13 Martin Heidegger, *Introduction to Metaphysics*, trans. Gregory Fried and Richard Polt (New Haven: Yale University Press, 2014).

the first item on the list, *Tool-Being* drives an explicit wedge between Heidegger and Bergson on the question of becoming, precisely because of the strong link I see between Heidegger and occasionalism with its succession of isolated instants. In short, I do not think that Heidegger has anything of interest to tell us about becoming. That leaves only "Being and the Ought." Given Wolfendale's allegiance to Wilfrid Sellars and the Pittsburgh School, preoccupied as it is with questions of "normativity," I can see why he would wish I had dealt with the issue of norms in *Tool-Being*. But then he simply ought to have said so, instead of exaggerating the supposed one-dimensionality of my book's treatment of Being. This brings us to one of the major problems with Wolfendale's book, as I see it: the low likelihood that it will receive a sufficient amount of the constructive critical feedback that young authors need. The most avid readers of the book will be those who hate me, OOO, or both, and these are not the right people to rein him in when his claims stray beyond the available evidence. Certainly it will not be Brassier who does this, judging from the unseemly flattery of Wolfendale that fills up the final page of his postscript (421).

I am also left breathless when Wolfendale praises himself for "discursive charity" in his reconstruction of my views (30). An example of his less-than-charitable charity comes when the author claims that "our current task is thus to draw [Harman's arguments] out of hiding and expose them to the light of reason" (29), which anyone will recognize as condescension rather than charity. This is a problem throughout the book. Rather than just saying that he strongly disagrees with what I say about a given topic, and giving reasons for why, he invariably presents himself in the guise of an enlightened hero in unique relation to reason who will now show where a lesser figure has botched everything in sight—although "reason" is usually just shorthand for "Wolfendale's own philosophical commitments." An example of this is his assertion that "Harman gives us little in the way of phenomenological methodology" (32). There is no trace in this statement of my original interpretation of Husserl's phenomenology, centered in my argument that his true enemy is British Empiricism and its "bundles of qualities" rather than psychologism. There is also my further claim that Husserl wrongly links the essential qualities/adumbrations pair with the thought/sensation pair. Both of these points are stark departures from the chain restaurant phenomenology one usually encounters, and on some level Wolfendale must know it. Genuine "discursive charity" would not pass over these matters in silence while claiming that I give the reader "little in the way of phenomenological methodology" (32). Wolfendale's real worry only becomes clear on the following page, with this bit: "This sidelining of methodological issues is rather worrying given Harman's unapologetic calls to return to the problems of precritical metaphysics" (33). This is already not quite right. No one should cite my view that pre-Kantian metaphysical problems should be fair game once more without also noting that I endorse the existence of the Kantian thing-in-itself, the ultimate remedy to all pre-critical dogmatism. What the author really seems to worry about in my supposed "sidelining of methodological issues" is the weakened status of *epistemology* in OOO. All his various putdowns about methodology rest on his claim that epistemology must be the starting point for any real philosophy. This, finally, is a philosophical argument; unlike insults, it can be challenged via counterargument.

Wolfendale calls his own philosophy "transcendental realism," and it easy to see what he means by each of these terms, which together form the heart of Modern Onto-Taxonomy. "Transcendental" means that we must begin with the self-reflexivity of the human subject and ask how this subject is even able to know the world, just as happens with Meillassoux's frequently overlooked embrace of the correlational circle. Wolfendale realizes this similarity and soon tells us about it, "I agree with Quentin Meillassoux that the essence of correlationism is epistemological rather than metaphysical, and that it must be challenged on this terrain rather than dismissed as ontologically arrogant" (36). OOO does not agree. Indeed, OOO does not accept the existence of a self-justified subfield called "epistemology" at all, but interprets it as a bad ontology that takes the thought–world relation to be the basis of all others. By "realism," Wolfendale means a realism in which science has the ultimate say about the real. Although he and Brassier like to pretend that the term "scientism" is meaningless or vacuous, a perfectly good definition of the term is given by James Ladyman and Don Ross in chapter 1 of *Everything Must Go*—namely, that science ought to be the ultimate authority on all the problems usually treated by metaphysics.[14] And while Brassier likes to complain further that OOO conflates scientism with naturalism, any nuance on this point is irrelevant, given that both he and Wolfendale wholeheartedly endorse a Ladyman/Ross form of *scientism,* according to which—for example—OOO is forbidden to speak about causation beyond the limits of current discussions in natural science. This is a thoroughly scientific form of scientism, demanded solely for scientism's sake. To summarize, Wolfendale thinks philosophy should begin with epistemological reflections on what thought is able to know in the first place ("transcendental") before ending in a deferential attitude towards science ("realism"), except maybe on a few scattered ethical and aesthetic problems, if even there. This is a textbook version of Modern Onto-Taxonomy, and for this reason I regard the author's 400+ pages against OOO as issuing from a philosophically retrograde stance. Speaking of history, Wolfendale sees fit to "commend" me for "wielding [the] method [of historical exposition] with some skill" (31). The reader can almost hear him swallow hard as he makes this concession, and of course he quickly flips it into a negative: "this method […] can easily slip from licit *exposition* to illicit *justification* in the form of arguments from authority. […] (equivalent to saying 'you need to go read Aristotle/Hegel/Heidegger etc. before we can talk seriously about this')" (31). But he gives no examples of such "illicit justification" in my work, and thus I have to wonder how many he found. On the whole, I think my books do a good job of wearing their erudition lightly, giving readers just enough historical background to

---

14 James Ladyman and Don Ross, *Every Thing Must Go: Metaphysics Naturalized* (Oxford: Oxford University Press, 2007), 61.

understand the context of an idea without making them feel excluded from the discussion. No doubt I do this more effectively in some cases than in others; that is the nature of the beast when writing books. We all know there are authors in philosophy who use their learning to bully readers into submission, but I would bet that vanishingly few readers, Wolfendale included, consider me to be one of them. I expend a great deal of effort in writing user-friendly prose, or at least as user-friendly as prose in books of metaphysics can be. To say the least, neither Wolfendale nor Brassier would have an easy time claiming they are more approachable writers than I am.

As a final initial point, I call attention to a second mistake in a footnote already mentioned (33n23). En route to Wolfendale's false claim that I "almost entirely [elide] the general sense referring to the Being of objects *as such* with which Heidegger himself is principally concerned" (33), he says that all I cover is the being of *specific* beings as well as the being of the totality of all objects. As for the first claim, I do not think there is any "Being of objects *as such*" apart from specific beings — though for different reasons from Derrida — and give multiple arguments to this effect. Hence there is no "elision" of Being as such in *Tool-Being*, but an explicit discussion of why I see no such distinction in Heidegger as the one that Wolfendale demands. As for the second, I explicitly reject the notion of a totality of objects, as Wolfendale himself acknowledges later in the book. In making his claim about my supposed focus on totality, Wolfendale sends the reader to page 294 of *Tool-Being*. But on that page I *criticize* Heidegger for treating tools as belonging to a single global system, and try to show how his account of how tools break works against any holism of equipment. More generally, I reject the notion that all objects belong to one encompassing largest object, as seen in a 2010 article (which Wolfendale has read) that talks about how the uppermost level of reality consists of "dormant" objects that are not currently in relation with anything else and thus do not form part of a larger object.[15] What Wolfendale really seems to be saying is that I wrongly accuse *Heidegger* of treating Being as a single large object, though he leaves the point ambiguous at this early stage of his book. I will return to the topic shortly. This is a related problem that recurs repeatedly throughout the book. Quite often Wolfendale will cite my view on a single point, or my failure to discuss a certain point, and make it sound as if this were ridiculous on its face and a sign of innate carelessness on my part. Yet more often than not, these critiques are based on some philosophical agenda of his own that he does not announce until much later, though it would have been helpful to know from the start how it motivates a particular complaint. In the present case, by saying that through my focus on beings I "almost entirely [elide] the *general* sense referring to the Being of objects *as such* with which Heidegger himself is principally concerned," he tries to make it look as if I have messed up badly as an interpreter by failing to account for something obtrusively obvious in Heidegger's own writings. We are a good way down the road before Wolfendale clarifies the nature of his own investment in a sharp distinction between Being as a whole and the being of particular beings. For only in chapter 3 does he admit that "I doubt whether it is possible to think beings as such directly without either implicit definition, metaphorical allusion, or a highest genus of being," a significant concession to my position, despite the hastily added caveat that he would "hesitate to claim that it is strictly impossible" (319). By shifting to the Whole, Wolfendale thinks he can also shift from the indirect and the allusive to the direct mastery available to "logic." To summarize, he belatedly admits that I am right about individual entities, and would prefer to change the topic to one where he thinks he has the upper hand. A *fairer* way to introduce our disagreement on page 33 would have been something like this:

---

15 Graham Harman, "Time, Space, Essence, and Eidos: A New Theory of Causation," *Cosmos and History* 6, no. 1 (2010): 15.

Here we see for the first time an important disagreement between me and Harman that will have significant ramifications for this book. Harman chooses to focus on the structure of individual beings while downplaying any notion of Being as such. But while I concede that he largely gets it right about these individuals — in terms of the difficulty or even impossibility of gaining direct access to them — I still hold that direct access *is* possible to something like the structure of Being as a whole. In this way, Harman's attempt to downplay the role of knowledge when it comes to Being is undercut, given that his allusively accessible withdrawn beings are dependent on a prior logic of Being in general that is perfectly knowable.

This is how intellectual disputes ought to be conducted, not by pretending that an opponent's disagreement with us is merely an outrageous blunder, before admitting three hundred pages later that he was at least half-right all along.

Perhaps the most programmatic statement in the introductory pages of Wolfendale's book comes in the final two points of a six-point list that he directs against me. I refer to the following:

> (v) I predict that a return to metaphysical speculation without the methodological awareness accompanying an answer to the question "What is metaphysics?" is doomed to failure; and (vi) I think that there can be no viable 'realism' without a *definition* of 'real' more subtle than "that which is always other than our knowledge of it." (36)

Anyone can make "predictions" about what will happen in the near future of philosophy. More than that, everyone *does* make such predictions, since any philosophical career amounts to a bet placed on the relative long-term importance or unimportance of different currently available research programs. In point (v), with its insistence on "methodological awareness," Wolfendale is telling us that he has staked his own career on the need for epistemological preliminaries if philosophy is to be rigorous. In this he scarcely departs from Meillassoux's surprising allegiance — which I regard as ill-considered — to the "correlational circle," or from Brassier's fondness for what he now terms "good correlationism" (412), another synonym for epistemology. But this is not the only possible method for philosophy, and Wolfendale ought to just call it what it really is — his own preferred epistemological starting point. This only makes sense if one holds (as I do not) that the thought–world relationship is the one through which all others must be processed, so that to speak of the collision between two billiard balls self-reflexively means to speak of *my thought* of the collision of two billiard balls. OOO rejects this way of proceeding and considers it to be what is "doomed to failure." Moreover, this is not just a "prediction" on my part, but follows from a systematic rejection of Modern Onto-Taxonomy.

We move now to point (vi), "there can be no viable 'realism' without a *definition* of 'real' more subtle than 'that which is always other than our knowledge of it.'" This is simply another version of the old "negative theology" canard that OOO can only tell us what an object is not, not what it is. It is mistaken on two levels. First of all, there are other features of the object we can deduce aside from its being "other than our knowledge of it." Knowledge is Wolfendale's own obsession. For OOO, the object is other than any relation *anything* might have with it; this already does important work in broadening the initial scope of philosophy beyond the thought–world dyad in which Onto-Taxonomists like Wolfendale have imprisoned it. Beyond that, for OOO there must be multiple objects and not just one, meaning it has already taken a position on a question that Kant apparently considers insoluble. Objects are also torn by a rift between themselves and their own qualities, which takes us beyond the ambient British Empiricism in which even post-Husserlian philosophy tends to operate. There are other features of both real and sensual objects that can be deduced, but I would prefer to leave the full list for a different occasion.

But the second problem concerns Wolfendale's — and not only Wolfendale's — inability to distinguish between *philosophia* and knowledge. To accuse someone of "negative theology" when they reject the primacy of discursively available properties of things is to fall into the trap of Meno's Paradox. The reader will recall that this paradox amounts to the Sophist's view that we either know something or we do not, and therefore it is pointless to search for what is not already contained in our starting point. Socrates responds with his central teaching about the status of human beings in the cosmos: that we are both in the truth and not in the truth. OOO's way of addressing the issue is with the impossibility of exhausting any object through undermining, overmining, or their simultaneous employment in duomining.[16] Wolfendale, instead, wants to see philosophy as another form of *knowledge* (i.e., of mining) in continuity with the natural sciences. This is not how Socrates saw it, and Wolfendale's later footnote depicting my reading of Socrates as some sort of catastrophic inversion ("a parody of Socrates as bad as Aristophanes' *The Clouds*") is a mere assertion based on his own deeply modernist vision of what philosophy ought to be: namely, an epistemological *consigliere* to the heavy-hitting Dons of natural science (335n426). There is no trace here of Socrates' harsh remarks in the *Phaedo* on Anaxagoras's physical explanations.[17] On this note, we turn to Wolfendale's analysis of withdrawal, the fourfold, and vicarious causation in chapter 2 of his book. They make up the heart of his criticism of OOP before he claims in chapter 3 to determine the more general pattern of its errors and, in chapter 4, to poetic laments about the catastrophe that looms if the principles of my philosophy are widely adopted. Before discussing chapter 2, I should note that its respective sections on withdrawal, the fourfold, and vicarious causation are of uneven length and uneven seriousness. The part on withdrawal is where Wolfendale fires what he thinks is his heaviest artillery, trying to show that my writings are plagued with ambi-

16 Graham Harman, "Undermining, Overmining, and Duomining: A Critique," in *ADD Metaphysics*, ed. Jenna Sutela (Aalto: Aalto University Design Research Laboratory, 2013), 40–51.
17 Plato, *Euthyphro, Apology, Crito, Phaedo*, trans. G.M.A. Grube, in *Complete Works*, ed. J.M. Cooper (Indianapolis: Hackett Publishing Company, 1997), 49–100.

guities, equivocations, and inconsistencies, though generally all he shows is that his own presuppositions about philosophy are not the same as mine. Contrary to his usual rhetoric, it is I who needed to perform extensive reconstructive surgery on these pages, since they are mostly tedious lessons masked as displays of remorseless logic. The part on the fourfold is less interesting, though it begins with a tiny ray of agreement, and mostly involves Wolfendale claiming that I misread Heidegger, Husserl, and Saul Kripke. The final section on vicarious causation is especially short, and largely limits itself to affirming the Onto-Taxonomical assumption that science deserve its current monopoly on discussions of the inanimate world, and that all vicarious causation offers by contrast is an "introspective theory of emotional intensity," thereby repeating the usual scientistic cliché that aesthetics is about nothing more than "emotion." Accordingly, my pages on withdrawal will be longer than the others.

Withdrawal

Wolfendale is right when he says that "Harman has several arguments for his account of withdrawal. By far the most famous is the reading of Heidegger's tool-analysis presented in his first book, *Tool-Being*" (39). He knows that OOO arose from my reading of the tool-analysis and tells us in a footnote that in *Towards Speculative Realism*, which contains pieces of writing from both before and after my debut book, "[eight] out of [eleven] essays contain truncated summaries of the tool-analysis"[18] (39n28). That is not surprising to hear.

Wolfendale's disagreement with my interpretation shapes everything that happens in the rest of the book, as concerns both content and method. His favorite trope when discussing my work is that everything is so hopelessly mixed together that he himself had to clean up my arguments before critiquing them. This rather self-congratulatory description of his activi-

---

18 Graham Harman, *Towards Speculative Realism: Essays and Lectures* (Winchester: Zero Books, 2010).

ties is often picked up by his supporters and repeated as if it were fact rather than self-congratulation. Here is one of his early versions of that claim:

> despite the fact that the tool-analysis is referred to and summarized to different degrees throughout Harman's work, it remains fairly opaque in its logical structure. [… A]lthough it is referred to as if it were a single argument, Harman's version is really a blend of a number of distinct arguments, mixing all three forms of exposition discussed above: historical, phenomenological, and metaphysical. (39)

This claim to have conducted a painstaking inquiry into the many tangled threads of my writings is really just a rhetorical sleight of hand; given how frequently it recurs in this form, it needs to be called out from the start. Let's begin with the assertion that I "mix" historical, phenomenological, and metaphysical approaches in my reading of Heidegger. As for the first, we have already seen that Wolfendale concedes that I handle the method of historical exposition "with some skill." We saw that he adds the pejorative caveat that this method could be used to bully readers into submission, though he never provides any evidence that I do so. Therefore, the "historical" ingredient of my "mix" is not relevant to his polemic, which thus consists of two terms rather than three: a "mixing" of the phenomenological with the metaphysical. All that Wolfendale really means with these two terms is that I conflate the ontological and epistemological registers. This, in fact, is one of *just two* major arguments structuring his book as a whole. If my first supposed mistake is mixing the epistemological and the ontological, my second is daring to hold that philosophy might have something to say about inanimate objects that is not already done better by the natural sciences. In short, Wolfendale is a loyal devotee of the two pillars of Modern Onto-Taxonomy, (a) correlationism and (b) science-worship, and thus his originality is very much in question.

The reason this needs to be mentioned here is that at the end of his book, Wolfendale will make great efforts to "brand" me as some sort of mainstream degenerate continental who peddles easy forms of skepticism for people who have been left behind by the greatness of science (401–6). He will tell us that if I am giving continental philosophy what it *wants*, he knows what it *needs*. However, it is rather disappointing to learn that what he thinks continental philosophy "needs" is more analytic philosophy and more science. He will also tell us that the "good" part of Gilles Deleuze and Alain Badiou is their interest in mathematics, while the "bad" part comes when Deleuze works with crazy Félix Guattari and Badiou talks about events (353–57). In short, what Wolfendale has to offer is not some novel vision for philosophy, but a fairly standard "rationalist tough guy" mix of epistemology, mathematism, and scientism. I do not say this in defense of present-day continental philosophy, which — God knows — is decadent enough. But if there is anything on which the analytic and continental traditions fundamentally agree, it is the two pillars of Modern Onto-Taxonomy, which I have said are (a) correlationism and (b) a monopoly for science on discussions of the world. Both traditions follow Kant in beginning with reflections on human thought or language as instruments of knowledge. And while analytic philosophy celebrates science in a way that the continental tradition does not, the latter adopts an agnostic silence about the world itself that allows science-worship to continue without resistance.

In short, it is not I but Wolfendale who adheres to the basic principles of both analytic *and* continental orthodoxy, and he as well who accepts the two underlying dogmas of modern philosophy. This guarantees in advance that he will receive an easy hearing from any readers who join him in these biases. Earlier we encountered Shaviro's claim that panpsychism is enough to get one branded a crackpot, but in fact it is not even necessary to endorse panpsychism to receive that particular insult. To be called a crackpot, all one needs to do is object to *either* of the pillars of Modern Onto-Taxonomy, arguing either that we should not begin with the thought–world relation *or* should not allow science to monopolize discussions of the inanimate world. OOO argues for both points, and thus it defends a position much bolder than the mainstream epistemological scientism that Wolfendale and Brassier take to be some sort of daring challenge to orthodox thought. In this way, they run the serious risk of being mere products of their era.

Well then, we have seen that Wolfendale attempts to disguise the bland and false charge that I "conflate the epistemological with the ontological" by adding a third term (the historical) that I never conflate with anything. This is augmented in his book with needlessly technical language masquerading as nuanced tenacity. I refer above all to his practice of taking any of my chief points and claiming to split them up into discrete Arguments, "The Argument from X," "The Argument from Y," "The Argument from Z." This enables him to pose as an uncompromising logician picking apart the sloppy reasoning of OOO, though more often than not it is simply a sign of boring pedantry. We will see how this plays out in his complaints about my interpretation of Heidegger.

Before we get to those complaints, allow me to list my basic objections to Wolfendale's own manner of proceeding. Let's begin with something he gets right: "Harman is very clear that his version of the tool-analysis is not one that Heidegger himself would endorse, and that as such it must be assessed on its own merits" (40). He says that this is precisely what he will do, but before long he is back to the accusation that I get Heidegger's *intentions* wrong, and he makes this charge in fairly severe form:

> It is possible to read thinkers against themselves, but this requires that there is some essential element present in their work that the work itself fails to live up to. But the element that Harman tries to unearth in Heidegger's tool-analysis is not even there. [… H]e has stripped [the] relation [of Dasein to its tools] of everything that makes it recognizably Heideggerian. (48)

In giving his reasons for saying so, he will try to make it look as if his own subtler account of the tool-analysis has unmasked a labyrinth of self-complicating errors in mine. But in fact, his only reason for saying so is that he thinks the tool-analysis *really is* about *Dasein* rather than about all beings, and thus that I have "completely abandoned the semantic and epistemological framework within which the encounter with the tool is described" (48). In other words, it is only by presupposing precisely what I dispute — that the tool-analysis is "semantic" and "epistemological" — that he can claim my reading of that analysis has run off the rails. For the very same reason, he is able to beat his favorite drum and accuse me of conflating the phenomenological and metaphysical registers. A related problem is that, although Wolfendale claims I have stripped the tool-analysis of anything remotely resembling Heidegger, he says this not on the basis of careful attention to Heidegger's own words, but on philosophical prejudices drawn mostly from Brandom.

Be that as it may, he at least begins the chapter with a helpful list of the five main points on which he disagrees with my reading of Heidegger:

1. Harman reads "Heidegger's critique of presence as championing a complementary notion of execution."

2. Harman takes the ontic/ontological distinction to be the same as that between present-at-hand and ready-to-hand.

3. Harman claims that "world" is not a phenomenological horizon.

4. Harman holds that *Dasein* is not central to Heidegger's ontology.

5. Harman identifies the encounter with the broken tool with the as-structure. (40)

All in all, this is not a bad list. None of these five statements distorts my position, though some clarification is needed. Furthermore, Wolfendale seems to miss that his list really boils down to just two basic disagreements, though there is a good deal of interplay between them. Points 1, 2, and 5 have to do with the opposition I call real/sensual. Usually, the distinction between *Vor-* and *Zuhandenheit* in Heidegger is read as a difference between the explicit awareness of something and implicit use of it. The key to my reading of the tool-analysis is that this is too anthropocentric to be a good starting point for philosophy; unfortunately, the anthropocentric reading is exactly the one that Wolfendale gives. The surfeit of detail in his critique tends to conceal that it is based entirely on his own *Dasein*-centric prejudice.

Points 3 and 4 give us this prejudice in more open form — Wolfendale does think "world" in Heidegger is a phenomenological horizon and does think that *Dasein* is at the center of the tool-analysis. But this, of course, is Modern Onto-Taxonomy incarnate: we cannot begin with a discussion of all beings, but must first consider the way these beings manifest themselves to *Dasein*. It was Descartes who launched modern philosophy by arguing that what is present to thought is more unshakably true than the mediated deductions we draw about anything outside thought. In the *Meditations on First Philosophy* and elsewhere, we must first pass through God and his goodness to realize that he is not an evil deceiver, with the result that if we make sure to use our reason correctly, we already have everything we need to reach correct conclusions about the world.[19] Wolfendale drops the "God" part, like most modern rationalists, but keeps the trust in reason as capable of giving us things the way they really are. After Descartes we have Malebranche, Spinoza, and Leibniz, for whom human thought is not quite as special as it was for Descartes, although they remain rationalists. But it is really from Kant onward that human thought becomes the obligatory starting point, so that anyone straying from this method can only look like a crackpot. The most refreshing exception is Whitehead, who *for this very reason* is not warmly welcomed by either analytic or continental philosophy despite being one of the most original thinkers of the twentieth century.

---

19 René Descartes, *Meditations on First Philosophy,* trans. Donald A. Cress, 3rd edn. (Indianapolis: Hackett Publishing Company, 1993).

Before saying more about the Kantian era, I would call the reader's attention to another problem with Wolfendale's point 3, to the effect that "world" as shown in the tool-system should be taken as a phenomenological horizon rather than an ontological claim by Heidegger. One problem this introduces is that if the tool-system is a horizon, then orthodox Husserlians are right, and Husserl already saw whatever Heidegger sees in the tool-analysis. While this claim is not obviously absurd, it misses Heidegger's uniqueness in a way that Derrida already did — as seen in the chapter on Peter Gratton — when claiming that the horizon of intentionality already gives Husserl everything called for by Levinas under the name of "alterity." Now, we saw with Derrida that the gist of the claim for Husserl having gotten there first is that we can never have an "adequate" intention of the horizon, since it is the primal source from which all intentions well up, though this is probably not how Wolfendale would put it. While this does succeed in treating the horizon as an amorphous background that can never be fully objectified, it does not address the key difference between Husserl and Heidegger: the fact that Being in Heidegger, as that which withdraws, is not even *potentially* the correlate of an intentional act, not even in the sense of a *telos* toward which we are forever striving without success. In short, the Husserlian horizon is an idealist structure whereas Being is a realist one, even if Heidegger always couples it with *Dasein*. Wolfendale would certainly not agree with everything that Husserlians say on the matter, but he will have a hard time explaining why Husserl is not already enough, and why the tool-analysis marked a step forward.

Returning now to the question of the Kantian era in philosophy, one of the easiest ways to rank the many great philosophers is as follows. The handful of really pivotal philosophers redefine the very terms in which philosophy works, while the great thinkers a half-notch below extend the application of those terms without quite redefining them. In this respect, the central role of *Dasein* in Heidegger's own philosophy — and I do not deny it is there — means that he is still working in the space carved out by Kant; great as Heidegger is, I would say that he is not quite at the level of Kant. For this very reason, I have recently been reconsidering my career-long assertion that Heidegger is the greatest philosopher of the twentieth century, and am now inclined to say it was Whitehead instead. Although I am no Whiteheadian, for reasons explained in my discussion of Steven Shaviro in chapter 2, it is Whitehead rather than Heidegger who struck a body blow against the Kantian assumptions in which Modern Onto-Taxonomists — including Brandom, Brassier, and Wolfendale — conduct their business. What I mean to say is that Wolfendale's five-point list just cited should be condensed into a single point — his Onto-Taxonomoical allegiance to the principle that "epistemology" is where we must start. When he says that what I draw out of Heidegger "is not really there," all he means is that I reject the Kantian assumptions that Heidegger takes for granted. Since Speculative Realism is often unfairly portrayed as an exercise in "Kant-bashing," I should remind the reader of my view that the *Ding an sich*, which almost no post-Kantians accept, is the one portion of his doctrine that *must* be preserved. The Onto-Taxonomical assumption that any talk of object-object relations must be processed through a prior thought-object relation is the part that must be rejected. In Meillassouxian terms, it is Wolfendale who is the real correlationist, not I. For he accepts a version of the correlational circle, while I do not.

Let's now consider how Wolfendale goes wrong in challenging me on the five points listed above. The first has to do with "execution," a term I took from José Ortega y Gasset's essay on metaphor.[20] Although Wolfendale apparently concurs with my criticism of mainstream Heidegger scholarship for treating *Vor-* and *Zuhandenheit* as a catalogue of different *kinds* of beings — as if the ready-to-hand were speaking only about hammers and screwdrivers as opposed to other sorts of entities — he does not think I am justified in arguing that the executant real-

---

20 José Ortega y Gasset, "An Essay in Esthetics by Way of a Preface," in *Phenomenology and Art*, trans. Phillip W. Silver (New York: Norton, 1975), 127–50.

ity of beings is what is deeper than presence. He thinks I have created a false either/or between the mainstream scholars and myself on this point. What is the alternative? In Wolfendale's own words, "it is possible to view [Heidegger's distinction ...] as a distinction between different modes of Being, [...] without reducing it to a distinction between mutually exclusive types of beings" (41). This is already strange, since I do consider presence and readiness-to-hand as two possible *modes* of all beings, corresponding to my sensual and real, and Wolfendale at this stage does not explain how his conception differs from mine. But he does get in a negative word about my linking of real beings with the tradition of *substance,* and it will turn out that by "modes," all he means is two different modes of things *for Dasein.* But this means that Wolfendale already accepts the major premise of mainstream Heidegger scholarship, for which it is an article of faith that we are confined to treating everything first in terms of how it is manifest to human being. At most, what Wolfendale adds to this standard picture is a greater reverence for science than what we find among Heideggerians, with their infamous dictum that "science does not think," a statement I do not admire.

Second, Wolfendale rightly notes that I do not think we should treat reality in terms of its intelligibility to *Dasein*. He claims that this amounts to the notion that intelligibility is a form of "seeming," though this is one of Wolfendale's pet words, not mine. On this basis, he claims that the mainstream Heideggerians and I are simply mirror-images of each other. We both think that Heidegger is mainly talking about meaningfulness for *Dasein,* though I attach a minus-sign to this and reject it while the mainstream simply affirms it. This leads him to the view that we both get something right even while missing the big picture: Heidegger thinks that being must be interpreted in terms of intelligibility, but also that it remains somewhat outside every interpretation. Wolfendale thinks this balance is best struck in "[Heidegger's] later work in particular" (42), given his increasing attention in later years to the strife between earth and world or concealing and clearing. In the first place, there is no reason to accept this developmentalist account of Heidegger: the duality in question is available in full-fledged form as early as 1919, in the Freiburg Emergency War Semester.[21] But more importantly, I do not treat the sensual or presence-at-hand as a mere "seeming." As seen in the previous chapter, I am interested in Levinas primarily as a philosopher of the *sensual* realm in all its sincerity and also hold that the sensual is the only place where causation can be triggered, given that real objects are cut off from all direct interaction. Hence, the idea that I disdain "intelligibility" is just an artifact of Wolfendale's intellectualist bias.

As for the third point, which concerns "horizon," Wolfendale shows less precision. He spends too much time countering my mockery of how mainstream scholarship follows Heidegger too closely in retreating from one horizon into another and on into another. Wolfendale objects that just because many scholars overdo it does not mean that there is no such regress into ever-deeper horizons in Heidegger's work. *Au contraire,* he tells us: Heidegger's analyses often "have an end point in some more or less well-delimited unitary structure (e.g., *Temporalität* in the early work, or *Ereignis* in the later work)" (43). At first it is hard to grasp his point, since I already accept the existence of a unitary structure in Heidegger, the tool-system. I simply deny that it should be called a "horizon," a phenomenological term which always refers to something already there before us as given, though without being the object of our explicit focus. But as mentioned earlier, if Wolfendale thinks the tool-system is a horizon, then he may as well stick with Husserl, who already discusses this concept with more precision than Heidegger himself. What is unique about Heidegger is that he points *beyond* any horizon, though it is unclear whether Wolfendale would contest this point in particular. What really bothers him is that I read what is "beyond the horizon" for Heidegger as a unity: "Harman's alternative is to read 'world' as a complete totality of entities rather than a phenomenological horizon within which

---

21 Martin Heidegger, *Towards the Definition of Philosophy,* trans. Ted Sadler (London: Continuum, 2008).

entities appear. This is a disastrous misreading, one that is explicitly counselled against by Heidegger" (43). Now, Wolfendale has already claimed that he accepts my procedure of not saying that Heidegger would agree with my reading of his work, and that he would therefore judge it on its own merits. Thus it is unclear why doing something "explicitly counselled against by Heidegger" would amount to a "disastrous misreading."

The same problem immediately arises with Wolfendale's fourth point. When I say that although *Dasein* is obviously central for Heidegger, we can easily broaden his analysis to cover all entities, his rejoinder is as follows: "This is indicative of a really pernicious misunderstanding of Heidegger's project that underlies the other points addressed so far" (43). It is always a bad sign when adjectives are asked to do too much work, and so it is with "pernicious" here. Let's rewrite Wolfendale's sentence without it: "This is indicative of a misunderstanding of Heidegger's project that underlies the other points addressed so far." From this we can see that Wolfendale is back to the claim that I misunderstand what Heidegger is really doing, though he conceded at the start that I do not wish to read the tool-analysis in terms of Heideggers's self-understanding. Perhaps aware that this contradicts his earlier claim to read my interpretation on its own merits, he adds the word "pernicious," as if to imply that more than a matter of getting Heidegger's own intentions wrong, there is some sort of deeper philosophical rot in our midst, though he does not say exactly what it is. Having already strayed into the realm of "what Heidegger really meant to say," Wolfendale summarizes what he meant in terms that merely reflect his own biases, "what characterizes *Dasein qua Dasein* (*Existenz*) is that set of conditions (*Existentiale*) without which *Dasein* could not count as freely choosing, and thus acting in any real sense" (44). Freely choosing? Acting? This already looks like a mainstream, *Dasein*-centric reading of *Being and Time*, which is precisely what I announced in *Tool-Being* I did not intend to follow. In other words, Wolfendale pretended that he would play along to see what happens with my reading, but quickly recurs to the point that I cannot read the tool-analysis without

223

Dasein because Heidegger meant it to be about Dasein. The technical name for this maneuver is "begging the question." It enables Wolfendale to defend Heidegger's rather weak distinction between world-forming humans and world-poor animals in 1929/30 by saying that "[Harman] fails to see that [with animals] Heidegger is describing entities which have similar behavioral capacities to *Dasein* (drives) but which nevertheless lack the specific conditions of organization that enable choice (as opposed to mere disinhibition)"[22] (44). In short, Wolfendale — like Heidegger — is simply presupposing the commonsensical assumption that animals have drives but only humans make choices. More than presupposing it, he *ontologizes* it, so that human "choice" is something so different from anything found in any other creature that it needs to be built into the very fabric of philosophy. It is the Game of Hurdles again. Wolfendale falsely implies that I recognize no difference at all between animals and humans (high hurdle for me), but since there do seem to be such differences (low hurdle for himself), they must rip an ontological chasm between humans and everything else (*non sequitur*). Worse yet, this is really just a fancy way of restating Brandom's own painfully commonsensical sapience/sentience distinction, while shedding no new light on the human/animal distinction and merely repeating extant rationalist commonplaces about choice, reason, and the like. It is even more disastrous when Wolfendale continues to project these biases back onto Heidegger himself. World for Heidegger, Wolfendale tells us, is "an internally articulated space of possible action (i.e., the projection of what is possible), involving a grasp of both generality and particularity (e.g., the possibilities of pens *as such* vs. the possibilities of *this* particular pen)" (44). This sounds a lot more like Brandom than Heidegger, and insofar as it relates to Heidegger, the argument amounts to nothing more than "Harman thinks the tool-analysis can be extended to all beings, but obviously

---

22 Martin Heidegger, *Fundamental Concepts of Metaphysics: World — Finitude — Solitude,* trans. William McNeill and Nicholas Walker (Bloomington: Indiana University Press, 1995).

it's supposed to be about *Dasein*." This is circularity at its worst, and given that Wolfendale shamelessly accuses me of circularity throughout his book, he ought to have been more aware of his own rampant indulgence in *petitio principii*. He soon repeats the exercise, combining it with another misstatement of my views: "Harman cannot see that differences in modes of Being [...] are not simple differences between types of beings, because he does not see the different ways they are supposed to be individuated as actualities within the world qua space of possibility" (44–45). This gets nothing right. I do not say that *Vor-* and *Zuhandenheit* are differences between *types* of beings, since this is exactly what I reject in the mainstream readings of *Zuhandenheit* as limited to specific items of hardware; indeed, this point is one of the best-known trademarks of my interpretation. As for the attempt to lecture me about seeing that the modes being are "individuated as actualities within the world *qua* space of possibility," this is both (a) a conflation of Heidegger with Brandom and (b) the presupposition of a *Dasein*-centric Heidegger whose validity I deny from the start. In fact, this passage is one of those places in Wolfendale's book where I am equally astonished and annoyed that it has been taken by his supporters for some sort of devastating critique.

His fifth point mixes the interesting with the uninteresting. Let's begin with the latter. Wolfendale again slips into the complaint that I misunderstand Heidegger's intentions, despite his purported acceptance of my announcement that I am not attempting to reveal Heidegger's self-understanding but to show what his analysis really entails. In his own words, "[Harman] misunderstands Heidegger's account of the as-structure and its relation to the broken tool encounter" (45). This is bad enough, but we are now familiar with this gesture and are probably no longer surprised. What makes matters worse is the utter triviality of how we are told the as-structure *should* be understood: "The crucial point is that Heidegger distinguishes between the hermeneutic 'as' and the apophantic 'as,' and associates these with the ready-to-hand and the present-at-hand, respectively. [... T]his is essentially a matter of the relation between the *im-*

plicit and the *explicit*" (46). In this passage, three of the worst features of Wolfendale's argument are combined: (a) presupposing a *Dasein*-centric reading of Heidegger when that is what we were supposed to be debating, (b) reducing Heidegger to an implicit/explicit distinction that conflates him with Husserl by ignoring that Being for Heidegger is not just "implicit," but phenomenologically inaccessible; (c) dragging in another of Brandom's obsessions, this time the implicit/explicit distinction. The situation is simple: if you presuppose that the tool-analysis can only be about what is hidden or present to *Dasein* because "that's obviously what Heidegger meant," then you cannot possibly follow my argument for how, on its own terms, the tool-analysis really tells us a lot more than it claims. You have remained inside the Kantian transcendental thought-object dogma with Heidegger himself, while suppressing everything in Heidegger that pushes us beyond it. When Wolfendale goes on to speak about the movement from implicit interpretations to abstract linguistic generalities, he is merely capitalizing on the limitations of his own starting point, rather than — as he evidently thinks — teaching a masterclass to ignoramuses who fail to see that the tool-analysis is all about the difference between human praxis and human rationality. I cannot imagine a more mainstream reading of Heidegger than this.

The more interesting part of Wolfendale's fifth point is his confrontation with my claim that the tool-analysis can be extended to questions of causation. In denying that the analysis of equipment has anything to do with "use," I am indeed saying that it "should be understood as a matter of reliance upon equipment" (45). That much is correct. But Wolfendale now mounts what he seems to regard as a devastating counterattack:

> It is the fact that reliance is an essentially *causal* notion that underpins Harman's claim that all interactions between entities can be described as entities "understanding" one another "as" something, and the development of this into the further notion that all such interactions are analogous to the encounter with the broken tool. (45)

It is not clear why Wolfendale puts "understanding" and "as" in scare-quotes in this passage. Presumably he is trying to insinuate that I am arguing for a full-blown panpsychism of a sort that even Shaviro, Strawson, and Chalmers would not accept, as if rocks could "understand" the water into which they are thrown. As demonstrated earlier, I make no such claim. My argument, instead, is that while Heidegger's discussion of understanding and the as-structure presents itself as an analysis of the basic features of *Dasein,* that analysis turns out to have highly general features that can easily be extended into the causal realm as well. Whatever differences there are between humans and non-humans — and there are many — they have to be redefined in terms of a prior flat ontology that tells us what is common to *all* relations. Above all, if we start by assuming with Brandom and Wolfendale that what characterizes the human vis-à-vis animals (let alone rocks) is interpretation, choice, reason, and the implicit/explicit distinction, then we are left with nothing but commonsensical, pre-ontological anecdotes about human specialness when we ought to be digging much deeper. Such digging Wolfendale does not do. He merely reports that it takes "special linguistic equipment" to "[extricate] the causal capacities of entities from the normative functions through which our everyday understanding grasps them," as if I were claiming that language is present everywhere in the cosmos (46). It again gets worse when Wolfendale says that "the exemplars of the present-at-hand are those entities posited by science independently of any role they could have in everyday practices (e.g., electrons, black holes, mitochondria, etc.)" (47). We are now very far from Heidegger himself, who, to say the least, was not inclined to praise the scientific objectification of the world. Once more it is Brandom speaking through Wolfendale's lips, not Heidegger himself. Nor does Heidegger speak of any "exemplary" form of presence-at-hand: all forms of which belong, for him, to the dark and grievous reign of ontotheology and technology. One can certainly argue that Heidegger is much too harsh on presence-at-hand, but that is already what I do in my own work. Yet there is no question that for Heidegger all forms of presence-at-hand share one basic point in common, in that they forget the *being* of that which they present.

Wolfendale clearly dislikes this flat sense of presence, since it is an obstacle to his valorization of science, so palpably impossible within a Heideggerian framework. And as too often happens, rather than mount a sustained argument against it, he resorts to an adjectival insult: "Science is thus hardly the domain of pure presence in this vacuous sense, but rather the forerunner of our attempt to work out what is really possible, over and above the expectations implicit in our parochial forms of life." (47; italics modified). "Vacuous?" Oh my. But Wolfendale nowhere demonstrates that it is "vacuous" to consider that there is a problem with presence, one that must be countered by something other than presence, which happens to be exactly what Heidegger thinks. Instead, Wolfendale simply adopts mainstream Heideggerianism with an opposite valence. As he has it, we start with "parochial" everyday habits, and this implicit parochialism becomes more and more explicit, until finally we have the "good presence" of scientific research. And I for one find this interpretation… vacuous. This is not because it disagrees with what Heidegger meant, but because the praxis/theory distinction is simply not very deep to begin with, and to read the tool-analysis as a contrast between implicit and explicit is to humanize it beyond repair. That is what *Tool-Being* is all about. Thus, I am unmoved when Wolfendale concludes that "[Harman] has excised the structure of understanding wholesale, and thereby completely abandoned the semantic and epistemological framework within which the encounter with the tool is described" (48). The words "semantic" and "epistemological" are at least as foreign to Heidegger as any of my own terminology. But more importantly, we recall once more that Wolfendale began with the boast that he would show that my interpretation fails by its own lights. Far from it. He simply asserts or rather presupposes that the tool-analysis is obviously about *Dasein* in its practical and theoretical existence, which is exactly what I deny from one end of *Tool-Being* to the other. He ought to have made actual counterarguments rather than simply projecting his own rationalist wish list onto *Being and Time*.

Almost thirty pages still remain in Wolfendale's repetitious account of why his interpretation of the tool-analysis is better than my own. We have already seen that his basic strategy is nothing but a table-pounding insistence that the analysis is about humans, and ultimately about the great achievements of "explicit" human science. The pounding continues from pages 49 through 78, and rather than listening to more of it, I propose instead that we leaf through those pages and look for possible signs of a new line of attack. It turns out that none of what comes next is entirely new, since it all somehow involves the claim that I am conflating phenomenology with metaphysics, or epistemology with ontology. But now and then they have a slightly different spin and are thus worth answering directly.

In his pages on what he calls "The Argument from Execution," Wolfendale is concerned with what he sees as a slippage in my analysis. In arguing that objects "withdraw from all *epistemic* and *causal* contact," I am said to "[provide] no clarification of [my] phenomenological method" (49). But the point is that the method here is not phenomenological in the first place; it is Wolfendale's requirement, not mine, that we begin with the phenomenology of how equipment appears to *Dasein*. To state my argument briefly, the fact that we ourselves are humans who use equipment in the world *is not* the basis for understanding that humans do not encounter tool-beings directly. Instead, this is something we deduce, not only through the fact that the tools often surprise us but more so from the realization that to use something is not to be it, and that to encounter something is not to encounter the whole of its being. But this very same deduction works for entities other than ourselves. We can deduce that other humans and animals are also unable to encounter the whole of the beings with which they interact, and can even do the same for entities that presumably have no conscious awareness at all: as in my oft-repeated example, drawn from Medieval Islamic thought, of fire burning cotton. It is not because of human "awareness" of the cotton that we fail to do justice to its being — this is the central dogma of Kant — but simply because no relation can exhaust its relata. By contrast, Wolfendale defends the modern dogma by complaining that I extend the as-structure to entities "that lack anything that could be construed as *awareness* of the thing depended upon" (51). But this is precisely the point. I have already argued that "awareness" is not needed for anything to be finite, and thus there is no reason to restrict the term "finitude" to humans in the first place. He complains further that I slide from the properly active sense of equipment to a rather different sense of *passive reliance* upon it: "Gone is the emphasis upon equipment *actively deployed* toward a goal […] to be replaced with a focus upon 'equipment' necessary to *passively sustain* a given state" (50). Wolfendale half-concedes that passive reliance might be "as eligible a goal as achieving one" (50), but in doing so he remains loyal to a notion of "goal" that merely reflects his own anthropocentric bias. The point of my reading of the tool-analysis is simply that all *relations*, whether human, animal, or inanimate, are equally unable to exhaust that to which they relate. Goal-oriented behavior is not unique in this respect, unless one begins like Wolfendale by assuming that the tool-analysis can only be about humans because Heidegger says so. Again, my point is not that rocks and comets have "goals," but that the analysis of relationality must also apply to relations that are far more primitive than goal-oriented praxis. When Wolfendale adds that "we can already see the pretense of phenomenology slipping here" (51), he is forgetting that I never made any such pretense. The idea that the tool-analysis must be a "phenomenology" of tools is Wolfendale's own bias, since for me the analysis is primarily about what can never appear. He concludes with a pointless warning that the tool-analysis is supposed to be about "comportments that [lack] a specific *kind* of awareness, rather than lacking awareness as such" (51). What makes it pointless is that I never claim the contrary. From the early pages of *Tool-Being* it is clear that I do not intend to remain within the *Dasein*-centric motivations of Heidegger himself, but will show that his tool-analysis cannot remain restricted to human-specific cases such as the opposition between implicit and explicit. Since that is a matter of record for anyone even loosely familiar with my work, Wolfendale is merely bursting through a paper door with such claims. To think that finitude requires full-blown conscious awareness is the dogmatic kernel in Kant that was torn asunder by Whitehead at last.

After conceding that I am right that to rely on something requires that it have a specific causal capacity, he adds that "the way in which it is introduced and used by Harman is questionable precisely insofar as it is metaphysical rather than phenomenological" (52). Nothing new here so far. The grain of novelty comes in his follow-up claim: "Harman is already straying into metaphysics in describing the thing as *consisting* in this capacity, rather than simply *possessing* it" (52). Here he confuses me with George Molnar and other metaphysicians of powers.[23] By no means do I think that an object *consists* in its causal capacity, since for me this is too much a derivative, relational conception of objects; the object is a specific simplification of the pieces of which it is composed and not *primarily* a causal agent. Indeed, I specifically theorize *dormant* objects that exist despite having no causal effect on anything at present and perhaps even in the future.[24] Since Molnar is a respectable analytic philosopher, I would guess that Wolfendale would not object to *him* doing metaphysics. It seems that the real difference between me and Molnar in Wolfendale's eyes stems from his false accusation about my "pretense" of doing phenomenology while covertly mixing it with metaphysics. He sees traces of such pretense in my use of the word "invisibility" to refer to withdrawn objects, though I normally use this term to refer to the human use of equipment and simply as a way of illustrating that particular point. But Wolfendale overdetermines this term, by way of claiming that invisibility to humans does not entail withdrawal of things from each other. True enough, but that is not how my argument proceeds. It is not "humans cannot see

---

23 George Molnar, *Powers: A Study in Metaphysics,* ed. Stephen Mumford (Oxford: Oxford University Press, 2003).
24 Harman, "Time, Space, Essence, and Eidos."

tools when they are using them, and therefore inanimate things cannot make contact with each other either." Instead, it is this: "the invisibility of equipment to humans does not just refer to an 'implicit' character in our use of them, but allows us to see that the implicit use of things does not grasp them any more directly than explicit perception of them does. And the same holds for causal interaction, which also does not deploy the full reality of interacting objects."

Wolfendale goes on to say that there is a "*general paradox* of the accessibility of inaccessibility" in my model, along with the "*more specific* paradoxes of modality and temporality" (55). He mocks these paradoxes as akin to "a zen master wielding a koan: a pure act rests beyond any superficial acts, a pure actuality grounds all potential actualities. One hand claps slowly" (55). Let's take these one at a time, bearing in mind that I reject Wolfendale's equation of the paradoxical with the nonsensical; I would say, instead, that the emergence of a paradox is often the best index that we have hit on something real. As for the "general paradox" of the accessibility of inaccessibility, this is just the usual maneuver of invoking the correlational circle. Derrida uses it against Levinasian alterity, the German Idealists against Kant's *Ding an sich,* and Meillassoux against the weak correlationist. It always runs roughly as follows: "if something is said to be inaccessible, than we have already accessed it somehow, and thus there is a performative contradiction; to know a limit is already to be beyond it." The point is that there a difference that is almost always elided between direct and indirect access. To say "there is something outside thought" is indeed itself a thought, but this does not mean that the thing referred to by thought is thereby also a thought; Wolfendale's own ally Brassier often makes a similar point when dismissing the argument known as "Stove's Gem."[25] In Heideggerian terms, the fact that the tool becomes manifest in malfunction does not mean that it consists in its manifestness. We know this in everyday life through

---

25 David C. Stove, *The Plato Cult and Other Philosophical Follies* (Oxford: Blackwell, 1991).

instances of allusive and figurative language and the rhetorical use of enthymemes, which give us access to things as absent rather than as present, and which for this very reason tend to be unusually powerful. As for the "more specific" paradoxes of "a pure act [...] beyond any superficial acts, [and] a pure actuality [grounding] all potential actualities," this is mostly a matter of Wolfendale overreading the language of certain passages in *Tool-Being*. To be more specific, I only describe the executant reality of objects as an "act" in the early sections of the book, as Wolfendale himself soon recognizes. "Act" normally implies having effects on something else, and the point of my real objects is that they are real even when they are not having such effects; once this is seen, there is no paradox at all. Objects must exist in order to act, and they must exist regardless of any "potentiality" they might have, because potential also implies a relationality that is excluded from real objects.

There are just three remaining points in Wolfendale's pages on withdrawal. The first is his claim that I botch the argument for Heidegger's tool-system by claiming that it is tantamount to a single large entity. His main argument here is, once again, the old chestnut that I conflate the phenomenological and metaphysical registers. This is possible only because Wolfendale again makes rather mainstream assumptions about the tool-analysis being limited to *Dasein,* which he conceals — here as usual — with the term "modal," his chicken soup cure for the realization that he is now repeating himself. The second is his rejection of what he calls my "argument from excess," that the object can never be exhausted by any theoretical, practical, *or* causal contact for the same reason in all three cases. Here he will have recourse to a distinction between "qualitative" and "quantitative" excess, with Wolfendale championing the latter. Third and finally, he goes after my argument that since complete knowledge of a tree would not itself be a tree, knowledge can only be a translation of the tree rather than a form of direct access. Wolfendale cites this argument from my article on James Ladyman and Don Ross, though it appeared again later in the Pelican book *Object-Oriented Ontology,* where it would be criticized by Stephen Mulhall (see chapter 8 in this text). The often needlessly technical character of Wolfendale's analyses of these three points conceals a fairly basic philosophical disagreement, while giving his own argument a false air of precision and mine a fake aroma of carelessness. I will take them in order.

In considering my analysis of how a bridge — on Heidegger's terms, not mine — becomes a single holistic entity, Wolfendale neglects to cite the single most relevant passage from *Being and Time*: "Taken strictly, there 'is' no such thing as *an* equipment. To the Being of any equipment there always belongs a totality of equipment, in which it can be this equipment that it is."[26] There is a sense in which my entire reading of Heidegger aims to oppose this single passage, which is by no means a textual outlier, but explains perfectly well what happens in the tool-analysis. Heidegger takes presence-at-hand to mean isolation, and indeed a false isolation. Obviously I disagree with this view, since for me *Vorhandenheit* is primarily about *relation*, whether to *Dasein* or something else. But Heidegger really does mean to say that presence-at-hand is about entities considered in abstraction from all other entities, and the reason he introduces his ultra-relational conception of equipment is to counter the *Vorhandenheit* that in his view has dominated Western philosophy since Plato. By contrast, Wolfendale does not want to read *Being and Time* as an argument against presence-at-hand *tout court*, because he prefers an outcome in which there is a "good" form of presence-at-hand for Heidegger: namely, scientific knowledge. That is all Wolfendale is after whenever he employs the wowie-zowie term "modal," which simply refers to his belief that the tool-analysis is all about the difference between "parochial" practice and admirable cognitive abstraction. This is one weapon he uses against my analysis of the bridge in *Tool-Being*. The other is his attempt to show that I contradict myself by relying on the "functional" sense of tools before contradicting myself and saying that tools are "deeper" than any functionality. But more than just claiming I say two different things at different times, he wishes to imply

26 Heidegger, *Being and Time*, 97.

that the step to what is "deeper" than functionality itself *relies* on functionality, and therefore the argument destroys itself. Yet matters are considerably simpler than this.

When covering the so-called "Argument from Execution," we saw that Wolfendale complained about a "modal tension" in *Tool-Being,* in the sense that I refer to tools as an activity, though one that is deeper than any *particular* activity. But this is nothing more than an artifact of his misreading of the pedagogical structure of the book. As Wolfendale admits, despite the early pages in which I refer to tool-beings as actions or executions, the following passage appears later in the book:

> [T]he time has come to admit to the reader that I have been guilty of a deliberate over-simplification […]. In fact, it is impermissible to replace the tool/broken tool distinction with the difference between causality and visibility. For it turns out that *even brute causation already belongs to the realm of presence-at-hand.*[27] (62)

Although Wolfendale calls this an attempt to "resolve the contradiction between functional fixity and apparent change" (62), what it actually shows is that all of his previous complaints about the apparent contradictions of the "argument from execution" are cleared up in the pages of *Tool-Being* itself. Although I still like the term "execution," what Wolfendale calls the "argument from execution" is simply the provisional stage of the argument in chapter 1 of the book before I lead the reader to the central idea of *Tool-Being* in the passage just cited — causation reduces entities to presence-at-hand no less than praxis and theory do. Therefore, the sense in which objects are executant simply cannot be a "functional" one, given that functions are also relations.

In any case, the reader of *Tool-Being* reaches page 221 and finds the passage cited by Wolfendale above: "For it turns out that *even brute causation already belongs to the realm of presence-*

---

27 Graham Harman, *Tool-Being: Heidegger and the Metaphysics of Objects* (Chicago: Open Court, 2002), 221.

at-hand." This means that causal function is now framed as derivative of a prior reality of the things, without which they could never have any effects at all. Any functional descriptions of tool-being prior to that point in the book are only preliminary, as I openly state, and no knowledge of how the book was written is necessary to see that a provisional analysis has been replaced by a final one. The notion of objects as completely withdrawn did emerge *biographically* for me from the initial working hypothesis that functionality was the deep being of things, but there is no *logical* dependence of one on the other. I could have rewritten the book so that it started instead with the claim that even causal relations occur on the level of presence-at-hand, but did not do so because I thought it would be too much for the reader to swallow in the opening pages.

However, this move from the functional/causal to the withdrawn is *my own* move, not Heidegger's, and he clearly means his tool-analysis in the functional sense. Thus, when Wolfendale discusses my use of the language of function/effect/reference to describe tool-beings, while this is not my own position, it is in fact how Heidegger himself should be read. "Taken strictly, there 'is' no such thing as *an* equipment." This means that although Wolfendale summarizes my account of the bridge as some sort of misunderstanding of what Heidegger was up to, it is a perfectly accurate account of the intentions of *Being and Time*. Here is Wolfendale summarizing my interpretation from pages 22 to 25 of *Tool-Being*: "The various girders, nuts, and bolts that compose a bridge are simultaneously depended upon by the bridge and captured in executing their functional role in sustaining the bridge as a systematic effect upon which further things depend" (56). Everything here is correct, although his critical follow-up remark is not: "It is this interpretation of reference relations that collapses Heidegger's account of world into a simple totality" (56). Why does he interpret my reading as a "collapse" of Heidegger's account of world, given that Heidegger's lucid phrase "taken strictly, there 'is' no such thing as *an* equipment" supports me so strongly here? We are led back to the thoroughly mainstream character of Wolfendale's own interpretation, in which the tool-analysis shows us "a complex horizon that involves relations between both types and instances, understood in terms of their possible states" (56). I have already said why Heidegger's analysis cannot be interpreted in terms of a "horizon," for reasons having to do with the need to keep Heidegger distinct from Husserl. A horizon is an implicit background for the human observer, one that perhaps cannot be fully objectified, but is still governed by Husserl's rejection of any reality that might not be the possible correlate of an intentional act as an "absurd" notion. Heidegger does sometimes use the word "horizon" in a positive sense, as when he speaks of time as the possible horizon for the question of the meaning of being. But Hans-Georg Gadamer, who when all is said and done is still one of the best readers of Heidegger we have ever seen, already saw through this device very well:

> True, as the ideas of *Being and Time* unfolded, it seemed at first simply an intensification of transcendental reflection, the reaching of a higher stage of reflection, where the horizon of being was shown to be time. [...] But it was more than that. Heidegger's thesis was that being itself is time. This burst asunder the whole subjectivism of modern philosophy.[28]

I doubt whether one can find even five or six other passages of Heidegger commentary as profound as this one. What it implies is that to speak of Heidegger's analyses in terms of "horizons" is to yield too much ground to "the whole subjectivism of modern philosophy," of which Wolfendale's interpretation is an excellent example in view of his stubborn humanizing of the tool-analysis. As a reminder, this is the sort of thing that Wolfendale habitually says about that analysis:

> Heidegger provides us with an intricate modal epistemology. He builds a phenomenological framework within which he

---

28 Hans-Georg Gadamer, *Truth and Method,* trans. Joel Weinsheimer and Donald G. Marshall, 2nd edn. (London: Continuum, 2004), 247–48.

> analyzes both our understanding of the entities we encounter in terms of both the *normative features* through the practices we are socialized into, the unthematic understanding of the *causal features* of these entities that is implicit in this, and the various levels of thematic understanding that can be developed out of it. His analysis of the encounter with the broken tool is a subtle demonstration of the interface between these levels of modal understanding. (65)

Again we see that it is Wolfendale's interpretation, not mine, that has nothing to do with Heidegger. The role of "normativity" in his reading comes from Brandom, not Heidegger; his mention of "the practices we are socialized into" sounds like it was cribbed from Hubert Dreyfus, not from Heidegger.[29] It already falls well short of what Gadamer saw nearly six decades ago in the passage cited above: that the analytic of *Dasein* is simply the gateway to a discussion of Being itself, and not just Being as the correlate of *Dasein*'s "implicit" understanding. Stated briefly, Wolfendale reduces Heidegger to someone who gives an anthropological account of how various kinds of knowledge emerge, with science his ultimate version of the ascent of man. My procedure is exactly the opposite — by showing that the ideas deployed in the tool-analysis hold good for much more than tools, we can continue to "burst asunder the whole subjectivism of modern philosophy" rather than reinforcing it with tedious "epistemological" and "semantic" scaffolding in the manner of Wolfendale.

In the example I give of the bridge, we see that nuts, girders, cables, and panels support the lateral position of scaffolds, panels, and concrete. For Heidegger, these pieces are not treated as independent units, but as swallowed up into the work they do. The bridge is complete, and in turn enables further actions by the *Dasein* who is not consciously aware of the smoothly functioning bridge. "Taken strictly, there 'is' no such thing as

---

29 Hubert Dreyfus, *Being-in-the-World: A Commentary on Heidegger's Being and Time, Division I* (Cambridge: MIT Press, 1991).

an equipment." Wolfendale objects further that I conflate someone's "mereological" or internal dependence on their own internal organs with "environmental" or external dependence on factors such as gravity or oxygen. I acknowledge no such difference. Someone's crossing of the bridge would be halted equally by a heart attack, the sudden disappearance of all oxygen from the world, or the collapse of one of the bridge pillars. In any of these cases, no matter whether "mereological" or "environmental," the streamlined interlocking of the bridge-system with my own potentiality for being would be ruptured. Wolfendale claims further that I "even [go] so far as to incorporate *negative* dependence relations (e.g., my dependence on a meteorite *not* falling from space into me)" (57). This sounds more like Whitehead's "negative prehensions" than anything I would say. In any case, Wolfendale cites no page reference that can be double-checked, and I certainly say nothing of the kind during the discussion of the bridge from pages 22 to 24 of *Tool-Being*.

He also goes on to speak of a "tension" between what I take to be Heidegger's global holism and my focus on individuals, though he is soon using "tension" instead to refer to a purported problem internal to my own argument. He correctly notes that for Heidegger the individual bridge-pieces are individuated by their place in the total functional system, while for OOO the real individuality is *prior* to any such deployment (58). He then adds, inexplicably, that "the tension becomes manifest in the way Harman connects totality and invisibility through the characterization of execution as functional role" (58). This is hardly a tension, but a smooth demonstration of how the principle that "taken strictly, there 'is' no such thing as *an* equipment" shows us exactly what the tool-analysis is doing. The functional totality of the bridge-system is one and the same as its invisibility, despite Wolfendale's nagging insistence that "invisibility" is merely an epistemic term: apparently forgetting that *Dasein* is always the terminus of any tool-system for Heidegger, and thus that the invisibility of something for *Dasein* is one and the same as its participation in a larger system whose details are suppressed by it. He then makes a false argument against my ontologizing of the situation: "We focus upon what we are doing with the hammer […] rather than the mechanics of the hammer and our use of it. Nevertheless, this phenomenological insight is not meant to preclude the possibility of our turning our attention to any of these easily overlooked details" (58). In other words, Wolfendale argues that the hammer ceases to be invisible as soon as we decide to look at it, neglecting to notice two important complications. First, if we turn from the bookshelf we are building to the hammer, we are now simply inside a new tool-system, one in which the hammer is the terminus, though all of its sustaining parts and environmental conditions (there is no important difference between the two) are still suppressed from view. And second, to look at the hammer is not to eliminate its execution, since we are still objectifying it in our specific *Dasein*-futural manner. This is why the Brandom–Wolfendale implicit/explicit distinction carries no water in this case. Ultimately, whether *Dasein* uses the hammer implicitly or stares at it explicitly, both of these uses fall short of the hammer itself. Yet Wolfendale continues to grant exceptional powers to consciousness awareness: "Our *awareness* of the task as an articulated whole enables us to shift our attention back to any aspect of it" (59). Great. So now we turn our attention from the bookshelf to the hammer, but in doing so we have simply shifted the population of the tool-system and have not converted it into "explicit" awareness.

At this point he announces that "the strangest move is yet to come" (59). What is this uncanny maneuver that I am about to foist upon my readers? "[For Harman,] it is not merely the *visibility* of the parts but their *distinctness* that collapses into the whole — *vanishing* becomes *absorption*" (59). At first this looks like just another repetition of the complaint about conflating the phenomenological (vanishing) with the ontological (absorption), though again Wolfendale misses that it is *Heidegger* who does this for us by treating *Dasein* (phenomenology) as the terminus of a tool-system in which each item of equipment only is what it is within the system, not a substance held in reserve. "Taken strictly, there 'is' no such thing as an equipment." But it is worse than this. For Wolfendale also wants to claim that I am guilty of a logical contradiction, since my reading of the tool-analysis requires the *discreteness* of bolts, girders, and cables, although I then conclude that they are not discrete at all. He comments on this as follows: "This is highly problematic [...]. We would be forgiven for insisting upon a *reductio ad absurdum* of some, if not most, of Harman's premises at this point" (59–60). I will forgive but not forget, before noting the shoddy character of his argument. The point of my mentioning individual bridge-pieces is to show that *the tool-analysis* makes no allowance for their individuality in the first place, but swallows them up into the total system of the bridge. "Taken strictly, there 'is' no such thing as an equipment." I mention the various pieces not to affirm that Heidegger acknowledges their individual character, but to show that this individuality is lost by his tool-analysis from the start. There is no tension at all in Heidegger but rather a contradiction, since he simply dissolves all items of equipment into whatever whole they are serving, which is ultimately some whole for *Dasein*. "Taken strictly, there 'is' no such thing as an equipment." My argument is that this makes a poor fit with his insight into how tools *break,* which shows that taken strictly, *there is* such a thing as *an* equipment! If a trestle of the bridge collapses, it is the trestle that collapses, not the bridge as a whole, and thus we can speak only of a fragile tool-system that depends on the individual reserve of each of its pieces not going wrong. In short, the "live contradictions hovering in the background" (60–61) are not mine but Heidegger's, and that is exactly why I wrote *Tool-Being* and what it is about. Quite simply, Heidegger wants it both ways. Taken strictly, there both *is not* and *is* such a thing as *an* equipment. This is the inherent failure of the most important thought experiment of twentieth-century philosophy. We can either explore its consequences, or we can explain them away in terms of a supposed difference between "phenomenological" and "ontological" levels, even though Heidegger himself erases this distinction by making tools dependent upon their position in the system and the system dependent in turn on *Dasein*. It is Wolfendale who takes the easy way out by artificially separating the two, claiming that Heidegger is merely giving us a "modal" phenomenology of the causal, the implicit, and the "normative." He has not risen to the challenge posed by the case at hand.

After pedantically claiming that he will deal with my argument "one contradiction at a time" (61), he is soon back to trivializing the tool-analysis as giving us a difference between implicit and explicit in the sense of *human awareness* (61), even though Heidegger passed this point long ago by locating "implicitness" in the way that tools fuse into one another in the system. We cannot say that this is merely "phenomenological," as if it could somehow be supplemented with the commonsense assumption of a real world outside the system made up of discrete physical individuals, because Heidegger's relational ontology is far more ambitious than that. Any idea of pre-existent individuals that are only "phenomenologically" one for a *Dasein* using tools must assume the existence of presence-at-hand things outside the tool-system, when in fact Heidegger takes such things to be a derivative *byproduct* of the system as a whole.

Wolfendale goes on to cite the "move" I make with the example of an appliance sitting on a frozen lake. This appliance too, I argue, encounters the lake only as a stable surface (sensual object) whose easy resting on the ice is haunted by a fragility that the appliance does not currently register. When the ice begins to melt, the readiness-to-hand of the surface collapses, and its innate fragility unleashes severe consequences for the appliance, which sinks to the bottom of the lake. As I have already argued, this requires no "awareness" of the lake by the appliance; there is no panpsychism here. The sheer causal dependence of the appliance on the ice turns out to have been just another form of presence-at-hand, just like the presence of phenomena before the mind for Husserl. Instead of claiming to find a contradiction here, Wolfendale returns to another typical anti-OOO trope, "negative theology." As he puts it, "We are once more told what execution is not, but are none the wiser about just what it *is*" (64). Rather than repeating my response to the negative theology charge, I want to ask why Wolfendale still makes a point of using the word "execution," even though *Tool-Being* has already passed beyond the functional sense of this term to treat it as deeper than any function, cause, or effect. Wolfendale falsely states that, "[Harman] does not stop characterizing execution in terms of function. He continues to think of objects in terms of systematic unity" (64). But I *do* stop characterizing execution as function, we have seen, as soon as I note that causation is still a relational notion that therefore belongs at the level of presence-at-hand. In the case of the appliance sitting stably on the frozen lake, the "execution" of the lake *is clearly not* characterized in terms of function, since its current function is to stabilize the appliance, but that function will soon cease, with dire results for the appliance. As for the second claim, that I "continue to think of objects in terms of systematic unity," that is a direct result of Heidegger's own approach. "Taken strictly, there 'is' no such thing as *an* equipment." But it is obviously not my own position, which emphasizes the other side of Heidegger: the thinker of *broken* tools.

I will speak more briefly of Wolfendale's remaining points, starting with the "Argument from Excess." This is not actually a distinct argument that Wolfendale needed to "tease out" (his phrase) of *Tool-Being*. As soon as we realize that execution is not function but what is deeper than any function, it is *already* the argument from excess. Neither *Dasein,* nor a goose, nor a frozen appliance sitting on a lake can relate to another object in its totality. Wolfendale speaks: "the identification of theory and praxis paves the way for the more controversial identification of knowledge and causation" (67). One page later he asserts that I proceed from the "*obvious fact* that the causal capacities of an object can exceed our understanding of them" to the "*contentious claim* that we cannot encounter the real objects in which this excess consists, but only the distinct sensual objects that they withdraw behind" (68). But in the first place, my case is now well beyond the "obvious fact" that the "causal capacities" of an object "can" exceed our understanding of them. For it is not my argument at this stage of *Tool-Being* that real objects consist in causal capacities; that was true only in chapter 1, only as a pedagogical device, before I later said that even causation belongs to the realm of presence-at-hand. The real objects are not just "capacities," which entails possible relations to other objects, but something deeper than capacities. But second and more importantly, what makes it so "contentious" for Wolfendale that causal limitation and epistemic limitation would be conceived in the same terms? Not surprisingly, it his assertion — a mere assertion — that I am "equivocating" between phenomenology and metaphysics, "collapsing" them into one another (69). To repeat, this claim puts Wolfendale at a pre-Heideggerian level by merely assuming that the withdrawal of entities into the tool-system is nothing but a "phenomenological" description of *Dasein*'s experience, although Heidegger's reduction of individuality to presence-at-hand says exactly the opposite.

Another way he puts it is to say that I turn "factual" excess into "essential" excess (69). What he means is basically this: "hey, of course we don't know everything about the objects around us, but that doesn't mean we can't learn it if we try!" What he is obviously trying to preserve here is the claim that science can know the real directly, and therefore we cannot say that there is anything "essentially" unknowable in the things. He also introduces some terminological hair-splitting with the claim that we need not take the objects of encounter to be "intrinsically" unknowable, since they are really just "extrinsically" unknowable to a finite knowing subject. He soon rewrites this as a distinction between "qualitative" and "quantitative" excess, implying that the latter is all that really faces us. As he summarizes his position, "It could simply be the case that the subject can only grasp a finite number of the infinity of features belonging to each thing, but that there is no *particular* feature that is in principle ungraspable" (70). For Wolfendale, then, we are dealing only with an extrinsic and quantitative unknowability. The fact that we cannot grasp *all* the features of a thing does not mean that we cannot grasp, say, 3,000 of them. Wolfendale is right that I favor instead what he calls an "intrinsic" and "qualitative" version of the ungraspable as equivalent to the "substantial reserve" of any thing, though as expected, he blames this on a conflation of epistemic and causal excess, which we have seen repeatedly is really the only argument in his toolbox. He puts it as follows: "The equivocation between knowledge and causation thus disguises an illicit leap from quantitative to qualitative excess, along with the mysterianism it invokes" (72).

Let's deal first with the charge of "mysterianism." As argued throughout this book, the charge only holds if we confine ourselves to Meno's Paradox and think that either we know something or we don't. This basically rationalist position is best expressed in words from Adrian Johnston that I have cited often enough, though it is worth doing so again here:

> [N]umerous post-idealists in the nineteenth and twentieth centuries end up promoting a facile mysticism whose basic underlying logic is difficult to distinguish from that of negative theology. The unchanging skeletal template is this: there is a given "x;" this "x" cannot be rationally and discursively captured at the level of any categories, concepts, predicates, properties, etc.[30]

The problem with this passage is its false dualism between "unknowable x" and "discursive capture at the level of categories, concepts, predicates, or properties." This is precisely the duality that Socrates rejects. For we are in the truth and not in the truth, and although Wolfendale would presumably wish to read this as a merely "quantitiative" excess, so that Socrates already knows a number of things but does not yet know the rest, this is not a very rigorous sense of *philosophia*. Socrates' proclamations of ignorance clearly do not mean "I only know 3,000 things but do not yet know the other 54 million." What it does mean is that we must approach reality obliquely or sideways, and know it indirectly rather than directly. This is not the way that natural science likes to proceed, but there are many other modes of human cognition that do so, from art and architecture criticism,

---

30 Adrian Johnston, "Points of Forced Freedom: Eleven (More) Theses on Materialism," in *Speculations IV*, eds. Michael Austin et al. (Earth: punctum books, 2013), 93.

to biography, to wine tasting. In these cases it is not a matter of "quantitative" failure to reach all the facts, but a question of whether the topic has to do with facts at all, in the sense of that which is "discursively capturable." In the arts and humanities we easily find the "qualitative" access that Wolfendale disdains precisely because he assumes, contra Socrates, that philosophy ought to serve as a private secretary to natural science.

Perhaps more importantly, as concerns "quantitative" ungraspability, Wolfendale recognizes the similarity of his argument to a related objection I often face. Against my argument that direct relations are impossible, many critics have countered that "relations are direct but partial." Since I already discussed this point in connection with Bryant — in the chapter on Shaviro above — I will not review it here in full. But it may be helpful to restate it in Wolfendale's own epistemic terms, rather than the causal ones that arose in debate with Bryant. What Wolfendale basically claims is that I can know some of a thing even if I cannot know all of it. So, let's say I am a botanist who knows 1,000 facts about roses. Wolfendale concedes that there may be "infinitely" many more facts about roses than that, though here I think he is guilty of leaping straight to the infinite sublime, when it may simply be a question of a very large finite number of facts à la Morton in *Hyperobjects*. But to know any given fact about a rose is already an abstraction from the rose as a whole, one that has been removed from the rose itself and has taken up residence in my mind. The reason this cannot entail merely an "extrinsic" unknowability about the rose is that the rose is not composed of a finite or even infinite number of "facts" any more than a house, as Merleau-Ponty wrongly thinks, is made up of an infinite number of possible views. We saw that the house is what makes the views possible even while not being itself a view, and the same holds for the rose: all possible facts about a rose will never add up to a rose.

This leads us directly to Wolfendale's last effort to "tease out" of one of my arguments, which again is not distinct from the others, despite his book-long pretension that I mix different arguments together and thereby force him into Herculean labors of philology. The new, supposedly separate argument is the so-called "Argument from Identity." Although Wolfendale cites its appearance in my article on Ladyman and Ross, its original target was the mathematism of Meillassoux. The reader will recall that Meillassoux holds that the primary qualities of things are those which can be mathematized. He is quick to preempt any charge that this amounts to Pythagoreanism, and to this end develops a theory of mathematics as consisting of "meaningless signs" (an argument found already in Badiou). Stated differently, Meillassoux says he is not claiming that *reality itself* is mathematical, but only that mathematics *indexes* the real primary qualities of things in their own right. The problem is that to do so, he needs to posit the old standby "dead matter" as the external medium in which these primary qualities inhere. As is known to readers of my books, I see no legitimate motivation for any concept of "dead matter." As self-evidently meaningful as dead matter may seem, it has been used primarily to deny accusations of idealism from those who object to the idea of knowledge as extracting forms from the world and bringing them into the mind. Thus, I have objected to Meillassoux that without his arbitrary positing of "dead matter," he would in fact be a Pythagorean, since he would be claiming that perfect knowledge of a lemon and the lemon itself are one and the same thing. For otherwise, the same primary qualities would exist both in the lemon and in our knowledge of it.

Now, Wolfendale splits my counterargument into no less than five separate propositions and tries to map the purported logical blunders that lead me to infer some of them from the others. But the argument is really much simpler than he thinks, as we will see again with Mulhall in chapter 8 in this text. The sole question at issue is this: what is the difference between the forms in the object and the forms in our knowledge of the object? Meillassoux's answer is effectively: no difference. We can mathematize the primary qualities of things (its forms), and this is not Pythagoreanism because the things also consist of dead matter which does not come into the mind along with the forms. For anyone who rejects the concept of dead or even living matter, as I do, this argument does not work. Meillassoux has simply posited "matter" as a bulwark against Pythagoreanism, aided in this effort by the fact that "matter" will no doubt sound to his readers like a good "materialist" principle that supports science, Enlightenment, and the political Left. Thus he is unlikely to get much pushback, except from hardliners like me who see no reason to accept the existence of anything like matter as distinct from form in the first place.

Wolfendale's argument looks somewhat different, though at bottom it is the same. He begins by conceding the difficulty of knowing *all* the forms of the things, perhaps because his preferred model is natural science rather than mathematics, and in science it is more difficult to claim to have exhausted any given topic. There is always an Einstein to follow a Newton, and while new branches of mathematics open up all the time, it is exceedingly rare for well-plowed mathematical fields to collapse completely. That is why these days there are various attempts to reconceive science in mathematical terms by claiming that a certain mathematical core remains even when scientific paradigms collapse: "structural realism," as this strategy is generally known, of which Ladyman and Ross offer just one variant. I hold that these attempts fail. In any case, Wolfendale's argument differs from Meillassoux's through his greater willingness to concede a vast number of unknown properties in the things, even though he calls their unknowability "extrinsic" and "quantitiative," meaning that they may become knowable through future developments in science and technology.

But at bottom their argument is one and the same. For both Meillassoux and Wolfendale, there is no *intrinsic* way in which the forms in the things differ from the forms in our knowledge of those things. And this is precisely what I deny, for reasons related to Latour's famous phrase that there is "no transport without transformation." To extract facts from roses is like taking different viewpoints on a house — it does not get us any closer to the rose than the views of a house get us to the house. It increases our amount of sensual information on these objects, and though Wolfendale claims I conflate sensual with "empirical" information, this is a mere assertion of the superiority of theory over the senses in getting closer to the real, which is precisely what is under dispute. A fact about a rose is a form in my mind, but is incommensurable with the forms in the rose itself. The reason is that any fact about the rose is actually a fact about my *relation* with the rose, which OOO argues is a new object in its own right, just as water is a new object formed from hydrogen and oxygen. Meillassoux's "dead matter" is a poor solution to the specter of Pythagoreanism, but Wolfendale's solution also veers dangerously close to Pythagoras. For while he concedes that we cannot know *all* the qualities of the rose, he offers instead a local Pythagorean theory in which the qualities I do know are the same in both my mind and the rose. And without the assumption of "dead matter" somewhere in the background, he will not be able to explain why my knowledge of the rose's mechanism for feeding is not the same as that feeding itself. An object is not a bundle of thousands of forms that can be peeled away one at a time and directly known, but a system of forms that cannot be abstracted from the object without becoming different forms.

The Fourfold

Wolfendale's pages on my interpretation of the fourfold begin on a shockingly positive note:

> Harman's reading of the fourfold is to be praised for refusing either to sideline it as an unimportant feature of Heidegger's work, or to deny the numerical specificity of the categories constituting it. Moreover, it is to be commended for interpreting these categories as the result of the intersection of two distinctions that it basically gets right: cleared/concealed, and multiple/unitary. (79)

Are we entering a section of the book where Wolfendale thinks I am largely right about something? Of course not. The familiar negative affect quickly resurfaces: "It is in [Harman's] interpretation of these distinctions that everything goes wrong" (79).

Not just certain things, mind you. *Everything* goes wrong. I am reminded again of Detective Marlowe's lament, "All tough guys are monotonous. Like playing cards with a deck that's all aces. You've got everything and you've got nothing."[31] Let's examine Wolfendale's deck of fifty-two aces to see if any of them are real.

He finds that there are two initial problems with my reading of *das Geviert*. "The most serious problem is that Harman conflates the more well-known [1949] fourfold [...] with another fourfold schema found earlier in Heidegger's works — namely, in his lecture course during the Freiburg Emergency War Semester of 1919"[32] (80). But that is not all: "This is complicated by the fact that Harman also misreads the 1919 schema, reading its concern with the 'something' as a matter of singularity as opposed to universality, of beings as opposed to Being" (80). He adds the related complaint that I suppress all trace of the fourfold in the Heidegger of the 1930s, even though that decade would supposedly have provided my best evidence: "Harman overlooks ['The Origin of the Work of Art' and *Contributions to Philosophy*] for the most part, in favor of his attempt to read a continuity with the 1919 schema. It is ironic, then, that his interpretation of the twin distinctions that constitute the fourfold gains more traction upon these works"[33] (81).

Let's begin with the last point. The reason for my focusing so heavily on the 1919 course is to show that the fourfold, usually thought to be an enigma exclusive to the "later" Heidegger, is already fully operative in a lecture course he gave at the age

---

31 Chandler, *The Long Goodbye*, 483.
32 The original source on the 1949 fourfold is Heidegger, "Insight into That Which Is," in *Bremen and Freiburg Lectures: Insight into That Which Is and Basic Principles of Thinking*, trans. Andrew J. Mitchell (Bloomington: Indiana University Press, 2012). The 1919 version can be found in Martin Heidegger, *Towards the Definition of Philosophy*, trans. Ted Sadler (London: Continuum, 2008).
33 Martin Heidegger, "Origin of the Work of Art," in *Off the Beaten Track*, eds. and trans. Julian Young and Kenneth Haynes (Cambridge: Cambridge University Press, 2002), 1–56; Martin Heidegger, *Contributions to Philosophy: Of the Event*, trans. Richard Rojcewicz and Daniela Vallega-Neu (Bloomington: Indiana University Press, 2012).

of twenty-nine. To my knowledge this had not been noticed previously by scholars, although Theodore Kisiel had made a similarly bold claim that the term *Ereignis* (event) — also normally seen as confined to the later period — is the key to the earliest lecture courses as well.[34] Indeed, scholarly commitment to a pivotal "turn" in Heidegger's thinking, and to a corresponding sharp distinction between "early" and "later" periods, is so widespread that to oppose it is already a risky stance. 1919 and 1949 give us the original and ultimate versions of Heidegger's fourfold structure, and thus we need to keep our eyes on these two specific moments in his career. Naturally, it would also be interesting to write a career-long history of this concept in his philosophy. But if I were to do so, I would not follow Wolfendale's rather conventional path of focusing on the "Origin of the Work of Art" and *Contributions to Philosophy*. Instead, I hold that there are two other points in the development of the fourfold that are more important. One of them, unmentioned by Wolfendale, is the portion of *Gesamtausgabe* Volume 50 entitled *Nietzsches Metaphysik*, dating from 1941/42.[35] There we are introduced to a *fivefold* reading of Nietzsche, though it is recognizably Heidegger's own *Geviert* with the addition of an overarching fifth term, seldom used by Nietzsche himself: *Gerechtigkeit* (justice), presumably an allusion to the pre-Socratic thinker Anaximander.[36] Stripped of its fifth term, the remaining fourfold goes on to dominate (however covertly) the whole of Heidegger's more famous multi-volume work on Nietzsche.[37] The bigger omission by Wolfendale, though I discuss it explicitly in *Tool-Being*, is the key role of the twin 1929 pieces "What

---

34 Theodore Kisiel, *The Genesis of Heidegger's* Being and Time (Berkeley: University of California Press, 1995). The reader is referred to Kisiel's Appendix D, "Genealogical Glossary of Heidegger's Basic Terms, 1915–1927," 490ff.

35 Martin Heidegger, *Nietzsches Metaphysik/Einleitung in die Philosophie* (Frankfurt am Main: Vittorio Klostermann, 2007).

36 Martin Heidegger, "The Anaximander Fragment," in *Early Greek Thinking: The Dawn of Western Philosophy*, trans. D.F. Krell and Frank A. Capuzzi (New York: Harper & Row, 1984), 13–58.

37 Martin Heidegger, *Nietzsche*, 4 vols., trans. David Farrell Krell (New York: Harper & Row, 1979–82).

Is Metaphysics?" and "On the Essence of Ground," which again draw our attention to the double axis that first appeared in the 1919 lecture course.[38]

Let us now consider Wolfendale's claim that I "conflate" the 1919 and 1949 versions of the fourfold. Here a preliminary word is in order. Earlier in the book, when referring to our 2010 email disagreement about his blog posts, he tells us that "my own [philosophical] commitments […] are quite different from Harman's, and this leaves little ground for praise on my part" (35). This misses the point, which is not "praise," but *fairness*. One could imagine a book or article filled with nothing but severe criticism that would still be perfectly fair; more than "imagine" it, we have all actually read fine examples of this critical genre. Now, what is it that makes Wolfendale's book not just lacking in "praise" but so fundamentally unfair? It is not just that most of his sections append gratuitous insult to arguments that ought to be left to stand or fall on their own merits. More importantly, the unfairness is found in the various ways that Wolfendale tries to position himself in advance on a pedestal of superior rationality, rather than simply pitting counterarguments against my own arguments and seeing what happens. In his critique of my reading of the fourfold, for instance, he adopts the air of a seasoned veteran marking the efforts of an apprentice with red ink, though it is perfectly clear from the details that my interpretation was the inspiration for his own. One would never realize from reading Wolfendale that the fourfold had been either ignored or trivialized in the decades since its appearance, and that along with the fine efforts of the late Jean-François Mattei in Nice, my interpretation of the fourfold in *Tool-Being* was among the first to treat it as Heidegger's central theme.[39]

---

38 Martin Heidegger, "What Is Metaphysics?" in *Pathmarks*, ed. William McNeill (Cambridge: Cambridge University Press, 1998), 82–96; Martin Heidegger, "On the Essence of Ground," in *Pathmarks*, ed. William McNeill (Cambridge: Cambridge University Press, 1998), 97–135.

39 Jean-François Mattei, *Heidegger et Hölderlin: Le Quadriparti* (Paris: Presses Universitaires de France, 2001).

Yet this sort of failure to give credit where it is due is simply a familiar feature of the brashness of youth; no doubt we have all been guilty of it at some point in our lives. A more important example of unfairness is Wolfendale's claim that I "conflate" 1919 and 1949, since this implies to the reader not just that we disagree about how to interpret these two models, but that I foolishly hold they are one and the same. We will see shortly that this is a falsehood. There is also Wolfendale's claim that I suppress the role of "Origin of the Work of Art" and *Contributions to Philosophy* in an "attempt to read a continuity" (81) between the two models, which again we will see is not true. It is also somewhat odd, given that Wolfendale has read *The Quadruple Object,* and in that book it is made abundantly clear that I do not think the 1919 and 1949 fourfolds are the same.[40] The reader is asked to turn to page 88 of that book and consider the following contrast in the bullet-pointed list:

- 1919: "there is a duel between the apple as 'something at all' and its specific apple-qualities,"

- 1949: "there is a duel between reality as a whole and apple-qualities."

Far from "conflating" the two models, I make perfectly clear that the 1919 fourfold ascribes a separate unity to each individual object, while in 1949 it is the unity of reality as a whole, echoing Heidegger's treatment of *Angst* in *Being and Time* and "What Is Metaphysics?" But not only do I not "conflate" the two models, I treat the 1949 model as a *regression* from 1919, and describe the earlier version as much closer to OOO. As stated in the book, I still think the earlier model can be faulted for treating the "unitary" side too much in accordance with Humean "bundles of qualities." This demonstrates my overriding point that Heidegger simply overlooked Husserl's greatest discovery — the

---

40 Graham Harman, *The Quadruple Object* (Winchester: Zero Books, 2011), 87–91.

tension between intentional objects and their sensual qualities or adumbrations. In this specific respect, Husserl remained the more advanced thinker. In more technical terms, Heidegger's 1919 "formal-logical objective something" (*formallogisches gegenständliches Etwas*) is the same for each and every thing. If we consider the case of an apple, "there is nothing especially applesque about its 'something at all' pole [...] This makes the 'something at all' disturbingly close to Hume's 'bundle,' which does not differ qua bundle in our respective experiences of cotton, dogs, melons, or trees."[41] It is also misleading when Wolfendale says that "Harman underplays Heidegger's version of the cleared/concealed and multiple/unitary axes in order to draw a continuity with his own fourfold" (82), since I make it clear that this is not the case. Only in his footnote 92 does Wolfendale finally make the fair point that I am less explicit about this in *Tool-Being* than in *The Quadruple Object*. I have just gone back and reread the relevant passages and can see that this is true. But I no longer recall whether this was strategic simplification while writing *Tool-Being,* or whether I did not become fully conscious of this difference between my model and Heidegger's until later. That said, from Wolfendale's account one might assume I had missed this point completely.

That brings us to Wolfendale's final major complaint about my reading of the fourfold: "the fact that Harman also misreads the 1919 schema, reading its concern with the 'something' as a matter of singularity as opposed to universality, of beings as opposed to Being" (80). As seen previously, this is not a question of a "misreading," but of a philosophical disagreement between me and Wolfendale as to whether it makes sense to speak of Being in general apart from specific beings. In any case, he draws conclusions that lead him astray. He does begin with the correct observation that "Harman does not so much think that the whole conceals itself, as that it doesn't exist" (83). From this correct premise he proceeds to something fundamentally incorrect: namely, that "Harman's rejection of the whole turns on in-

---

41 Ibid., 88.

terpreting it as a single being composed out of all other beings [...]. This makes Heidegger's position into a variant of what he would call onto-theology, insofar as it comprehends Being in terms of a single privileged Being" (83). He then claims further that I thereby "blend" two separate distinctions, before using a footnote to accuse me of "convoluted transitions" that are "beyond the scope of [his] book" (83n95).

But here it is Wolfendale who "blends" and "convolutes" three separate issues. First, we know that Wolfendale wants to speak of "Being as a whole" without its being treated as a single object. As seen in the previous section, the reason this cannot be done is that Heidegger himself treats the tool-system as a holistic unity; I argued this point above and will not do it again here. Second, Wolfendale conflates Heidegger's aspirations with his own; for we have seen it is Wolfendale who will later concede my point that *beings* can only be known through allusion or other modes of indirect access, while arguing that Being itself is more amenable to direct intellectual treatment. Yet this is merely an epistemological wish, one that makes a poor fit with Heidegger's own insistence that Being must not be confused with any *concept* of it, a point where Derrida shows superior prudence. Third and finally, to say that Heidegger's tool-analysis treats Being as a single entity is not to ascribe "onto-theology" to him, as Wolfendale claims. Although it is true that he blames onto-theology for "[comprehending] Being in terms of a single privileged Being," this is not an argument against *monism*—which Heidegger often verges on himself, given his own conflation of withdrawal with unity—but against *presence*. For Heidegger the problem with onto-theology is less its concern with "a single privileged Being" than with the assumption that this privileged Being can be made directly present to the mind. As seen in my remarks on Gratton, we cannot understand the notion of onto-theology without grasping that it primarily marks Heidegger's break with phenomenology. This is clear from *History of the Concept of Time* and its discussion of why Husserl missed the *Seinsfrage*—the fact that the older thinker interprets being in the sense of "possible correlation with an intentional act."

Let's turn in closing to the remaining sections of Wolfendale's pages on the fourfold, which in typical, needlessly technical fashion he calls "The Argument from Eidos" (84–88) and "The Argument from Essence" (88–95). As a reminder, all of the many sections in his book entitled "The Argument from X" are efforts to support his overriding rhetorical conceit that my arguments are so unclear and intertwined that he had to isolate them for me, though the unbiased reader will invariably find that my arguments are clearer than Wolfendale's own.

He begins with what looks like a surprising concession to my double-axis model: "Harman *does not really need to argue* for the distinctions between objects and qualities, at least insofar as it is a correlate of the *intuitive distinction* between subjects and predicates" (84; italics added). What does need further examination, he thinks, is the way this distinction plays out along the other axis, real/sensual. For the moment, at least, he seems to accept that the object/qualities distinction is not just a correct interpretation of Husserl, but even an accurate diagnosis of intentionality itself. In other words, for now he is granting my claim that the object-pole is distinct for each sensual individual. Since we already know he complains about my doing so on the *real* level, where I also individualize the object-pole rather than making it a general "Being" shared by everything, the current state of his argument seems to be as follows: "It may work on the sensual level, but on the real level it effaces the generality of Being that Heidegger demands." His further summary of my interpretation of Husserl (84–86) is faintly sarcastic, but he mostly lets it pass with no sign of disagreement, aside from an exception I will now consider.

That exception comes with the SO–RQ tension that I call *eidos*. As Wolfendale correctly notes, although I argue that SO–SQ consists of purely accidental qualities that can be subtracted from the sensual object, this cannot be done to SO–RQ without stripping objects of any essential qualities at all, something I could obviously never accept. His objection is not to this point, but to my neighboring rejection of Husserl's claim that sensual qualities are known through the senses and eidetic qualities through the intellect. I recall his asking an astonished question about this very point when I gave my 2012 lecture at the Summer School in Bonn, and it came as no surprise. For Wolfendale, a dyed-in-the-wool rationalist, if the intellect cannot gain direct access to the real then philosophy is doomed.[42]

His horror at my denial of Husserlian intellectual intuition leads him to three additional claims that cloud the discussion further. First, he argues that "Husserl's concept of eidos is an account of general essence, as opposed to the account of individual essence that Harman is attempting to develop" (86). This is clear in *Ideas I*, the only source Wolfendale cites in opposing me, though I refer throughout my argument to the *Logical Investigations.* In this way he opens up a can of worms concerning the relation between the Husserl of 1900/1901 and the Husserl of 1914, a span of time during which he famously shifted from a half-hearted *faux* realism to a full-blown idealism. Given my view that Husserl was already an idealist in the 1890s, I am perfectly willing to entertain the notion that in the *Logical Investigations* eidetic qualities are also meant in the sense of knowable universals. But the point is irrelevant, since I make no claim to be a Husserlian in the first place. I have already discarded his strong opposition between sensual and categorial intuition, and have equally little concern with whether I am being loyal to Husserl's own theory of qualities. Even if Wolfendale could prove to my satisfaction that the treatment of the theme in *Logical Investigations* is not all that different from the later account in *Ideas I,* my response would simply be: "All right then, I disagree with Husserl on this point as well." My homage to Husserl is limited to his crucial threefold distinction between sensual object, sensual qualities, and eidetic qualities, phrased in OOO terminology as SO–SQ/SO–RQ. I take this to be a decisive blow to the empiricist "bundles of qualities" model, and a wonderfully paradoxical recognition that an element of the real (namely, RQ) is embedded in the heart of sensual existence itself. I am under

---

42 My lecture day at Markus Gabriel's Summer School in Bonn was July 10, 2012.

no obligation to accept the additional baggage of Husserl's philosophy, of which his idealism is merely the heaviest.

Yet, and this is my second point, Wolfendale persists in his assumption that I claim to be Husserlian but really am not. This is clear from the end of the section, where he complains that my model "bears no resemblance to the Husserlian phenomenological method on which it is supposedly based" (88). *No* resemblance? He exaggerates once again. Like any other philosopher, I have the right to agree with Husserl on some points but not others, and thus I am free to draw the SQ-SO–RQ triad from him while not accepting his assumption that RQ can be penetrated by the intellect. So offended is Wolfendale by my non-rationalist approach that he echoes Gratton in the false remark that in this way, my argument "seemingly conflates *allure* […] with *theory*" (88). Not at all. The two are completely different. Allure is an RO–SQ fusion produced by the aesthetic withdrawal of a real object, so that the observer has to perform the missing object, as in the case of metaphor. There is no such performance in theory, which occurs along the totally different axis of SO–RQ. To repeat, allure is RO–SQ, and theory is SO–RQ, which means that they share *not a single term*. The only resemblance is that both contain a real element (RO in allure, RQ in theory) which means that there is something that eludes the intellect in both cases. The fact that Wolfendale equally dislikes my accounts of both does not mean they are "conflated" in my treatment of them. That would merely be an "Argument from Emotional Effect" of the sort that Wolfendale otherwise disdains. In short, this is yet another case of Wolfendale disagreeing with me on philosophical grounds while portraying the disagreement as an interpretative blunder on my part.

Let's turn now to Wolfendale's third point, which already bothered Brassier even in the 2007 heyday of our joint collaboration on Speculative Realism. Given my treatment of qualities as individual or specific rather than universal, Wolfendale complains further that "this dearth of generality means that there is no basis for the process of comparison, insofar as there are no qualities that could possibly be shared" (87). That brings us to the following punch line: "this makes the basis of the process of subtraction entirely mysterious, as there are *no criteria* for sorting accidents from eidos. In essence, what Harman does is capitalize upon this mystery" (87; italics added). Here Wolfendale declares his allegiance to an aspect of Modern Onto-Taxonomy that I have called "epistemism." Epistemism is the brand of realism that does not care at all about the real except insofar as it can be *known,* hence Wolfendale's ungenerous reaction to my interpretation of Socrates. Since I insist that Socrates never attains knowledge and does not even mean to attain knowledge, in Wolfendale's eyes this means I am calling Socrates a worthless sophist, in what he calls a perverse misinterpretation of our disciplinary hero equal to that of Aristophanes. Again, this hinges on Wolfendale's "implicit" acceptance of Meno's Paradox, since he thinks something is either knowable or unknowable, and what is unknowable is not even worth talking about: Wittgenstein's "what must be passed over in silence."[43] But in this way Wolfendale merely abandons philosophy for epistemology, throwing *philosophia* into the ditch for the Greater Glory of Science. Yet there are numerous ways to get at the real without knowing it, and not all such efforts are equal. To say that we need "criteria" for distinguishing between the accidental and the essential is to assume that a number of propositions are arrayed equally before us, some of them true and others false, and that valid epistemological criteria are needed to sort the wheat from the chaff. Here we are essentially at the level of Sellars's manifest and scientific images: we confront many images, and some are scientific and others less so. Needless to say, this disappointing metaphysics of images is not how OOO frames the problem. In my model, both allure and theory contend with an element of the real (but not the *same* element — real objects for allure, real qualities for theory) that the intellect cannot touch any more directly than the senses. Here Wolfendale will no doubt fall back on accusations of "negative theology." But we do face the necessity of

---

43 Ludwig Wittgenstein, *Tractatus Logico-Philosophicus,* trans. D.F. Pears and B.F. McGuiness (London: Routledge, 1974), 89.

inventing methods for *indirect* detection of the real, since that is all the real permits. One example of how this can be done is developed in my book *Immaterialism*. If we ask for "criteria" for the essential and inessential elements in the history of the Dutch East India Company, such criteria could never be better than external and accidental: which news made the biggest noise at the time, which battles had the largest body counts, which shipments earned the most money. We have seen that Wolfendale likes to pretend that I never discuss methodology, though in fact I do so frequently. In the case of *Immaterialism* — and there are ramifications well beyond that book — what is sought are moments of irreversible symbiosis between the Company and something else. And here, external "criteria" are not enough. What is required instead is some touch and agility of the sort that Socrates so often showed.

We turn at last to what Wolfendale calls "The Argument from Essence." Here he argues that my interpretation of Saul Kripke's theory of reference "seriously [warps]" (93) Kripke in the same way that I seriously warped Husserl. In the latter case we saw that there was no warping of Husserl, but simply the arbitrary dictate by Wolfendale that since I reject Husserl's theory of the intuition of essence, I am forbidden to borrow anything from him at all. It was a curious argument in that case, and his "Argument from Kripke" has curious features of its own. He again begins by way of Husserl: "[Harman] interprets Husserl's claim that all other intentional acts are founded upon nominal acts as saying that in any intentional relation we are *acquainted* with an immediate 'this' (sensual object) that in turn refers to a shadowy 'this' (real object)" (89). I was confused when reading this because, as Wolfendale ought to know, I do not think Husserl has any conception of real objects at all, given his *a priori* exclusion of objects that might not be the potential correlate of an intentional act. Hence, I followed his citation back to pages 28 to 29 of *Guerrilla Metaphysics,* and immediately found that he got me wrong. Here is what I wrote: "Echoing Aristotle and anticipating Saul Kripke, Husserl holds that names are 'fixed appellations' (cf. 'rigid designators') referring directly to an underlying shadowy 'this' rather than to any particular set of sensual-material qualities."[44] (28). In fairness to Wolfendale, he was probably misled by the word "shadowy," which I normally use when speaking of the real rather than the sensual. But the ensuing passage about Husserl's example of a blackbird flying in the garden makes it abundantly clear that I am speaking, with Husserl, of the blackbird as distinct from its numerous visible properties, not of a real blackbird distinct from the sensual one. Nominal acts, like everything else in Husserl's philosophy, simply have no traffic with the withdrawn real objects that are completely excluded from his model of the cosmos.

Wolfendale continues, with the aid of Fregean terminology: "Names [for Husserl in Harman's reading] are attached to [sensual objects] as if they are the *senses* that determine their reference. This means that *distinct* sensual objects can refer to the *same* real object insofar as one thing can have many names"[45] (89). What Wolfendale probably has in mind is Frege's famous example of "morning star" and "evening star" as two different names for Venus. But in light of Husserl's idealism, some qualifications are obviously needed. Since there are no real objects for Husserl, Venus can never be anything more than a sensual object, though of course we can still call it the "reference" of both "morning star" and "evening star." This cannot be a relation between two sensual objects and a real one (since no such distinction exists in Husserl) but only between two adumbrations and a sensual one. That is to say, I encounter a morning-time adumbration of a bright planet near the horizon, and later in the year I encounter a night-time adumbration of a bright planet. Once I learn they are both Venus, I decide that these two adumbrations refer to one and the same sensual object rather than two different ones. Any talk of real objects simply cannot apply to Husserl. Wolfendale is right in his follow-up point that I do not think

---

44 Graham Harman, *Guerrilla Metaphysics: Phenomenology and the Carpentry of Things* (Chicago: Open Court, 2005), 28.
45 Gottlob Frege, "Über Sinn und Bedeutung," *Zeitschrift für Philosophie und Philosophische Kritik* 100 (1892): 25–50.

descriptions are needed to become acquainted with sensual objects, but I am not sure who would say the contrary, unless it were a philosopher who sees language at work even in immediate perception. Wolfendale is also right that I relate Ortega's term "feeling-things" to sensual objects, insofar as any such object has a unified effect on us prior to any analysis of that effect. Unfortunately, however, I suspect that he makes this connection mostly to associate me with the word "feeling," which fuels his eventual attack on the supposed "emotional introspection" of ooo. But Ortega's feeling-things are not restricted to "emotions" any more than Husserl's intentional objects are; rather, they are interwoven with all manner of features of these objects, including those achieved through theoretical inference. Despite his confusing use of the phrase "real objects" with respect to my reading of Husserl, Wolfendale is well aware that Kripke at least *looks* like a different case. As he frames it, whereas for Husserl the difference is between a name and its sense, with Kripke it amounts to the difference between a name and its reference, so that it looks as if we are headed outside the thought-world correlate and toward reality itself (90). This would appear to be on the right track, although Wolfendale's follow-up gloss of this claim ends up in avoidable error: "Whereas the immediate 'this' [in Husserl] is something more than the *particular descriptions* that give us purchase upon it, the shadowy 'this' is something deeper than every *possible description*" (90). What makes this confusing is that Husserl's sensual object is already deeper than "every *possible* description," which is precisely why Husserl grounds all expressions of a thing in the prior nominal act through which it is given. Whether Kripke's theory refers to the real rather than just the sensual is a separate question, but the difference between him and Husserl is certainly not that between "every possible description" and "particular descriptions."

It is also worth a devoting a paragraph to a genuine point of surprise on my part. Although Wolfendale rarely misses the chance to accuse me of a mistake, he completely misses the biggest one in *Guerrilla Metaphysics,* which I noticed soon after publication: the ambiguity in that book as to whether Kripke's rigid designator points to a real object or a sensual one. There are two passages where I seem to be arguing that it is the real object: (a) "Ortega holds that the inwardness of things is a depth that can absolutely never be fathomed, insofar as it is not interchangeable with any sum of its attributes (cf. Kripke's objection to Russell's theory of names)";[46] (b) "the rigid designator is pointing to a subterranean President Nixon with real [qualities], though by definition it is impossible in the case of real objects to determine exactly what these [qualities] are."[47] By contrast, perhaps the clearest passage arguing that rigid designators point at sensual objects instead is the following:

> What we have with proper names as rigid designators are the feeling-units "gold" or "Nixon," not gold and Nixon in themselves, since these consist only in executing their own reality and can never be reduced to names or thoughts any more than to definite descriptions. A proper name is simply not the thing itself, even if it points more closely to that thing than does an adjective.[48]

As a reminder, the term "feeling-units" is drawn from Ortega's theory of metaphor, and I have argued that it is analogous to Husserl's intentional objects and my own sensual ones. Now, it may seem obvious that by the standards of OOO, reference in Kripke's theory cannot be pointing to real objects. We need only consider his view that the essence of gold is to have seventy-nine protons, a basically scientistic result having nothing in common with an elusive deep essence of the thing. Most probably, what I had in mind when writing the two contrary and misleading passages was that Xavier Zubíri both speaks of the deep non-relational reality of essence *and* locates that essence in a thing's "atomic-cortical structure."[49] Since this sounds a similar scien-

---

46 Harman, *Guerrilla Metaphysics*, 105.
47 Ibid., 199.
48 Ibid., 109.
49 Xavier Zubíri, *On Essence*, trans. A. Robert Caponigri (Washington, DC: The Catholic University of America Press, 1980).

tistic note to Kripke's seventy-nine-proton gold-essence, perhaps I was willing to think that both authors were concerned with a withdrawn essence nonetheless. At present, however, I would argue that Zubiri is much closer to such a possibility than Kripke. The question was best illuminated by Niki Young in Malta, whose knowledge of OOO is vast to the point of unnerving. As he put it in an email to me, rigid designation is obviously not a form of allure, and therefore it must point to sensual objects, not real ones.[50] Here I think Young gets it right.

We return to the main topic. Wolfendale sees me as producing an illegitimate combination of one point from Leibniz and another from Kripke. The Leibnizian point, taken from *Monadology* §8, is that although all monads are one they must also have numerous qualities. For otherwise, (a) they could not even exist, (b) they would not be able to change, and (c) they would all be alike. As Wolfendale accurately summarizes my argument, "if sensual qualities are unable to compose these essences, there must be an entirely distinct type of quality capable of doing so" (92). Nor does he seem to reject this argument; his real gripe is with how I use Kripke. As he puts it, "[for Harman,] because Kripke shows that the *reference* of names is somehow independent of our beliefs about their qualities, the *individuation* of the objects they refer to cannot have anything to do with these beliefs" (91). But this is less a matter of properly understanding Kripke than of the usual disagreement between me and Wolfendale. He thinks that both the true and false qualities of things are available to the mind and we need criteria for sorting them; I think that all the qualities available to the mind come up short of the things, and this is why "our beliefs" can never be isomorphic with what our beliefs are about. Wolfendale thinks this leads to skepticism and negative theology, while I think it compels fresh methods of indirect access to reality. One example of this difference is Wolfendale's point that Kripke merely means rigid designation in a "modal" sense, referring to counterfactual cases such as those in which Aristotle might have been clean-shaven

---

50 Niki Young, personal communication, February 20, 2019.

or chose not to study with Plato, while he calls my own use of these designators "epistemic." As he nicely puts it, "[Kripke, unlike Harman] thus does not think that grasping the essence of a thing is impossible, but simply that it is distinct from grasping the *meaning* of a name that refers to it" (94). But here as with Husserl, I am not sure why Wolfendale thinks I am bound to *all* aspects of Kripke's theory just because I accept some of them. At the 2007 Goldsmiths workshop I called Kripke's position "disappointing realism," and this is the reason why.[51]

On this basis, Wolfendale claims that my position should be called "stubborn designation" rather than "rigid designation," since "[for Harman] names not only refer to the same thing throughout counterfactual variations, but across *all* possible appearances" (94). What is the point of this witticism? For Wolfendale, of course, it is a question of "criteria": if we are to distinguish between the essential and inessential features of things, then all of these features must be equally accessible in order to be judged with blue or red ink, as the case may be. This is what Wolfendale is after when he says that the same property can be essential for one thing and accidental for another: "a living cell's salinity [...] must remain within a narrow range for it to function [... while] a cooked pasta's salinity [...] can vary well outside of this range without dissolution" (92–93). But note that to say this he must treat "salinity" as a universal accessible to the mind, one that can be either essential or accidental; for me, as Wolfendale himself already complained, essential qualities are peculiar to the individual object, a level where even he admits that only something like allure can help us. For OOO, since we know that the essential is inaccessible, what we need are not "criteria," but methods for getting at the essential qualities indirectly, as in the case of the Dutch East India Company. Thus my rejection of "criteria" as the heart of the matter does not mean, as he implies throughout his book, that anyone can say anything they please. Instead, it only means that the real qualities

---

51 Ray Brassier et al., "Speculative Realism," in *Collapse III*, ed. Robin Mackay (Falstaff: Urbanomic, 2007), 379–80.

of things require a more indirect means of access. But of course, Wolfendale's dogmatic rationalist commitment to a continuity between philosophy and science means that he can only view indirect access as negative theology.

His final claim in this connection is an attempt to strike at the heart of OOO's concern with individuals. In the absence of "criteria," he holds, we cannot even know if beings are many rather than just one: "Even more worryingly, perhaps, we are left wondering why we must affirm the reality of discreteness at all, rather some single *Apeiron* underlying a plurality of discrete appearances" (95). His case seems to be that my argument is circular, and to establish this point he quotes me as referring to the "glaringly obvious fact" of the existence of numerous discrete entities. He does not give a citation for this phrase, and I am unable to find this exact wording during word-searches of both *Tool-Being* and *Guerrilla Metaphysics*. The closest I can find is a passage referring to sincerity in Levinas, which runs as follows:

> As Levinas puts it, life is a sincerity, contending not just with a total equipmental system, but with an innumerable variety of distinct elements. The problem is that, for now, we can only concede this existence of individual objects as a glaring experiential fact — no room has been found for it yet in the context of Heidegger's theory.[52]

But the reference here is to a glaring *experiential* fact, which means I am discussing *sensual* objects. Presumably even Wolfendale would admit that at the level of *experience* there seem to be many individual things, and this is the level at which sensual objects are relevant. Obviously, what Wolfendale means is that a plurality of individual sensual objects does not prove that the *real* is not just a One. True enough, but I have never called multiplicity at the level of the real a "glaring experiential fact"; quite the contrary, since the real is for me something deeper than sensory, theoretical, or pragmatic experience. An argument is in

---

52 Harman, *Tool-Being*, 43.

fact needed for plurality on the level of the real; I gave it already in the chapter on Gratton, in connection with Derrida, and will not repeat it here. But I gave the same argument against Ladyman and Ross in "I Am Also of the Opinion That Materialism Must Be Destroyed," an article Wolfendale has clearly read but never refutes. He not only cites it in his book, but was even in the audience in Dundee, Scotland when it was first presented it as a lecture.[53]

Vicarious Causation

The pages on vicarious causation (97–105) are the shortest and least interesting of the three sections considered here, mainly because Wolfendale thinks this theme is motivated by "arguments [he has] already considered and rejected" (97). More specifically, we can say that Wolfendale rejects vicarious causation because of his persistent allegiance to the twin pillars of Modern Onto-Taxonomy, (a) the correlational circle and (b) science-worship. Point (a) is used to deny that object–object interactions are of the same philosophical order as thought–object interactions; given his insistence on an epistemological starting point, he thinks that the thought–object correlate (or "phenomenological horizon") is where all rigorous philosophy must begin. We have seen that this is also the case for Meillassoux, in view of his often overlooked *admiration* for the correlational circle. It is equally true for Badiou's opposition between inconsistent and consistent multiplicity, since the former is treated as only the retroactive effect of a "count," and there is no evidence in his

---

53 My Dundee conference lecture was held on March 27, 2010 at a conference entitled "Real Objects, or Material Subjects? A Conference on Continental Metaphysics." Wolfendale and I were still on reasonably good terms at that point, and I remember him approaching me afterward with the claim that Deleuze is neither an underminer nor an overminer. I was too exhausted from the lecture to respond at the time and excused myself from the room; perhaps he was irked by that incident too, though I meant no harm.

writings that anything but a human can perform the count.⁵⁴ I mention all this to emphasize that here Wolfendale is squarely in the continental mainstream, despite the closing chords of his book that depict me as the calculating purveyor of rampant continental prejudice. While he will claim that OOO is guilty of the most extreme form of correlationism, this is only because he, like Meillassoux, takes correlationism to be the equivalent of finitude, and therefore as something that can only be overcome by securing access to direct knowledge of reality. For my part, I think this *is not* the main problem with Kantian correlationism, which consists instead in a false attitude that is widely taken for a truism: that we cannot speak of any object-object relations without treating them as derivative versions of the relation between objects and human thought. As for point (b), what I mean by science-worship is the notion that only science is permitted to speak about object–object interactions, and that science is doing this so well that philosophers ought to shut up about the matter and merely comment on the results of "the best science we have." Thus, Wolfendale's quick dismissal of vicarious causation is a natural consequence of the rather commonplace biases built into his starting point. If you accept the same biases, then you are likely to give Wolfendale too easy a hearing and not push back with tough questions.

He begins by quoting a passage from *Guerrilla Metaphysics*: "Once it was conceded that the world is made up of withdrawn objects, utterly sealed in private vacuums but also unleashing forces upon one another, all the other problems emerge in quick succession. Let anyone who does not agree with the strategies of guerrilla metaphysics specify clearly which of its initial steps is invalid."⁵⁵ His response to this is immodest: "This is precisely what I have done. None of these initial steps has proved valid, let alone all of them. This seems to rule out vicarious causation by default" (97). But as mentioned, what Wolfendale considers

---

54 Alain Badiou, *Being and Event*, trans. Oliver Feltham (London: Continuum, 2005), 25.
55 Harman, *Guerrilla Metaphysics*, 97.

to be a demonstration of the invalidity of vicarious causation is really just a result of his own biased commitment to the Onto-Taxonomical Two-Step, (a) the correlational circle and (b) scientific monopoly on discussions of the world itself. Let's take a brief look at how this plays out in his breezy eight pages on the theory of vicarious causation.

Wolfendale turns first to the historical context I supply for the problem. Earlier we saw that he concedes I deploy the method of historical contextualization "with some skill," though he then immediately warns that this "could" lead to attempts to intimidate readers unfamiliar with the sources I describe, without giving examples of this ever happening in my work. In the present section he makes a half-hearted attempt to insinuate that I try to intimidate readers on the present topic, though he never comes right out and makes the claim. He begins as follows: "[Harman] provides a further historical narrative regarding the tradition of *occasionalist* accounts of causation, which is meant to suggest that the problem his theory responds to emerges from a broader range of concerns than his own" (97–98; boldface changed to italics). Far from merely "suggesting" it, I have given a number of analyses of the similarities and differences between the different variants of occasionalism found in early Islamic speculation (the Ash'arites), the seventeenth-century continentals (Descartes, Malebranche, Spinoza, Leibniz) as well as Berkeley, whose occasionalism is just as pronounced as that of the others. Whitehead is added to the list as a fascinating historical outlier, a twentieth-century thinker who ascribes a central causal role to God as the mediator (by way of eternal objects) of all prehensions (relations). Wolfendale rightly adds that I read Hume and Kant as providing a different sort of occasionalism, though with the mind rather than God as the sole causal mediator. This argument is important for me, since it demonstrates that occasionalism is not just the laughably outdated religious theory it is often taken to be, but that by transferring causal monopoly to the human mind, Modern Onto-Taxonomy (including Wolfendale's version) remains a derivative form of occasionalism without knowing it. This has the added merit of suggesting a paradoxical secret dependence of modern European rationalism on the most radical theories of medieval Islam, which opens up new avenues of historical research. All of this leads Wolfendale to make the following, unsurprising statement: "Now, although this strikes me as presenting a somewhat perverse reading of Kant and Hume, insofar as it reads their epistemological concerns in metaphysical terms they would abjure, there are definite continuities here" (99). Let's deal first with the charge of "perversity," and second with the apparent concession that "there are definite continuities here."

The supposed perversity of my reading of Hume and Kant hinges entirely on Wolfendale's presupposition of a gulf between epistemology and metaphysics. As already seen, I refuse such a strict division, which is based on an acceptance of the correlational circle that I reject outright. But let's play along for a moment and see where it takes us. It is easy to see why someone would make the charge of perversity. After all, the theological occasionalists all make positive claims about the way causation really works in the world: for the Ash'arites of medieval Basra, God is so mighty that he must be the only causal agent and not just the only Creator; for Descartes He provides a bridge between the two distinct finite substances; for Malebranche it is closer to the Ash'arite view that God mediates relations between *any* two things; for Spinoza, God is the sole substance and everything happens inside God or nature; for Leibniz, what seems like causation is the result of the pre-established harmony between monads ordained by the Lord; for Berkeley, God is the sole producer of apparent regularities that cannot result from the things themselves, which are mere images with no hidden causal powers; for Whitehead as well, all relations pass through God. Obviously, these are all strong metaphysical claims that would count as "pre-critical" or "dogmatic" by present-day standards. But is it not altogether different for Hume and Kant, who merely say that we cannot *know* what causation really is, or know if it even exists, and therefore must focus our attention instead on how something like causality seems to appear to the mind?

The difference is not as great as it seems, and certainly cannot be proven with the terminological artifice of saying that the first group makes claims about the world itself and the second only about human experience of the world. The reason is that the decision to start from what is given to us and not speculate about the shadowy beyond is itself an *ontological* doctrine. Epistemology is merely a name for a specific ontology, not an entirely separate branch of philosophy. Namely, the epistemologist simply assumes that we have direct access to the thought–world relation but no direct access to world–world relations between inanimate things, and thus we cannot philosophize without first examining the capacities of one *specific* entity (the mind) to make contact with the world. The epistemologist and the theological occasionalist are perfectly alike in holding that there is some ultimate important entity whose various relations with reality are *different in kind* from the relations of other entities. Yes, the epistemological standpoint is far more respected today than the theological one; after all, no one has seen God directly, though all of us have conscious experience, and therefore the second alternative looks like a far more rigorous starting point. But the problem is as follows. The fact that we begin (like Hume and Kant) with doubt about whether our own experience provides evidence of causal relations existing outside us *is not* something we glean from our experience of the world, except in the trivial sense that an entity without experience could not philosophize at all. Instead, this very doubt requires an *inference* that there may be a difference between our experience and a world outside it. And by the same token, we can make the very same inference about object–object relations, just as the old occasionalists did. Whenever Wolfendale accuses me of cloudy "methodology," this is all he really means: he is fully on board with the Onto-Taxonomists in assuming that we have direct access to the thought–world relation but not to the world–world kind. Against this prejudice, the OOO methodology is clear — to infer a possible difference between our experience and reality, and to infer another possible difference between the relations of objects and their independence from those relations, is one and the same inference. If we are prepared to give up the possible idealist monism of solipsistic experience (and otherwise science would never work) then by the same token we must give up the notion of direct contact *between non-human entities*. Stated more provocatively, Wolfendale can proclaim a respectable atheism all he likes, but with his insistence on "epistemology" as our starting point, he remains in the basically theological tradition of a single super-powered super-entity that is the root of all other causation.

Aside from that, he strangely admits that "there are definite continuities here," meaning that he basically grasps my point and sees some merit in it. Naturally, he does not pause to appreciate this result and credit me for seeing it. But it is one of the chief historical results of OOO method, and to my knowledge it has never been seen as clearly by historians of philosophy as it has been here, although Steven Nadler has written a fine piece on the occasionalist roots of Hume in the writings of Nicolas d'Autrecourt.[56] Instead, here as always, Wolfendale explores every possible path to saying something negative about my procedure even in cases where he agrees. He does so by changing the subject and saying that all of these thinkers had different *motivations* for considering indirect causation, as if I had not already made this point at length in my pages on occasionalism. As he puts it, "There are overlapping themes that seem to motivate a similar account of causation, insofar as they all demand some form of *causal mediation*. However, this demand does not arise from a single *problem* held in common by the various sub-traditions that make up this narrative" (99). No kidding. It should hardly be a surprise that philosophers can end up in the same place after starting from different motivations, and Wolfendale knows this: do all realists have the same motivations for realism, or all theologians the same motives for believing in God? Do we then need a different name for every occasional-

---

56 Steven Nadler, "'No Necessary Connection': The Medieval Roots of the Occasionalist Roots of Hume," in *Occasionalism: Causation among the Cartesians* (Oxford: Oxford University Press, 2011).

ist system instead of referring to them with a single term? That would be historically disabling. Perhaps sensing that this line of critique is headed nowhere, Wolfendale changes the subject yet again, saying that "we still need some good reasons, above and beyond this narrative, to accept the problematic status of unmediated causal relations" (99). This seems to imply that I think the historical narrative of previous thought on indirect causation is sufficient reason to embrace it once more, though of course I never say such a thing and have never thought it. Rather, the reverse was the case: I came to the need for indirect causation along my own philosophical path, and only then did the homework that confirmed I was not the first to run up against this problem.

Now, Wolfendale knows full well that I came to indirect causation through the *argument* that thought–object and object–object relations are not ontologically different in kind. Rather than contenting himself with a counterargument, he adopts his usual pretense that my argument is so convoluted that he had to expend precious time in carefully distilling it from my writings. We can see this from his typical habit of giving an artificially technical-sounding, analytic philosopher's sort of name to an argument I already make clearly enough: "The Argument from Independence," he calls it in this case. Naturally, he then goes on to call it a "tangle of claims about epistemic access and causal interaction" (100), though here as usual he begs the question by simply assuming the radical difference between epistemology and ontology that OOO always contests. He then promises to demonstrate "a non-sequitur underlying the other arguments" (100).

What is this crushing *non sequitur*? Wolfendale gets off to a bad start by ascribing yet another view to me that I have never held. Namely, he says that my "conflation" of causation and knowledge "[treats] things as *striving* for ends" (100). But I have never claimed that inanimate objects "strive" to have effects on other entities, as my cautious attitude toward panpsychism shows. His argument seems to be as follows: while reference can obviously be either successful or unsuccessful, to say the same thing about causation is an illegitimate anthropomorphization of inanimate beings. The source of this claim in my writings is unclear, for it is not something that Wolfendale found in the underbrush of my "tangle of claims," but something he invented himself. For my part, I see nothing wrong with saying "the fire failed to burn the cotton because it was wet," or even "the fire was unsuccessful in burning the cotton because it was wet." And even if Wolfendale wishes to adopt a highly puritanical attitude towards metaphor — as Onto-Taxonomists always do — and claim that "failure" and "success" should be ascribed only to free conscious agents, we could easily remedy this problem. Namely, we can let him restrict these words to humans if he pleases, however stylistically boring the result, and introduce other language that presumably would not offend him: such as "the speaker *did not* actually refer to an object in the world" and "the fire *did not* burn the cotton." I sincerely hope Wolfendale will not claim further that "did not" should only refer to humans and not be illegitimately extended to inanimate objects, because that would amount to the arbitrary dictate that no words can apply equally to both human and non-human entities, much like German uses *essen* for human eating but *fressen* for eating done by animals. This would be nothing more than an attempt to enforce Onto-Taxonomy with an artificial demand for two parallel languages. In any case, OOO has never claimed that objects "strive" toward anything, which sounds more like the dynamicist modifications of OOO that I reject. Having merely restated a prejudice rather than making an argument, Wolfendale concludes with the air of someone who has successfully accomplished the latter: "It is the equivocation between the standards of representational success and causal success that allows [Harman] to convert epistemic excess into causal independence" (101).

When a question is under dispute, and one party builds his own view in advance into the standards for how the question is to be adjudicated, this is called "begging the question." It is exactly what Wolfendale does here. He seems to know this on some level, since he concludes the section with additional insults rather than further argumentation. My model, he says, is "more like access to *narcotics* than access to *information*" (102).

Of course he will get away with it among many of his readers, since they came for laughs and for the negative affect of the book, not because they want to weigh carefully the respective cases for and against vicarious causation. And though he ends with the claim that "[Harman's] non sequitur is hidden by blatant circularity" (102), we have already seen that Wolfendale is the one trapped in a circle, arguing for a vast rift between the epistemic and the causal by way of *presupposing* this very rift. His lone remaining sentence in the section is simply a mistake: "Harman's aesthetics is an introspective theory of emotional affection" (102). To repeat, I explicitly deny the priority of first-person introspection over third-person scientific description, and treat both as equally derivative of a prior zero-person reality of things.[57] Furthermore, Wolfendale's identification of aesthetics with "emotion" is a scientistic parody of what aesthetics is about, as even a quick re-reading of the *Critique of Judgment* would have clarified; already in Kant it is a question of the disinterest of taste, not the "emotion" of it. At least this misstep reveals the deeply emotional presupposition behind Wolfendale's own biases: namely, that science is cold, hard, and rigorous, while the arts are populated by airy-fairy wussies who can say whatever they want without being refuted. There has never been a more emotional basis for a philosophy than this; in the work of Wolfendale's master, the glowering Brassier, it takes on even more emotional form.

Again offering a needlessly technical name for an argument I make perfectly well, with the aim of insinuating that he has discerned my argument better than I have myself, Wolfendale now turns to what he calls "The Argument from Supplementation" (102). He begins by summarizing my views with perfect accuracy, though I have already done it more effectively elsewhere: "[Harman] defends philosophy's right to tackle the same topics as the sciences by claiming that it can approach them through

---

57 Graham Harman, "Zero-Person and the Psyche," in *Mind That Abides: Panpsychism in the New Millennium*, ed. David Skrbina (Amsterdam: John Benjamins, 2009), 253–82.

other means" (103). Wolfendale takes the opposite view, of course, given his advance commitment to the Onto-Taxonomical division of labor: only science is allowed to discuss object–object relations (and look at how successful it has been!) while philosophers must remain content with transcendental-epistemological reflection on the thought–world relation. As usual, he tries to call my view into question with a redundant reference to the "difficulties we have encountered in determining Harman's methodology so far," which now as always is nothing more than Wolfendale reporting how aghast he is at my not joining him inside the correlational circle of epistemology.

Now citing another passage from *Guerrilla Metaphysics*, in which I complain that naturalism treats causation as "essentially a physical problem of two material masses slamming into each other or mutually affected through fields,"[58] Wolfendale pretends to be appalled at this "incredibly crude version of the sciences" (103), citing "phase space modelling, statistical analysis, information theory, etc." (104) as topics excluded from my "crude" view of science. But Wolfendale knows I was not trying to give an exhaustive catalogue of existing scientific approaches, and even he leans too heavily on the "etc." in the passage above. More importantly, he knows I mean that science as we know it has not explicitly formulated the idea that perhaps all causation is *indirect*. If he somehow thinks it has, then this would only *strengthen* the case for the immediate scientific relevance of OOO. But that is not what he thinks, since he goes on to complain bizarrely about the "crude misunderstanding" that I think science is confined to indirect knowledge whereas *philosophy* can somehow do it directly: "on second thought, the real problem is that Harman's approach precludes him from paying attention to [science] anyway. As far as he is concerned, the sciences don't tell us anything about *reality*. They only talk about it as it *seems,* whereas philosophy can talk about it as it *is*" (104). It is hard to imagine a teaching less compatible with OOO than this. Note first that Wolfendale plays the Game of Hurdles by claim-

---

58 Harman, *Guerrilla Metaphysics*, 18.

ing that I do not think the sciences teach us anything about reality (high hurdle for me) although obviously they must (low hurdle for himself). But in fact, Wolfendale has a rather high hurdle to clear in assuming that science tells us everything we can possibly say about the real better than any other discipline, which is not a difficult proposition to refute. As soon as one demonstrates that the intrinsic reality of any entity cannot be exhausted by any means, then neither science nor any *non*-scientific field can claim mastery of a particular category of objects. And by no means do I think that philosophy has direct access to reality, which is why I argue again and again — unlike Wolfendale himself — that philosophy is *philosophia,* the polar opposite of any claim to direct knowledge. Wolfendale gets his feet even muddier with his more detailed claim that OOO "[seeks] out a special kind of intuition unknown to the sciences" (104). What? For me there is no direct access to reality by any field, whether it be science, mathematics, poetry, or philosophy: which, by the way, is why scientism rather than OOO is close to mysticism in its claim of direct access to truth. OOO does not argue for anything like a Bergsonian or even Husserlian direct "intuition of the real," and I believe I am even on record in support of Brassier's critique of intellectual intuition in Meillassoux's work.[59]

At the end of his pages on vicarious causation, Wolfendale returns to his strange assertion that OOO "amounts to the practice of introspective metaphysics" (104) and even "provides us with an introspective theory of causation modelled upon emotional intensity" (105). To repeat, OOO is fiercely opposed to any priority of first-person, introspective experience — recall that this was one of my arguments against Shaviro — and denies, with Kant, that aesthetics is primarily about emotion. In more recent writings I have treated all art as inherently *performance,* but this is not the same thing as emotion; a dry accountant or lawyer also performs what they do, though with as little emotion as possible. There is also a perfectly obvious difference

---

59 Ray Brassier, *Nihil Unbound: Enlightenment and Extinction* (New York: Palgrave, 2007), 83–94.

between calm and histrionic art, as explored among others by Nietzsche in *The Birth of Tragedy*.[60] What is again telling in this section of Wolfendale's book is that he is so little confident in his argument that he adopts the "rhetorical" method of ending the section with an insult: "The phenomenological trappings in which Harman's metaphysical introspection are clothed are at best a bad disguise, as if an unusually pensive crook were to don a rubber Husserl mask to preserve his anonymity during a hold-up" (105). It would be a fine and amusing image, if not that OOO is a realism rather than a phenomenology, and if not that it denies the privilege of introspection, despite Wolfendale repeatedly belaboring the contrary claim.

General Remarks

That is far from the end of Wolfendale's book. He goes on for almost 300 more pages, taking me to task for a variety of purported philosophical blunders, before giving a bleak depiction of the philosophical wasteland that would result if my ideas were to gain ascendancy. I am portrayed not only as a slick manipulator and a philosophical clown, but as a socially dangerous threat to the ongoing Enlightenment project. Although Wolfendale seems to think that nearly everything I say is erroneous, he also views me as such an insidiously powerful figure lurking in the shadows that at times he seems driven to despair. By the end of the book I no longer recognize any resemblance of his vitriolic portrait to what I know myself to be: a hard-working student of the history of philosophy with a relatively classical orientation toward the theory of substance, who happens to reject the view that science deserves the sole word on the inanimate universe, who also loathes boring philosophical prose of the sort found in many of Wolfendale's heroes (Brandom, Willard Van Orman Quine), and who therefore employs a variety of stylistic means

---

60 Graham Harman, *Art and Objects* (Cambridge: Polity, 2020); Friedrich Nietzsche, *The Birth of Tragedy*, trans. Douglas Smith (Oxford: Oxford University Press, 2008).

to keep the reader awake, alert, and engaged. I suspect this is also a good match for what most readers find in my books. Not content simply to disagree with the basic principles of OOO, Wolfendale chooses to depict me as the grim horseman of an impending new era of darkness. But as complex and detailed as his exposé of my stealthy maneuvers may seem, recall that everything boils down to his acceptance — and my rejection — of the two basic features of Modern Onto-Taxonomy, (a) the correlational circle or epistemological starting point for philosophy and (b) science-worship, where worship means the view that science deserves not only the final word but the *sole* word on anything lying outside human thought. If you accept these two principles, then you are a modernist who belongs on Wolfendale's side of the quarrel. But since I do not accept them in the first place, most of the detail of his book reads to me like an attempt at ruthless deduction from false axioms.

For this reason I will not analyze chapter 3, with its specific discussions of such topics as semantics, qualia, relations, ontological liberalism, and the definition of metaphysics. I have neither the space nor the interest to chase Wolfendale around the arena and answer tit-for-tat after he gets off so badly in chapter 2, though he occasionally makes some interesting claims that I reserve the right to address elsewhere. Instead, the closing pages of this chapter will address the charge that OOO is engaged in what he calls "ersatz interdisciplinarity" (377). Like Brassier himself, Wolfendale has apparently noticed that OOO has been picked up and utilized in numerous disciplines outside philosophy, and seems to be worried about it. Since this is normally an excellent sign of the fertility of a philosophical theory, the Urbanomic publishing circle has no choice but to attack this well-known strength of OOO and portray it as a symptom of weakness. Wolfendale does so with respect to science (377–79), politics (379–83), and art (383–90), and OOO is said to have had a disastrous impact in all three of these areas. Let's consider these themes in order.

His discussion of the supposedly corrupting influence of OOO in its attitude toward science is short, presumably because he thinks he has already made the case earlier in his book. That case, such as it is, amounts to a twofold complaint. In the first place, OOO tries to privilege "introspection" over empirical results, thereby "[providing] more than an escape route for those who have been left behind by physicists' penetrating investigations of traditionally metaphysical topics (e.g., space/time, order/chaos, causality, etc.)" (378). In passing, this is yet another example of how tiresome it is to hear Wolfendale complain online and elsewhere that "scientism" is a "vacuous" term. For his assumption that physics can now take over all considerations of space/time, order/chaos, and causality while pushing philosophy to the side is precisely what scientism means. I would certainly not say the reverse and claim that philosophy has nothing to learn from physics, but the implicit view that one discipline must "dominate" shows the essentially political character of scientism. Brassier's demand that science must be given "maximal authority" is just an especially clear example.[61] In the second place, Wolfendale complains that OOO provides "an elaborate excuse to suggestively dabble in physics" (378). What this means is that it "allows one to claim the support of physics wherever it seems consistent with one's views, while eschewing the reciprocal responsibility to make one's views cohere with physics" (379). As a result, for OOO "it becomes more important to cultivate a taste for the weird and wonderful in physics than to develop an *understanding* of its consequences" (379).

Let's begin by addressing the accusation that OOO buries itself in "introspection." We have seen that this is a perfect example of begging the question, since philosophy can only be called "introspection" if one has decided in advance that it is stranded in the "epistemological" realm of the thought–world relation. In order to get outside thought, Wolfendale assumes, we need *science,* since only science is allowed to speak of object–object relations in which humans are not one of the active terms. Phe-

---

61 Ray Brassier, "Concepts and Objects," in *The Speculative Turn: Continental Materialism and Realism,* eds. Levi R. Bryant, Nick Srnicek, and Graham Harman (Melbourne: re.press, 2011), 64.

nomenology also claims to cover the whole of reality, of course, but it would not be unfair to call it "introspective," given that it limits the whole of reality to the field of possible intentional objects. OOO accepts no such limitation, but has the whole of reality as its theme, including the withdrawn real objects that Husserl simply forbids. As seen repeatedly in this book, OOO is severely critical of the first-person introspective approach and equally critical of Wolfendale's own great love, the third-person scientific standpoint. Both are forms of description that cannot account for the zero-person reality that underlies both. The same holds of course for the overrated Sellarsian distinction between the "manifest" and "scientific" image, an ontology of images as extreme as Bergson's in *Matter and Memory*, despite its veneer of hard-nosed methodological prudence.[62] To invoke Sellars on the "myth of the given" as Wolfendale does works best on Hume, not so well on Husserl, and poorly indeed in the case of OOO, which is perfectly happy to grant the intertwining of perception with theory, since that is what the sensual realm is. Remember, the sensual refers to sensual enjoyment rather to sense-perception, and also includes theory under its rubric.[63] Wolfendale is on even thinner ice when he counters OOO with "the (neuro)psychological reduction of consciousness to the functional architecture of the brain promised by cognitive science" (377). The word "promised" plays an unusual role in this sentence, bribing our confidence with money not yet earned. Wolfendale would certainly be the last person to grant any credence to an intellectual "promise" made by me. It should also be noted that a reduction of consciousness to the functional architecture of the brain is nowhere near in sight. Read Thomas Metzinger's deliberately ominous book *Being No One*, and you will find with comical regularity that he is forced to admit, for one property of consciousness after another, that no "minimally

---

62 Wilfrid Sellars, "Philosophy and the Scientific Image of Man," in *In the Space of Reasons*, eds. Kevin Scharp and Robert B. Brandom (Cambridge: Harvard University Press, 2007), 369–408.

63 Wilfrid Sellars, *Empiricism and the Philosophy of Mind* (Cambridge: Harvard University Press, 1997).

sufficient neural correlates" have yet been found.[64] I would not wish to compare science to a religion, but *scientism* displays the very same features one expects of Calvinist zealotry. The elect are already sure of the eventual Grace of Father Neuroscience, while the others are damned in advance and not worth saving.

We turn now to the charge of an "opportunistic" relation to science, defined as using science only from time to time in order to bolster one's case; the same charge has frequently been levelled at Meillassoux. All the trouble here is caused by one of Wolfendale's own arbitrary assumptions — namely, the Onto-Taxonomical dogma that philosophers have a responsibility "to make [their] views cohere with physics" (379). The problem is that, while no one would wish to propose a philosophy that runs directly counter to basic physics, Wolfendale smuggles in the further tacit dictum that "coherence with physics" applies to philosophy in a *maximalist* sense. Now, it would be foolish indeed for a philosopher to propose that Newton was wrong, and that celestial and terrestrial motions are governed by two different kinds of forces rather than a unified one called gravity. In this respect Newton had important consequences for philosophy, and the same holds for Darwin, whose theory destroyed the philosophers' assumption that the number and identity of life forms has always been the same. Another case of a philosopher being *directly* influenced by a discovery in physics is Whitehead's conclusion that we must listen to Einstein and no longer speak straightforwardly of the simultaneity of different events: "According to modern relativistic views, we must admit that there are many durations [that include an occasion] M — in fact, an infinite number, so that no one of them contains all M's contemporaries."[65] The exact nature of how philosophy and science influence each other is a fascinating though still somewhat obscure topic, and only the most dogmatically scientistic phi-

---

64 Thomas Metzinger, *Being No One: The Self-model Theory of Subjectivity* (Cambridge: MIT Press, 2004); Graham Harman, "The Problem with Metzinger," *Cosmos and History* 7, no. 1 (2011): 7–36.

65 Alfred North Whitehead, *Process and Reality* (New York: Free Press, 1978), 320.

losopher would hold that the philosopher must march in lockstep with contemporary mainstream science. The constant appeals to "the best science we have" forget that the best science is not always the same thing as the consensus science we have, and that sometimes it takes decades if not centuries to sort the matter out.

A good example comes to mind. Although I have never written on the topic, I could imagine myself inclined — on the basis of OOO itself, not "the best science we have" — to argue that time and space cannot have been created. After all, for me these result from the inner strife of objects, and I see no reason to postulate an initial creation of objects *ex nihilo*. In Wolfendale's eyes, this would be an automatic absurdity, since it entails speculating against the grain of "the best science we have," which currently tells us that the universe was created in a singularity or Big Bang rather than having always been present. But why should philosophy limit its speculations to the *current* "best" science, rather than exploring conceptual possibilities on their own terms, possibilities that science may someday eventually need. In the famous dispute between Leibniz and Newton's proxy Samuel Clarke, there is no question that Newton's theory of space and time as empty containers was closer to "the best science we have" of that time. The best science in question, after all, was Newton's own. But the Leibnizian relational theory was much closer to what a clairovyant at the time might have called "the best science we *will* have, once Einstein overthrows Newton two centuries from now."[66] I also doubt very much that Wolfendale would demand that mathematics limit itself to "the best science we have." For if Bernhard Riemann had waited to develop his curved-space geometries until Einstein demonstrated the physical relevance of such space, then neither Riemann nor Einstein would have made their discoveries, since Einstein needed Riemann to get there first. Somehow, philosophy alone is supposed

---

66 G.W. Leibniz and Samuel Clarke, *Correspondence,* ed. Roger Ariew (Indianapolis: Hackett Publishing Company, 2000).

to limp along after whatever science has done in the past few years, always behind and never ahead.

In chapter 5 I will cite a counterargument from the Italian physicist Carlo Rovelli when considering Toscano's objection to "neo-monadological" philosophies such as mine and Latour's. Here I will cite instead a typical remark from the physicist Lee Smolin, who frequently asks philosophers to challenge physicists more boldly and openly. Smolin had the following to say about philosophy, during a heated 2012 debate in the comments thread of Richard Woit's blog:

> I believe that the pendulum is swinging back because many of us [physicists] have learned that an engagement with philosophy does greatly aid a serious assault on the key questions physics faces such as quantum gravity, the foundations of quantum theory and questions as to the choice of laws and cosmological initial conditions.[67]

This is the polar opposite of the "maximal authority" for science demanded by Wolfendale and Brassier. To be sure, other scientists have agreed with these two about the relative uselessness of philosophy in questions of nature — most recently Stephen Hawking, but at an earlier point such luminaries as Richard Feynman and Freeman Dyson.[68] But this dispute will continue, and it cannot be dissolved by the Modern Onto-Taxonomy to which Wolfendale adheres and which he tries to force on me as well. This is true even on topics about which science has nothing

---

67 Lee Smolin, comment to Richard Woit, "Much Ado about Nothing," *Not Even Wrong*, April 27, 2012, https://www.math.columbia.edu/~woit/wordpress/?p=4623&cpage=1#comment-109957.

68 Matt Warman, "Stephen Hawking Tells Google 'Philosophy Is Dead,'" *The Telegraph*, May 17, 2011, http://www.telegraph.co.uk/technology/google/8520033/Stephen-Hawking-tells-Googlephilosophy-is-dead.html. For a response to Hawking, see Graham Harman, "Concerning Stephen Hawking's Claim That Philosophy Is Dead," *Filozofski Vestnik* 33, no. 2 (2012): 11–22.

to say, such as the vicarious/indirect causation that is motivated for me by a problem not even considered by present-day physics.

Another point concerns the supposed "opportunistic" use of physics by OOO. Here it is telling that Wolfendale does not even quote from my own work, perhaps because he has noticed that I tend to be cautious about appealing to the current findings of natural science. Instead he cites Timothy Morton from *Realist Magic*, a marvelous book hated by the scientistic wing of Speculative Realism due to its treatment of causation as analogous to literary forms of allure. I have seen at least one generally abusive tweet by Wolfendale directed at Morton, but in his book he seems most offended by this passage from my OOO colleague: "quantum theory and relativity are valid physical theories to the extent that they are object-oriented."[69] Wolfendale would have done well to provide some context for this statement. As he knows, the usual "opportunistic" use of quantum theory in philosophy is to treat it as proof of a correlationist or outright idealist ontology (Barad, Žižek), usually with reference to the famous double-slit experiment concerning the wave/particle duality of light.[70] Against these anti-realist readings, Morton makes the perfectly valid point that quantum theory tells us reality is made of discrete packets, and hence that this theory is more legible as one in which the *properties* of things are defined by measurement rather than the things themselves.[71] And furthermore, what would a "non-opportunistic" use of quantum theory even look like? For Wolfendale, it would apparently require that we do no more than report what is said by quantum theorists themselves. But this is made rather difficult by the fact that they do not agree among themselves on the key issues, so

---

69 Timothy Morton, *Realist Magic: Objects, Ontology, Causality* (Ann Arbor: Open Humanities Press, 2013), 30.

70 Karen Barad, *Meeting the Universe Halfway: Quantum Physics and the Entanglement of Matter and Meaning* (Durham: Duke University Press, 2007); Slavoj Žižek, *The Parallax View* (Cambridge: MIT Press, 2006).

71 See also Timothy Morton, *Hyperobjects: Philosophy and Ecology after the End of the World* (Minneapolis: University of Minnesota Press, 2013).

that "the best science we have" is not only ontologically but also *physically* inconclusive.

As for politics, Wolfendale introduces OOO's relation to the theme as follows: "There is a peculiar pressure in Continental circles to secure the worth of one's philosophical insights by demonstrating their political applicability" (379). What he neglects to mention is that the "peculiar pressure" at issue is a pressure toward some recognizable permutation of Leftism, and that any theory with even a whiff of Leftness about it is more likely than others to receive a sympathetic hearing in continental circles. Unfortunately, this is equally the case whether the Left position in question is a natural outgrowth of the philosophy as a whole, or whether someone just vaguely waves a black or red flag to show team allegiance, as if it were a question of choosing arbitrarily between Beşiktaş or Manchester United. Wolfendale's master Brassier gives us an especially egregious sample of this tactic when he calls Bruno Latour a "neo-liberal" and shouts vaguely for "revolution" instead.[72] Aside from the fact that Latour is not a neo-liberal but a rather severe critic of *homo economicus,* the main problem here is that "revolution" as a political act is never explicitly justified in Brassier's books, and by no means follows naturally from his pessimistic nihilism.[73] In short, Brassier caved in to "the peculiar pressures in Continental circles" and simply waved the flag of Manchester United to curry favor with his teammates. No substantive political argument can be found anywhere in Brassier's writings to date, and thus his purported commitment to the Left remains pure *doxa,* without philosophical significance. By contrast, OOO has shown patience and courage in not succumbing to demands for a quick and familiar Leftist result.

---

72 Ray Brassier, "Concepts and Objects," 53.
73 A good chunk of Bruno Latour's *An Inquiry into Modes of Existence: An Anthropology of the Moderns,* trans. Catherine Porter (Cambridge: Harvard University Press, 2013) is devoted to the decomposition of economics into the three distinct modes of [ATT]achment, [ORG]anization, and [MOR]ality. To say the least, this is not a "neoliberal" gesture but one of the harshest critiques of neoliberalism in recent philosophy.

Naturally, Wolfendale has nothing to say about this "peculiar" incident involving his friend, but points the political finger at me and Latour instead. I have no problem with Wolfendale calling OOO "the paragon of contemporary ontological liberalism" (380), especially since he is quick to add — I assume sincerely — that there is no direct link between ontological and political liberalism. He makes no direct criticism of my attitude toward politics, but is content with blaming me for "[catalyzing] the development and appropriation of Latour's social theory [… which] threatens to let a methodological mutation in one area explode into a full-blown methodological metastasis across the social sciences" (380). Aside from the intellectual swear word "metastasis," a grotesque rhetorical maneuver designed to compare me and cancer survivor Latour to the horrors of cancer itself, Wolfendale has two specific political complaints about us. The first is that we attempt "to project some form of *ontological egalitarianism* into the political sphere" (381), meaning that we treat inanimate things as "agents" just like humans. According to Wolfendale, this amounts to "[turning] this defunct analogy into an unruly metaphor that confuses our understanding of the very problem we are supposed to be solving" (383), The second is that we indulge in the "political convenience in reducing every social situation to a series of interlocking trials of strength (i.e., a resurrected and rebranded *will to power*)" (381), Although Wolfendale rarely if ever tips his own political hand — though I know from the blogosphere that we share a common disdain for Donald Trump — we can deduce his deepest commitments by simply reversing his two criticisms of Latour and me. Namely, Wolfendale sees politics as revolving around humans rather than all actors equally, and also holds that might and right must not be conflated: there is an "ought" in politics, just as in ethics and science. How do these commitments stack up against Latour's and my own?

Let's begin with the relation between politics and flat ontology. One of Latour's most important contributions to political theory is his idea that "society" is not just made up of humans, but of a heterogeneous series of actors. We see this in early career in his important co-authored article with the primatologist Shirley Strum, where they conclude that baboons are even more condemned to social existence than we are, given that human society is largely stabilized by inanimate entities such as driver's licenses, wedding rings, guns, and the like.[74] In his 1999 book *Politics of Nature,* Latour tries to incorporate the new entities discovered by science into the political sphere, on the same footing as the oppressed and abject human outsiders to whom moralists call our attention.[75] More recently he has been inspired, by the Gaia theory of climatologist James Lovelock, to call for assembling a new collective of humans and non-humans in the face of the threatening Anthropocene.[76] While I do think Latour has already reached interesting results along this path, perhaps its greatest significance stems from its historical novelty. When Wolfendale complains about a flattening of political agency in both Latourian actor-network theory and OOO, he is effectively saying that politics is a human concern whose definition must revolve around human rationality, an utterly Onto-Taxonomical view of the situation. Perhaps without his realizing it, this puts Wolfendale back in the comfortable mainstream of modern political theory, which is centered in the question of whether human nature is inherently good or evil. Jean-Jacques Rousseau is the classic example of a "humans are good" theorist who blames our corruption on society, with Thomas Hobbes a good example of the reverse position.[77] The opposition between these two stances is perhaps best captured by Carl Schmitt:

---

74 S.S. Strum and Bruno Latour, "Redefining the Social Link: From Baboons to Humans," *Social Science Information* 26, no. 4 (1987): 783–802.

75 Bruno Latour, *Politics of Nature: How to Bring the Sciences into Democracy,* trans. Catherine Porter (Cambridge: Harvard University Press, 2004).

76 James Lovelock, *The Ages of Gaia: A Biography of Our Living Earth* (New York: Norton, 1995); Bruno Latour, *Facing Gaia: Eight Lectures on the New Climatic Regime,* trans. Catherine Porter (Cambridge: Polity, 2017); Bruno Latour, *Down to Earth: Politics in the New Climatic Regime* (Cambridge: Polity, 2018).

77 Jean-Jacques Rousseau, *Discourse on the Origin of Inequality,* trans. Donald A. Cress (Indianapolis: Hackett Publishing Company, 1992); Thomas Hobbes, *Leviathan,* ed. J.C.A. Gaskin (Oxford: Oxford University Press, 1996).

"One could test all theories of state and political ideas according to their anthropology and thereby classify these as to whether they consciously or unconsciously presuppose man to be by nature evil or by nature good [... by their] answer to the question whether man is a dangerous being or not, a risky or a harmless creature."[78] Although Latour draws heavily on Hobbes for his own political theory, and to a lesser extent on Schmitt, there is a sense in which his theory entails that Hobbes, Schmitt, and Rousseau have all equally missed the point. Whether we think that human nature is good or actually evil, in both cases we assume that politics is primarily about human nature. Yet this was never really plausible, and is even less so as technological and other means of mediation begin to multiply. By insisting with the moderns that politics remain a purified human realm, void of non-human contaminants, Wolfendale misses the chance to approach political philosophy from a fresh angle.

The other point concerns Wolfendale's fear that a Latourian flat ontology of actants would amount to little more than a power struggle between various human and non-human entities, with no overriding principle of right and wrong. This is one of the central topics of my book *Bruno Latour: Reassembling the Political*; since it was published shortly before Wolfendale's own book, he could not have known what I would say there, although a brief summary will at least show what he misses. As mentioned early in *Reassembling the Political,* one of the four referees who reviewed my book proposal expressed the same worry as Wolfendale, to the effect of "go ahead and write the book and see what happens, but I doubt you will find more to Latour's politics than 'might makes right.'"[79] As it happened, I found a lot more than that. The Latour of the 1970s and 1980s does take pleasure in mocking morality and stressing the "pathetic" character of being right without having the might to

---

78 Carl Schmitt, *The Concept of the Political,* trans. George Schwab (Chicago: University of Chicago Press, 1996), 58.

79 Graham Harman, *Bruno Latour: Reassembling the Political* (London: Pluto Books, 2014), 13.

make anything happen. This comes through most emblematically in his 1981 article with fellow youngster Michel Callon, "Unscrewing the Big Leviathan."[80] Yet everything changes with *We Have Never Been Modern* in 1991.[81] Here he openly confronts Steven Shapin and Simon Schaffer's argument that Hobbes was right and Boyle was wrong, that society trumps science because society itself decides the definition of what counts as good science.[82] And while this is the same sort of argument that Latour himself had formerly made, he suddenly feels horrified by the asymmetry of it. Thus he now claims that if we deconstruct science, we must be prepared to deconstruct "power" as well, placing the two on equal footing. From 1991 forward, Latour is no advocate of "might makes right" but is always alert to what lies outside the currently formatted networks of power. In this respect, we could even say that his politics has become the most ontologically realist side of his philosophy. We have seen that in *Politics of Nature* it is a question of detecting new human and non-human entities wrongly excluded from the political assembly. A few years later, under the influence of Noortje Marres's re-reading of the Lippmann/Dewey debate, Latour is on the scent of the never fully visible object of politics, culminating in what his major book *An Inquiry Into Modes of Existence* will call an "object-oriented politics."[83] In Latour's later writings on cli-

---

80 Michel Callon and Bruno Latour, "Unscrewing the Big Leviathan: How Actors Macrostructure Reality and How Sociologists Help Them To Do So," in *Advances in Social Theory and Methodology: Toward an Integration of Micro- and Macro-Sociologies*, eds. Karin Knorr Cetina and Aaron V. Cicourel (Boston: Routledge and Kegan Paul, 1981), 277–303.

81 Bruno Latour, *We Have Never Been Modern*, trans. Catherine Porter (Cambridge: Harvard University Press, 1993).

82 Steven Shapin and Simon Schaffer, *Leviathan and the Air-Pump: Hobbes, Boyle, and the Experimental Life* (Princeton: Princeton University Press, 1985).

83 Noortje Marres, "No Issue, No Public: Democratic Deficits after the Displacement of Politics," PhD diss., University of Amsterdam, The Netherlands, 2005; Walter Lippmann, *The Phantom Public* (New Brunswick: Transaction Publishers, 1993); John Dewey, *The Public and Its Problems: An Essay in Political Inquiry*, ed. Melvin L. Rogers (University Park: Penn State University Press, 2012); Bruno Latour, *An Inquiry into Modes of Existence:*

mate there is a return to Schmitt's modernism, but only because he thinks we face an existential struggle with global warming deniers. After the initial Schmittian gesture of cutting off these pettifogging opponents as the "enemy," he is back to proposing networks of human and non-human actors, not calling for amoral power struggles.[84] Given Latour's agreement with Dewey that the objects of politics never become fully transparent, he pursues a non-rationalist political philosophy rather than the rationalist one Wolfendale no doubt prefers. But if there is any arena in which rationalism is doomed to fail, it is surely politics. While it is not the case that science is more deconstructible than politics, the fact remains that the decision about what is "rational" in any situation is often determined precisely through political struggle. No epistemologist, not even Brandom himself, will ever be in a position to settle the rival claims to Kashmir, legal abortion, or a Nobel Prize. These will always be, with differing levels of intensity, political struggles sorted out by political means.

We turn in closing to Wolfendale's remarks on OOO and art, which are the weakest and most cynical of them all. Here he makes little reference to my own extensively published views on art, but focuses instead on the supposedly grim effects of my work on artistic and curatorial practice: "The greatest effect that OOP [Object-Oriented Philosophy] has had lies, no doubt, in its appropriation by artists, architects, curators, and the discourses that cater to their theoretical needs" (383–84). The word "cater" is manipulative, since it implies — without evidence — an unscrupulous pandering to the ingrained biases of these aesthetic professions. Like Brassier, Wolfendale sees no especial cognitive value in the arts, and thus he seems unconcerned by how offensive his view of the arts is likely to be. He baldly states, without argument or textual basis, that the "foundational status" OOO gives to aesthetics suggests that "artists can do philosophy *sim-*

An Anthropology of the Moderns, trans. Catherine Porter (Cambridge: Harvard University Press, 2013), 337.
84 Latour, *Facing Gaia.*

ply by doing art" (384). No source in my writings is given for this sweeping proclamation, for the simple reason that I have never said or even fleetingly thought such a thing. All I recall saying on the topic is that philosophy in its original sense of Socratic *philosophia* — for me the pre-Socratics are magnificent but undermining forerunners of philosophy, rather than philosophers proper — is more closely related to aesthetics than to any form of knowledge, given that all knowledge amounts to some kind of undermining, overmining, or duomining. Nowhere have I suggested that an artwork is a piece of philosophy. The great works of Édouard Manet or Pablo Picasso must be called art, not philosophy. Nor do I know any practicing artists who even aspire to be called philosophers, and thus I strongly doubt that this non-existent blurring of disciplinary boundaries is what draws artists to OOO.

But no matter. As mentioned, Wolfendale is less concerned to criticize my own conception of art than to claim, rather insultingly to artists, that they have no clear idea what OOO is all about. In particular, he sees art-world figures as having utilized my explicitly non-relational philosophy as a means of combatting the *Nonrelational Aesthetics* of the curator Nicolas Bourriaud.[85] This too he calls "opportunistic," since "the concept of relation is being deployed differently in each case" (385). A nice point indeed, but one I have already made more clearly myself in an article entitled "Art without Relations."[86] Since Wolfendale does not bother to spell out the different "deployments" of the term "relational," I will have to do it for him. When Bourriaud praises relational aesthetics, he is talking about something that would more appropriately be called "convivial aesthetics," since he is referring to art designed to produce social interaction between gallery visitors. I have nothing *a priori* against such artworks, since the only "relational" approach to art I oppose is the sort that thinks art consists entirely in its socio-political effects

---

85 Nicolas Bourriaud, *Relational Aesthetics* (Dijon: Les Presses du Réel, 1998).
86 Graham Harman, "Art without Relations," *ArtReview* 66 (September 2014): 144–47.

or in the precise reaction of its beholders. Although Wolfendale hints at mass misunderstanding by artists and curators of this nuance, he provides no evidence for his claim, and seems to be relying on limited anecdotal evidence.

There is further cloudiness when he says that "OOP provides a pseudo-aesthetic justification for the Duchampian gesture after its conceptual innovativeness has waned" (386). In the first place, it is unclear whether Wolfendale means to claim that I have purposely bolstered "the Duchampian gesture" in my work, or whether I have simply had a bad unintended effect. If he knew my writings on art a bit better, he would recognize the obvious point that my sympathies are with the explicitly *anti*-Duchampian currents of formalist criticism embodied in the writings of Clement Greenberg and Michael Fried.[87] It would be an understatement to say that the influence of these two critics has been highly marginalized in the arts from the 1960s through the present, and hence it is bizarre to imply that I "cater" to contemporary artistic practice by giving it the exact opposite of what it has demanded for the past fifty years. If anything, I throw down the gauntlet to contemporary practice. This was seen clearly by at least one working artist, Hasan Veseli in Munich, who wrote to me as follows:

> My art friends and I can't understand why you go on and on about Greenberg, although we do get your point (background, flatness). In retrospect it feels that his writings were already assigned an expiration date at the time that he wrote that stuff (probably because of his problems with subject matter, making art just a formalist exercise). Notable critics, from today's perspective, are the likes of Rosalind Krauss, David Joselit, Hal Foster, Arthur Danto.[88]

---

[87] Graham Harman, "Greenberg, Duchamp, and the Next Avant-Garde," in *Speculations V,* eds. Ridvan Askin et al. (Earth: punctum books, 2013), 251–74; Harman, *Art and Objects.*

[88] Hasan Veseli, personal communication, December 4, 2016.

Furthermore, ooo in no way promotes or encourages what Wolfendale calls "curatorial interest in diverse arrays of intriguing objects transplanted from their native contexts" (388). Again, I have nothing *a priori* against such displays; here as with any genre, there are likely to be both successes and failures. Wolfendale is simply indulging in equivocation between "object" in the ooo sense and "object" in the sense of a medium-sized physical entity that might be used as part of an artwork, though I have frequently warned against this in print. Thus, when he claims further that "Harman is entirely happy to supply his own brand of sugar pills" (388) to anyone who uses mid-sized, decontextualized objects in art, he has strayed into the realm of polemical fantasia. For good measure, he adds the emptily cynical innuendo that "there is a surprising amount of money to be made" (388) in such efforts, though I have yet to see much of this purported financial windfall. More importantly, Wolfendale has no knowledge of my communications with professional artists, in all of which I am more the learner than the teacher. Unfortunately, his own philosophical biases are likely to exclude him from such informative dealings with artists, since no one enjoys the sort of belittlement he routinely aims in their direction no less than mine.

Worse yet, Wolfendale completely misses that his own fixation on the "conceptual" side of art puts him much closer to the biases of the contemporary art world than my own approach. For it is he, not I, who sides with Duchamp's bias against "retinal art" and in favor of art that "makes us think," even if he is quick to add that in contemporary art the conceptual focus has "waned." He seems unaware that his notion that art should primarily be a prod to "thinking" runs counter not only to my views and those of the formalist critics I so admire, but to Kant's own view in the *Critique of Judgment*. Worse yet, he does not think that art based on concepts is very good thinking anyway; in keeping with his commitment to Brandomian dogma, any thinking provoked by art is little more than "implicit" and needs to be turned into "explicit" conceptuality, presumably with the aid of epistemology.[89] But it hardly matters, since few artists are likely to have much interest in this set of prejudices, or even take much note of them.

---

[89] Robert B. Brandom, *Making It Explicit: Reasoning, Representing, and Discursive Commitment* (Cambridge: Harvard University Press, 1998).

PART TWO

ALBERTO TOSCANO

Let's begin Part Two by responding to an unusually brief criticism of OOO by Alberto Toscano of Goldsmiths, University of London, a productive researcher of a distinctly Leftist stripe. Although Toscano is close to Brassier and his circle, he has always maintained a level of professionalism in disagreement that is seldom in evidence from the others. Toscano's 2006 debut book *The Theatre of Production* shows speculative talent and an advanced awareness of the up-to-date philosophy of the time; in particular, it remains a go-to source on the philosophy of Gilbert Simondon for those who cannot read his still untranslated major works in French.[1] As mentioned earlier, it was Toscano who organized the 2007 Speculative Realism workshop at Goldsmiths, and he as well who filled in for Quentin Meillassoux when the latter declined to attend the follow-up 2009 workshop in Bristol.[2] The same year saw the publication of Toscano's Eng-

---

1 Alberto Toscano, *The Theatre of Production: Philosophy and Individuation between Kant and Deleuze* (London: Palgrave Macmillan, 2006).
2 Alberto Toscano, "Against Speculation, or, a Critique of the Critique of Critique: A Remark on Quentin Meillassoux's *After Finitude* (After Colleti)," in *The Speculative Turn: Continental Materialism and Realism,* eds. Levi R. Bryant, Nick Srnicek, and Graham Harman (Melbourne: re.press, 2011), 84–91.

lish translation of Alain Badiou's important *Logics of Worlds*.³ Toscano was also on the guest list for my February 2008 discussion with Bruno Latour at the London School of Economics, later published as *The Prince and the Wolf*.⁴ In that capacity, he was one of ten guests who accepted our invitation to submit written questions. I will focus here on two specific passages from Toscano's questions, which the interested reader can find on pages 139–40.

> Does the endeavor to avoid "modernist" practices of abstraction, separation and reductionism for the sake of a neo-monadological theory of actants not undermine any attempt to speculate about "the structure of reality"?
>
> Doesn't the more-or-less panpsychist dramatization of the alliances of actants in jauntily anthropomorphic terms enact the ultimate reduction, whereby objects and things are thought as analogies of human action, in ways far less challenging or surprising than the "reductive" explanations of mechanists and determinists?⁵

Let's treat these objections in order, keeping in mind that the responses that follow are solely my own. Latour would likely respond to Toscano's remarks in a different way.

The first problem with Toscano's term "neo-monadological" is that the prefix is asked to do too much work. He could simply have referred to Latour's position and my own as "monadological," thereby conveying accurate information about some similarities between both of us and Leibniz.⁶ By smuggling in the "neo-" beforehand, he adds a derisive element with the insinu-

---

3   Alain Badiou, *Logics of Worlds: Being and Event II,* trans. Alberto Toscano (London: Continuum, 2009).
4   Bruno Latour, Graham Harman, and Peter Erdélyi, *The Prince and the Wolf: Latour and Harman at the LSE* (Winchester: Zero Books, 2011).
5   Ibid., 140.
6   G.W. Leibniz, "The Principles of Philosophy, or, the Monadology," in *Philosophical Essays,* trans. Roger Ariew and Daniel Garber (Indianapolis: Hackett Publishing Company, 1989), 213–25.

ation that we are merely recycling a historical philosophy that is rightly dead and buried. In so doing, he fails as a critic on two separate counts. The first is that there are highly significant differences between my and Latour's positions and that of Leibniz, significant enough to speak strongly against our being in any sort of "neo-" relationship with the great German thinker. Above all, Leibniz is a philosopher of substance, while Latour is as anti-substance as one can be, since he allows for no enduring entity beyond the series of unending actions that make up the life of any actant. Unlike Latour, I am a philosopher of substance and happily ally myself with the Aristotelian tradition to which Leibniz belongs. Nonetheless, Leibniz draws a rather rigid distinction between naturally occurring "substances" and artificially produced "aggregates," which makes it impossible for him to speak of compounds, machines, or events as objects in the way I do. There is also the not unimportant fact that Leibniz's monads were all created at the beginning of time in order to spare God superfluous labor, an idea that has no analogue in Latour's ontology or my own, given that neither of us recognizes eternal entities despite our shared unpolemical attitude toward religion. Furthermore, the windowless monads of Leibniz hark back to the occasionalist tradition of a constantly intervening God, despite his variant doctrine of "pre-established harmony," while Latour and I both take a secular approach to how contact between two entities is always mediated by a third. Leibniz also leaves little room for free will in his philosophy, and while neither Latour nor I have published a full-blown theory on this central philosophical topic, one would be hard-pressed to find anything resembling determinism in our works. It seems to me, at least, that a theory should only be called "neo-monadological" if it is significantly closer to Leibniz than this.

The second problem is that, in his apparent assumption that monadologies all deserve to have a "neo-" affixed to their name, Toscano fails to grasp why this sort of philosophy might reasonably recur three centuries after Leibniz. As I see it, the chief virtues of monadic philosophies persist to this day, and are as follows. First, they flatten the world in a way that allows us to consider the character of all individual things, without the hasty modern assumption that human thought is radically different in kind from everything else. Latour and I, like Whitehead, offer much flatter monadologies than that of Leibniz, given his reluctance to extend monads beyond entities that exist by nature rather than artifice. This is already a significant revision of Leibnizian philosophy. Second, monadologies try to strike an effective balance between the core individuality of things and their involvement in relations with other entities. Some theories of this kind stress the "windowless" character of monads to a large degree (Leibniz), while others treat relations between entities as much easier to produce (Latour). In Latour's case nothing can touch anything else without the presence of a mediator, as when politics and neutrons were brought together in pre-war France only through the mediation of the physicist Frédéric Joliot-Curie.[7] These being the two chief virtues of monadologies, whoever sweepingly dismisses such theories must not see the point of these virtues. Either the critic does not see the point of a flat ontology, does not see why such a complex theory is needed to account for relations, or both.

Such a person is no doubt a *modernist,* and that brings us to Toscano's complaint about the Latourian critique of modernity, of which I am an enthusiastic adherent.[8] Above all else, the modernist is an *Onto-Taxonomist* who accepts the existence of two and only two basic kinds of things: (a) human thought and (b) everything else. Naturally, the modernist position is not quite as ridiculous as it sounds when stated in this form. The taxonomy is grounded not just in human vanity, though this plays a role, but in René Descartes's effort to produce a philosophy of compelling mathematical rigor.[9] Everything I ob-

7   Bruno Latour, "Science's Blood Flow: An Example from Joliot's Scientific Intelligence," in *Pandora's Hope: Essays on the Reality of Science Studies* (Cambridge: Harvard University Press, 1999).
8   Bruno Latour, *We Have Never Been Modern,* trans. Catherine Porter (Cambridge: Harvard University Press, 1993).
9   René Descartes, *Meditations on First Philosophy,* trans. Donald A. Cress, 3rd edn. (Indianapolis: Hackett Publishing Company, 1993).

serve in the outside world may be purely illusory, but the fact that I am thinking cannot be refuted, since I must be thinking even to be deluded: the famous "I think, therefore I am." Thus the modern taxonomy could be rewritten as: (a) that which is immediately evident and (b) that whose existence is known in mediated fashion. However we write it, the result is the same. Any flat ontology will now look foolish, since human thought supposedly has special status as the immediately evident entity in which all others are grounded; thus it deserves an ontology of its own, rather than being forced to share one with such riff-raff as lobsters, rocks, unicorns, and square circles. And as soon as we turn from "human thought" to "everything else," philosophy has no important role to play, since the natural sciences already enjoy undisputed success in their dealings with inanimate reality. Therefore, philosophy from now on must concern itself only with the relation between human and world, while relations not involving humans will be reserved for science. The twofold taxonomy becomes a twofold division of labor. And when philosophy is thereby converted into critical theory, to which Toscano himself is very much committed, one of the philosopher's major tasks is to detect illegal anthropomorphisms and fetishes that result from improper transgression of one sphere on the other. Monadology, which adopts a false flat ontology and a nonexistent problem of relations between beings, becomes the perfect example of a philosophical joke.

But the counterarguments are as follows. First, the fact that I as a human can only undergo human experience does not entail that I can say nothing about object–object relations not involving humans. For it is not by virtue of inhabiting human experience that I know of my finitude or of the separation of entities into an object-pole and a qualities-pole. These are deduced by means of philosophical arguments, and such arguments work just as well for inanimate interactions as for my reflections on my own thinking activity. Stated differently, I do not need *to be* fire or cotton to know that these entities fail to exhaust one another through interacting. And second, the apparent success of natural science in dealing with such entities does not mean that philosophy has no right to discuss them in its own way. For note that the sciences deal largely with the mathematizable properties of entities occupying space-time, which means that they deal largely with the *relational* properties of things rather than their intrinsic ones. Coleman, following Bertrand Russell in a certain period, speaks to this point: "the concepts of physics only express the extrinsic natures of the items they refer to […] The question of their intrinsic nature is left unanswered by the theory, with its purely formal description of micro ontology."[10] Modern Onto-Taxonomy actually has little in its favor other than its lingering status as a majority position among intellectuals, a situation dating to the era of Hume and Kant.

That brings us to Latour's critique of modernity, which the modernist Toscano obviously views with disfavor. One of the most intriguing features of recent French philosophy is that Latour and Meillassoux are joined in their view that Kant was a philosophical disaster, but say so for *opposite* reasons.[11] For Meillassoux, Kant is a correlationist who excessively *binds* thought and world while forbidding us to treat them in their independence, so that our access to world will never be more than relative or fideistic. For Latour, by contrast, the problem with Kant is that he creates an artificial *separation* between thought and world, although everywhere we find *hybrids* in which the natural and cultural elements are difficult to disentangle. I hold that Latour's view is superior on this point, since human beings are such a minor element in the cosmos that it makes little sense to grant them dominance over fifty percent of ontology. Yet his particular solution to the problem is unfortunate: for Latour, the way to get over the Kantian separation between nature and culture is to insist that they are always bound together, so that *everything* is a hybrid. As a result, he sometimes forces himself into outlandish claims: Ramses II cannot have died of tuberculosis,

10 Sam Coleman, "Being Realistic: Why Physicalism May Entail Panexperientialism," in *Consciousness and Its Place in Nature: Does Physicalism Entail Panphychism?*, ed. Anthony Freeman (Exter: Imprint Academic, 2006), 52.
11 See also Graham Harman, "The Only Exit from Modern Philosophy," *Open Philosophy* 3 (2020): 132–46.

since it had not yet been discovered in ancient Egypt, as if tuberculosis could not exist in its own right before being "hybridized" through its emergence in a cultural-scientific process.[12]

Nonetheless, Latour's diagnosis of modernism remains on target; there is no reason to treat the human and non-human zones as two mutually forbidden territories not to be combined under penalty of death. Toscano is evidently among those who see this as running the risk of anthropomorphism, as when the new monadological theories speak of inanimate entities "negotiating" or engaging in "trials of strength." But this is only a problem if we insist on both a puritanically literal use of language and an utter incommensurability of humans and non-humans, both of which flat ontology denies. It was Jane Bennett who gave the best response to this worry: "Maybe it is worth running the risks associated with anthropomorphizing [...] because it, oddly enough, works against anthropocentrism."[13] Toscano is also quick to assume that monadological theory necessarily leads to panpsychism, but this hinges entirely on what we mean by "psyche." As mentioned above, Skrbina has shown both that panpsychism is more common in Western philosophy than is generally believed, and that psyche can refer to a number of different capacities that must be carefully distinguished and enumerated.[14] Although I do hold that inanimate objects oversimplify each other in their actions no less than humans do, and though I am not nearly as allergic to panpsychism as Toscano and others, we saw in the case of Shaviro that there is an important reason why I do not consider myself a panpsychist. Namely, in the whole debate between panpyschism and anti-panpsychism, the unfortunate assumption is shared by both sides that human thought is something so ontologically pivotal that it must either be: (a) jealously hoarded for humans alone or

---

12 Bruno Latour, "On the Partial Existence of Existing and Non-existing Objects," in *Biographies of Scientific Objects,* ed. Lorraine Daston (Chicago: University of Chicago Press, 2000), 247–69.
13 Jane Bennett, *Vibrant Matter: A Political Ecology of Things* (Durham: Duke University Press, 2010), 120.
14 David Skrbina, *Panpsychism in the West* (Cambridge: MIT Press, 2005).

(b) made a ubiquitous property of every point in the cosmos. The rather different OOO principle that both human and nonhuman objects encounter each other as *sensual* objects rather than real ones does not require any sort of thought, perception, or other form of explicit representation. Therefore, the accusation that OOO is panpsychist tells us more about the fears of the critic than the actual content of OOO itself.

Finally, there is the fact that Toscano does not just accuse me of using anthropomorphic terms for nonhuman things, but of doing so in "jaunty" fashion. While this word is used less frequently in North America than in the United Kingdom, I understand him to mean that the supposed anthropomorphism is deployed in a carefree and light-hearted way, without the hesitant scruples the case requires. All I can do in response is remind him that OOO is the product of years of reflection and tens of thousands of pages of explication. It is no jocular contrarian stunt, but an attempt to rise to the joint "neo-monadological" challenge posed by flat ontology and the problematic status of relations. Toscano's Modernist Onto-Taxonomy is still far more common than my own position, but this is no basis for thinking it more intellectually serious than OOO. As for his further claim that our approach to objects is "less challenging or surprising" than that of the natural sciences, these are simply the words of someone who has too little faith in philosophical speculation. Luckily, not all practicing scientists agree, as seen from the words of the physicist Carlo Rovelli: "I wish that philosophers who are interested in the scientific conceptions of the world would not confine themselves to commenting [on] and polishing the present fragmentary physical theories, but would take the risk of trying to look ahead."[15] Such looking ahead is precisely what we lose when Modern Onto-Taxonomy is adopted as the form of present-day philosophy.

---

15 Carlo Rovelli, "Halfway through the Woods," in *The Cosmos of Science: Essays of Exploration*, eds. John Earman and John D. Norton (Pittsburgh: University of Pittsburgh Press, 1997), 182.

CHRISTOPHER NORRIS

Christopher Norris is based at the University of Cardiff in Wales, and has an unusual dual interest in Derridean deconstruction and scientific realism. To my knowledge, his most in-depth discussion of Speculative Realism can be found in an article in *Speculations,* a journal founded by Paul Ennis and co-edited with a cast of his associates.[1] Most realists will quickly agree with some parts of the article, such as Norris's scathing critique of the empiricism of Bas van Fraassen, which he dismisses as an "absurd position" for its claim that only what can be seen with the naked eye or relatively simple technological extensions can be regarded as real[2] (39). Unfortunately, Norris gets Quentin Meillassoux wrong in two important and inter-related ways, one concerning the "arche-fossil" and the other in reference to "correlationism." The arche-fossil is Meillassoux's term for those objects studied by natural science that antedate the emergence of all conscious life. As Norris interprets him, Meillassoux takes the arche-fossil "to offer a standing refutation of the basic anti-

[1] Christopher Norris, "Speculative Realism: Interim Report with Just a Few Caveats," in *Speculations IV,* eds. Michael Austin, Paul J. Ennis, Fabio Gironi, Thomas Gokey, and Robert Jackson (Earth: punctum books, 2013), 38–47. Subsequent page references are given between parentheses in the main text.
[2] Bas C. van Fraassen, *The Scientific Image* (Oxford: Clarendon Press, 1980).

realist idea that truth is coextensive with the scope and limits of attainable human knowledge, or that it cannot exceed the bounds of cognitive-linguistic representation" (38). Further, he claims that for Meillassoux the arche-fossil "[bears] witness to the basic realist claim that human beings and their particular […] powers of sensory, perceptual, or cognitive grasp are by no means prerequisite to the nature, structure or properties of what those beings sometimes manage to cognize" (39).

Norris sees this realist sentiment as the reason for Meillassoux's pejorative introduction of the term "correlationism," which is "nowadays bandied about by speculative realists with the tone of mixed pity and contempt that once, in the heyday of post-structuralism and postmodernism, attached to the term 'realism'" (40). Norris is unimpressed with this line of argument, which he treats as old news among philosophers of science; the first part of Meillassoux's *After Finitude* "[puts] the realist-objectivist case in a way that is perhaps more striking and forceful than genuinely radical or original" (41). He sees the second half of the book as veering into groundless speculation that conflicts with its purported realism. Meillassoux's theory of the sheer contingency of the laws of nature "is certainly not realism-compatible in any sense of 'realism' that will hold up again various well-honed lines of attack from the skeptical-relativist, constructivist, conventionalist, or anti-realist quarter," something Norris thinks is done more effectively by traditional appeals to "abduction" and "inference to the best explanation" (44). On this basis, "any readers who endorse the arguments to be found in the first part of *After Finitude* should find themselves at odds with, or utterly perplexed by, the arguments put forward in its second part" (45). More than once, Norris uses the term "broken-backed" to refer to this purported tension in the book, a term clearly not meant as a compliment (41, 45). He speculates that this internal contradiction is an environmental effect of post-war French philosophical prejudice against plain old scientific realism, and colorfully bemoans the way that Meillassoux blithely swings across, in the course of one short book, from a hard-line objectivist or ontological realism that takes absolutely no hostages from that Janus-faced adversary camp to a far-out speculative (quasi-)ontology of Heraclitean flux that offers no hold for any but a notional and explanatorily vacuous realism. (45–46)

He also claims in passing that Meillassoux's point about what *precedes* the emergence of consciousness is supplemented by Ray Brassier's assertion that the correlationist approach to science also forbids any knowledge of what happens at "the opposite end" of the time-scale, given Brassier's concern with the ultimate extinction of the universe at some point in the distant future (44).

Now, the central concern of the present book is to answer the critics of OOO, not of Speculative Realism as a whole. But as someone who has written an entire book reconstructing Meillassoux's arguments before criticizing them, I am struck by the remarkable sloppiness of Norris's interpretation. Let's begin with his two factual errors before getting to the more basic issues of misunderstanding. The first error is Norris's assertion that Meillassoux focuses solely on reality prior to consciousness and that it is Brassier who adds the futural point about the universe following the extinction of all matter. While it is true that Brassier's work contains a number of scientific points not found in *After Finitude,* this is not one of them. Norris seems to have completely missed the Meillassouxian term "dia-chronicity," introduced at the beginning of chapter 5 to cover events both prior to the emergence of thought *and* after the disappearance of thought.[3] The point is not a small one, and casts some doubt on Norris's level of familiarity with the second part of the book, about which he speaks so harshly. More damning evidence comes from his assertion that Meillassoux offers a "far-out speculative (quasi-)ontology of Heraclitean flux." Far from it. Meillassoux argues

---

3 Quentin Meillassoux, *After Finitude: An Essay on the Necessity of Contingency,* trans. Ray Brassier (London: Continuum, 2008), 112–13.

explicitly that contingency need not result in flux but could lead just as well to a frozen, cosmic stability. As the French philosopher puts it, "This is not a Heraclitean time, since it is not the eternal law of becoming, but rather the eternal and lawless possible becoming of every law. *It is a Time capable of destroying even becoming itself by bringing forth, perhaps forever, fixity, stasis, and death.*"[4] Once again, this is not a minor passage in *After Finitude*, but a pivotal moment in which Meillassoux tries to fend off one obvious possible misunderstanding of his notion of contingency. The fact that Norris steps so clumsily into this hole, despite Meillassoux patching it clearly and skillfully in advance, again calls into question the carefulness of Norris's reading and further undermines his authority as an interpreter. Indeed, it is so blatantly off the mark that one wonders how it escaped the red pen of Ennis at the journal's editorial desk.

But these mistakes are trivial compared to Norris's wholesale misunderstanding of the way *After Finitude* develops its argument. As he sees it, Meillassoux uses the arche-fossil to "prove" the objective existence of a world outside the mind and on this basis leads Speculative Realism into pity and contempt for the sad correlationist, before it skips analytic philosophy of science altogether and heads off into a land of hallucinatory speculation. This interpretation is worse than sloppy; it is, quite simply, rubbish. The point of introducing the ancestral arche-fossil in *After Finitude* is not to slap the correlationist's face with the cold, hard facts of scientific inquiry, but rather to note an *aporia*. The basis of *After Finitude* is the notion that the scientific realist *and* the correlationist both have a point to make, and Meillassoux sets himself to resolving their dispute. Otherwise, he could have become just another scientific realist much like Norris himself, though in that case his book would have been less interesting. Anyone with lingering doubts on this point simply needs to reread Meillassoux's presentation from the 2007 workshop at Goldsmiths, the entirety of which is a *defense* of what he takes to be the unsurpassable argument of the correlationist: if we think

4 Ibid., 64. Italics added.

something, it is given to us, and therefore we are not strictly thinking of it as "outside thought."[5] This holds no less for the arche-fossil, which Meillassoux, even in *After Finitude*, concedes can easily be reduced by the correlationist to an "in-itself-for-us."[6] In short, Meillassoux does not veer from "ontological realism" in the first part of the book to wild speculation in the second, because he never regards straightforward realism as an option in the first place: "On this point, we cannot but be heirs of Kantianism," as he puts it.[7] This is why it would be of no use for Meillassoux to engage closely with the standard literature of scientific realism, as Norris recommends. Instead, Meillassoux devotes his energy to a complex and ingenious argument for reversing what he calls Strong Correlationism into his own Speculative Materialist position. Now, I have argued in print that this ultimately leaves Meillassoux with nothing more than idealism. But Norris has not bothered to understand the argument, and it is shocking that he fails even to mention the distinction between Weak and Strong Correlationism, not to mention the key phrase "Speculative Materialism" itself.[8] That is to say, the central argument of *After Finitude* never so much as appears in Norris's article, and thus the condescending tone of his piece is puzzling rather than insufferable.

What is more insufferable than puzzling is Norris's treatment of my own object-oriented position, which lacks even the residual respect he occasionally shows to Meillassoux. For instance, "One sign that SR has grown up in a somewhat hermetic research environment is precisely the above-noted tendency, most visible in the writings of Graham Harman, to substitute the word for the deed — or the slogan for the detailed investigative work — when it comes to the real-world object domain" (46). What, exactly,

5   Ray Brassier, Iain Hamilton Grant, Graham Harman, and Quentin Meillassoux, "Speculative Realism," in *Collapse III*, ed. Robin Mackay (Falstaff: Urbanomic, 2007), 408–49.
6   Meillassoux, *After Finitude*, 3–4.
7   Ibid., 29.
8   Graham Harman, *Quentin Meillassoux: Philosophy in the Making*, 2nd edn. (Edinburgh: Edinburgh University Press, 2015), 139–41.

is his evidence for this charge? Nothing more than my stylistic habit of frequently giving lists of assorted objects. As Norris complains, "there is not much point in continually reeling off great lists of wildly assorted objects if the upshot is merely to remark on their extreme diversity, or irreducible thingness, without (as it seems) much interest in just what makes them what they are" (46). In an oddly flowery passage, Norris admits that this technique does allow me to distance myself from the pompous darkness of Heidegger's style: "Much better is [Harman's] light-touch way with Heidegger — his breezy (if somewhat routine) celebration of the sheer multiplicity of objects each flaunting its strictly irreducible *haecceitas* — than the Schwarzwald redneck's solemn lucubrations" (46). But despite granting me this small point of superiority to the "Schwarzwald redneck," Norris thinks I am still caught up "with depth-ontology in the *echt*-Heideggerian mode: that [I find] no room for anything like what a scientist (or science-led philosopher of science) would count as a contribution to knowledge or a claim worth serious evaluation in point of truth-content or validity" (46). This is Norris's first cluster of concerns about my work.

Here there are two separate issues, the first being my purported substitution of lists of objects for actual inquiry into what makes them what they are, and the second my supposedly excessive closeness to Heidegger in dismissing the merely "ontic" character of science in favor of a depth-ontology. Norris is not the first to dislike the lists of objects: or, I should say, to *pretend* to dislike the lists, since he seems to have as much fun as anyone else with the way they counter Heidegger's tone. Ian Bogost has given the name "Latour Litanies" to these lists, due to Bruno Latour's outstanding fabrication of them throughout his many publications. The lists are not meant as "arguments," but have a useful philosophical effect that I would be happy to call rhetorical, if not that "rhetoric" is no longer viewed in a serious way — as it was among Aristotle and other ancient thinkers — but has turned into the pejorative phrase "mere rhetoric" in purported opposition to rigorous scientific inquiry. As Aristotle shows, the point of rhetoric is to prepare the battlefield for argument by shifting attention to the unstated syllogisms ("enthymemes") presupposed by the listener.[9] My lists are not meant as a statement of sheer variety or *haecceity*, as Norris uninsightfully claims, but generally mix human, animal, vegetable, natural, and artificial elements in the same breath. The rhetorical purpose of this is to get my readers thinking in terms of a flat ontology that treats all objects as equally objects, rather than presupposing the Modern Taxonomy in which humans are one kind of entity and "natural" things another, with "artificial" objects such as plastics, oil refineries, hybrid corn, and battleships usually placed sloppily on the "human" side given that humans happen to have produced them. This taxonomy leads directly to the division of labor endorsed by Norris, according to which science should have the only word on the "nature" side. OOO's initial interest is not in the difference between humans and non-humans, but the preliminary equality between objects, and thus the various lists of objects do *bona fide* philosophical work by reframing the reader's conception of how objects might be apportioned into various zones.[10] Anyone who grasps the point early and grows bored with the lists is always free to skip them. Norris is wrong that there is nothing more to OOO's investigation of objects than that, and it is noteworthy that he makes no mention whatsoever of the fourfold OOO metaphysics of objects and qualities that marks a fresh forward step in doing objects justice.[11]

The second point is Norris's insinuation that I am too close to Heidegger in favoring a depth-ontology over science. Now, I am on record as denouncing Heidegger's unfortunate statement that "science does not think," and by no means do I regard science as a merely "ontic" procedure.[12] Since undergraduate days I

---

9 Aristotle, *Rhetoric*, trans. C.D.C. Reeve (Indianapolis: Hackett Publishing Company, 2018).
10 See also Levi R. Bryant, *The Democracy of Objects* (Ann Arbor: Open Humanities Press, 2011).
11 Graham Harman, *The Quadruple Object* (Winchester: Zero Books, 2011).
12 Graham Harman, *Heidegger Explained: From Phenomenon to Thing* (Chicago: Open Court, 2007), 146–47.

have been an enthusiastic student of the history of science, and have always tried my best to keep up with the latest scientific developments, while claiming no special technical proficiency in these areas. While I do agree with Heidegger on the special power of poetic language, this need not entail a superiority of poetic to scientific language. But science aims at knowledge, and I have frequently made the case that knowledge is not the only form of cognition, and that philosophy and the arts should not be understood as forms of it. Knowledge occurs in two and only two forms: "undermining" by reducing objects downward to their components or causal backstory, and "overmining" by reducing them to their effects or empirical observability.[13] I am a *realist* because I think the object itself cannot be fully replaced by any knowledge of it, and in this respect have some points in common with any number of scientific realists for whom Norris himself has high regard, including but not limited to Roy Bhaskar and Nancy Cartwright.[14] I have also developed what I think is a more detailed account of the relation between science and poetics than Heidegger himself, though that account is by no means complete.[15] Norris, being a shining example of a Modern Onto-Taxonomist, is apparently convinced that the modern division of labor gives science the sole right to discuss the sphere of reality that is unfortunately called "nature," whereas I hold that there are metaphysical features of objects that can be dealt with by philosophy alone and not by the natural sciences. Aside from this, many objects are already beyond any adequate scientific treatment, insofar as they are artificial, hybrid, or somewhat elusive. Above all, the tense separation between objects and their qualities, a central topic of my work, cannot possibly be dealt with by a natural science that is primarily concerned with

---

13 Graham Harman, "The Third Table," in *The Book of Books,* ed. Carolyn Christov-Bakargiev (Ostfildern: Hatje Cantz Verlag, 2012), 540–42.
14 Roy Bhaskar, *A Realist Theory of Science* (London: Verso, 2008); Nancy Cartwright, *How the Laws of Physics Lie* (Oxford: Clarendon Press, 1983).
15 Graham Harman, "Aesthetics Is the Root of All Philosophy," in *Object-Oriented Ontology: A New Theory of Everything* (London: Pelican, 2018), 59–102.

the spatio-temporal behavior of physical matter and fields. As I see it, these are all relational properties of objects, while OOO is concerned to isolate their non-relational properties, along with the interaction between the former and the latter. The fact that a philosophy deals with the physical universe in terms different from those of natural science means neither that it is unserious nor that it wishes to *replace* science with speculative ontology, as even Meillassoux has wrongly claimed.[16] Here, Norris would have been better-served by more patience and open-mindedness about work he seems not to know in much detail. It is certainly true that a dialogue between OOO and mainstream philosophy of science could be fruitful, but that will take place on my schedule rather than Norris's own.

Another misunderstanding comes when Norris says that I "get into problems […] when it comes to the issue of causality," and that I make "somewhat desperate recourse to a version of the old occasionalist doctrine—recast as a notion of 'vicarious causation,'" which Norris goes on to describe as "whacky" and "credibility-stretching" (47). Here he distorts and trivializes a topic on which I have worked far more seriously than he has. In the first place, to say that I "get into problems" with causality seems to imply that science and the philosophy of science already know everything there is to know about causation—a strange sentiment in the age of quantum theory and its long-standing tension with General Relativity—and that I "get into problems" by straying from this reliable path. The point is that I *pose* a problem about causality that has only rarely been posed. Namely, given my argument—never mentioned or cited by Norris—that real objects can only confront each other as sen-

---

16 Meillassoux, in "Iteration, Reiteration, Repetition," accuses both me and Iain Hamilton Grant of a "hyper-physics" that transgresses the proper terrain of science. But this only demonstrates his allegiance to the specific division of labor resulting from taxonomical dogma. Quentin Meillassoux, "Iteration, Reiteration, Repetition: A Speculative Analysis of the Meaningless Sign," trans. Robin Mackay and M. Gansen, in *Genealogies of Speculation: Materialism and Subjectivity since Structuralism*, eds. Armen Avanessian and Suhail Malik (London: Bloomsbury, 2016), 117–97.

sual caricatures, there is a problem with understanding how sensual influence can lead to real effects. I do not doubt that such real effects occur, and doubt only that the problem has ever been posed in this form. Admittedly, this particular framing of the causation problem is unlikely to be of immediate interest to present-day scientists. But as seen from the Carlo Rovelli passage cited in the previous chapter, it is by no means clear that philosophers should limp along after present-day science while singing its praises. We are more likely to be of use when pursuing our own interests, which could prove useful to some future state of science. As mentioned, it took nearly two centuries after Leibniz's relational theory of space and time for Einsteinian General Relativity to appear on the scene. By contrast, Norris's pets "abduction" and "inference to the best explanation" are unlikely to have similar imaginative impact on the physics of the future. These ideas are respectable efforts by professional philosophers to explain the extant achievements of science. But that sort of *ex post facto* success is precisely the sort of thing that Imre Lakatos associates with "degenerating research programs" (a term sometimes inaccurately applied to OOO itself) and no practicing scientist will learn much from it.[17]

The second problem comes when Norris refers to my "somewhat desperate recourse" to "the old occasionalist doctrine" (47). While he does note that I "recast" it as "vicarious causation," his reference to the "old" occasionalist doctrine suggests a poor understanding of the difference between the two. When he calls my theory "whacky" and "credibility-stretching," he invites the uninformed reader to imagine that I invoke God as a universal causal agent to escape a self-created jam; after all, everyone knows that this is what the "old" occasionalist doctrine did. Here again, Norris does the reader a disservice by not citing any of my arguments for vicarious causation, or any of my histori-

---

17 Imre Lakatos, *Philosophical Papers*, vol. 1: *The Methodology of Scientific Research Programmes*, eds. John Worrall and Gregory Currie (Cambridge: Cambridge University Press, 1978). See also Graham Harman, "On Progressive and Degenerating Research Programs with Respect to Philosophy," *Revista Portuguesa de Filosofia* 75, no. 4 (2019): 2067–102.

cal remarks about the "old" occasionalists.[18] The differences between these theories and mine are not only clear, but painstakingly enumerated in my writings on the subject. The traditional Islamic and Early Modern European occasionalists, as well as Alfred North Whitehead in the twentieth century, do appeal to God as a universal agent. We need not accept this theory today — I certainly do not — but there were already arguments for this view that deserve better than the off-hand treatment Norris gives them. He also neglects to mention my argument that Hume and Kant are themselves heirs of occasionalism, with the human mind replacing the old occasionalist God; in this sense all modern philosophers, Norris included, owe more to the occasionalists than they realize. My rejection of both the "old" occasionalism and the modern Hume–Kant variant is that both restrict causal power to a single kind of entity. Although the mind is a more generally respectable causal medium these days than God, and epistemology held in higher regard than theology, in both cases one *special* entity is posited as able to engage in direct causal relations though everything else is not. My solution is more consistent: nothing engages in direct relations with anything else, but everything real interrelates through a sensual object, and everything sensual through a real one. If Norris still objects to this, he should at least take the trouble to read my relevant pages on the topic before appointing himself as the enforcer of mainstream respectability.

Unfortunately, his manner of mentioning Speculative Realism only with arched eyebrows seems to have spread to his younger disciples. Norris's recent Ph.D. student Fabio Gironi sneaks the following dig into a footnote:

> Graham Harman, radicalizing Latourian "irreductionism," bemoans all anti-object standpoints "[which] try to reduce reality to a single radix, with everything else reduced to dust

18 See for example Graham Harman, "A New Occasionalism?" in *Reset Modernity!*, eds. Bruno Latour and Christophe Leclercq (Cambridge: MIT Press, 2016), 129–38.

[…]," since they generally fail to fully deliver the "weirdness" of reality, and declares himself happy to think "that electrical and geological facts are permeated by deeper metaphysical vibrations" than contemporary reductionist science can account for. It is hard to identify which kinds of theoretical virtues "weirdness" is supposed to index, and the reader might be excused for dismissing it as an up-to-date, secularized form of *credo quia absurdum*.[19]

While the unearned contempt — including for Latour, who has revolutionized multiple disciplines — is reminiscent of Norris's own style, in one respect Gironi's passage is worse, since it is written largely in bad faith. For although he feigns ignorance of "which kinds of theoretical virtues 'weirdness' is supposed to index," he is sufficiently familiar with my work to know the answer to this question in advance, and I therefore conclude he is mainly playing for laughs. As Gironi is well aware, "weirdness" is a precise technical term in my philosophy, one with both a solid etymological pedigree and an impressive canonical user in the person of William Shakespeare.[20] For OOO, the experience of the weird marks the important encounter with a rift between objects and their qualities, a rift that happens to lie at the center of my theory. It is something to be believed not "because it is absurd" but because it is compellingly strange, which is often enough the mark of ideas with staying power. Would it not be better for everyone if Norris and Gironi directly addressed my *arguments* for the object/quality split, drawn in part from the eminent pages of Leibniz and Husserl, rather than waving the flag of scientific rationalism while speaking in the snarky argot of schoolboys and aping deconstruction's overdependence on scare-quotes? Since Norris is the teacher in this case, I hold him personally responsible for the sloppy remarks and bad form of both.

19 Fabio Gironi, "Between Naturalism and Realism: A New Realist Landscape," *Journal of Critical Realism* 11, no. 3 (2012): 383, 79n.
20 Graham Harman, *Weird Realism: Lovecraft and Philosophy* (Winchester: Zero Books, 2012); William Shakespeare, *Macbeth*, eds. S. Clark and P. Mason (London: Bloomsbury, 2015).

DAN ZAHAVI

I will speak now of Dan Zahavi, who resembles Norris in his critical posture towards all that Speculative Realism represents, as seen from Zahavi's dismissive review of Tom Sparrow's *The End of Phenomenology*.[1] The title of that book being what it is, Sparrow was always destined for some negative feedback, and he was well aware of the risk. Phenomenology is a well-established school with a sophisticated bureaucratic apparatus, equipped with societies and publishing series overseen by presiding officers, gatekeepers, and expert technicians, none of them amused to hear the claim that they are defending a theory whose time has passed. In many cases, phenomenology's conflict with its newer critics simply displays the usual features of generational warfare. For this reason, Speculative Realism might well proceed by way of Max Planck's verdict that crabby, I've-seen-it-all opponents of any new theory are often best waited out rather than assaulted frontally. Yet this method will not work with Zahavi. According to published information he was born on November 6, 1967, which would put him in the same high school graduating class as Quentin Meillassoux and I. Despite Zahavi's relative youth,

---

1 Dan Zahavi, "The End of What? Phenomenology vs. Speculative Realism," *International Journal of Philosophical Studies* 24, no. 3 (2016): 289–309. Subsequent page references are given between parentheses in the main text.

he is an ambitious and prolific author, long regarded as one of the world's leading experts on phenomenology. In his review of Sparrow's book, he manages to take shots at each of the original Speculative Realist authors, although just as with Christopher Norris, it is OOO which takes the brunt of the criticism. Here I will summarize the key points of his attack, before explaining what he misses about Speculative Realism more generally.

Much of Zahavi's article is a critique of Sparrow. For reasons of space I will not spend much time here defending Sparrow, which he is perfectly capable of doing himself. I would just cite the following passage from Zahavi, since it contains both my chief agreement and disagreement with Sparrow: "[according to Sparrow,] speculative realism delivers what phenomenology always promised, but never provided: a full-fledged defense of realism. On the other hand, however, Sparrow also argues that phenomenology never really got started […] since no proponent of phenomenology has ever been able to adequately clarify its method, scope, and metaphysical commitments'" (290). I have already agreed with Sparrow's claim about realism. Edmund Husserl is quite serious in his claim to return to "the things themselves," but is unable to do so because of his disqualification of objects that could not be, in principle, the correlate of some intentional act. But such objects, which Kant calls the thing-in-itself and I call real objects, are the core subject matter of OOO. We reject the Modernist Onto-Taxonomy that feels obliged to begin from a transcendental standpoint and then somehow decides that the things themselves are already dealt with sufficiently and exhaustively by natural science. As for Sparrow's claim that no one has ever fully established what phenomenology is, I have agreed with him that "description" is too vague to do the trick, though I also think — like Zahavi, evidently (305n2) — that an airtight definition is too stringent a standard for any philosophical school to meet. As I see it, we are inside phenomenology as soon as we suspend the actuality of the real world (the phenomenological reduction) and focus on the tension between intentional objects and their adumbrations in an effort to reach their essential qualities (the eidetic reduction).

The reason I am not a phenomenologist, despite great sympathy for Husserl and his successors, is that I oppose the bracketing of the real and do not agree that the intellect can lead us to an intuition of essences any better than the senses can. In short, essences are not intuitable either sensuously or intellectually, but are accessed by way of allusion and other indirect means. Since Zahavi is a professional phenomenologist, it should come as no surprise that he would be hostile both to my view and to Sparrow's. For me the problem is not that "the reduction can never be completed," a view in which Zahavi draws on the support of Maurice Merleau-Ponty (291). Instead, the problem is that Merleau-Ponty *does* complete it, despite his disclaimer as summarized by Zahavi: "even the most radical reflection depends upon and is linked to an unreflected life" (291). This is not really the point, since the difference between radical reflection and unreflected life unfolds entirely within the human sphere, and thus Merleau-Ponty makes no room for the real. As proof of this, consider the way that his supposedly most futuristic doctrine, that of "the flesh" in *The Visible and the Invisible*, tells us merely that the world looks at us just as we look at it. Nothing is said about the interaction of parts of the world with each other, which is a key aspect of any *bona fide* realism. A mere "realism of the residue" like this one is not realism, but simply idealism with an alibi. Zahavi and Merleau-Ponty are both correct that even "Heidegger's analysis of being-in-the-world presupposes the reduction" (291), but this proves the opposite of what they think. Namely, it shows that Heidegger remains stuck in a transcendental-phenomenological standpoint, as is his clear from his own assumption that the difference between praxis and theory is some sort of major ontological rift, rather than simply two different ways of converting real things into sensual ones.

Turning now to Speculative Realism, Zahavi goes slightly astray in characterizing it as bitterly opposed to Kant (293). This largely holds for Meillassoux, though Zahavi only seems to know *After Finitude*, and thus misses Meillassoux's later extension of the term back to David Hume.² It is certainly true that Meillassoux bemoans the "Kantian catastrophe," and this puts him close to Alain Badiou's own claim that the Kant-event has "poisoned philosophy."³ This no doubt has something to do with their national preference for a resurgent French rationalism that takes alternative inspiration from René Descartes, for whom finitude is not a factor the way it is for Kant.⁴ Zahavi quotes five exemplary passages from Husserl by way of proudly admitting that, yes, Husserl was a correlationist (293–94). He also quotes Ian Bogost and me, accurately enough, as saying that the relation between objects is no different in kind from that between thought and world.⁵ After first noting the superficial similarity between this position and philosophical naturalism, he deftly cites Timothy Morton to show that there is actually a big difference between the two. In Zahavi's words, "if anything the aim seems the reverse [of naturalism's], namely to finally recognize that all objects, including fireplaces, lawnmowers or slices of rotting pork possess an inner infinity of their own"⁶ (295). Zahavi wonders whether such a move really suspends correlationism or simply spreads it throughout the cosmos. To his credit, he has read and understood my response to this objection — in those passages referenced in the Steven Shaviro chapter above — where I worry that panpsychism continues to assume that human psyche is so

---

2   Quentin Meillassoux, "Iteration, Reiteration, Repetition: A Speculative Analysis of the Meaningless Sign," trans. Robin Mackay and M. Gansen, in *Genealogies of Speculation: Materialism and Subjectivity since Structuralism,* eds. Armen Avanessian and Suhail Malik (London: Bloomsbury, 2016), 117–97.

3   Alain Badiou, *Logics of Worlds: Being and Event II,* trans. Alberto Toscano (London: Continuum, 2009), 535.

4   Quentin Meillassoux, *After Finitude: An Essay on the Necessity of Contingency,* trans. Ray Brassier (London: Continuum, 2008), 124; Badiou, Logics of Worlds, 535.

5   Graham Harman, *Guerrilla Metaphysics: Phenomenology and the Carpentry of Things* (Chicago: Open Court, 2005), 75; Ian Bogost, *Alien Phenomenology, or What It's Like to Be a Thing* (Minneapolis: University of Minnesota Press, 2012), 30.

6   Timothy Morton, "Art in the Age of Asymmetry: Hegel, Objects, Aesthetics," *Evental Aesthetics* 1, no. 1 (2012): 132.

important an ontological dimension that it must be found in germinal form in all entities. But Zahavi notes his "puzzlement" when I say that what is at issue is not psyche but *sincerity,* and when I add that this entails a *weird realism* (295). There is no reason to be puzzled, however, since I have often defined both sincerity and weirdness as technical terms. The mere fact that they are unfamiliar to Zahavi is no argument against them. Sincerity means that everything just is what it is, and that at any moment it confronts a given range of sensual objects while not confronting others. This idea is drawn from Emmanuel Levinas, while adding a Whiteheadian cosmic dimension. Here I am as a human being, having certain phenomenal experiences; over there is a rock, which need not be "conscious" in the panpsychist manner, but which does confront sensual objects rather than real ones, simply because any human or non-human relation is capable of nothing more. As for weird realism, this is the notion that metaphysical realism does not entail that direct knowledge of the real is possible, but rather the reverse: precisely *because* objects are real, they are different not only from any human or non-human relation to them, but even from their own qualities. In the book *Weird Realism* I explore this notion with reference to the fiction of H.P. Lovecraft.

Zahavi proceeds to give an account of my theory which, although hardly less critical than Peter Wolfendale's, is considerably more lucid. For instance, "on [Harman's] account, scientific naturalism is itself a form of correlationism" (295). And further, "on Harman's account, the real objects, the things-in-themselves, remain forever inaccessible" (295). And finally, drawing properly on two passages from *Guerrilla Metaphysics,* "everything is isolated from everything else; nothing is ever in direct contact with anything else. This principle holds not only on the inter-objective level, but even on the intra-objective level: an object also withdraws from and has no direct contact with its constituent parts" (295). From this he concludes that even though I accuse phenomenology of enchaining us to the phenomenal, it is actually I who do this, and that I contradict myself by "making various claims about the structure and nature of this inaccessible realm" (295). Here Zahavi overlooks two important points. The first is that I do not say we are limited to the phenomenal, but only that *direct* access to things is limited to the phenomenal. Indirect relation to the real happens frequently, and there is no contradiction in gaining indirect access to that which can only be accessed indirectly. As a secondary point, he switches back to the claim of "our" (human) access being restricted to the phenomenal, forgetting my broader claim that non-human objects also have no direct access to each other. But the point of OOO is that real relations occur *indirectly* between real objects by means of sensual mediators, as seen in my various discussions of allure and vicarious causation. With his final complaint, that I make claims about the nature of the inaccessible, this simply repeats the strong correlationist assumption that we can only speak about the phenomenal, and that any attempt to discuss the real is itself a thinking that immediately collapses back into the phenomenal. But the fact that someone makes statements about the nature of the real is not the same thing as claiming that the real must also be phenomenally accessible to them. This is the same taxonomical error that leads readers to conflate Kant's doctrine that we only have direct access to the phenomenal with the false corollary that we can therefore only talk about the relation between humans and world. These are two different points; I affirm the first while rejecting the second.

In passing, I should note that Zahavi misreads Meillassoux in the same way as Norris and most other critics: "[Meillassoux] insists that fidelity to science demands that we take scientific statements at face value and that we reject correlationism. No compromise is possible" (296). By no means. This is the view of straightforward realists like Paul Boghossian and John Nolt, not of Meillassoux himself. The latter is abundantly clear that the correlationist has a point too, and his entire philosophical position is an attempt to thread the needle between science and correlationism, through a complicated effort to radicalize strong correlationism into his own speculative materialism. Although I disagree strongly with both Meillassoux's method and his results, it is important that we get his position right and not misidentify him as a standard scientific realist. Zahavi follows this up by saying, "an even more extreme form of anti-correlationist scientism can be found in the work of Brassier," who treats the goal of enlightenment as a destruction of the manifest image (296). While this is true of Ray Brassier, the most intense opponent of phenomenology among the Speculative Realists, the phrase "an even more extreme form" wrongly implies a continuity between him and Meillassoux. They do have their agreements, but this is not one of them. For we have seen (at Goldsmith's most clearly) that Meillassoux is not an anti-correlationist, and also that his position deserves to be called mathematism rather than scientism. Peter Gratton has rightly noted that Meillassoux makes rather limited use of science in his philosophy. Oddly enough, Zahavi makes the same point himself toward the end of his article, though for polemical purposes: "as [Harald] Wiltsche has recently pointed out in a critical discussion of Meillassoux's work, the latter's treatment of an engagement with science is astonishingly sparse"[7] (302). But there is no contradiction here unless we assume that the passages on ancestrality and the archefossil are a form of scientific realism, which they are not. In any case, I am very much with Zahavi and against Brassier when it comes to the destruction of the manifest image, especially since Brassier merely wishes to replace it with a different kind of image: the scientific one. Thus, Brassier is primarily a *philosopher of images*, and to this extent he has more in common with phenomenology than he would care to admit.

I will close this chapter by dealing with Zahavi's final criticism of me and showing that he understates several important points of agreement between us. He first quotes a passage from *The Quadruple Object* in which I argue that the idealism of phenomenology is proven by the fact that many intentional objects are not real in the least. I might have added, more pertinently in this case, that there is no reason to assume that all objects are

---

7   Harald A. Wiltsche, "Science, Realism, and Correlationism: A Phenomenological Critique of Meillassoux's Argument from Ancestrality," *European Journal of Philosophy* 25, no. 3 (September 2017): 808–32.

necessarily available to intentionality—and in fact, I hold that no *real* objects are thus accessible. He responds as follows: "This criticism is unconvincing. It is an obvious non sequitur to argue that since some objects of intentionality are non-existing, all objects of intentionality are non-existing" (298). But this is not the argument, and only appears to be so because Zahavi has taken one passage out of context. The argument, instead, is that since an intentional object is something to which we relate directly, any intentional object that happens to be linked with some real object must differ in kind from it. Let's imagine an unusual case in which I am intending a white dog that links with a real animal that is actually here in the room, while simultaneously hallucinating a green dog. Zahavi claims that Husserl has the resources to deal with this. He quotes the following from *Logical Investigations*: "the intentional object of a presentation is the same as its actual object, and on occasion as its external object, and [...] it is absurd to distinguish between them"[8] (298).

The use of the word "absurd" is telling, since this is most often a table-pounding term rather than an argument. Even worse, Zahavi begs the question so hard that it probably phoned the police. For he simply asserts, along with Husserl, the supposed "absurdity" that there might be any objects that could not become the object of an intentional act. This goes back to Husserl's initial idealist turn in the 1890s in the essay "Intentional Objects," meant as a rejoinder to Kazimierz Twardowski's doubling of an object outside the mind with a content inside it. Husserl's motive in that essay, much like Zahavi's in rejecting my version of Speculative Realism as the worst of the bunch (despite my incorporation of numerous phenomenological insights) was the avoidance of "skepticism." Namely, Husserl worries that if an intentional Berlin is doubled up with a real Berlin outside the mind, no knowledge of Berlin would be possible. But the fact that this would pose complications for knowledge does not mean that it cannot be true, and thus Husserl's rejection of

---

8   Edmund Husserl, *Logical Investigations*, ed. Dermot Moran, trans. J.N. Findlay (London: Routledge, 2001), 2:127. Italics removed.

Twardowski is never convincing, though his resulting idealism does allow him to explore the concreteness of the ideal sphere more fully than any idealist before him. (A further note: "concrete" and "real" are not the same thing, though Zahavi consistently treats them as such.) Another way to put it is that Husserl's apparent use of nuanced and layered terminology in the passage above — his threefold distinction between intentional object, actual object, and external object — falsely suggests he has covered every base with his model, which is not true. What Husserl must exclude *tout court* from phenomenology, if the theory is to work as he wishes, is any possibility of a real object that is not potentially an intentional one. Rather than making an argument for this, Zahavi merely joins Husserl in dismissing the other option as "absurd" (which is just what the German Idealists did to the *Ding an sich*, though with more of an argument than Husserl ever gives) and calling his theory of knowledge "non-representationalist" (301). This term is certainly an apt description of Husserl, but it does not get either Husserl or Zahavi off the hook of explaining why it is "absurd" to ask if there might be something to represent apart from the non-representational sphere. What Husserl calls the "external" object in the passage above is only external in the sense that we have not yet fulfilled our intention of it, though in principle we might. This is not the real object, which is completely missing from his threefold schema mentioned above. Then again, Zahavi can still dismiss the real object as "absurd," and we can march forward into total idealism, resting easy in the assurance that it will enable us to avoid "skepticism" and "representationalism," whether justifiably or not.

Zahavi's next point shows him in slipperier form. He begins, "Whereas it is true that some phenomenologists have suggested that one should stay clear of the realism/anti-realism (idealism) controversy, it is certainly not a position shared by all" (298). This is already somewhat evasive, since Zahavi is well aware that it is at least the usual position found among phenomenologists, and one that is often stated explicitly by the two chief figures of the movement, Husserl and Heidegger. Indeed, it is a position Zahavi himself seems to share, given his agreement with the "absurdity" of positing objects beyond all intentional access. This remains the case despite the fig leaf of citing two of his own articles in which the question of whether phenomenology is compatible with some form of realism "is debated."[9] But rather than just telling us what he thinks about the matter, he quickly follows these citations by shifting to a "more important" topic. That topic is as follows:

> [M]any early phenomenologists (including members of the Münich and Göttingen circles of phenomenology, i.e. figures like Pfänder, Scheler, Stein, Geiger, Hildebrand and Ingarden) were committed realists who were disappointed by what they saw as Husserl's turn towards transcendental idealism. They considered this turn a betrayal of the realist thrust of phenomenology and very much saw themselves as defending realism. (298)

The name-drop is never an effective way to end an argument, though it does allow Zahavi a *segué* into his needlessly condescending conclusion that "ultimately one has to wonder whether [the Speculative Realists] are reliable and knowledgeable interpreters of the tradition they are criticizing" (299). I would say, instead, that ultimately one has to wonder whether Zahavi has a sufficiently robust sense of what "realism" means. Husserl's idealism did not begin with his turn toward transcendental phenomenology around the time of the First World War but nearly two decades earlier, in his proclamation of the "absurdity" of a real Berlin that could not be the correlate of an intentional act. It is true that most realists do not accept anything like the thing-in-itself, but we are speaking here of OOO, which does accept it (304). The various figures on Zahavi's list of "realist phe-

9 Dan Zahavi, "Phenomenology," in *The Routledge Companion to Twentieth-Century Philosophy*, ed. Dermot Moran (London: Routledge, 2008), 661–92; Dan Zahavi, "Husserl and the 'Absolute,'" in *Philosophy, Phenomenology, Sciences: Essays in Commemoration of Husserl*, eds. Carlo Ierna, Hanne Jacobs, and Filip Mattens (Dordrecht: Springer, 2010), 71–92.

nomenologists" differ greatly in the intensity of their commitment to realism, even if all of them –and he could have added Heidegger — preferred the *Logical Investigations* to the rampant idealism of *Ideas I*.[10] But it is at least probable that none of them would have disagreed with Husserl's claim of the "absurdity" of objects beyond all intentionality. Yet an express commitment to such objects is what object-oriented realism is about, rather than the "scientific realism" that Zahavi questions in the company of Hillary Putnam (299–301). Furthermore, Zahavi cannot have it both ways about ooo, claiming sometimes that it is a wild and fantastic speculative skepticism and at other times that it is "old hat" (303). On another point, he simply misfires:

> Heidegger is often portrayed by the speculative realists as an even more fierce idealist and correlationist than Husserl. This characterization, however, is by no means universally accepted by Heidegger scholars. Many see him as a realist. There are even those who interpret him as a scientific realist. Recently, even Husserl has been interpreted along similar lines. (299)

The point about Husserl was dealt with above. To say that "even Husserl has been interpreted" as a realist is not yet a realist case for Husserl, a case that Zahavi more or less admits he does not believe anyway. It amounts to nothing more than saying "you can't paint all phenomenologists with the same brush; there is great diversity amongst us!" Yet he simultaneously represses any diversity in the various Speculative Realist approaches to Heideggger, while also implying that since some people have treated Husserl and Heidegger as realists, therefore realist concerns have been adequately covered by phenomenological authors. As concerns Heidegger, Zahavi seems entirely unaware that I interpret Heidegger as posing one of the great realist challenges to correlationism. Although Zahavi generally seems to have done

---

10 Edmund Husserl, *Ideas for a Pure Phenomenology and Phenomenological Philosophy*, trans. Daniel O. Dahlstrom (Indianapolis: Hackett Publishing Company, 2014).

his homework in reading the key Speculative Realist texts, one glaring omission from his references is my debut book, *Tool-Being*. Thus, at least when it comes to Heidegger, ultimately one has to wonder whether Zahavi is "a reliable and knowledgeable interpreter" of the Speculative Realist tradition he is criticizing. Beyond this, the fact that a number of Heidegger commenters aside from me call Heidegger a realist (I happen to know the literature fairly well) tells us nothing about what kind of realism they defend, and many so-called realisms are rather feeble versions of the doctrine. For instance, there are those who call Jacques Lacan a "realist," despite the fact that his Real functions only as a trauma to the symbolic order. There are also numerous "realisms of the residue," which imply that the throwaway concession that something exists outside thought is enough to count as realism. Badiou is sometimes guilty of this trick, and Sparrow showed the same for Merleau-Ponty. There are also phenomenologies of "givenness" such as Jean-Luc Marion's, which imply that to call humans passive recipients of the given rather than active formatters of it is enough to make one a realist. And we have already met with Lee Braver's "transgressive realism," which is realism only in the sense that shock or resistance alert us to reality. But as Jane Bennett has argued effectively, such forms of "recalcitrance" are not enough to make room for the real.[11]

Zahavi is a leading scholar, highly accomplished at what he does. His article is much clearer and fairer in spirit, I would say, than the books of Gratton and Wolfendale. He took time from his active schedule to read a good bit of Speculative Realist literature and mount counter-arguments against us. But his article would have been better with less condescension, and with a more nuanced awareness of the different intensities of realism found among the various thinkers who claim to be realists. Beyond this, he should simply have owned his obvious idealist commitments, rather than pre-emptively farming out a hypo-

---

11 Jane Bennett, *Vibrant Matter: A Political Ecology of Things* (Durham: Duke University Press, 2010), 61.

thetical phenomenological realism to a glittering roster of third parties. Amidst his recurrent claims that the Speculative Realists make unfair generalizations, he ought not to have generalized unfairly about the Speculative Realist attitude toward Heidegger, given his apparent unawareness — and its coals-to-Newcastle outcome — of my numerous publications on Heidegger's realist impulses. Zahavi would also have done well to engage with the reading of Husserl by the only original Speculative Realist who has offered such a reading, in a book he already cites in his article.[12] That would have been a conversation to relish.

Finally, there is Zahavi's strange concluding lament that, even if the Speculative Realists have a point about phenomenology's in-built idealism, we still ought to celebrate phenomenology's fruitful impact on countless disciplines (302). This might be worth saying to Brassier, who would be perfectly happy to see phenomenology wiped from the face of the earth. But such a needed confrontation is rendered impossible when Zahavi clumsily cites Brassier's boorish remark about the "online orgy of stupidity" of Speculative Realism, unaware of the complex human situation that lies behind that remark (304). More importantly, how could Zahavi have read my book *Guerrilla Metaphysics* — he does cite it — and still think I see nothing of value in phenomenology? And beyond that, if he demands recognition for the fruitfulness of phenomenology, why is he unwilling to appreciate a similar impact of Speculative Realism across nearly as many disciplines, allowing for its much shorter lifespan so far? My sense is that Sparrow's book put Zahavi into a defensive mood, and thus he was unable to let his guard down and engage in some good old give-and-take. I hope there will still be an opportunity for more substantive discussion with Zahavi in the future, especially since I love phenomenology as much as he does, whatever my reservations.

---

12 Harman, *Guerrilla Metaphysics*.

8

STEPHEN MULHALL

My book *Object-Oriented Ontology: A New Theory of Everything* was published under the Pelican label in the spring of 2018. On September 27th of that year, it received a critical assessment in the *London Review of Books* from Stephen Mulhall of Oxford.[1] Along with Mulhall's work on Martin Heidegger and Ludwig Wittgenstein, readers of the present book may know him for his editorship of *The Cavell Reader*.[2]

Let's turn directly to Mulhall's review, which is just over 5,000 words in length, but manages to make multiple objections to the theory advanced in my Pelican book. Drawing on Wittgenstein in the *Philosophical Investigations,* Mulhall begins by questioning the value of "theories of everything" such as the one promised by OOO.[3] If we say that every tool "modifies something," this is clear enough in the case of a hammer or saw, but in what sense do a glue pot or ruler also "modify" something? In expanding the sense of "modify" to cover a greater number of cases, the

---

1   Stephen Mulhall, "How Complex is a Lemon?" *London Review of Books*, September 27, 2018, https://www.lrb.co.uk/the-paper/v40/n18/stephen-mulhall/how-complex-is-a-lemon. Since I am quoting from the online rather than the print version of this article, no page numbers will be listed.
2   Stephen Mulhall, ed. *The Cavell Reader* (London: Wiley-Blackwell, 1996).
3   Ludwig Wittgenstein, *Philosophical Investigations,* trans. G.E.M. Anscombe, 3rd edn. (London: Pearson, 1973).

meaning of the word becomes "increasingly loose and baggy," so that we end by "evacuating the theory of any content." There is a twofold way in which this complaint might apply to OOO. In *Tool-Being,* a book Mulhall seems to know at first hand, my method was of just the sort that Wittgenstein complains about, since I argue there that Heidegger's "tool-analysis" cannot be limited to hammers, saw, glue pots, rulers, or any other familiar "tools"; instead, I hold that Heidegger's analysis hold good for any object whatsoever. In the Pelican book sixteen years later, I presented a global theory of objects, which is exactly what OOO is. Mulhall responds to such efforts with blanket skepticism: "This is the trouble with philosophical theories of everything, whether it's in a given domain (tools, say, or language) or absolutely everything. It isn't so much that their generality increases the risk of incorporating erroneous claims; it's that they risk failing to make a claim at all." But this is not true. If it were, then philosophy (or at least ontology) would be impossible. The broader the theory, the more it must abstract from the fine-grained detail of any specific locale. We do not need Heidegger's tool-analysis to build a tree house any more than I need a globe to drive from my home in downtown Long Beach to my office in downtown Los Angeles. But a globe is surely not "vacuous" just because it shifts us to a different level, and neither is the tool-analysis "vacuous" when I apply it to all entities. The tool-analysis shows, in my reading, that entities withdraw not only from our theoretical awareness, which is as far as Heidegger goes, but also withdraw from our practical handling and even from each other in causal contact. One can argue that this theory is *wrong,* as Mulhall does elsewhere in his review, but it would be hard to claim it says nothing at all. If that were the case, then I would not have been challenged repeatedly by relational ontologists, such as Bruno Latour or Steven Shaviro, who understand perfectly well what I am saying and argue the opposite instead.

For the sake of illustration, imagine Mulhall giving the same sort of verdict about Immanuel Kant: "by claiming that *everything* is an appearance according to space, time, and the categories as opposed to the thing-in-itself, Kant risks failing to make a claim at all. For he thereby loses the distinction between some things that are very easy to see directly, like chairs and dogs, and others that transcend our understanding, such as God, the inside of a black hole, or what happens after death." This would be a strange thing to say, and a good Kantian would crisply retort that noumenon/phenomenon is a distinction that goes well beyond the empirical question of how easy various things are to know. If philosophy is not permitted to explore the basic background features shared by everything that exists, then I am not sure what it is supposed to do, or even what Mulhall thinks it is supposed to do. A blogosphere critic once told me that "if everything is an object, then nothing is an object," but this is both platitudinous and false. It is simply untrue that we know what things are only by contrast with other things. Ontology in its first steps works primarily not by drawing contrasts but by asking what all things share *qua* things.

All right, then: what is shared by all things, or — in OOO terminology — by all objects? Mulhall begins on a charitable note, "Harman's opening attempts to specify what he means by ['object'] look promising." As he summarizes these attempts, "For Harman, an object is simply anything that is resistant to reduction: anything whose autonomous, unitary nature and existence cannot be explained away by being reduced to its component parts, or to its effects on the world, or to its relations with other objects." Mulhall never refers to my undermining/overmining/ duomining terminology, but that is what he means. Most critics, with Peter Wolfendale being a good example, cite my "non-reducible" definition of objects only to follow up immediately with something resembling a "negative theology" complaint: OOO can only say what an object is not, rather than what it is. But saying what something *is not* is at least a good start, especially when so many philosophies in the course of two-and-a-half millennia have given just the sorts of answers that I take to be the wrong ones: undermining everything into water or atoms or *apeiron,* overmining everything into ideas or relations or dialectical process. Furthermore, such preliminary negations are by no means all that OOO says about objects. We also argue for points such as the following: real objects are plural, they have both real and sensual qualities, they interact through the mediation of sensual objects, they have parts without incorporating all the features of those parts, they are destructible, and so forth. But the "negative theology" line does not figure prominently in Mulhall's review. Instead, there are two other problems that concern him about OOO's definition of objects.

The first has to do with whether or not this definition is useful. For "even at this early stage […] we might worry that Harman's strategic orientation towards objects is less distinctive than it seems. It's not clear, for example, that that his ontological open-mindedness in social theory generates anything terribly original in the way of insights into the nature and history of its distinctive objects." Or as he puts it shortly thereafter, "it's hard to see how conceptualizing matters in [Harman's] way helps the working historian." His assumption, then, is that history is something dealt with by historians, and it is unclear how my theory can help them. It is Mulhall's equivalent of the taxonomical argument employed earlier by Wolfendale and Christopher Norris, to the effect that nature is dealt with by scientists, and since OOO cannot do anything of obvious help to scientists, it should stay in its own lane and just talk about the thought-world relationship like other post-Kantian philosophers. But first of all, it is not clear that this is the case. OOO has enjoyed extensive interdisciplinary success precisely because practitioners of various disciplines have found my writings useful. It would not be at all surprising to hear that a group of historians somewhere had taken *Immaterialism* to heart and found ways to use it for some collective project or other, just as it was unsurprising when a group of organization theorists in Leicester held a special conference on my book *Dante's Broken Hammer*.[4] Something analogous holds for physics, which — as Mulhall, Wolfendale, and Norris may have heard — has been in a bit of a jam in

---

4 Graham Harman, *Dante's Broken Hammer: The Ethics, Aesthetics, and Metaphysics of Love* (London: Repeater Books, 2016). The conference on this book was held at Leicester University on June 19, 2017.

recent decades. There is simply no way to know whether such OOO concepts as vicarious causation or the fourfold structure of the object may prove useful to science in the future. But that is not even the point. The point is that there is no good reason to hold that each kind of object should be reserved for one specific discipline. We know that artists, art critics, art historians, and philosophers of art all deal with art, and that they do so in different ways, though this does not exclude a good deal of communicative overlap between them. As made clear in *Immaterialism*, which Mulhall also seems to have read, that book develops an *ontology* rather than a history of the Dutch East India Company, and there is nothing vague about what this means. The historian is concerned with figuring out what really happened as well as the actual causal relationships between various factors, and thus attempts to increase our knowledge about what occurred. The ontologist, by contrast, is less concerned with what happened then with the basic parameters of all the things that *might* have happened. The framework for these possibilities is what I call "symbiosis," which is not a "neologism" as Mulhall says, but is simply borrowed from the evolutionary theory of Lynn Margulis.[5] Unlike the historian, the ontologist tries to downplay the details of what really happened, so as to turn away from the numerous historical details of the Dutch East India Company toward the five or six of its transformations that really mattered. It is not hard to see how this might prove useful to the historian: by drawing greater attention to the distinction between important and unimportant events, by encouraging a more robust sense of the impermeability of the chief historical actors to most aspects of their environment, by enhancing our attention to the fact that historical objects tend to reach mature form fairly early in their lifespan, and by affirming that historical objects are unified rather than multiple (contra the widely admired method of

---

5   Lynn Margulis, *Symbiotic Planet: A New Look at Evolution* (New York: Basic Books, 1998).

Annemarie Mol).[6] None of this is hypothetical. I phrased my arguments in *Immaterialism* explicitly against actor-network-theory, and explored the very real consequences for historians that result.

Mulhall's second worry about my definition of objects is that it turns out to be not very different from what it opposes. After all, it could turn out that the things I think are real objects are ultimately reducible after all. To give an example of my own, a OOO-inspired sociologist might write a study treating the generation known as Millennials as an object, but then future demographic studies show conclusively that there are two distinctive generations blended together under that name, and therefore Millennials never really existed. While it is true that something like this could easily happen, Mulhall draws needlessly severe conclusions: "the real range and variety of object-oriented ontology is always hostage to its' opponents ability to make good on their aspirations [...] Being a reductionist and being a proponent of OOO are thus perfectly compatible: the sole distinguishing feature of OOO turns out to be nothing of the kind." In one of just two truly condescending moments in Mulhall's review, he depicts my argument as boiling down to a triviality:

> What we're left with is the following principle: don't assume in advance that the unitary phenomena that appear to populate any given domain of reality are reducible, but don't assume in advance that they're not. In other words, don't let your assumptions get in the way of seeing what is really there. Good advice, Polonius, but hardly a radical breakthrough.

A real knee-slapper, that one! The problem is that my expositions of undermining, overmining, and duomining all make the same point in advance. Many reductions are justified. I am perfectly happy to undermine "morning star" and "evening star" into the single planet Venus, and equally happy to overmine "witch"

---

6 Annemarie Mol, *The Body Multiple: Ontology in Medical Practice* (Durham: Duke University Press, 2003).

into a number of coincidental events not caused by some evil black-magicking woman who must be burnt at the stake. Being cautious about what we reduce and non-reduce is a prudent principle indeed, and one not as universally followed as Mulhall seems to assume. However, the OOO approach to reduction does not just amount to saying, "Boris Johnson real, Sherlock Holmes unreal." What is original in OOO does not consist in its awareness that we are fallible in our reductions and non-reductions, but in its theory of the *nature* of whatever is taken to be non-reducible. For even if a reductionist admits that Boris Johnson exists, they will still treat him by reducing him downward (to his background, history, DNA) and upward (to the commotions he has caused, the effects he has on various possible Tory coalitions). But this is precisely what an object-oriented ontologist will not do. In short, reduction is not just about whether or not we think something exists, but about what we conclude from our view that it *does* exist.

After giving a brief account of my fourfold ontology of objects and qualities, Mulhall notes that this ontology "also generates two other, more richly elaborated, metaphysical proposals that are worth dwelling on here," which is not to say that he agrees with them. "The first," he tells us, "results from the apparently innocuous claim that a truly realistic ontology must not privilege relations between real objects and subjects over relations between real objects." In passing, I would hardly say that my claim is "innocuous," since it strikes at the very basis of Modern Onto-Taxonomy, which is precisely why OOO has been so controversial. It troubles me, for instance, that the usual definition of realism is "belief in a reality *outside the mind*." This already concedes too much to the idealist or correlationist position, since it implies that we are first secure *in our minds* and that we then somehow make the leap *outside our minds*. But the mind is not the only thing with an outside, nor is it even the first thing with an outside, and therefore we ought to redefine realism in terms of there being a reality outside *any relation*. Mulhall makes the common argument that this puts me dangerously close to panpsychism, though he is well aware that I distinguish this from what I call polypsychism.

The second result of OOO covered by Mulhall is the discussion of metaphor and aesthetics provoked by my interpretation of José Ortega y Gasset.[7] Mulhall is right to say that in the OOO theory of metaphor developed from Ortega's own, one term occupies the object-pole while the other provides the qualities, and the combination of the two creates a paradoxical combination, as in Ortega's example "the cypress is like the ghost of a dead flame." Mulhall's sole error here comes on a point of detail: namely, he says "since Harman (unlike Ortega) thinks the real cypress is necessarily inaccessible," although Ortega too treats the real cypress as an "executant" reality untranslatable into any image. As Mulhall notes, from the inaccessibility of the metaphorical cypress, I conclude that the reader herself must step in theatrically and perform the absent object by fusing with the qualities of the flame. This compelled performance, I argue, explains the great power of aesthetics by contrast with literal language and everyday experience.

This leads Mulhall to say that "it's amazing how quickly we've moved from an anodyne reminder that we should check our ontological privileging to an enthusiastic investment in polypsychism and in art as a metaphysically revelatory metaphorical theatricality." Here Mulhall is in such a hurry to make a witty remark that he utters two falsehoods en route. First, we saw that the supposedly "anodyne" view of OOO on objects resulted solely from Mulhall's inadequate claim that the reductionist and I both basically proceed according to the same methodology, which is not the case: for even when the reductionist agrees with me that a given object really exists, he will still conceive of it in reductionist terms whereas I will not. And second, the only "quick" transition from the definition of the object to the theories of polypsychism and metaphor is in Mulhall's review itself, with its

---

7   José Ortega y Gasset, "An Essay in Esthetics by Way of a Preface," in *Phenomenology and Art*, trans. Phillip W. Silver (New York: Norton, 1975), 127–50.

necessarily compressed account. There is no such quickness in my book, and certainly not the wild leaps of logic that Mulhall's ribbing demeanor in this passage implies.

In any case, Mulhall does not agree with my handling of either the polypsychist theme or the metaphorical one. As for the first, he rightly notes that

> Harman's polypsychism rests on a refusal to privilege subject-object relations over object-object relations [...]. But one could believe that object-object relations are all real, genuinely existent phenomena [...] and also believe that the two types of encounter are very different in kind, and in particular that subject-object encounters have ontological possibilities involving sense and intellect that object-object encounters lack.

This is strange, since I too believe that subject-object encounters "have ontological possibilities involving sense and intellect" that cannot be found in object-object encounters, though I would disagree if by "ontological" he means that this difference ought to be built into the foundation of ontology. Never have I argued that rocks and grains of dust think, dream, plan for the future, repress forbidden wishes, or have access to other higher cognitive functions. Indeed, this is one of the reasons I am leery of the term "panpsychism": as soon as you use this word, everyone quickly assumes that you want to eliminate *all* differences between humans and inanimate objects. What I attempt instead is to find the lowest common denominator between both kinds of objects, and this can be found in the fact that both of them *relate,* and that relations are never directly with the other object but only with a sensual translation of it. When I touch a cotton ball I only encounter a limited range of its features, and the same is true of the flame that burns that cotton. Like Mulhall himself, I see no reason to argue that the cotton is capable of the same range of complex subtleties as humans are when we feel cotton. But neither is there good reason to *ontologize* the difference between humans and cotton by saying that the rift is so deep and poignant that there are two and only two kinds of things in the universe, (a) human thought and (b) everything else. On this score, Mulhall is just another Modern Onto-Taxonomist.

His objection to my aesthetic theory is somewhat less to the point. After asking whether I think the real object is accessible or not, he gives a clear summary of my argument. Unfortunately, he lists the steps of that argument with an air of impatient incredulity, as if to suggest an impossible tangle of rushed contradictions: "First, [Harman] tells us that the real cypress cannot be accessible to us because it's real; then that the subject, which is a real object, is always genuinely and truly present in aesthetic experience, and so can substitute for the absent real cypress; and then that the only real object involved in such experiences is not the subject but the newly amalgamated object of which it is a part." Yes, Mulhall gets me right, but I fail to see why he detects a contradiction in any of this. The real cypress is withdrawn; I, the reader, as a different real object stand in for it; finally, this results in a new real object through my performing the flame-qualities that had been ascribed by the metaphor to the cypress. Mulhall got it right the first time without much difficulty, despite his vaudeville gesticulations of someone being asked to perform a ridiculous and impossible task by a chaotic author.

Apparently, Mulhall's question is how there can be any philosophy if we are simply erecting new objects on top of old ones — as my theatrical model suggests — rather than gaining knowledge of pre-existent ones. The answer is that, while I do think there is knowledge of pre-existent objects through the modes of undermining, overmining, and duomining, I do not agree that philosophy or art are forms of knowledge. This is easy enough to see in the case of art, where no one becomes angry when the artist doesn't just come out and tell us what they meant to say, since everyone knows there are many possible readings of the art object and it is not equivalent to any of them. It is only in connection with *philosophy* that people tend to become angry about my model, since they want philosophy to be an extension of that marvelous magnificent miraculous pursuit called "science," and if philosophy produces no knowledge then it cannot be a science. To this I respond that *it is not a science.* Above all, philosophy is *philosophia,* a desire that never attains its object. As to whether or not the objects "pre-exist" the philosopher's own performance of philosophy, we have some reason for doubt thanks to the insights of existentialist and para-existentialist thinkers such as Pascal, Kierkegaard, Nietzsche, and Lacan, for all of whom philosophy presupposes an *act* and not just a theoretical content that unveils a pre-existent outside world. This focus on the act is what Alain Badiou calls "anti-philosophy," and given that Badiou himself tries to combine a philosophy of truth with a philosophy of human fidelity to truth, his work can be read as the fusion of philosophy and anti-philosophy.[8] Ultimately, I think some form of such fusion is inescapable. Just as Max Scheler shifts the unit of ethics from the autonomous human to a hybrid made up of humans and the objects they love, Badiou shifts the unit of truth from a fact outside the mind to a hybrid made up of an event and a human commitment to it.[9] That is why I do not worry much about the consequences of my theatrical model of beauty, which can easily be expanded into a theatrical model of truth.

Unfortunately, Mulhall chooses to prolong the trope that I jump ceaselessly from one point to another: "Such unclarities return us to the larger puzzle of how we got from a quietist conception of an object as whatever resists reductionism to the claim that there are exactly two kinds of object and two kinds of quality that yield precisely four distinct but internally related rifts that together generate the flat, pluralist ontology of everyday life." To repeat, the idea that objects are defined by OOO merely as "whatever resists reductionism"—without positive characteristics—is nothing more than Mulhall's own insufficient reading of the situation. We recall as well his mis-

---

8 Alain Badiou, *Lacan: Anti-Philosophy 3*, ed. Kenneth Reinhard, trans. Susan Spitzer (New York: Columbia University Press, 2018); Graham Harman, "Alain Badiou, Lacan: Anti-Philosophy 3," *Notre Dame Philosophical Reviews,* May 27, 2019, https://ndpr.nd.edu/news/lacan-anti-philosophy-3/.

9 Max Scheler, "Ordo Amoris," in *Selected Philosophical Essays,* trans. David R. Lachterman (Evanston: Northwestern University Press, 1992), 98–135.

taken claim that the reductionist and the OOO anti-reductionist end up in the same position. Quite apart from all this, Mulhall does not really seem very "puzzled" by the fourfold structure, which throughout his article he continually gets right without much effort. I suspect that most readers have the same good luck with it, since even the hostile Wolfendale does. As Mulhall puts it, "the crucial motivation is Harman's belief that we can properly acknowledge the reality of real objects only if we deny their accessibility to human subjects; for this is what leads him to introduce his second category of sensual objects, and to define them as necessarily veiling real objects. But why should the accessibility of objects threaten their reality?" To answer the final question first, to have access to a thing is to relate to it, and our relation to anything is by definition not the thing itself. A relation has two terms, whereas the thing itself is just one, and to identify my perception of a lemon with the lemon itself is like identifying water with hydrogen. Admittedly, there is a difference between my relation to the lemon (two terms) and the lemon as it appears to me in this relation (one term). But this apparent lemon is not the same as the real lemon that exists in the world, because the real lemon is sour and acidic, and the apparent lemon is neither. At best, one could argue for a certain correspondence or connection between the two rather than an identity, though William James — like Henri Bergson in *Matter and Memory* — makes a failed attempt to treat the image of a dog as if it were identical to the real dog in the world.[10]

The issue will return at the end of Mulhall's article, when he accuses me of setting too high a bar for knowledge. We can deal with this later, after first noting that his own bar for knowledge is much too low. For here is what he means by the interplay of the inaccessible and the accessible:

10 William James, "A World of Pure Experience," in *Essays in Radical Empiricism* (Lincoln: University of Nebraska Press, 1996), section II; Henri Bergson, *Matter and Memory,* trans. Nancy Margaret Paul and W. Scott Palmer (Mineola: Dover, 2004); Graham Harman, "Object-Oriented Philosophy vs. Radical Empiricism," in *Bells and Whistles: More Speculative Realism* (Winchester: Zero Books, 2013).

We think that the apple on my desk continues to exist when I'm not perceiving it; that I may misperceive some of its attributes under certain conditions, and that others may or may not be in a position to correct me; that no matter how much knowledge of it we acquire, there may be more to discover; that our best current theory of its nature may turn out to be wrong, either in small details or large [...]; and even that some aspects of reality might resist our understanding indefinitely.

He concludes that all of this "looks like a pretty robust acknowledgement of the autonomy and independence of real objects," but that unlike the OOO version of autonomy, this less exacting one has the advantage of permitting us to "sometimes grasp their real properties and nature." For "at least some of our representations of the apple are accurate at least some of the time," and "Harman never explains why this kind of sober acknowledgment of our finitude as knowers [...] is such a threat to its independent reality."

I would say instead that knowledge of a thing is no threat to its reality at all, because a thing and knowledge of it are of two completely separate orders, in a sense more important than Mulhall's distinction between the apple on my desk when I'm looking and when I'm not looking. If he had pushed just a bit further, he would have repeated Quentin Meillassoux's distinction between an ancestral or arche-apple prior to the emergence of all consciousness and the apple for us here and now. Nonetheless, autonomy does not just refer to the existence of a thing when I'm not looking at it, but to its existence when *I am* looking. Mulhall is aware that this is my position, since he cites a passage from *Object-Oriented Ontology* in which I make this very point:

Any real orange or lemon, as I perceive it, is a vast oversimplification of the real citrus objects in the world that are submitted to rough translation by the human senses and human brain. [...] All of the objects we experience are merely fic-

tions: simplified models of the far more complex objects that
continue to exist when I turn my head away from them, not
to mention when I sleep or die.[11]

Unfortunately, this is the occasion for Mulhall's second condescending remark. He pulls out his flute and plays a familiar academic tune: "My Opponent Is So Mixed Up That I Hardly Know Where to Begin." Mulhall's own lyrics to the song run as follows: "So many dubious ideas are compressed into these remarks that it's hard to know where to start [unpacking] them." Despite the "many" dubious ideas Mulhall claims to find in the passage above, by my count he gives just four. The first dubious idea is that by pointing to the simplifications contained in our experience of a lemon, I omit to mention that when we perceive a lemon we still get *some* things right about it, and therefore am seemingly committed to the "bizarre idea that anything less than an absolutely complete representation of an object must absolutely misrepresent it." The second dubious idea is that I call our perception of a lemon "fictional," despite the fact that the obviously fictional Sherlock Holmes corresponds to nothing in the world, while the lemon-perception does. Here Mulhall comments as follows: "Harman's policy of treating 'simplified-translated-distorted-false-fictional' as a chain of synonyms conflates importantly distinct ideas, and thereby implicates the respectable ideas towards the beginning of the chain with the flaws we associate with those towards the end." The third dubious idea is that by mentioning the human senses and brain in the passage above, I "implicitly privilege the case of material objects, rather than maintaining the assumption of ontological plurality to which [I claim] to adhere." But "for the phenomenologists Harman most respects, the assumption that modelling or representing is our most basic relation to the world is a distinctively modern fallacy. And more generally, erecting metaphysics on the basis of physics […] is a version of the scientism that Har-

---

11 Graham Harman, "A New Theory of Everything," in *Object-Oriented Ontology: A New Theory of Everything* (London: Pelican, 2018), 34.

man begins his book by denouncing." The fourth and final dubious idea is that there seems to be a performative contradiction in my claims, since I "treat [my] theory as a truthful account of the reality of human perception, when by [my] own lights it must be entirely fictional." This leads him to speculate that I was secretly influenced by Nietzsche's famous essay "On Truth and Lying in the Extra-Moral Sense."[12] (For the record, I was not.)

Let's take the purportedly dubious points in reverse order. The idea that there is a performative contradiction in any philosophy that does not admit of direct access to truth stems from the assumption that this claim must itself pose as a direct access to truth. Yet this merely begs the question. Although Mulhall praises Heidegger, at my expense, for actually giving specific analyses of the ontology of equipment despite his view that Being hides itself, others are not so kind to the German thinker. It is not uncommon, for instance, to hear people say that the concealment of Being openly contradicts Heidegger's ability to write a book about it at all. But this critique misfires, since Heidegger does not claim that his tool-analysis takes the form of a direct presentation of truth, but takes care to say that the analysis is hermeneutic in character and is undertaken from a specific, historically rooted moment. In short, the rationalist assumption that the denial of truth must present itself as a truth is just another version of the correlationist argument that the inapparent must appear in order for us to talk about it. But the fact that we talk about something does not prove that it appears *directly* to us. I could say "Mulhall will face consequences for his review of my book," without that being anywhere near a direct inventory of such consequences, much as when Vito Corleone in *The Godfather* speaks of making someone "an offer he can't refuse." Thus it is simply false that OOO is merely fictional in the sense of having no relation to reality at all. Insofar as it is "fictional," a term I do use in the passage cited by Mulhall, this sim-

---

12 Friedrich Nietzsche, "On Truth and Lying in an Extra-Moral Sense," in *Friedrich Nietzsche on Rhetoric and Language*, trans. Sander L. Gilman, Carole Blair, and David J. Parent (Oxford: Oxford University Press, 1989).

ply means there is no isomorphy, no identity of form between reality and anything we say about it. It is not the case that any system of statements needs to be grounded on an initial axiom of direct contact with reality.

The third dubious idea is simply a misunderstanding on Mulhall's part. The fact that the passage he cites speaks of the workings of the brain and the senses is merely an *ad hoc* example I chose and does not reflect a grounding of ooo in scientism. At least this accusation is a new one! But I could just as easily have spoken of two rocks colliding in outer space and encountering distorted versions of each other. In that case there would have been no accusation of scientism, and Mulhall would quickly have changed his tune and called me a wild panpsychist instead. He turns phenomenology against me, noting that I "admire" it, while citing this school's denial that there is a real thing-in-itself that the phenomena can never reach. Yes, phenomenology has a non-representationalist conception of truth, but I have tried to show that the price of this conception is idealism. To offer a realist and representationalist model instead, as I do, has nothing to do with scientistic materialism. There are good reasons that no one ever accused me of such a thing before Mulhall did.

The second dubious idea was related to Mulhall's complaint that I use the words "simplified," "translated," "distorted," "false," and "fictional" as synonyms, thereby occluding important differences of meaning between all these terms. I would say, first, that I favor precise differentiation of the meaning of terms only in cases where there is good reason to do so. Otherwise, needless distinction between words is not only pedantic but deprives the writer of synonyms — an important stylistic resource for preventing fatigue in the reader. That is to say, simplified, translated, distorted, false, and fictional are not functioning as technical terms in the passage cited by Mulhall. Or rather, they are all functioning as one and the same technical term, just as when a single god is described by thousands of honorific titles. If the situation involved an actual discussion of the ontology of fictional characters, then I would have said something like this: "By real person, I mean the following… By fictional character,

I mean the following...." But truth be told, Mulhall seems less bothered by the purported confusion of terms than by the simple fact that I treat the real object as utterly different in kind from any manifestation of it, whether in fiction or in theory. And this brings us to the final point of supposed dubiety.

The first dubious idea, and the most important of all, was the view Mulhall rightly ascribes to me, the "bizarre idea that anything less than an absolutely complete representation of an object must absolutely misrepresent it." My idea is actually even more bizarre than that, for as Mulhall already knows, I happen to think that even a *complete* representation of an object would absolutely misrepresent it. He zeroes in on this issue in the penultimate paragraph of his review:

> [T]he picture shaping Harman's thinking only needs to be plainly articulated for its peculiarity to become apparent. His conviction about the inherent inaccessibility of reality seems ultimately to rest on assuming that genuine knowledge of an object would have to become wholly and fully identical with that object: fusing with it, actually realizing the theatrical method-acting aspiration that he claims is internal to the experience of metaphor [...]. This is a strangely idealist assumption for a putatively realist ontology, and one which would abolish the independent reality of subject and object if it were realized.

Here Mulhall basically gets the theory right, though are there significant problems with his portrayal of it. By no means do I think that genuine knowledge of an object would require fusing with it and becoming identical with it. My point, instead, is that even the best possible knowledge of a thing *would not* be such a fusion, since it would still be separated from that thing by an unbridgeable gulf. To say so is not some empty game of defining "thing" and "knowledge" in deliberately incommensurate ways without meaningful effect. Instead, it is ultimately meant as an assault on the classical opposition between form and matter. Namely, those such as Meillassoux who think the primary qualities of a thing are accessed by mathematizing it can say all they like that they are not Pythagoreans, that mathematics is merely a set of meaningless signs that *index* a reality outside mathematical formulation, and so forth. But at the end of the day, their view of the difference between a lemon and perfect knowledge of the lemon is that the former "inheres in dead matter" and the latter does not. In short, the lemon-form can in principle be transported from the lemon into my mind, even if various fallibilist provisos are added about the never-ending task of science or (as with Edmund Husserl) the unfulfillability of intentional acts. The OOO model, instead, is that there is no such thing as matter, but only forms and more forms everywhere. The difference between 100 real Thalers and 100 imaginary ones is not just a difference "of position" but a difference of form, one stemming from the fact that even if their outward visual look is utterly identical, the real and the imaginary Thalers are composed of different parts and different causal backstories that result in entirely different objects. Here a new strategy for dealing with the ontological argument also suggests itself. But in any case, OOO has never opposed knowledge, which is the obsession of Mulhall and other moderns who like to see themselves as the good neighbors of science. By contrast, OOO sees itself as a closer neighbor of aesthetics and Socratic *philosophia,* and these disciplines do not pursue knowledge, but forms that can never be converted into knowledge.

This leads us to a second and related error in the passage cited above. When Mulhall says I demand of knowledge that it "actually [realize] the theatrical method-acting aspiration that [I claim] is internal to the experience of metaphor," he is wrong on two counts. First, the theatrical model pertains to aesthetics and not to knowledge, which always remains literal. And second, the theatrical fusion with an object in metaphor — with a cypress, for example — is not some sort of "becoming one" with it, but a temporary identification with it solely for the purpose of fusing with its flame-qualities. In aesthetics I do not fuse with a pre-existent object, but impersonate such an object in order to create an entirely different one.

From these points it is also clear why Mulhall is wrong to accuse me of "a strangely idealist assumption for a putatively realist ontology [...] one which would abolish the independent reality of subject and object if it were realized." For it is not the case that I treat knowledge as a way of fusing with its object. And even in the aesthetic realm, there is no fusion of beholder with artwork. The work is the work, and the beholding of the work contains the work as one of its elements, just as water contains hydrogen as one of its elements without becoming hydrogen.

BIBLIOGRAPHY

Acuto, Michele, and Simon Curtis, eds. *Reassembling International Theory: Assemblage Thinking and International Relations.* Basingstroke: Palgrave Macmillan, 2014.

Ameriks, Karl. "Husserl's Realism." *The Philosophical Review* 86, no. 4 (October 1997): 498–519.

Andersen, Hans Christian. "The Emperor's New Clothes." In *Stories and Tales,* translated by H.W. Dulcken, 81–84. London: Routledge, 2002.

Aristotle. *Physics.* Translated by Robin Waterfield. Oxford: World's Classics, 1996.

———. *Rhetoric.* Translated by C.D.C. Reeve. Indianapolis: Hackett Publishing Company, 2018.

———. *The Metaphysics.* Translated by Hugh Lawson-Tancred. London: Penguin, 2004.

Austin, Michael. "To Exist Is to Change: A Friendly Disagreement with Graham Harman on Why Things Happen." In *Speculations I,* edited by Paul Ennis, 66–83. Earth: punctum books, 2010.

Auxier, Randall E., and Gary L. Herstein. *The Quantum of Explanation: Whitehead's Radical Empiricism.* London: Routledge, 2017.

Badiou, Alain. *Being and Event.* Translated by Oliver Feltham. London: Continuum, 2005.

———. *Lacan: Anti-Philosophy 3*. Edited by Kenneth Reinhard. Translated by Susan Spitzer. New York: Columbia University Press, 2018.

———. *Logics of Worlds: Being and Event II*. Translated by Alberto Toscano. London: Continuum, 2009.

Barad, Karen. *Meeting the Universe Halfway: Quantum Physics and the Entanglement of Matter and Meaning*. Durham: Duke University Press, 2007.

Barcan Marcus, Ruth. "Modalities and Intensional Languages." *Synthese* 13, no. 4 (1961): 303–22. DOI: 10.1007/BF00486629.

Bateson, Gregory. *Steps to an Ecology of Mind: Collected Essays in Anthropology, Psychiatry, Evolution, and Epistemology*. Chicago: University of Chicago Press, 2000.

Baudrillard, Jean. *Seduction*. Translated by Brian Singer. London: Palgrave Macmillan, 1991.

Beiser, Frederick C. *German Idealism: The Struggle Against Subjectivism, 1781–1801*. Cambridge: Harvard University Press, 2008.

Bennett, Jane. *Vibrant Matter: A Political Ecology of Things*. Durham: Duke University Press, 2010.

Bergson, Henri. *Matter and Memory*. Translated by Nancy Margaret Paul and W. Scott Palmer. Mineola: Dover, 2004.

———. *Time and Free Will: An Essay on the Immediate Data of Consciousness*. Translated by F.L. Pogson. Mineola: Dover, 2001.

Berkeley, George. *A Treatise Concerning the Principles of Human Knowledge*. Edited by Kenneth P. Winkler. Indianapolis: Hackett Publishing Company, 1982.

Bhaskar, Roy. *A Realist Theory of Science*. London: Verso, 2008.

Bloom, Harold. *The Anxiety of Influence: A Theory of Poetry*. 2nd edition. Oxford: Oxford University Press, 1997.

Boghossian, Paul. *Fear of Knowledge: Against Relativism and Constructivism*. Oxford: Oxford University Press, 2006.

Bogost, Ian. *Alien Phenomenology, or What It's Like to Be a Thing*. Minneapolis: University of Minnesota Press, 2012.

———. "Time, Relation, Ethics, Experience: Some Responses to the Alien Phenomenology Reading Group." July 4, 2012. http://bogost.com/blog/time_relation_ethics_experienc/.

Böhme, Gernot. *The Aesthetics of Atmospheres*. Edited by Jean-Paul Thibaud. New York: Routledge, 2017.

Bourriaud, Nicolas. *Relational Aesthetics*. Dijon: Les Presses du réel, 1998.

Brandom, Robert B. *Making It Explicit: Reasoning, Representing, and Discursive Commitment*. Cambridge: Harvard University Press, 1998.

———. *Reason in Philosophy: Animating Ideas*. Cambridge: Belknap Press, 2009.

Brassier, Ray. "Concepts and Objects." In *The Speculative Turn: Continental Materialism and Realism,* edited by Levi R. Bryant, Nick Srnicek, and Graham Harman, 47–65. Melbourne: re.press, 2011.

———. "I Am A Nihilist Because I Still Believe in Truth." Interview by Marcin Rychter. *Kronos,* March 4, 2011. http://www.kronos.org.pl/index.php?23151,896.

———. *Nihil Unbound: Enlightenment and Extinction*. New York: Palgrave, 2007.

——— "Postscript: Speculative Autopsy." In Peter Wolfendale, *Object-Oriented Philosophy,* 407–21. Falstaff: Urbanomic, 2014.

Brassier, Ray, Iain Hamilton Grant, Graham Harman, and Quentin Meillassoux. "Speculative Realism." In *Collapse III,* edited by Robin Mackay, 306–449. Falstaff: Urbanomic, 2007.

Braver, Lee. *A Thing of This World: A History of Continental Anti-Realism*. Evanston: Northwestern University Press, 2007.

———. "A Brief History of Continental Realism." *Continental Philosophy Review* 45, no 2 (2012): 261–89. DOI: 10.1007/s11007-012-9220-2.

———. "On Not Settling the Issue of Realism." In *Speculations IV,* edited by Michael Austin, Paul J. Ennis, Fabio Gironi,

Thomas Gokey, and Robert Jackson, 9–14. Earth: punctum books, 2013.
Brentano, Franz. *Psychology from an Empirical Standpoint.* Edited by Linda L. McAlister. Translated by Antos C. Rancurello, D.B. Terrell, and Linda L. McAlister. London: Routledge, 1995.
Bruno, Giordano. *Cause, Principle, and Unity.* Edited and translated by Robert de Lucca. Cambridge: Cambridge University Press, 1998.
Bryant, Levi R. *Difference and Givenness: Deleuze's Transcendental Empiricism and the Ontology of Immanence.* Evanston: Northwestern University Press, 2008.
———. *The Democracy of Objects.* Ann Arbor: Open Humanities Press, 2011.
———. "The Time of the Object: Derrida, Luhmann, and the Processual Nature of Objects." In *The Allure of Things: Process and Object in Contemporary Philosophy,* edited by Roland Faber and Andrew Goffey, 71–91. London: Bloomsbury Academic, 2014.
———. "The Interior of Things: The Origami of Being." *Przeglad Kulturoznawczy* 29, no. 3 (2016): 290–304.
Callon, Michel, and Bruno Latour. "Unscrewing the Big Leviathan: How Actors Macrostructure Reality and How Sociologists Help Them to Do So." In *Advances in Social Theory and Methodology: Toward an Integration of Micro- and Macro-Sociologies,* edited by Karin Knorr Cetina and Aaron V. Cicourel, 277–303. Boston: Routledge and Kegan Paul, 1981.
Cartwright, Nancy. *How the Laws of Physics Lie.* Oxford: Clarendon Press, 1983.
Chalmers, David J. *The Conscious Mind: In Search of a Fundamental Theory.* Oxford: Oxford University Press, 1996.
Chandler, Raymond. *The Long Goodbye.* In *Later Novels and Other Writings,* 417–734. New York: Library of America, 1995.
Coleman, Sam. "Being Realistic: Why Physicalism May Entail Panexperientialism." In *Consciousness and Its Place in*

Nature: Does Physicalism Entail Panphychism?, edited by Anthony Freeman, 40–52. Exter: Imprint Academic, 2006.

de Saussure, Ferdinand. *Course in General Linguistics*. Translated by Wade Baskin. New York: Columbia University Press, 1994.

DeLanda, Manuel. *A New Philosophy of Society: Assemblage Theory and Social Complexity*. London: Continuum, 2006.

———. *Intensive Science and Virtual Philosophy*. London: Continuum, 2002.

DeLanda, Manuel, and Graham Harman. *The Rise of Realism*. Malden: Polity Press, 2017.

Deleuze, Gilles. *Bergsonism*. Translated by Hugh Tomlinson and Barbara Habberjam. New York: Zone Books, 1990.

———. *The Fold: Leibniz and the Baroque*. Translated by Tom Conley. Minneapolis: University of Minnesota Press, 1992.

———. *The Logic of Sense*. Edited by Constantin V. Boundas. Translated by Mark Lester. New York: Columbia University Press, 1993.

Deleuze, Gilles, and Félix Guattari. *A Thousand Plateaus: Capitalism and Schizophrenia*. Translated by Brian Massumi. London: Continuum, 2004.

Derrida, Jacques. "Différance." In *Margins of Philosophy*, translated by Alan Bass, 1–27. Chicago: University of Chicago Press, 1982.

———. *Of Grammatology*. Translated by Gayatri Chakravorty Spivak. Baltimore: Johns Hopkins University Press, 2016.

———. "*Ousia* and *Grammē*: A Note on a Note from *Being and Time*." In *Margins of Philosophy*, translated by Alan Bass, 29–67. Chicago: University of Chicago Press, 1982.

———. "Signature Event Context." In *Margins of Philosophy*, translated by Alan Bass, 307–30. Chicago: University of Chicago Press, 1982.

———. "Violence and Metaphysics: An Essay on the Thought of Emmanuel Levinas." In *Writing and Difference*, translated by Alan Bass, 79–158. Chicago: University of Chicago Press, 1978.

———. *Voice and Phenomenon: Introduction to the Problem of the Sign in Husserl's Phenomenology*. Translated by Leonard Lawlor. Evanston: Northwestern University Press, 2010.

———. "White Mythology: Metaphor in the Text of Philosophy." In *Margins of Philosophy*, translated by Alan Bass, 207–71. Chicago: University of Chicago Press, 1982.

Descartes, René. *Meditations on First Philosophy*. Translated by Donald A. Cress. 3rd edition. Indianapolis: Hackett Publishing Company, 1993.

Devitt, Michael. *Realism and Truth*. 2nd edition. Princeton: Princeton University Press, 1997.

Dewey, John. *The Public and Its Problems: An Essay in Political Inquiry*. Edited by Melvin L. Rogers. University Park: Penn State University Press, 2012.

Dickens, Charles. *Bleak House*. Edited by Nicola Bradbury. London: Penguin Books, 2003.

Doyle, Arthur Conan. *The Sign of Four*. Scotts Valley: CreateSpace Independent Publishing Platform, 2018.

Dreyfus, Hubert. *Being-in-the-World: A Commentary on Heidegger's Being and Time, Division I*. Cambridge: MIT Press, 1991.

Dunham, Jeremy, Iain Hamilton Grant, and Sean Watson. *Idealism: The History of a Philosophy*. Montreal: McGill-Queen's University Press, 2011.

Eldredge, Niles, and Stephen Jay Gould. "Punctuated Equilibria: An Alternative to Phyletic Gradualism." In *Models in Paleobiology*, edited by Thomas J.M. Scopf, 82–115. New York: Doubleday, 1972.

Faber, Roland, and Andrew Goffey, eds. *The Allure of Things: Process and Object in Contemporary Philosophy*. London: Bloomsbury Academic, 2014.

Fakhry, Majid. *Islamic Occasionalism and Its Critique by Averroës and Aquinas*. London: Allen & Unwin, 1958.

Ferraris, Maurizio. *Manifesto of New Realism*. Translated by Sarah De Sanctis. Albany: SUNY Press, 2014.

Fichte, J.G. *The Science of Knowledge.* Edited and translated by Peter Heath and John Lachs. Cambridge: Cambridge University Press, 1982.

Frege, Gottlob. "Über Sinn und Bedeutung." *Zeitschrift für Philosophie und Philosophische Kritik* 100 (1892): 25–50.

Gabriel, Markus. *Fields of Sense: A New Realist Ontology.* Edinburgh: Edinburgh University Press, 2015.

Gadamer, Hans-Georg. *Truth and Method.* Translated by Joel Weinsheimer and Donald G. Marshall. 2nd edition. London: Continuum, 2004.

Galloway, Alexander R. "The Poverty of Philosophy: Realism and Post-Fordism." *Critical Inquiry* 39, no. 2 (Winter 2013): 347–66. DOI: 10.1086/668529.

Garcia, Tristan. *Form and Object: A Treatise on Things.* Translated by Mark Allan Ohm and Jon Cogburn. Edinburgh: Edinburgh University Press, 2014.

Gironi, Fabio. "Between Naturalism and Realism: A New Realist Landscape." *Journal of Critical Realism* 11, no. 3 (2012): 361–87. DOI: 10.1558/jcr.v11i3.361.

Golumbia, David. "'Correlationism': The Dogma That Never Was." *boundary 2* 43, no. 2 (May 2016): 1–25. DOI: 10.1215/01903659-3469889.

Grant, Iain Hamilton. "Mining Conditions: A Response to Harman." In *The Speculative Turn: Continental Materialism and Realism,* edited by Levi R. Bryant, Nick Srnicek, and Graham Harman, 41–46. Melbourne: re.press, 2011.

———. *Philosophies of Nature after Schelling.* London: Continuum, 2008.

Gratton, Peter. "Interviews: Graham Harman, Jane Bennett, Tim Morton, Ian Bogost, Levi Bryant, and Paul Ennis." In *Speculations I,* edited by Paul Ennis, 84–134. Earth: punctum books, 2010.

———. *Speculative Realism: Problems and Prospects.* London: Bloomsbury Academic, 2014.

Hallward, Peter. "Anything Is Possible: A Reading of Quentin Meillassoux's 'After Finitude'." In *The Speculative Turn: Continental Materialism and Realism,* edited by Levi R. Bryant,

Nick Srnicek, and Graham Harman, 130–41. Melbourne: re.press, 2011.

Harman, Graham. "Aesthetics as First Philosophy: Levinas and the Non-Human." *Naked Punch* 9 (Summer/Fall 2007): 21–30.

———. "Aesthetics Is the Root of All Philosophy." In *Object-Oriented Ontology: A New Theory of Everything*, 59–102. London: Pelican, 2018.

———. "A Festival of Anti-Realism: Braver's History of Continental Thought." *Philosophy Today* 52, no. 2 (Summer 2008): 197–210. DOI: 10.5840/philtoday200852234.

———. "Alain Badiou, Lacan: Anti-Philosophy 3." *Notre Dame Philosophical Reviews*, May 27, 2019. https://ndpr.nd.edu/news/lacan-anti-philosophy-3/.

———. "A New Occasionalism?" In *Reset Modernity!*, edited by Bruno Latour and Christophe Leclercq, 129–38. Cambridge: MIT Press, 2016.

———. "A New Theory of Everything." In *Object-Oriented Ontology: A New Theory of Everything*, 19–58. London: Pelican, 2018.

———. *Art and Objects*. Cambridge: Polity, 2020.

———. "Art without Relations." *ArtReview*, November 4, 2014. https://artreview.com/september-2014-graham-harman-relations/

———. *Bruno Latour: Reassembling the Political*. London: Pluto Books, 2014.

———. "Concerning Stephen Hawking's Claim That Philosophy Is Dead." *Filozofski Vestnik* 33, no. 2 (2012): 11–22.

———. "Conclusions: Assemblage Theory and Its Future." In *Reassembling International Theory*, edited by Michele Acuto and Simon Curtis, 118–31. New York: Palgrave Macmillan, 2014.

———. *Dante's Broken Hammer: The Ethics, Aesthetics, and Metaphysics of Love*. London: Repeater Books, 2016.

———. "Fear of Reality: Realism and Infra-Realism." *The Monist* 98, no. 2 (April 2015): 126–44. DOI: 10.1093/monist/onv001.

———. "Greenberg, Duchamp, and the Next Avant-Garde." In *Speculations V*, edited by Ridvan Askin, Paul J. Ennis, Andreas Hägler, Philipp Schweighauser, 251–74. Earth: punctum books, 2013.

———. *Guerrilla Metaphysics: Phenomenology and the Carpentry of Things*. Chicago: Open Court, 2005.

———. *Heidegger Explained: From Phenomenon to Thing*. Chicago: Open Court, 2007.

———. "I Am Also of the Opinion That Materialism Must Be Destroyed." *Environment and Planning D: Society and Space* 28, no. 5 (2010): 772–90. DOI: 10.1080/1600910X.2017.1373686.

———. *Immaterialism: Objects and Social Theory*. Cambridge: Polity, 2016.

———. "Levinas and the Triple Critique of Heidegger." *Philosophy Today* 53, no. 4 (Winter 2009): 407–13. DOI: 10.5840/philtoday20095348.

———. "Materialism Is Not the Solution: On Matter, Form, and Mimesis." *The Nordic Journal of Aesthetics* 47 (2016): 94–110. DOI: 10.7146/nja.v24i47.23057.

———. "Object-Oriented Philosophy vs. Radical Empiricism." In *Bells and Whistles: More Speculative Realism*, 40–59. Winchester: Zero Books, 2013.

———. "On Interface: Nancy's Weights and Masses." In *Jean-Luc Nancy and Plural Thinking: Expositions of World, Ontology, Politics, and Sense*, edited by Peter Gratton and Marie-Ève Morin, 95–108. Albany: SUNY Press, 2012.

———. "On Progressive and Degenerating Research Programs with Respect to Philosophy." *Revista Portuguesa de Filosofia* 75, no. 4 (2019): 2067–102.

———. "On the Undermining of Objects: Grant, Bruno, and Radical Philosophy." In *The Speculative Turn: Continental Materialism and Realism*, edited by Levi Bryant, Nick Srnicek, and Graham Harman, 21–40. Melbourne: re.press, 2011.

———. "On Vicarious Causation." In *Collapse II*, edited by Robin Mackay, 171–205. Falstaff: Urbanomic, 2007.

———. *Quentin Meillassoux: Philosophy in the Making.* 2nd edition. Edinburgh: Edinburgh University Press, 2015.

———. "Response to Shaviro." In *The Speculative Turn: Continental Materialism and Realism,* edited by Levi Bryant, Nick Srnicek, and Graham Harman, 279–90. Melbourne: re.press, 2011.

———. *Speculative Realism: An Introduction.* Cambridge: Polity, 2018.

———. "Strange Realism: On Behalf of Objects." *St. John's University Humanities Review* 12, no. 1 (Spring 2015): 3–18.

———. "The Current State of Speculative Realism." In *Speculations IV,* edited by Michael Austin, Paul J. Ennis, Fabio Gironi, Thomas Gokey, and Robert Jackson, 22–28. Earth, punctum books, 2013.

———. "The Enduring Importance of the Analytic/Continental Split." *Gavagai* 3 (2017): 158–60.

———. "The Only Exit from Modern Philosophy." *Open Philosophy* 3 (2020), pp. 132-146.

———. "The Problem with Metzinger." *Cosmos and History* 7, no. 1 (2011): 7–36.

———. *The Quadruple Object.* Winchester: Zero Books, 2011.

———. "The Road to Objects." *continent* 1, no. 3 (2011): 171–79.

———. "The Third Table." In *The Book of Books,* edited by Carolyn Christov-Bakargiev, 540–42. Ostfildern: Hatje Cantz Verlag, 2012.

———. "Time, Space, Essence, and Eidos: A New Theory of Causation." *Cosmos and History* 6, no. 1 (2010): 1–17.

———. *Tool-Being: Heidegger and the Metaphysics of Objects.* Chicago: Open Court, 2002.

———. *Towards Speculative Realism: Essays and Lectures.* Winchester: Zero Books, 2010.

———. "Undermining, Overmining, and Duomining: A Critique." In ADD *Metaphysics,* edited by Jenna Sutela, 40–51. Aalto: Aalto University Design Research Laboratory, 2013.

———. *Weird Realism: Lovecraft and Philosophy.* Winchester: Zero Books, 2012.

———. "Whitehead and Schools X, Y, and Z." In *The Lure of Whitehead,* edited by Nicholas Gaskill and A.J. Nocek, 231–48. Minneapolis: University of Minnesota Press, 2014.

———. "Zero-Person and the Psyche." In *Mind That Abides: Panpsychism in the New Millennium,* edited by David Skrbina, 253–82. Amsterdam: John Benjamins, 2009.

Hegel, G.W.F. *Phenomenology of Spirit.* Translated by A.V. Miller. Oxford: Oxford University Press, 1977.

Heidegger, Martin. *Contributions to Philosophy: Of the Event.* Translated by Richard Rojcewicz and Daniela Vallega-Neu. Bloomington: Indiana University Press, 2012.

———. *History of the Concept of Time: Prolegomena.* Translated by Theodore Kisiel. Bloomington: Indiana University Press, 1985.

———. *Identity and Difference.* Translated by Joan Stambaugh. Chicago: University of Chicago Press, 2002.

———. "Insight into That Which Is." In *Bremen and Freiburg Lectures: Insight into That Which Is and Basic Principles of Thinking,* translated by Andrew J. Mitchell, 3–73. Bloomington: Indiana University Press, 2012.

———. *Introduction to Metaphysics.* Translated by Gregory Fried and Richard Polt. New Haven: Yale University Press, 2014.

———. *Kant and the Problem of Metaphysics.* Translated by James S. Churchill. Bloomington: Indiana University Press, 1965.

———. *Nietzsches Metaphysik/Einleitung in die Philosophie.* Frankfurt am Main: Vittorio Klostermann, 2007.

———. *Nietzsche,* Vol. 1: *The Will to Power as Art.* Translated by David Farrell Krell. New York: Harper & Row, 1979.

———. *Nietzsche,* Vol. 2: *The Eternal Recurrence of the Same.* Translated by David Farrell Krell. New York: Harper & Row, 1984.

———. *Nietzsche,* Vol. 3: *The Will to Power As Knowledge and As Metaphysics.* Translated by David Farrell Krell. New York: Harper & Row, 1987.

———. *Nietzsche,* Vol. 4: *Nihilism.* Translated by David Farrell Krell. New York: Harper & Row, 1982.

———. "On the Essence of Ground." In *Pathmarks,* edited by William McNeill, 97–135. Cambridge: Cambridge University Press, 1998.

———. "The Anaximander Fragment." In *Early Greek Thinking: The Dawn of Western Philosophy,* translated by D.F. Krell and Frank A. Capuzzi, 13–58. New York: Harper & Row, 1984.

———. *The Basic Problems of Phenomenology.* Translated by Albert Hofstadter. Bloomington: Indiana University Press, 1988.

———. *The Fundamental Concepts of Metaphysics: World – Finitude – Solitude.* Translated by William McNeill and Nicholas Walker. Bloomington: Indiana University Press, 1995.

———. "The Origin of the Work of Art." In *Off the Beaten Track,* edited and translated by Julian Young and Kenneth Haynes, 1–56. Cambridge: Cambridge University Press, 2002.

———. "The Thing." In *Poetry, Language, Thought,* translated by Albert Hofstadter. New York: Harper & Row, 1971.

———. *Towards the Definition of Philosophy.* Translated by Ted Sadler. London: Continuum, 2008.

———. "What Is Metaphysics?" In *Pathmarks,* edited by William McNeill, 82–96. Cambridge: Cambridge University Press, 1998.

Hobbes, Thomas. *Leviathan.* Edited by J.C.A. Gaskin. Oxford: Oxford University Press, 1996.

Hopkins, Burt C. *Intentionality in Husserl and Heidegger: The Problem of the Original Method and Phenomenon of Phenomenology.* Dordrecht: Kluwer Academic Publishers, 1993.

Husserl, Edmund. *Ideas for a Pure Phenomenology and Phenomenological Philosophy.* Translated by Daniel O. Dahlstrom. Indianapolis: Hackett Publishing Company, 2014.

———. "Intentional Objects." In *Early Writings in the Philosophy of Logic and Mathematics*. Translated by Dallas Willard, 345–87. Dordrecht: Kluwer Academic Publishers, 1994.

———. *Logical Investigations*, 2 vols. Translated by J.N. Findlay. London: Routledge, 1970.

———. *Logical Investigations*, 2 vols., edited by Dermot Moran. Translated by J.N. Findlay. London: Routledge, 2001.

———. *The Phenomenology of Internal Time-Consciousness*. Edited by Martin Heidegger. Translated by James S. Churchill. Bloomington: Indiana University Press, 2019.

Ippolit Belinski. "Slavoj Žižek & Graham Harman Duel + Duet (Mar. 2017)." *YouTube,* March 2, 2017. https://www.youtube.com/watch?v=r1PJo_-n2vI.

Ivakhiv, Adrian. *Shadowing the Anthropocene: Eco-Realism for Turbulent Times*. Earth: punctum books, 2018.

James, Ian. "The Relational Universe." In *The Technique of Thought: Nancy, Laruelle, Malabou, and Stiegler after Naturalism*, 55–120. Minneapolis: University of Minnesota Press, 2019.

James, William. "A World of Pure Experience." In *Essays in Radical Empiricism*. Lincoln: University of Nebraska Press, 1996.

Johnston, Adrian. *Adventures in Transcendental Materialism: Dialogues with Contemporary Thinkers*. Edinburgh: Edinburgh University Press, 2014.

———. "Points of Forced Freedom: Eleven (More) Theses on Materialism." In *Speculations IV,* edited by Michael Austin, Paul J. Ennis, Fabio Gironi, Thomas Gokey, and Robert Jackson, 91–98. Earth: punctum books, 2013.

Joyce, James. *Ulysses*. Scotts Valley: CreateSpace Independent Publishing Platform, 2017.

Kant, Immanuel. *Critique of Judgment*. Translated by Werner S. Pluhar. Indianapolis: Hackett Publishing Company, 1987.

———. *Critique of Practical Reason*. Translated by Mary Gregor. 2nd edition. Cambridge: Cambridge University Press, 2015.

———. *Dreams of a Spirit-Seer: Illustrated by Dreams of Metaphysics*. Edited by Frank Sewall. Translated by Emanuel F. Goerwitz. London: Forgotten Books, 2012.

Kisiel, Theodore. *The Genesis of Heidegger's Being and Time*. Berkeley: University of California Press, 1995.

Knorr Cetina, Karin, and A.V. Cicourel, eds. *Advances in Social Theory and Methodology: Toward an Integration of Micro- and Macro-Sociologies*. London: Routledge, 1981.

Kripke, Saul A. *Naming and Necessity*. Cambridge: Harvard University Press, 1980.

Lacan, Jacques. *The Sinthome: The Seminar of Jacques Lacan, Book XXIII*. Edited by Jacques-Alain Miller. Translated by A.R. Price. Malden: Polity, 2016.

Ladyman, James, and Don Ross. *Every Thing Must Go: Metaphysics Naturalized*. Oxford: Oxford University Press, 2007.

Lagebesprechungen. "Graham Harman and Slavoj Zizek: talk and debate: On Object Oriented Ontology." *YouTube*, December 6, 2018. https://www.youtube.com/watch?v=6GHiV4tuRt8.

Lakatos, Imre. *Philosophical Papers, Vol. 1: The Methodology of Scientific Research Programmes*. Edited by John Worrall and Gregory Currie. Cambridge: Cambridge University Press, 1978.

Latour, Bruno. *An Inquiry into Modes of Existence: An Anthropology of the Moderns*. Translated by Catherine Porter. Cambridge: Harvard University Press, 2013.

———. *Down to Earth: Politics in the New Climatic Regime*. Cambridge: Polity, 2018.

———. *Facing Gaia: Eight Lectures on the New Climatic Regime*. Translated by Catherine Porter. Cambridge: Polity, 2017.

———. "Irreductions." Translated by John Law. In *The Pasteurization of France*, translated by Alan Sheridan and John Law, 153–238. Cambridge: Harvard University Press, 1988.

———. "On the Partial Existence of Existing and Non-existing Objects." In *Biographies of Scientific Objects*, edited by Lorraine Daston, 247–69. Chicago: University of Chicago Press, 2000.

———. *Politics of Nature: How to Bring the Sciences into Democracy.* Translated by Catherine Porter. Cambridge: Harvard University Press, 2004.

———. "Science's Blood Flow: An Example from Joliot's Scientific Intelligence." In *Pandora's Hope: Essays on the Reality of Science Studies,* 80–112. Cambridge: Harvard University Press, 1999.

———. *We Have Never Been Modern.* Translated by Catherine Porter. Cambridge: Harvard University Press, 1993.

Latour, Bruno, Graham Harman, and Peter Erdélyi. *The Prince and the Wolf: Latour and Harman at the LSE.* Winchester: Zero Books, 2011.

Latour, Bruno, and Steve Woolgar. *Laboratory Life: The Construction of Scientific Facts.* Princeton: Princeton University Press, 2013.

Leibniz, G.W. "The Principles of Philosophy, or, the Monadology." In *Philosophical Essays,* translated by Roger Ariew and Daniel Garber, 213–25. Indianapolis: Hackett Publishing Company, 1989.

Leibniz, G.W., and Samuel Clarke. *Correspondence.* Edited by Roger Ariew. Indianapolis: Hackett Publishing Company, 2000.

Levinas, Emmanuel. *Basic Philosophical Writings.* Edited by Adriaan Peperzak, Simon Critchley, and Robert Bernasconi. Bloomington: Indiana University Press, 1996.

———. *Discovering Existence with Husserl.* Translated by Richard A. Cohen and Michael B. Smith. Evanston: Northwestern University Press, 1998.

———. *Existence and Existents.* Translated by Alphonso Lingis. Pittsburgh: Duquesne University Press, 2001.

———. *Otherwise Than Being, or Beyond Essence.* Translated by Alphonso Lingis. Pittsburgh: Duquesne University Press, 1998.

———. *Totality and Infinity: An Essay on Exteriority.* Translated by Alphonso Lingis. Pittsburgh: Duquesne University Press, 1969.

Lingis, Alphonso. "A Phenomenology of Substances." *American Catholic Philosophical Quarterly* 71, no. 4 (Autumn 1997): 505–22.

———. "The Levels." In *The Imperative*, 25–38. Bloomington: Indiana University Press, 1998.

Lippmann, Walter. *The Phantom Public.* New Brunswick: Transaction Publishers, 1993.

Locke, John. *An Essay Concerning Human Understanding.* 2 vols. New York: Dover, 1959.

Lovelock, James. *The Ages of Gaia: A Biography of Our Living Earth.* New York: Norton, 1995.

Luhmann, Niklas. *Social Systems.* Translated by John Bednarz Jr. with Dirk Baecker. Stanford: Stanford University Press, 1996.

———. *Theory of Society.* 2 vols. Translated by Rhodes Barrett. Stanford: Stanford University Press, 2012.

MacDonnell, Kevin. "Interview: Some Differences Between Object-Oriented Philosophy and Onticology." Interview by Levi R. Bryant. *St. John's University Humanities Review* 12, no. 1 (Spring 2015): 65–72.

Margulis, Lynn. *Symbiotic Planet: A New Look at Evolution.* New York: Basic Books, 1998.

Marion, Jean-Luc. *Being Given: Toward a Phenomenology of Givenness.* Translated by J.L. Kosky. Stanford: Stanford University Press, 2002.

Marres, Noortje. "No Issue, No Public: Democratic Deficits after the Displacement of Politics." PhD diss., University of Amsterdam, Amsterdam, 2005.

Mattei, Jean-François. *Heidegger et Hölderlin: Le quadriparti.* Paris: Presses Universitaires de France, 2001.

Maturana, Humberto. *Autopoiesis and Cognition: The Realization of the Living.* Dordrecht: Kluwer Academic Publishers, 1980.

McGinn, Colin. "Hard Questions: Comments on Galen Strawson." In *Consciousness and Its Places in Nature: Does Physicalism Entail Panpsychism?*, edited by Anthony Freeman, 90–99. Exeter: Imprint Academic, 2006.

McLuhan, Marshall. *The Gutenberg Galaxy: The Making of Typographic Man*. Toronto: University of Toronto Press, 1962.

———. *Understanding Media: The Extensions of Man*. Cambridge: MIT Press, 1994.

Meillassoux, Quentin. *After Finitude: An Essay on the Necessity of Contingency*. Translated by Ray Brassier. London: Continuum, 2008.

———. "Appendix: Excerpts from *L'Inexistence divine*." In Graham Harman, *Quentin Meillassoux: Philosophy in the Making*, 175–238. Edinburgh: Edinburgh University Press, 2015.

———. "Iteration, Reiteration, Repetition: A Speculative Analysis of the Meaningless Sign." Translated by Robin Mackay and M. Gansen. In *Genealogies of Speculation: Materialism and Subjectivity since Structuralism*, edited by Armen Avanessian and Suhail Malik, 117–97. London: Bloomsbury, 2016.

Merleau-Ponty, Maurice. *Phenomenology of Perception*. Translated by Colin Smith. London: Routledge, 2002.

———. *The Visible and the Invisible*. Translated by Alphonso Lingis. Evanston: Northwestern University Press, 1968.

Metzinger, Thomas. *Being No One: The Self-model Theory of Subjectivity*. Cambridge: MIT Press, 2004.

Mol, Annemarie. *The Body Multiple: Ontology in Medical Practice*. Durham: Duke University Press, 2003.

Molnar, George. *Powers: A Study in Metaphysics*. Edited by Stephen Mumford. Oxford: Oxford University Press, 2003.

Moran, Dermot. *Introduction to Phenomenology*. London: Routledge, 2000.

Morton, Timothy. "Art in the Age of Asymmetry: Hegel, Objects, Aesthetics." *Evental Aesthetics* 1, no. 1 (2012): 121–42.

———. *Hyperobjects: Philosophy and Ecology After the End of the World*. Minneapolis: University of Minnesota Press, 2013.

———. *Realist Magic: Objects, Ontology, Causality*. Ann Arbor: Open Humanities Press, 2013.

Mulhall, Stephen, ed. *The Cavell Reader*. London: Wiley-Blackwell, 1996.

———. "How Complex Is a Lemon?" *London Review of Books*, September 27, 2018. https://www.lrb.co.uk/the-paper/v40/n18/stephen-mulhall/how-complex-is-a-lemon.

Nadler, Steven. "'No Necessary Connection': The Medieval Roots of the Occasionalist Roots of Humen." In *Occasionalism: Causation among the Cartesians*. Oxford: Oxford University Press, 2011.

Nagel, Thomas. "What Is It Like to Be a Bat?" In *Mortal Questions*, 165–80. Cambridge: Cambridge University Press, 1991.

Nietzsche, Friedrich. "On Truth and Lying in an Extra-Moral Sense." In *Friedrich Nietzsche on Rhetoric and Language*, translated by Sander L. Gilman, Carole Blair, and David J. Parent. Oxford: Oxford University Press, 1989.

———. *The Birth of Tragedy*. Translated by Douglas Smith. Oxford: Oxford University Press, 2008.

Nolt, John. "An Argument for Metaphysical Realism." *Journal for General Philosophy of Science* 35 (2004): 71–90. DOI: 10.1023/B:JGPS.0000035149.31235.79.

Norris, Christopher. "Speculative Realism: Interim Report with Just a Few Caveats." In *Speculations IV*, edited by Michael Austin, Paul J. Ennis, Fabio Gironi, Thomas Gokey, and Robert Jackson, 38–47. Earth: punctum books, 2013.

Ortega y Gasset, José. "An Essay in Esthetics by Way of a Preface." In *Phenomenology and Art*, translated by Phillip W. Silver, 127–50. New York: Norton, 1975.

———. "Preface for Germans." In *Phenomenology and Art*, translated by Phillip W. Silver, 24–70. New York: Norton, 1975.

Peñas López, Miguel. "Speculative Experiments: What If Harman and Simondon Individuate Together?" In *Speculations*

V, edited by Ridvan Askin, Paul J. Ennis, Andreas Hägler, and Philipp Scweighauser, 225–47. Earth: punctum books, 2014.

Perler, Dominik, and Ulrich Rudolph. *Occasionalismus: Theorien der Kausalität im arabisch-islamischen und im europäischen Denken.* Göttingen: Vandenhoeck & Ruprecht, 2000.

Plato. *Euthyphro, Apology, Crito, Phaedo.* Translated by G.M.A. Grube. In *Complete Works,* edited by J.M. Cooper, 49–100. Indianapolis: Hackett Publishing Company, 1997.

———. *Meno.* Translated by G.M.A. Grube. In *Plato: Complete Works,* edited by John M. Cooper, 870–97. Indianapolis: Hackett Publishing Company, 1997.

Povinelli, Elizabeth. *Geontologies: A Requiem to Late Liberalism.* Durham: Duke University Press, 2016.

Rancière, Jacques. *The Emancipated Spectator.* Translated by Gregory Elliott. London: Verso, 2011.

Rousseau, Jean-Jacques. *Discourse on the Origin of Inequality.* Translated by Donald A. Cress. Indianapolis: Hackett Publishing Company, 1992.

Rovelli, Carlo. "Halfway through the Woods." In *The Cosmos of Science: Essays of Exploration,* edited by John Earman and John D. Norton, 180–223. Pittsburgh: University of Pittsburgh Press, 1997.

Sallis, John. "Levinas and the Elemental." *Research in Phenomenology* 28 (1998): 152–59. DOI: 10.1163/156916498X00092.

Scheler, Max. "Ordo Amoris." In *Selected Philosophical Essays,* translated by David R. Lachterman, 98–135. Evanston: Northwestern University Press, 1992.

Schmitt, Carl. *The Concept of the Political.* Translated by George Schwab. Chicago: University of Chicago Press, 1996.

Seager, William. "The 'Intrinsic Nature' Argument for Panpsychism." In *Consciousness and Its Place in Nature: Does Physicalism Entail Panpsychism?,* edited by Anthony Freeman, 129–45. Exeter: Imprint Academic, 2006.

Sellars, Wilfrid. *Empiricism and the Philosophy of Mind.* Cambridge: Harvard University Press, 1997.

———. "Philosophy and the Scientific Image of Man." In *In the Space of Reasons,* edited by Kevin Scharp and Robert B. Brandom, 369–408. Cambridge: Harvard University Press, 2007.

Shakespeare, William. *Macbeth.* Third Series (The Arden Shakespeare), edited by S. Clark and P. Mason. London: Bloomsbury, 2015.

Shapin, Steven, and Simon Schaffer. *Leviathan and the Air-Pump: Hobbes, Boyle, and the Experimental Life.* Princeton: Princeton University Press, 1985.

Shaviro, Steven. *Discognition.* London: Repeater Books, 2015.

———. *The Universe of Things: On Speculative Realism.* Minneapolis: University of Minnesota Press, 2014.

———. *Without Criteria: Kant, Whitehead, Deleuze, and Aesthetics.* Cambridge: MIT Press, 2009.

Simondon, Gilbert. *L'individuation à la lumière des notions de forme et d'information.* Grenoble: Jérôme Millon, 2005.

Skrbina, David. *Panpsychism in the West.* Cambridge: MIT Press, 2005.

———. "Zero-Person and the Psyche." In *Mind That Abides: Panpsychism in the New Millennium,* edited by David Skrbina, 253–82. Amsterdam: John Benjamins, 2009.

Smith, Barry. *Austrian Philosophy: The Legacy of Franz Brentano.* Chicago: Open Court, 1994.

Smolin, Lee. Comment to Richard Woit, "Much Ado About Nothing," *Not Even Wrong,* April 27, 2012. https://www.math.columbia.edu/~woit/wordpress/?p=4623&cpage=1.

Sparrow, Tom. *Levinas Unhinged.* Winchester: Zero Books, 2013.

———. *Plastic Bodies: Rebuilding Sensation after Phenomenology.* Ann Arbor: Open Humanities Press, 2015.

———, ed. *The Alphonso Lingis Reader.* Minneapolis: University of Minnesota Press, 2018.

———. *The End of Phenomenology: Metaphysics and the New Realism.* Edinburgh: Edinburgh University Press, 2014.

Spencer-Brown, George. *Laws of Form.* Leipzig: Bohmeier Verlag, 2008.

Stengers, Isabelle. *Thinking with Whitehead: A Free and Wild Creation of Concepts*. Translated by M. Chase. Cambridge: Harvard University Press, 2011.

Stern, Robert. *Hegel, Kant and the Structure of the Object*. New York: Routledge, 1990.

Stern, William. "Psychische Präsenzzeit." *New Yearbook for Phenomenology and Phenomenological Research* 5 (2007): 310–51.

Stove, David C. *The Plato Cult and Other Philosophical Follies*. Oxford: Blackwell, 1991.

Strawson, Galen. "Realistic Monism: Why Physicalism Entails Panpsychism." In *Consciousness and Its Place in Nature: Does Physicalism Entail Panpsychism?*, edited by Anthony Freeman, 3–31. Exeter: Imprint Academic, 2006.

Strum, S.S., and Bruno Latour. "Redefining the Social Link: From Baboons to Humans." *Social Science Information* 26, no. 4 (1987): 783–802. DOI: 10.1177/053901887026004004.

Suarez, Francis. *On Individuation: Metaphysical Disputation V: Individual Unity and Its Principle*. Translated by Jorge J.E. Gracia. Milwaukee: Marquette University Press, 1982.

Thacker, Eugene. *In the Dust of This Planet: The Horror of Philosophy*. Winchester: Zero Books, 2011.

Toadvine, Ted. *Merleau-Ponty's Philosophy of Nature*. Evanston: Northwestern University Press, 2009.

Toscano, Alberto. "Against Speculation, or, a Critique of the Critique of Critique: A Remark on Quentin Meillassoux's *After Finitude* (after Colleti)." In *The Speculative Turn: Continental Materialism and Realism*, edited by Levi R. Bryant, Nick Srnicek, and Graham Harman, 84–91. Melbourne: re.press, 2011.

———. *The Theatre of Production: Philosophy and Individuation Between Kant and Deleuze*. London: Palgrave Macmillan, 2006.

Twardowski, Kazimierz. *On the Content and Object of Presentations: A Psychological Investigation*. Translated by R. Grossmann. The Hague: Martinus Nijhoff, 1977.

van Fraassen, Bas C. *The Scientific Image.* Oxford: Clarendon Press, 1980.
Warman, Matt. "Stephen Hawking Tells Google 'Philosophy Is Dead.'" *The Telegraph,* May 17, 2011. https://www.telegraph.co.uk/technology/google/8520033/Stephen-Hawking-tells-Google-philosophy-is-dead.html.
Weisman, Alan. *The World without Us.* New York: Picador, 2008.
Whitehead, Alfred North. *Adventures of Ideas.* New York: Free Press, 1967.
——— . *Modes of Thought.* New York: Free Press, 1938.
——— . *Process and Reality.* New York: Free Press, 1978.
——— . *The Concept of Nature.* Amherst: Prometheus Books, 1920.
Whorf, Benjamin Lee. *Language, Thought, and Reality.* Edited by John B. Carroll. Cambridge: MIT Press, 1956.
Wiltsche, Harald A. "Science, Realism, and Correlationism: A Phenomenological Critique of Meillassoux's Argument from Ancestrality." *European Journal of Philosophy* 25, no. 3 (September 2017): 808–32. DOI: 10.1111/ejop.12159.
Wittgenstein, Ludwig. *Philosophical Investigations.* Translated by G.E.M. Anscombe. 3rd edition. London: Pearson, 1973.
——— . *Tractatus Logico-Philosophicus.* Translated by D.F. Pears and B.F. McGuiness. London: Routledge, 1974.
Wolfendale, Peter. *Object-Oriented Philosophy: The Noumenon's New Clothes.* Falmouth: Urbanomic, 2014.
Young, Niki. "On Correlationism and the Philosophy of (Human) Access: Meillassoux and Harman." *Open Philosophy* 3 (2020): 42–52. DOI: 10.1515/opphil-2020-0003.
Zahavi, Dan. "The End of What? Phenomenology vs. Speculative Realism." *International Journal of Philosophical Studies* 24, no. 3 (2016): 289–309. DOI: 10.1080/09672559.2016.1175101.
——— . "Husserl and the 'Absolute.'" In *Philosophy, Phenomenology, Sciences: Essays in Commemoration of Husserl,* edited by Carlo Ierna, Hanne Jacobs, and Filip Mattens, 71–92. Dordrecht: Springer, 2010.

———. *Husserl's Phenomenology*. Stanford: Stanford University Press, 2003.

———. "Phenomenology." In *The Routledge Companion to Twentieth-Century Philosophy*, edited by Dermot Moran, 661–92. London: Routledge, 2008.

Žižek, Slavoj. *Less Than Nothing: Hegel and the Shadow of Dialectical Materialism*. London: Verso, 2012.

———. *The Parallax View*. Cambridge: MIT Press, 2006.

Zubíri, Xavier. *Dynamic Structure of Reality*. Translated by Nelson R. Orringer. Urbana: University of Illinois Press, 2003.

———. *On Essence*. Translated by A. Robert Caponigri. Washington, DC: The Catholic University of America Press, 1980.

www.ingramcontent.com/pod-product-compliance
Lightning Source LLC
Chambersburg PA
CBHW071733150426
43191CB00010B/1564